THE
SHINING SEA

THE
SHINING SEA

David Porter and the
Epic Voyage of the U.S.S. *Essex*
During the War of 1812

GEORGE C. DAUGHAN

BASIC
BOOKS

A MEMBER OF THE PERSEUS BOOKS GROUP
NEW YORK

Book design by Linda Mark
Text set in 11pt JansonText Pro

Library of Congress Cataloging-in-Publication Data

Daughan, George C.
   The shining sea : David Porter and the epic voyage of the U.S.S. Essex during the War of 1812 / George C. Daughan.
      pages cm
   Includes bibliographical references and index.
   ISBN 978-0-465-01962-5 (hardback)—ISBN 978-0-465-06994-1 (e-book)
   1. Porter, David, 1780-1843. 2. Essex (Frigate) 3. United States—History—War of 1812—Naval operations, American. 4. United States. Navy—History—War of 1812. 5. United States. Navy—Officers—Biography. I. Title.
   E353.1.P7D38 2013
   973.5'2573—dc23
                                                              2013018564

10 9 8 7 6 5 4 3 2 1

For Kay, Mary, Mark, Alex, and Tyler

The love of fame for the founders
was the ruling passion of the noblest of minds.

ALEXANDER HAMILTON

CONTENTS

INTRODUCTION

THE WAR OF 1812

ALTHOUGH ONE OF AMERICA'S LESSER-KNOWN CONFLICTS, THE War of 1812 was one of her most important. Beginning on June 18, 1812, the fighting continued unabated for a grueling thirty-two months before ending on February 17, 1815. The struggle spread over a wide area, including all of the United States east of the Mississippi, many parts of Canada, the Great Lakes, and Lake Champlain, as well as most of the world's oceans. Despite being underappreciated, the war had a profound effect on the nation's future. It brought about a rapprochement between Britain and America that changed world history. The enmity that had characterized their relationship since the War of Independence ended. In the final year of the war, the United States demonstrated a military capacity that secured Britain's respect and caused her to fundamentally alter her North American policy. By winning battles at Fort Erie in the Niagara area, at Plattsburgh on Lake Champlain, at Baltimore, and at New Orleans, the United States forced London to confront a new international reality—a strong republic on the other side of the Atlantic.

Led by their prescient foreign minister, Lord Castlereagh, Britain dealt with this new phenomenon by changing her policy toward America from confrontation to accommodation. Castlereagh recognized, before any other British statesman, the critical importance of maintaining friendship with the United States. Instead of treating her as a rival and a potential enemy, where every dispute might become lethal, he sought ways to build amicable relations. He feared that if Britain and America remained enemies, they could be fighting over one issue or another for the next hundred years. Prime Minister Robert Jenkinson (Lord Liverpool) and the rest of the cabinet followed his lead. The two great English-speaking countries never fought again. The serious disagreements they had during the nineteenth century—over boundaries with Canada, the westward expansion of the United States, Texas, the Mexican War, the American Civil War, and a fiercely competitive maritime rivalry—were all resolved peacefully.

The new diplomatic reality spawned by the War of 1812 eventually made possible the remarkable collaboration, indeed partnership, of the two countries during the twentieth and twenty-first centuries, a partnership that was to be of incalculable benefit to themselves and to the world.

Perhaps as important as beginning a new era in relations with Britain, the war strengthened the country's democratic impulses while solidifying respect for the Constitution. The franchise was extended. Property qualifications were lowered so that all those who fought the war could vote. And just as important, President James Madison led the fight without becoming a dictator, which many in Europe thought he would be forced to do. Throughout the struggle, he scrupulously observed the constitutional limits placed on the presidency and gave the country confidence that it could manage its most challenging problems without altering or discarding its form of government.

The heroic efforts of the American navy were critical in winning the war and the peace. Victory in the key battles at Plattsburgh, Baltimore, and New Orleans would have been impossible without the navy. It's true that the Battle of New Orleans was fought (on January 8, 1815) after the peace treaty had been signed at Ghent, on December 24, 1814. But the lopsided outcome at New Orleans showed the potential of American arms and had a major impact on Castlereagh. The navy's part in the battle is not well known, but the hero of the Battle of New Orleans, General Andrew Jackson himself, was the first to acknowledge that the tiny naval contingent played a key part in securing a tremendous victory.

The war revealed hidden strengths that made the small American fleet far more potent than its meager size would indicate. Several factors accounted for its surprising success. To begin with, the ships were as good as, and often better, than their British counterparts, and so were their crews. American men-of-war were manned by volunteers who were required to sign on for only two years, unlike British tars who were forced to serve until the war was over. American seamen exhibited an inspiring degree of patriotism, willingly enduring unbelievably harsh conditions. British seamen were patriotic, too, but their unusually high rate of desertion demonstrated, as nothing else could, how brutal conditions were aboard their ships. American desertions, by comparison, were minuscule. There were no impressed men aboard American men-of-war as there were in the Royal Navy. And the treatment of the crews was far better in the American fleet. Pay, health, food, and discipline were all superior.

Perhaps the most important factor accounting for the success of the American navy was its superb officer corps. Unlike the army, which had not fought (except against small numbers of poorly armed Indians) since the Revolution, the navy's leaders were experienced fighters, having begun their baptism of fire during the Quasi-War with France from 1798 to 1800. Their skills were further honed during the war with Tripoli, which lasted from 1801 until 1805.

A strong naval tradition, dating back to the War of Independence, added to the navy's strength. Heroes like John Paul Jones, John Barry, Silas Talbot, and many, many others inspired the young officers. So, too, did their fathers and uncles who fought with distinction in the Continental and state navies during the Revolution. Lesser-known heroes, like Christopher Perry, Stephen Decatur Sr., George Farragut, and David Porter Sr. inspired their sons to follow in their footsteps. The navy's young stars also benefited from gifted mentors like Thomas Truxtun and Silas Talbot during the Quasi-War and Edward Preble during the war with Tripoli.

David Porter Jr. was among the navy's more promising young officers. He had joined the service in 1798 and had been in the thick of the fight during the Quasi-War and the war with Tripoli. When he sensed the War of 1812 coming, he wanted, more than anything else, to be a part of it.

He viewed it as an opportunity to achieve everlasting fame, one that might never come again. His chance came early in the fighting, and he eagerly grasped it. Beginning in October 1812, he began a seventeen-month cruise in the USS *Essex* that would become the most famous voyage of the war, and one of the most spectacular in the entire age of fighting sail. What follows is the remarkable story of his unforgettable odyssey.

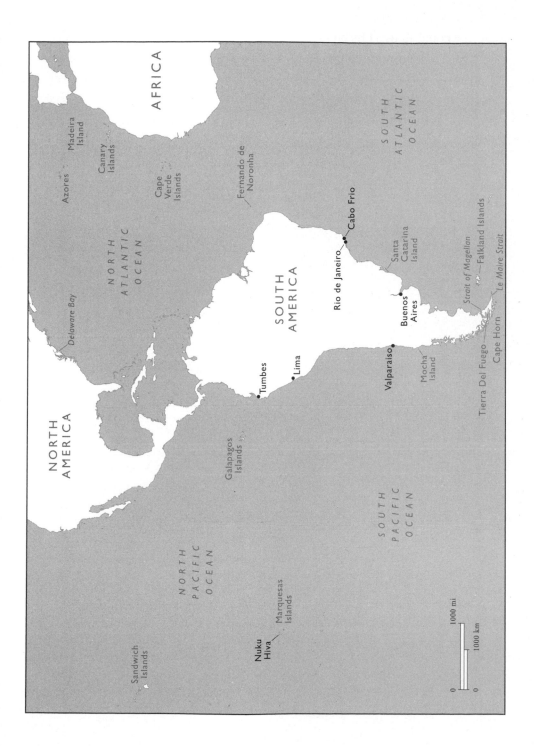

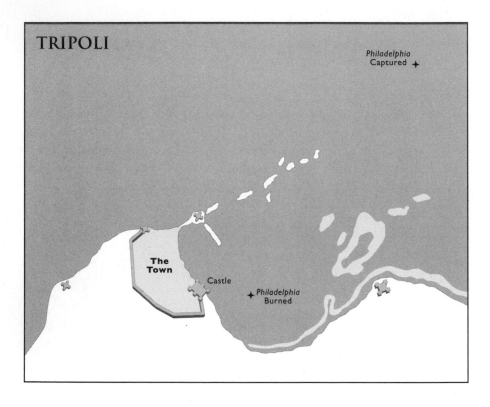

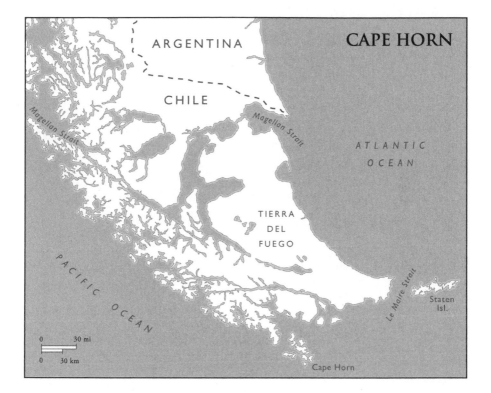

ARGENTINA

CAPE HORN

CHILE

Magellan Strait

Magellan Strait

ATLANTIC
OCEAN

PACIFIC

OCEAN

TIERRA
DEL
FUEGO

Le Maire Strait

Staten
Isl.

0   30 mi

0   30 km

Cape Horn

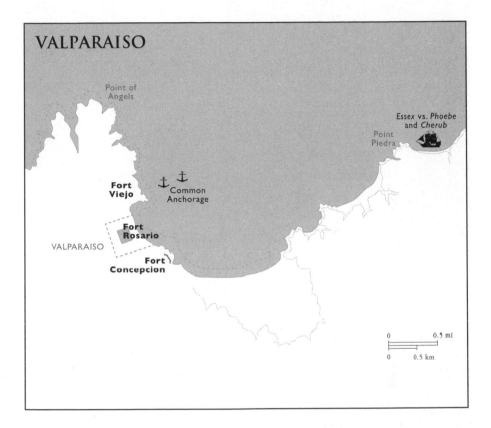

VALPARAISO

Point of
Angels

Essex vs. *Phoebe*
and *Cherub*

Point
Piedra

**Fort
Viejo**

Common
Anchorage

**Fort
Rosario**

VALPARAISO

**Fort
Concepcion**

0   0.5 ml

0   0.5 km

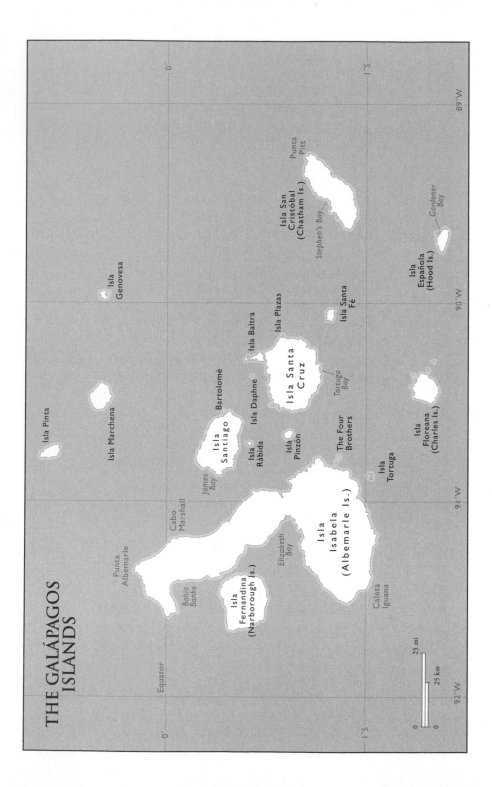

THE GALÁPAGOS
ISLANDS

Equator

Punta
Albemarle

Bahía
Banks

Isla
Fernandina
(Narborough Is.)

Cabo
Marshall

Elizabeth
Bay

Caleta
Iguana

Isla
Isabela
(Albemarle Is.)

Isla Pinta

Isla Marchena

Isla
Santiago

James
Bay

Bartolomé

Isla
Rábida

Isla
Pinzón

The Four
Brothers

Isla
Tortuga

Isla Genovesa

Isla Daphne

Isla Baltra

Isla Plazas

Isla Santa
Cruz

Tortuga
Bay

Isla Santa
Fé

Isla
Floreana
(Charles Is.)

Punta
Pitt

Isla San
Cristóbal
(Chatham Is.)

Stephen's Bay

Isla
Española
(Hood Is.)

Gardener
Bay

0°

0°

1°S

1°S

89°W

90°W

91°W

92°W

25 mi

25 km

0

0

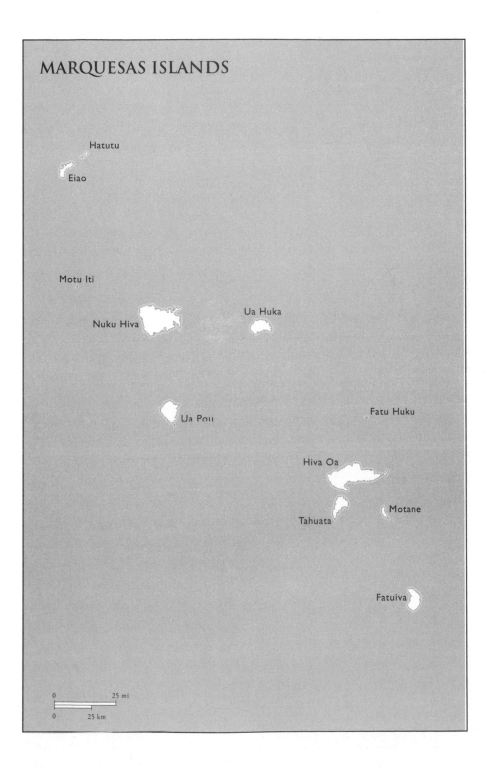

MARQUESAS ISLANDS

Hatutu

Eiao

Motu Iti

Nuku Hiva

Ua Huka

Ua Pou

Fatu Huku

Hiva Oa

Motane

Tahuata

Fatuiva

0   25 mi

0   25 km

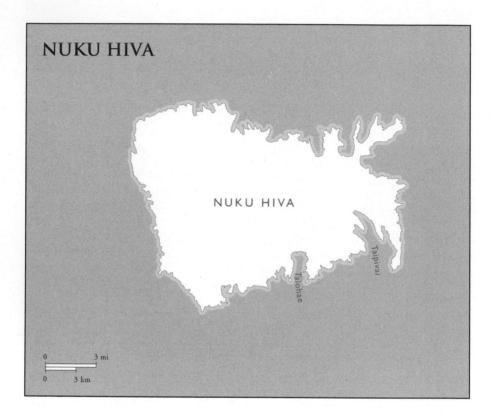

THE SAILS OF A SQUARE-RIGGED SHIP

1. Flying jib
2. Jib
3. Fore topmast staysail
4. Fore staysail
5. Foresail, or course
6. Fore topsail
7. Fore topgallant
8. Mainstaysail
9. Maintopmast staysail
10. Middle staysail
11. Main topgallant staysail
12. Mainsail, or course
13. Maintopsail
14. Main topgallant
15. Mizzen staysail
16. Mizzen topmast staysail
17. Mizzen topgallant staysail
18. Mizzen sail
19. Mizzen topsail
20. Mizzen topgallant
21. Spanker

Prologue

FIRST VICTORY

IT WAS 9:30 ON THE MORNING OF AUGUST 13, 1812, FIFTY-SIX days after the United States had declared war on Great Britain. Captain David Porter, a short, wiry intense man of thirty-two, was standing on the quarterdeck of the 32-gun American frigate *Essex*, looking through his telescope at an interesting ship to windward. She appeared to be an armed West Indiaman, but he suspected she was something else—a poorly disguised British man-of-war, hoping to take him by surprise.

The *Essex* was camouflaged herself. She was sailing in latitude 41° north and longitude 38° 10' west, roughly halfway between New York and Portugal. Porter wanted his ship to look like an easy target. Her gun ports were closed, the topgallant masts were housed, and the sails were trimmed in the careless manner of a merchantman. If the stranger was an enemy warship, Porter wanted to encourage her to attack. The *Essex* had British colors flying, and Porter kept them up, hoping the stranger would think they were a clumsy ruse by an American merchant. Satisfied with his disguise, he quietly cleared for action, while concealing every appearance of doing so.

The approaching stranger was a much smaller ship than the *Essex*, the 20-gun sloop of war HMS *Alert*, based in St. John's, Newfoundland. As the *Alert* drew closer, Porter could see how tiny she was, but he did not believe size would matter to her captain. The Royal Navy had a well-deserved reputation for successfully attacking larger enemy warships. It was a tradition in the British navy—going back to Sir Francis Drake in the sixteenth century—for enterprising captains to ignore the odds and attack. Every major and minor navy in Europe and the Mediterranean had suffered galling defeats at the hands of what looked like inferior British men-of-war. Nonetheless, Porter wanted to make sure that this captain did not back off. As the *Alert* got closer, Porter made it look as if the *Essex* was making a run for it. He shook out the reefs from the topsails and hoisted the topgallant yards, but while doing so, he put out drag sails from the stern unseen to slow the *Essex*.

Nothing Porter did had the slightest effect on the *Alert*. She continued to bear down, her sails straining to capture every bit of wind. Despite her array of canvas, she looked slow, which made her an even easier target than Porter originally thought. When the *Alert* drew near, she made a signal and hoisted British colors. Her gun ports were open and cannon thrust out, obviously poised to attack. By 11:30 she approached to within pistol shot on the *Essex*'s starboard quarter, intending to rake her. At which point, Porter hoisted the Stars and Stripes and wore short around, causing the enemy to pass under his stern to a position off his lee quarter. Suddenly, the *Alert*'s crew gave a loud shout and fired a full broadside of canister and grape shot. But by then she was too far abaft the *Essex*'s beam and delivered only a glancing blow.

Porter quickly put up the *Essex*'s helm and brought her deadly larboard carronades to bear. The *Alert* responded by hauling her wind on the starboard tack. Porter wore again and brought his starboard guns to bear. By this time, the enemy was on the starboard tack, trying to prevent the *Essex* from getting alongside and boarding.

Porter countered by standing on a wind on the starboard tack until the ships were separated by about a musket shot (a hundred yards). He then wore suddenly and raked the enemy with his powerful 32-pound carronades, delivering a devastating blow. The *Alert*'s tars were stunned. They got so rattled they panicked. And so did their first lieutenant, Andrew

Duncan, who led the frightened tars aft to the quarterdeck and pleaded with the captain to strike the colors. He refused. Instead, he attempted to escape, but Porter was right after him; making more sail; hoisting his favorite flag with the motto "FREE TRADE AND SAILORS RIGHTS"; and ranging up to within pistol shot on the *Alert*'s starboard quarter. From there, it was certain that every shot from the *Essex* would find its target. Porter was about to deliver a final crushing fusillade, when the British captain—seeking to avoid the dreadful consequences of the broadside he knew was coming—prudently struck his colors. The battle had lasted less than twelve minutes.

The *Alert* turned out to be a former collier the Royal Navy had purchased in 1804. A sturdy, well-built vessel, she had been used to carry coal from Newcastle to London, which she did a good job of, but she was too slow for combat. The British had been at war with the French for twenty years, first in the French Wars and then the Napoleonic Wars. The Royal Navy was so desperate for ships that it was forced to acquire a few colliers and turn them into men-of-war. When the *Alert* was converted, she carried twenty 18-pound carronades, making her nominally a sloop of war, but without the fighting capacity of Britain's other sloops, which had heavier guns and were much faster.

Porter sent First Lieutenant John Downes to take possession of the *Alert*, and while he did, her captain, Thomas L. P. Laugharne, came aboard the *Essex* to surrender his sword. Before doing so he told Porter that the *Alert* had six feet of water in the hold and was in danger of sinking. Porter reacted quickly, ordering her wore round on the other tack to bring her shot holes above water, and he sent carpenters to plug the holes, which they did rather easily.

When Lieutenant Downes arrived on the *Alert* with his party he found what he expected—her hull, sails, and rigging badly damaged. But he did not expect her crew to be in the excellent physical shape they were. Only three of her ninety men were seriously wounded and none were dead. What surprised him more, however, was the extent to which discipline had broken down. Once Captain Laugharne left the ship, his crew went wild, breaking into the spirits room, the purser's room, other store rooms—even the captain's cabin and stores, drinking as much liquor as they could, and throwing overboard whatever they could not consume.

The *Essex* for her part suffered no casualties. She had a few small musket and grape shots in her hull, but otherwise she remained untouched, except for her cabin windows, which had been broken by the concussion of her own guns.

Porter took the *Alert*'s officers and the better part of her crew aboard the *Essex*, and appointed Second Lieutenant James P. Wilmer as prize master to take charge on the sloop. His instructions were to proceed in company with the *Essex* to America. Porter hoped that the navy would buy the *Alert* and turn her into a guard or block ship, but not a cruising man-of-war.

The *Alert* was the American navy's first victory of the war over a British warship, which was surprising, since the Royal Navy was supposed to win every encounter regardless of the odds. Even more amazing was Porter's success before he met the *Alert*.

Since leaving New York on July 3, he had hunted in the North Atlantic between Bermuda and Newfoundland, ranging as far west as 38 degrees longitude. The game was plentiful. Before running across the *Alert*, he had taken eight other prizes. On July 11 he took the troop ship *Samuel & Sarah* (Captain L.T. Somes). She was part of a small convoy of seven, sailing under the protection of the 32-gun frigate, HMS *Minerva* (Captain Richard Hawkins). When Porter first saw the *Samuel & Sarah*, she was trailing the rest of the convoy, and a single shot across her bows brought her to. Seeing this, the *Minerva* broke away from the rest of the convoy and stormed after the *Essex*. Porter was delighted. He wanted nothing more than to fight an enemy frigate of equal size, and here was one coming right for him—and only a few days into the war.

Suddenly, as Porter was hastily preparing for the *Minerva*'s onslaught, Captain Hawkins changed his mind, reversed course, and returned to the troop ships, all of which were well armed. Porter could not believe it. He was furious, but there was nothing he could do—attacking the entire convoy would have been suicide.

Hawkins undoubtedly wanted to fight as much as Porter did. The contempt for American men-of-war in Britain, and particularly in the Royal Navy, was palpable. Hawkins must have felt confident of a quick victory and easy prize money, not to mention plaudits from the Admiralty. Yet, at the same time, his orders required him to shepherd the First Regiment of

Royal Scots infantrymen from Barbados to Quebec, where they were desperately needed, and battling the *Essex* could compromise his mission. Even if he succeeded, he might get so banged up that his convoy would be at risk. So, unquestionably with great reluctance, he declined combat and continued on his way. The *Samuel & Sarah* and all her troops were left to their fate.

The easy capture had presented Porter with a big problem—what to do with 197 new prisoners. He had no wish to keep them aboard the *Essex* and have them gobble up his supplies, or attempt to take the ship, so he threw the transport's armament overboard, put her crew and soldiers on parole of honor (which meant they could not fight against the United States until formally exchanged for American prisoners), and sent her on her way with a ransom bond of $14,000.

The *Samuel & Sarah* soon disappeared over the horizon, and Porter continued his remarkable cruise, capturing one prize after another. Between July 13 and August 1 he took the brigs *Lamphrey* and *Leander*, which he sent into port as prizes. On August 2 he caught the *Nancy*, which he also sent into port as a prize. On the same day he seized the tiny brig *Hero*, which he burnt. She was of little value. The next day, August 3, Porter stopped the brig *Brothers* and found to his surprise and delight that famed Revolutionary War hero Joshua Barney, sailing in the privateer *Rossie*, had previously captured her and was sending her into port with a prize crew. The *Brothers* had sixty-two of Barney's prisoners from five other prizes on board. Porter turned her into a cartel ship (a vessel with only one signal gun, whose sole mission was to exchange prisoners), added twenty-five of his own prisoners, and sent her to St. John's Newfoundland under the command of Midshipman Stephen Decatur McKnight. It was a challenging assignment for the young midshipman, but his captain was confident he'd be up to the task. Sailing and command were in McKnight's blood, after all. He was the nephew of Porter's great contemporary, Commodore Stephen Decatur.

Porter captured two more prizes, the *King George* and the *Mary*, before running into the *Alert* on August 13. He sent the *King George* into port as a prize and burnt the *Mary*. He kept the *Alert* with him, however, and sailed with her in company toward the Delaware Capes. It was a passage fraught with peril. A large number of prisoners were now aboard, and they presented a huge problem that soon developed into a crisis. As was their duty, they planned an escape. Captain Laugharne's coxswain took the lead.

On the night of the planned breakout, the cox suddenly appeared standing beside the hammock of Midshipman David Farragut with a pistol in his hand. He stared down at Farragut, who luckily had spotted him approaching and remained perfectly still with his eyes shut. Satisfied that Farragut was asleep, the cox moved on. As he did, Farragut slipped out of his hammock and crept noiselessly to the captain's cabin and warned Porter, who sprang from his cot and ran to the berth deck, shouting, "Fire! Fire!"

The ensuing hubbub startled the prisoners, but not the *Essex* crew, who numbered three hundred and twenty. Part of Porter's training of them had been to sound fire alarms at odd hours of the night. He even had smoke created in the main hold to make the exercise more real. During the drills, when the alarm sounded, each man repaired to his quarters with a cutlass and blanket to await the captain's orders. Porter conducted the exercise frequently, so that the ship would be prepared for any emergency. This was the first occasion he had to put the exercise to the test, however, and the crew's performance was near perfect. Outnumbered, utterly confused, the prisoners became disoriented. In a short time they were back under control.

Porter knew before the uprising that having so many hostile tars aboard was asking for trouble, and with provisions and water running low, he decided to send them to Newfoundland. Captain Laugharne readily agreed to the terms. They meant that Laugharne and his men would escape a potentially long confinement in an American prison. On August 18 Porter dispatched the *Alert* as a cartel ship with Lieutenant Wilmer still in charge. Aboard were Captain Laugharne, his officers, and entire crew. Porter directed Wilmer to take the *Alert* to St. Johns and return to New York with whatever Americans he could acquire in exchange. Porter was counting on the admiral in Newfoundland (Sir John T. Duckworth) to cooperate. It was an assignment fraught with peril for Wilmer, but he was eager for it.

Porter now turned for home to Chester, Pennsylvania. Situated on the Delaware River, between Philadelphia and Wilmington, Chester was the oldest town in the state. There, Porter would refurbish and resupply the *Essex*. There too his family awaited, at Green Bank, their mansion on the Delaware. He expected that traveling to Chester would be tricky business. He imagined that the British had established a blockade along the American coast. Since their base at Halifax was close to New

England and New York, he assumed their ships would be stationed outside the important ports north of the Hudson River, and possibly as far south as the Delaware Capes, and even Chesapeake Bay.

His fears appeared to be confirmed on September 4 when he ran into what he thought were British warships off the tail of Georges Bank. After a lookout aboard the *Essex* spotted three suspicious ships, Porter went aloft and observed them for a time, before concluding that they were indeed enemy warships. Two larger ones were to the southward and a brig to the northward. The brig was racing after an American merchantman. Porter set out after the brig, which instantly gave up chasing the merchant and dashed for the protection of the two larger men-of-war. Porter cut her off, however, and forced her to sail northward. He continued to chase her, but had to give up when the wind slackened and the brig got out sweeps (long oars).

Meanwhile, the larger warships, seeing what Porter was up to, went after him. A sudden change of wind allowed them to come up fast. By four in the afternoon they had gained his wake. Porter kept straining to stay beyond their reach, hoping that night would arrive before they got within striking distance, and he could disappear into the darkness. They continued gaining on him, however. The largest was still some distance to windward, but the other was only five miles astern, bearing S by W, working hard to catch up before nightfall. Porter did everything he could to keep beyond her reach, planning to heave about as soon as it was dark and pass right by her in the opposite direction. If he found it impossible to sneak by, he intended to fire a broadside into her and lay her on board. He organized boarding parties, and when he revealed his plan, the crew responded with three cheers.

Porter was able to keep ahead of his closest pursuer until seven when it finally grew dark. At 7:20 he hove about and stood SE by S until 8:30, whereupon he bore away SW, and the British ships miraculously vanished. Porter was dumbfounded. He considered their disappearance remarkable, and all the more so since a pistol was accidentally fired by an officer on the *Essex* at the moment when Porter thought he was but a short distance from the nearest ship. Greatly relieved, he made for the Delaware Capes. He never considered going to New York or Rhode Island, where he imagined British blockaders would be swarming.

As the *Essex* traveled home, Porter felt a deep sense of satisfaction. The accomplishments of his ship and crew on this first cruise of the war were exceptional. He estimated that his captures were worth in excess of $300,000, a handsome figure, made even more impressive by the fact that he had taken 424 prisoners. He also felt vindicated. His promotion to captain (the highest rank in the navy at the time) had been long delayed, and had not actually been granted until July 2, the day before he left New York. His performance during the *Essex*'s first cruise was additional proof in his mind that his numerous requests for promotion should have been granted long before they were. One thing he did not feel satisfied with, however, was his triumph over the *Alert*. She was not enough of a challenge. He longed to do battle with a frigate of at least the size of the *Essex*, and he became fixated on accomplishing this goal.

The *Essex* reached the Delaware Capes without further incident. British blockaders were nowhere in sight. Porter was mistaken about there being a blockade. None would be in place for months, although he continued to believe one was. When he dropped anchor off Chester, in the middle of September, he was anxious to repair and resupply the *Essex* and get right back to sea before he got trapped. He was also anxious about the fate of Midshipman McKnight and Lieutenant Wilmer. He need not have been. Both accomplished their difficult missions without mishap and returned to the *Essex* while she was still in the Delaware River preparing for her next cruise. Neither Porter nor any of his crew suspected that they would be getting ready for what would become one of the most famous voyages in American history, an oceangoing saga unsurpassed in the Age of Sail.

PRESIDENT MADISON'S
WAR PLAN

D AVID PORTER'S VICTORY OVER THE *ALERT* CAME AS A
surprise to President James Madison. When Congress had declared
war with Britain on June 18, 1812, the president did not think the navy
would play a significant part in it. The fleet was so small that almost no
one outside the navy's professional officer core expected much from it.
The United States had only twenty warships, while Britain had five to six
hundred continually at sea, and many more in shipyards being repaired
or built. Eighty-three British warships were in bases within striking distance of the American coast at Halifax, Nova Scotia; St. Johns, Newfoundland; Port Royal, Jamaica; and Antigua, West Indies. Although Madison
could not say so publicly, he expected that if he allowed the American
fleet to venture out of port, the Royal Navy would make quick work of it,
capturing, or sinking it, as they had during the War of Independence. He
thought it likely that America's men-of-war would be blockaded in their
harbors for the entire war.

Instead of counting on his navy, the president was relying on Napoleon
Bonaparte, a man he detested, to force Britain into negotiating with the

United States. For months Madison had watched as the French emperor amassed an army of over 600,000, the largest in history to that time, along the Polish border with Russia. Everyone expected Napoleon to launch an all-out attack before the end of June, and he did, on June 24. Everyone assumed he would compel Tsar Alexander I to ask for terms in a matter of weeks, certainly before the end of September. After that, Bonaparte was likely to turn his attention to his longtime nemesis, Great Britain. He had threatened to invade England twice in the past and had pulled back because of the insuperable power of the Royal Navy. But if Napoleon tried again with all of Continental Europe under his control, he would likely be able to amass enough sea power to drive a massive army across the Channel, occupy London, and dictate terms.

Madison had his own terms. He wanted to force London to negotiate an end to three issues that had precipitated his call to arms—the Royal Navy's wholesale impressment of American seamen, London's brazen attempt to control American trade, and its support of the Indian nations fighting to preserve their territory. The president was convinced that the British would not want to be fighting America at the same time they were facing a Napoleonic invasion.

To bring added pressure on London, Madison planned to attack Canada as soon as war was declared. Although he had an inexperienced, poorly led regular army of a mere seven thousand, he intended to augment it with enough militiamen to seize at least part of Canada during the summer of 1812. He thought the British would be so preoccupied with Europe they would be unable to defend Canada. Only a small contingent of His Majesty's regulars were stationed there. Madison assumed they would be inadequate, and that Canadian militiamen would be of little practical value. In addition, Madison believed that the many Americans who had emigrated to Canada—lured by land grants and promises of low taxes—would not oppose an American invasion. He thought that if he acquired even a portion of Canada he would have a strong lever to use in any negotiation with London.

Madison intended to bring even more pressure on Britain. He would unleash hundreds of privateers to attack her commerce, as the patriots had done so successfully during the Revolutionary War. Instead of relying on the navy, he thought privateers would provide America's muscle on the high seas. During the War of Independence, the Continental Navy had contributed almost nothing to America's victory, whereas privateers had been of great service. As the Revolutionary War progressed, shipbuilding centers like Salem, Massachusetts, had increased the size and quality of their privateers, until by the early 1780s some of them were carrying twenty guns—the equivalent of Britain's powerful sloops of war. Hundreds of American privateers (the exact number has always been in dispute) set out during the Revolution and ravaged enemy merchantmen, contributing to the war weariness in Britain that eventually forced a reluctant king to accept American independence. The president anticipated that privateers would perform the same service during this war, which many believed was America's second War of Independence.

Madison much preferred negotiating to fighting. He had been extremely reluctant to go to war, but he felt that he had no choice. London had pushed him beyond the breaking point. The issues in dispute had been souring relations for years, and despite Madison's determined attempts to resolve them peacefully, the reactionary Tory government of Spencer Perceval refused to seriously negotiate. Perceval was confident that he could keep impressing whomever he pleased, interfering with American trade, and supporting the Indians without suffering any consequences. America's pitifully small army and navy, and deep political divisions between the Federalist Party (which remained pro-British) and Madison's own Republican Party, elicited Perceval's contempt.

Right up until Congress declared war, London believed that Madison would never actually issue a call to arms, no matter how often he threatened to. The president became so frustrated with Britain's unwillingness to take America's complaints seriously that he decided the only way to bring Perceval to the negotiating table was to actually declare war. Thus, on June 1, 1812, an exasperated president urged Congress to vote for war, and after a bitter eighteen-day-long debate it did.

Commander in chief was a role Madison was ill-prepared for. He had done everything he could to avoid a war, and now he had to lead the republic in the most perilous undertaking in its short history. He was not

counting on the navy in any way. His lack of interest in the fleet was due
in part to his expectation that the war would be over quickly. He even entertained the idea that actual combat might not be necessary. He hoped
that the threat from Napoleon, the potential loss of Canada, and massive
privateer attacks, would force Britain to come to terms before the war had
progressed very far. It would not matter, in his view, whether America
had a strong navy or not.

IRONICALLY, THE NAVY'S WEAKNESS WAS A DIRECT RESULT OF
Madison's own policies and those of his mentor, Thomas Jefferson. They
had always opposed building a respectable fleet. When President George
Washington proposed creating a new federal navy in 1794, Jefferson (even
though he was Washington's secretary of state) and Madison (the leader
of the House of Representatives) opposed him. America had not had a
navy since the end of the Revolutionary War, and by 1794 President
Washington thought it was time the country built one. America was
strong enough financially, in his view, and international conditions made
it imperative. The Barbary pirate state of Algeria was seizing American
merchantmen with impunity; Britain was impressing American seamen
and interfering with her trade, while revolutionary France was aggressively
trying to involve the United States in her war against monarchical Europe.
Washington planned to use the new navy to force all three nations to respect American rights on the high seas, and her neutrality in the French
Revolutionary Wars then consuming Europe.

Jefferson, Madison, and their supporters fought Washington every
step of the way. They could not prevent him from starting a navy, but
they did succeeded in keeping the number of ships to a bare minimum.
President John Adams also ran into stiff opposition from the same quarter
in 1798 when he tried to expand and strengthen the navy to fight the
Quasi-War with France. Adams was temporarily successful, but once the
war was over in 1800, he drastically reduced the fleet, hoping that Jefferson,
his successor, would not confiscate it altogether.

When Jefferson took office in 1801, he could not do away with the
navy, as he might have liked. Tripoli had declared war on the United
States, and he had to use the warships the country still had to fight the pirate state. Nonetheless, he, and then Madison (his hand-picked successor),

had, with the support of most Republican congressmen, deliberately kept the navy small. They were afraid that a larger fleet would never be large enough to stand up to a European navy, particularly the Royal Navy. They felt it would be too expensive, embroil the country in unnecessary wars, be a powerful instrument in the hands of an ambitious executive, and, in short, be a threat to the Constitution. Thus, when the War of 1812 began, the United States had practically no navy. The largest of her twenty warships were old frigates, every one of them built in the 1790s prior to Jefferson taking office. No frigates, or much of anything else—except tiny gunboats of limited use and a few small warships—had been built in American yards since 1801.

President Madison soon found out that he was wrong about the need for a potent navy, however. As with most conflicts, once the War of 1812 began, nothing went as the president had planned, except for the privateers. They put to sea in significant numbers only days after Congress declared war. But Napoleon's push into Russia did not have the immediate success Madison expected. Tsar Alexander's badly outnumbered army successfully avoided the early showdown that Bonaparte wanted. Instead, the Tsar conducted a masterful retreat, coupled with a scorched-earth policy that drew the French deeper into Russia during a blisteringly hot summer that deprived Napoleon of desperately needed supplies, and consumed his troops in significant numbers. And the Canadian invasion, which was also supposed to be easy and quick, turned into a disaster. On August 15 an American army under General William Hull suffered a major defeat at Detroit.

The president had planned a simultaneous, three-pronged invasion of Canada. The first thrust was to come from Detroit, across the Detroit River to Amherstburg in Lower Canada. The second was to be a dash across the Niagara River. The third was an attack on Montreal. Nothing was working out, however. Not only did General Hull fail, but the other invasions never took place when they were supposed to, and each eventually ended in total failure.

When Madison heard of General Hull's ignominious surrender at Detroit, he was aghast. His war strategy was falling apart, and 1812 was an election year. The president now faced electoral defeat, as well as a war that was spinning out of control.

His fortunes were miraculously reversed, however, when he received help from an unexpected quarter—the United States Navy. On August 19, while Porter and the *Essex* were making their way toward the Delaware Capes, Captain Isaac Hull (General Hull's nephew) won a convincing victory over a British frigate—a feat that was never supposed to happen and that amazed the world. Sailing in the 44-gun heavy frigate USS *Constitution* in latitude 41° 42' N and longitude 55° 48' W, Hull fought and crushed the 38-gun frigate HMS *Guerriere*, one of the Royal Navy's premier warships, commanded by a capable skipper, Captain James Dacres, in half an hour.

The totally unexpected victory had a profound impact on both countries. Britain was shocked. The Royal Navy's aura of invincibility was of supreme importance. The *Constitution*'s easy triumph threatened to destroy it. Britain's contempt for the American navy made the wound cut even deeper.

Isaac Hull's triumph was so popular throughout the United States—even in areas like New England, where the Federalists were strong and the war unpopular—that it resuscitated Madison's electoral hopes, and caused him to completely change his mind about the navy. His belief that the British would make quick work of America's warships had been proven wrong, and he began searching for ways to employ them more effectively. He also recognized for the first time the urgent need to expand the fleet.

The president had help from the navy's senior officers. Before war was declared on June 18, Commodores John Rodgers and Stephen Decatur Jr., the senior captains in command, had given the president their views on how to use the navy. They had provided him with markedly different proposals, but Madison—not considering the navy important at the time—had set them aside. Now he was ready to develop a real strategy for the fleet, and he looked again at the thinking of the two commanders.

Rodgers had written on June 3 that the country's few men-of-war should be grouped together and sent to sea. He expected that the available British warships at Halifax would immediately go after them, drawing the Royal Navy away from the east coast, preventing it from blockading major ports, and allowing the large American merchant fleet then at sea to return home. Rodgers suggested that after the merchant ships were safely in port, the navy could be sent to harass Britain's commerce along the approaches to the English Channel and the coasts of Ireland, Scotland, and Wales. He pointed out that Britain had most of her naval force overseas fighting Napoleon and servicing a far-flung empire. She was, paradoxically, most vulnerable in her home waters.

Stephen Decatur, the navy's most celebrated captain, had a different view. He wrote on June 8 that American warships ought to patrol alone or in pairs, attacking the enemy—both warships and merchantmen—over as wide an area as possible, making it impossible for the enemy to destroy the entire American fleet in a single encounter.

After the victory of "Old Ironsides" on August 19, Madison revisited the recommendations of Rodgers and Decatur. Only days later (before Porter and the *Essex* reached the Delaware Capes) the president decided that commerce raiding would be the navy's core mission. At the same time he adopted Decatur's recommendation and divided the blue-water fleet into three small squadrons of three warships each, led by Commodores Rodgers, Decatur, and William Bainbridge, a close friend of David Porter. The three commodores received orders to deploy their squadrons wherever they thought best. Porter and the *Essex* were assigned to Bainbridge, who planned to attack British commerce around their major base at St. Helena Island in the South Atlantic. It was a course recommended by his friend William Jones of Philadelphia, who would soon become secretary of the navy. Bainbridge's three-ship squadron would be composed of the *Constitution*, the *Essex*, and the sloop of war *Hornet*, under Master Commandant James Lawrence. When the president settled on his new strategy at the end of August, the *Constitution* and the *Hornet* were in Boston and would leave from there. The *Essex*, which was on her way to Chester, would have to rendezvous with them later.

Once Porter reached the Delaware River he was informed of his new assignment, and he set to work getting ready. Bainbridge notified him of potential meeting places—Porto Praia in the Cape Verde Islands (350 miles off the western extremity of Africa); the island of Fernando de Noronha (220 miles off the northeast coast of Brazil); Cape Frio near Rio de Janeiro; the island of St. Sebastian (200 miles south of Rio);

St. Catherine's Island (500 miles south of Rio); and St. Helena, 600 miles northwest of the Cape of Good Hope.

If none of these points of rendezvous worked out, and Porter was left on his own, he was directed to "act according to your best judgment for the good of the service on which we are engaged." It was a mandate that gave Porter, if he failed to meet Bainbridge, wide latitude, a possibility that must have excited his fertile imagination.

CHAPTER 2

THE MAKING OF A SEA WARRIOR

N O ONE WAS BETTER TRAINED OR MORE MOTIVATED TO fight the War of 1812 than Captain David Porter. His whole life had been a preparation for this great trial.

His father, David Porter Sr., was a redoubtable fighting sailor who had served in the American navy during the Revolutionary War. One of the elder Porter's more remarkable adventures occurred when he was a midshipman aboard the 32-gun Continental frigate *Raleigh*, whose skipper was the renowned John Barry. On September 26, 1778, off the coast of Maine, a powerful British squadron forced Barry to run the *Raleigh* ashore. He escaped with some of his men, but others were captured, including Porter, who was shipped off to New York Harbor in chains and thrown into the hellish prison ship *Jersey*. By a strange coincidence, Porter's brother Samuel was already there. He had been badly wounded in a sea fight, captured, and confined to the *Jersey*, where he received no care and was certain to die. His brother was there to comfort him in his last moments.

Porter spent all his prison time planning an escape. He was a gifted raconteur, and managed to ingratiate himself with the British tars who were his jailers. They must have hated the god-awful *Jersey* as much as he did. Eventually, he persuaded them to smuggle him off the ship in an empty water cask; after which, he went right back to fighting—mostly in privateers.

The elder Porter's sea stories caught the imagination of his son, who wanted nothing more than to follow in his father's footsteps. The third generation, David Jr.'s son, David Dixon Porter, would follow in those footsteps, too, into the naval service, becoming an admiral and a great hero during the Civil War. In 1875, he would write of his father: "The boy, at an early age, manifested the restless energy which ever afterwards characterized him, in that respect resembling his father, whose daring spirit would stop at nothing when there was any enterprise afoot." Young Porter began his naval career in 1796 at the age of sixteen, sailing—over his mother's strong objections—as a deck hand on the *Eliza*, a merchant-man his father commanded. The Porters shipped out of Baltimore and sailed to Hispaniola. At the port of Jérémie, they found plenty of trouble when an arrogant British captain from the privateer *Harriet* attempted to impress hands from their ship. British warships and privateers took American seamen off their vessels whenever they pleased, whether they were at war with the United States or not. The British usually had no trouble, and the *Harriet*'s captain was not expecting any this time. He was in for a surprise, however. When his unsuspecting pressgang climbed aboard the *Eliza*, Captain Porter and his men, including his son, attacked them, putting up a spirited fight with inferior weapons. During the bloody mêlée, young David saw a comrade right next to him shot dead. The Porters and their men fought with a ferocity that shocked the attackers. Resistance was so strong, the British raiders retreated.

This was young Porter's first encounter with impressment, and it left a lasting impression. He had another set-to with the British on his next voyage when he was seventeen and first officer aboard a merchant brig bound from Baltimore to Santo Domingo. A no-nonsense press-gang from a frigate boarded his vessel and hauled him off with a number of other men. Porter was determined to avoid joining the Royal Navy, however, and when he saw a chance to escape, he jumped overboard, swimming to a nearby Danish brig bound for Europe. He joined her crew and worked his passage across the Atlantic to Copenhagen. After landing, he quickly found a vessel returning to America, signed on, and made his way home, after a tempestuous, mid-winter passage. On a third voyage to the West

Indies, another British pressgang captured him, dragged him aboard another warship, and roughed him up. He escaped one more time, however, and again worked his way back to the United States.

Given his family background and experience, it was not surprising that Porter joined the fledgling American navy forming under President Adams and Secretary of the Navy Benjamin Stoddert in 1798 to fight the Quasi-War with France. Porter obtained appointment as a midshipman, and on April 16 boarded the frigate *Constellation* as her sixth midshipman. The captain was Thomas Truxtun, a storied veteran of the privateer fleet during the Revolutionary War and a favorite of George Washington. Truxtun was a demanding skipper, and Porter sometimes rebelled, although not openly, against his strict discipline.

In fact, Porter could not have found a better teacher, as he later acknowledged from time to time. Truxtun believed that the infant American navy had to pay special attention to the training of its young officers and future leaders. He watched over his brood with a sharp eye, tending to their seamanship and character development. More importantly, he showed them by example how to manage a ship of war with maximum effect. Porter was in his natural element, and soon became a favorite of both Truxtun and First Lieutenant John Rodgers.

Porter did not get along with one particular officer, however. After suffering continual harassment from Lieutenant Simon Gross, Porter, in his characteristically impetuous way, punched him in the face during an argument and knocked him to the deck. The surprised lieutenant rose, called for the sergeant of the guard, and grabbed a cutlass. He was about to slice up Porter when Captain Truxtun appeared. The lieutenant froze, as Truxtun took charge. After hearing what had happened, Truxtun had Porter arrested and sent below. Normally, a captain would have then ordered a court martial, and Porter would have been dismissed from the service for striking a superior officer. But Truxtun, who knew the men on his ship well, was not going to let a bully like Gross destroy a young man's promising career. Instead of punishing Porter, Truxtun put him back on duty, and saw to it that Gross—a sadistic drunk—was run out of the service.

On February 9, 1799, the *Constellation* became embroiled in the most famous fight of the Quasi-War. She was cruising off the Island of Nevis, two hundred miles south of Puerto Rico, when she fell in with the 40-gun French frigate *L'Insurgente*, one of France's finest warships. Midshipman Porter was in command of the foretop. In the ensuing battle an eighteen-pound ball smashed the foretopmast just above the cap. It threatened to break free and fall to the deck or go over the side with its yards and sails, damaging the ship and impeding Truxtun's ability to maneuver. With the smoke and din on the weather deck making it impossible to communicate the danger to the captain, Porter went aloft at great risk to himself, cut the slings holding the yards to the mast, and lowered the yards to the deck. In saving the mast, Porter allowed Truxtun to carry on and win a stunning victory.

After *L'Insurgente* surrendered, Truxtun ordered Lieutenant Rodgers, Midshipman Porter, and eleven men to take possession of the prize and transfer its 332 prisoners to the *Constellation*. When that dicey business was completed, and enough repairs were made on the damaged ships to get them to port, they crawled in company to St. Kitts, arriving three days later at Basseterre roadstead. There the British authorities gave them a warm reception (Britain was at war with France during that time, but not with the United States).

As the Quasi-War progressed, Porter continued to perform exceptionally well. On October 8, 1799, when he was only nineteen, the navy promoted him to lieutenant, and assigned him to the 20-gun schooner *Experiment* as her second officer. Unfortunately, the skipper, Lieutenant William Maley, was an incompetent coward—totally unlike Truxtun or Rodgers. His character soon became evident. On January 1, 1800, the *Experiment* was convoying four merchantmen, when she was becalmed in the Gulf of Gonaïves. Local pirates known as picaroons suddenly appeared in ten oar-propelled barges, sweeping out from dens on shore to attack the convoy.

The *Experiment* was disguised as a merchantman, and thinking she was one, the heavily armed pirates went after her. Maley saw that he was badly outnumbered and decided to surrender, but his officers, led by Porter, refused. First Lieutenant Joshua Blake supported Porter, and seeing this, Maley turned the ship over to Porter, who fought a bloody battle with the pirates for seven hours and eventually beat them off. Many of the picaroons were killed, but only two of the *Experiment*'s crew were wounded. Porter was one of them, receiving a musket ball in the shoulder. Unfortunately, while the fight raged on the *Experiment*, pirates captured two of the other merchantmen. For his disgraceful conduct, Maley was dismissed from the navy.

Porter's next ship was the *Constitution*. Her skipper was Silas Talbot, of Revolutionary War fame and one of the finest fighting captains ever to serve the United States. Aware of Porter's ability, Talbot gave him command of the armed tender *Amphitheatre*, a vessel the *Experiment* had captured. A short time later, Porter was back on the *Experiment* as first lieutenant under Lieutenant Charles Stewart, an officer with a brilliant future ahead of him. He and Porter formed a close friendship.

On September 1, 1800, the *Experiment* captured the eight-gun French privateer *Deux Amis*. Stewart ordered Porter and four seamen to take command of the prize. When Porter climbed aboard the *Deux Amis* he found forty Frenchmen. They would be problem enough, but soon Stewart and the *Experiment* disappeared—chasing another prize. Porter was left alone in a dangerous situation. The closest port was St. Kitts, at least three days away. Undaunted, he herded the prisoners below, kept cannon loaded with canister shot pointed at the hatches, and sailed to St. Kitts, where he arrived four days later.

The Quasi-War with France ended on March 3, 1801, the last day of John Adams's presidency. The country began demobilizing. President Adams, who had been defeated for reelection by Thomas Jefferson, drastically reduced the navy in the hopes that Jefferson would not do away with it entirely. The Peace Establishment Act, which Adams signed on his last day in office, was very much in tune with Jefferson's thinking. Under it, the navy's officer corps was cut: to nine captains, thirty-six lieutenants, and 150 midshipmen. Porter survived.

The new president wanted the navy to be as small as possible, but a new war restrained him. Just as Jefferson came into office, Tripoli declared war on the United States. He was forced to use what was left of the fleet to fight the pirate state. Nonetheless, Jefferson made sure the navy remained small.

The war with Tripoli, which lasted for four long years, proved to be a seminal event in the life of David Porter. In the early stages he performed remarkably well, as he had in the past, serving in a variety of ships under different commanders. In 1801, now twenty-one, he was first lieutenant aboard the 12-gun armed schooner *Enterprise* (the *Experiment*'s sister ship). Lieutenant Andrew Sterrett was the *Enterprise*'s skipper.

Sterrett and Porter had served together under Truxtun on the *Constellation*. Sterrett was well known in the navy for an extraordinary incident that had happened on that ship. During the *Constellation*'s battle with *L'Insurgente*, amid heavy fighting, seaman Neale Harvey became terrified and abandoned his cannon. The twenty-one-year-old Sterrett flew into a rage and ran his sword through him. Harvey was one of only two men killed aboard the *Constellation* during the fight.

Captain Truxtun did not reprimand Sterrett, nor did the navy. The young lieutenant's execution of a man under his command during combat was let stand. Sterrett suffered no punishment, not even to his career, which proceeded apace. His action never became a precedent, but it was never condemned either.

When Sterrett arrived in the Mediterranean with Porter, he was looking for a fight, and on August 1, 1801, he found one. The *Enterprise* was off Malta when she fell in with the 14-gun *Tripoli*, a polacre-rigged warship under Rais Mahomet Rous, commander of the Tripolitan navy. As soon as Sterrett recognized the flag, he closed to within pistol shot and blasted away, commencing a savage battle that lasted for three hours. The Tripolitans tried three times to board the *Enterprise*, but each time Sterrett, Porter, and their men beat them off. The *Tripoli*'s deck became an ugly sight; mangled bodies were strewn everywhere. With no hope remaining, Rous finally gave up and struck his colors. Porter led a boarding party to take the surrender, and he was appalled at the slaughter on the *Tripoli*'s decks. The *Enterprise* had no dead and no wounded. It was a complete rout.

The following year, Porter was assigned to the 36-gun *Chesapeake*, and then transferred in April 1803 to the 36-gun frigate *New York* as her second lieutenant. The *New York* was Commodore Richard Morris's flagship. Morris was commander of the Mediterranean fleet at the time, tasked by President Jefferson with protecting American commerce and defeating Tripoli. Porter was not pleased with the transfer; he had little respect for Morris, who appeared to have no appetite for fighting. Porter's unhappiness was relieved somewhat by his association with the *New York*'s first lieutenant, Isaac Chauncey, with whom he formed a close relationship. The two lieutenants had the same low opinion of Morris. During the first week of June 1803 Porter did get into some action, leading a night raid against Tripolitan vessels. His party was beaten off, however, and he was wounded. Midshipman John Downes participated in the raid, impressing Porter with his daring and courage.

By the summer of 1803, Morris's poor performance, combined with his unwillingness to communicate with Washington, had so frustrated Jefferson that he replaced him with Commodore Edward Preble. The president expected his new commander to end the war before his reelection campaign in 1804. Preble had fallen ill in Batavia (later Jakarta, Indonesia), and he had not fully recovered. In spite of his fragile health, he was far more aggressive than his lackluster predecessor. Even so, the economy-minded Jefferson—in spite of his looming reelection contest—still did not give Preble enough firepower to accomplish his mission. This did not stop Preble, of course; he did his best with what he had. His fleet consisted of the 44-gun *Constitution* (his flagship), the 36-gun *Philadelphia* (Captain William Bainbridge), the 16-gun *Argus* (Lieutenant Isaac Hull), the 12-gun *Enterprise* (Lieutenant Stephen Decatur Jr.), the 12-gun *Nautilus* (Lieutenant Richard Somers), the 12-gun *Vixen* (Lieutenant John Smith), and the 16-gun *Syren*, under Lieutenant Charles Stewart.

Preble may have had less firepower than he would have liked, but his captains were a superb group of young stars, which he soon realized. They had their doubts about him, however. He had a reputation for having a quick temper and a willingness to discipline subordinates with a heavy hand. In spite of this, he soon won their respect when he proved to be also brave, smart, decisive, willing to listen to men who had proven themselves, and above all, committed to winning. As time went by, a bond formed between the commodore and his young lions that allowed Preble to get the most out of the meager force assigned to him.

The *Constitution* arrived at Gibraltar on September 12, 1803. Preble was anxious to resupply and move on to Tripoli. He was delayed, however, when he discovered that the King of Morocco was secretly cooperating with the bashaw, of Tripoli, Yusuf Karamanli, seizing American vessels whenever he could. There were four Barbary States—Morocco, Algeria, Tunisia, and Tripoli—and Preble wanted to avoid fighting more than one of them at a time. So he adjusted his plans, sailing first to Tangiers, where he thought it would be relatively easy to convince the Moroccan king that peace with the United States, under the old treaty of 1786, was preferable to being attacked.

Preble realized he did not need the entire American squadron to bring the Moroccan king to heel. So he sent Captain Bainbridge ahead to Tripoli with the *Philadelphia* and the *Vixen* to begin a blockade. Preble expected to deal quickly with Morocco and then join Bainbridge for an attack on Tripoli. To strengthen Bainbridge's crew, Preble appointed David Porter, now twenty-three, as first officer on the *Philadelphia*. Preble had a high regard for Porter's fighting record. Needless to say, Porter was delighted with the prospect of finally taking decisive action against Tripoli.

The *Philadelphia* was a powerful frigate. She was one of the subscription warships built by the city of Philadelphia and given to the government in the wave of patriotic fervor that swept the country in the spring and summer of 1798 at the start of the Quasi-War with France. Together with the shallow draught *Vixen*, she could wreak havoc on Tripoli's commerce. The *Vixen* could patrol in areas that the larger *Philadelphia* could not, while the frigate could command the deeper waters outside the port.

Bainbridge and Porter worked well together. They trusted each other. Bainbridge recognized Porter's leadership ability, and gave him broad authority to run the ship. That was fine with the lower deck. Bainbridge, was a hard skipper, who never had good relations with a crew and never sought them. Sensitive and moody, he had a low opinion of seamen. He respected officers as gentlemen and had reasonably good relations with them, but ordinary sailors were another matter. His attitude would have been a significant handicap in getting the *Philadelphia* to perform at her best had it not been for Porter, who acted as an intermediary between a difficult captain and a wary crew.

Porter ran a tight ship, but he respected the men, and they were happy to serve under him. He had been brought up in the strict, but humane school of Thomas Truxtun and his first lieutenant, John Rodgers. Like them, Porter had high standards and was a disciplinarian, demanding attention to duty from everyone, and strict obedience. At the same time, he was fair. He did not play favorites, and he never hesitated to bend the rules when the situation required. Like Truxtun, he seldom resorted to physical punishment, as Bainbridge and Preble often did. Porter believed in leading by the force of his personality, rather than by terror, and he encouraged other officers to do the same. The result was a diverse crew that functioned as a cohesive unit ready for combat. As the *Philadelphia* plowed toward Tripoli, Porter was confident that she would make an important contribution to ending the war.

3

DISASTER IN TRIPOLI

DAVID PORTER WAS ANXIOUS TO DISTINGUISH HIMSELF IN Tripoli, and Bainbridge was as well. But Bainbridge's desire was far stronger than his first lieutenant's. Unlike Porter, whose career had been marked by continuous success, Bainbridge's, at least in his own estimation, had been a failure. His first disappointment had come on November 20, 1798, at the start of the Quasi-War. Then a lieutenant, Bainbridge, captain of the armed schooner *Retaliation*, was sailing off Guadeloupe with the sloop of war *Montezuma* (Commodore Alexander Murray) and the 18-gun brig *Norfolk* (Captain Thomas Williams). Suddenly, several sail were spotted. Two in the west appeared to be French. The *Montezuma* and *Norfolk* went after them, while Bainbridge in the *Retaliation* approached two in the east, who appeared to be friendly British cruisers. As Bainbridge got closer, however, he discovered that he'd made a dreadful mistake. The strangers were not British, but powerful French warships—the 40-gun frigate *L'Insurgente* and the 44-gun *Volontier*. *L'Insurgente* immediately sent up the French flag and opened fire, while the *Volontier* pulled alongside the *Retaliation* and ordered Bainbridge to haul down his colors. He had no choice but to comply. The French took the *Retaliation*, with Bainbridge and his crew aboard, to

Basse-Terre, the capital of Guadeloupe, and put them in prison for a time before exchanging them.

Bainbridge was understandably chagrined at being forced to surrender the *Retaliation* without a fight, but he was soon absolved of any blame and promoted to master commandant. Nonetheless, his failure to elude the French frigates or to fight them, rankled, and he yearned for a chance to wipe away the embarrassment by winning an important victory. He was given the opportunity when he was sent back into the fight against France as skipper of the *Norfolk*. He had some success with her—enough to get him promoted to captain on May 2, 1800—but it wasn't nearly enough for him; he wanted far more.

That was not to be, however. Immediately after receiving his promotion to captain, he was assigned the miserable duty of carrying tribute to the Dey of Algiers in accordance with a treaty signed with the pirate state in 1796. Bainbridge sailed to Algeria in the 24-gun *George Washington*—the first American warship to sail past Gibraltar and into the Mediterranean. Instead of simply delivering the tribute, Bainbridge sailed into the harbor at Algiers and put the *George Washington* within reach of the port's guns. It was a tactical error that gave the dey an opportunity to force Bainbridge into carrying gifts to the dey's master, the Sultan of the Ottoman Empire in Constantinople. The sultan was unhappy with the dey for making an untimely peace with France, and the dey was anxious to appease him. He compelled Bainbridge to fly the Algerian flag at the *George Washington*'s main while he sailed to Constantinople. It was a humiliation for Bainbridge and for his country, one that disturbed him far more than having to surrender the *Retaliation*. Fortunately for Bainbridge, Jefferson did not share his chagrin, and, believing that, given the circumstances, Bainbridge had acted wisely, the president did not even consider reprimanding him. In fact, he praised Bainbridge for his good judgment.

Soon after, Bainbridge became involved in the war with Tripoli as skipper of the *Essex*. He had a great desire to achieve the sort of distinction that would make up for what he considered his failure in Algeria. Sailing in company with the *Philadelphia* (Captain Samuel Barron) he looked into the harbor at Tripoli on September 28. In surveying the city, Bainbridge thought "it had a mean appearance, [looking] little better than a village. Their fortifications appear to cover a good deal of ground; it shows but few guns and apparently is slightly built." Little happened on this occasion for him to distinguish himself, and that remained the case until Preble gave him command of the *Philadelphia* and ordered him to blockade Tripoli. Bainbridge hoped the new assignment would be the means of ridding himself of the humiliation he continued to feel.

THE *PHILADELPHIA* AND THE *VIXEN* ARRIVED OFF TRIPOLI on October 7, 1803. The city's fortifications appeared much improved since Bainbridge first viewed them in 1801, but he saw nothing that would deter him. He wanted action right away, and so, of course, did Porter. The Tripolitans refused to accommodate them, however, keeping well clear of the powerful American warships. Bainbridge and his first mate became increasingly frustrated. "Made the coast of Tripoli on the 7th," he grumbled to Preble, "and have remained on this solitary station without the good fortune of seeing our enemies except under the refuge of well fortified works."

Aggravated by the inactivity and wanting to make some move before Preble arrived with the rest of the squadron, Bainbridge on October 19 sent the *Vixen* to patrol off Cape Bon Peninsula at the northeastern tip of Tunisia. There had been vague rumors of a Tripolitan warship in that area and American commerce being threatened. "My motives of ordering her off Cape Bon," he explained to Preble, were "to grant more efficient protection to our commerce, than I would by keeping her with me." It was a decision Bainbridge and Porter would deeply regret.

As the days went by, Bainbridge's annoyance at the inaction mounted. He kept searching for any opportunity—however small—to attack the enemy. On October 31 he saw his chance. "At 9 A.M., about five leagues eastward of Tripoli, [I] saw a ship in shore of us," he reported, "standing before the wind to the westward." She was obviously a Tripolitan vessel, sailing in waters honeycombed with shoals, sandbars, hidden rocks, and ledges. In spite of the dangers, Bainbridge gave chase with three leads continuously chanting soundings. His prey hoisted Tripolitan colors and continued on her course close to shore. "About 11 o'clock [I] had approached the shore to 7 fathoms of water, [and] commenced firing at her, which we continued by running before the wind until half past 11, being then in 7 fathoms water and finding our fire ineffectual to prevent her from getting into Tripoli, gave up the pursuit and was beating off the land when we ran on the rocks in 12 feet of water," he reported. An instant before grounding, Bainbridge, suddenly aware of the danger, ordered the helm put hard-a-port and the yards sharp braced. But it was too late. The frigate, making eight knots, ground to a halt in deep sand and rock on Kaliusa Reef—well-known to locals but not to Bainbridge, Porter, or any other officer. When the ship struck, Porter was half way up the mizzen rigging. The sudden jolt made him reverse course and return immediately to the quarterdeck, where he remained close to Bainbridge.

They both recognized that the *Philadelphia* was in serious danger. And she was alone; the *Vixen* was not around to help. She would have been of great service. "Had I not sent the schooner from us," Bainbridge wrote to Preble, "the accident might have been prevented: if not, we should have been able to have extricated ourselves."

Reacting quickly, Bainbridge, at Porter's urging, threw on all sails, hoping to move the ship forward into deeper water ahead, but all they succeeded in doing was planting her more firmly on the reef. The Tripolitans, in the meantime, had been studying the frigate's predicament, and they dispatched nine gunboats to assess the possibility of attacking her. They approached cautiously, of course. The *Philadelphia* could still sink them all fast.

As the enemy gunboats slowly closed in, Bainbridge asked Porter's opinion on what to do. He suggested that all the officers be consulted, and Bainbridge agreed. They advised lowering a boat to explore the depth of water in the immediate vicinity, which was done. Finding that the deepest water was astern, the officers urged Bainbridge to back the ship off, which he attempted to do by running the guns abaft, laying all the sails aback, loosening the topgallant sails, and setting a heavy press of canvas, hoping the wind would push the ship off the reef. But she did not budge. As a last desperate measure, a second council of officers advised cutting away the foremast, which Bainbridge did as well. As expected, the main topgallant mast toppled with it. But again, the *Philadelphia* would not move. Towing her off with the ship's boats, or using ketch anchors to accomplish the same thing was impractical; she was too deeply embedded, and the captain feared that the Tripolitan gunboats—getting closer all the time—would shoot the boat crews working the ketch anchors.

With Porter continuing to advise him, Bainbridge next cast three anchors off from the bows, started the water in the hold, and hove the big guns overboard, reserving only enough to resist the gunboats, which by now were firing on the ship. Nothing worked. Part of the stern was then cut away to allow the remaining guns to bear on the Tripolitan attackers, but that did not work either.

Four hours went by in this desperate struggle to free the ship, which had now heeled over to port. Porter described Bainbridge as acting during the entire time with "great coolness and deliberation." Their situation was now desperate. Enemy gunboats were becoming bolder. They took up positions on the *Philadelphia*'s starboard side, where they pummeled the helpless frigate with eighteen and twenty-four pounders, without the *Philadelphia* being able to reply. Her remaining guns on that side could only fire into the water.

It was now four P.M., and Bainbridge saw no hope of either getting the ship off the reef or fighting off the gunboats. At this moment of supreme peril, he called another meeting of officers—hardly unusual, even for the bravest, most self-assured skippers. Truxtun made it a practice to call them in extreme emergencies to decide or approve a course of action. John Paul Jones had done the same. So, for that matter, had George Washington. In fact, Bainbridge had been consulting right along, but now the fateful decision to surrender or fight to the death had to be made before the gunboats blew up the ship and killed all aboard, something the Tripolitans probably did not want to do, but might do inadvertently.

After laying out the options, Bainbridge, with a heavy heart, proposed to surrender the frigate rather than fight to the death, and Porter supported him. So did the others. Later, Porter would explain that Bainbridge had "coolly and prudently called a council of his officers who were unanimously of opinion that to save the lives of the brave crew there was no alternative but to haul the colors down and with tears in his eyes did that truly brave man submit to painful necessity."

"In such a dilemma, too painful to relate, the flag of the United States was struck," Bainbridge reported to Preble. Both Porter and Bainbridge were convinced that the only realistic alternative to putting themselves and their crew into the hands of the enemy was to blow up the ship. But neither Bainbridge nor Porter ever considered doing this. "Some fanatics,"

Bainbridge told Preble, "may say that blowing the ship up would have been the proper result. I thought such conduct would not stand acquitted before God or man, and I never presumed to think I had the liberty of putting to death the lives of 306 souls because they were placed under my command."

Before surrendering, Bainbridge ordered all the arms thrown overboard, the magazine drowned, and the signal books and everything else of value to the enemy destroyed. He also ordered the ship's carpenter to smash the pumps, bore holes in the hull, and scuttle the ship. He forgot to get rid of his personal papers, however, which the bashaw eventually retrieved and gleaned important information from, particularly about Preble's fleet.

Unfortunately, Bainbridge's humiliations were not over. The Tripolitans did not react to the colors coming down, so he was forced to send Porter and Midshipman James Biddle over to the gunboats under a white flag of truce and inform them that the *Philadelphia* had surrendered. When the two officers pulled alongside the lead gunboat, "Nearly twenty men of ferocious appearance, armed with sabers, pistols and muskets, jumped into the boat and at once commenced their work of insult and plunder," Porter reported. "Two of them snatched Mr. Biddle's sword, pulled off his coat, and began to fight for it, until at length, probably to decide their dispute, they returned it to him. His cravats were violently torn from his neck, his waistcoat and shirt opened, and his breast exposed, for the purpose, as he very naturally inferred, of perpetuating their horrid vengeance, though their intention, it appeared, was only to search for valuables that he might have concealed about his person. They searched all his pockets and took all his papers and money, except twenty dollars in gold which he had slipped into his boots and thereby secured."

Around six P.M., the Tripolitans swarmed aboard the frigate, robbing the sailors and officers of everything except the clothes on their backs— and they even ripped off some of those. During the evening, when they could plunder no more, the Tripolitans dragged the officers and crew ashore to the palace gates. The bashaw was understandably pleased to see them, for they represented a great deal of ransom money.

To add to Porter's misery and shame, the *Philadelphia* did not sink. The ship's carpenter had not succeeded in scuttling her. The pumps, which were supposed to have been made inoperable, actually continued working. The Tripolitans stopped up the holes. The frigate remained where she was, heeled over to port, stuck on the reef. But forty hours later, her tragedy was compounded immeasurably when a strong westerly wind brought on a violent storm and a high sea that allowed the Tripolitans, after a mighty effort, to float her off the reef and bring her into Tripoli Harbor, where they repaired her. The frigate's guns were also retrieved, and when cleaned (which they easily were), the bashaw had a fearsome 36-gun warship to sell or operate, as he chose, along with 307 Americans to ransom.

For Bainbridge, the defeat was shattering. "If my professional character be blotched," he wrote to his wife, Susan, "—if an attempt be made to taint my honor—if I am censured, if it does not kill me, it would at least deprive me of the power of looking any of my race in the face." Porter was deeply affected as well. As the years passed, he vowed that if he were ever in similar circumstances, he would never surrender.

Both Bainbridge and Porter were understandably concerned about Commodore Preble's reaction to their decisions. They knew he would be furious. Bainbridge had not only lost a frigate and all her men, but the American squadron—pathetically weak to begin with—was now reduced by another 30 percent, making it impossible for Preble to accomplish his mission. Adding to his chagrin was the fact that the frigate had been captured intact and could now be used against him. He wondered why Bainbridge had not succeeded in scuttling her, and why he and Porter had not led their men in a fight to the death, as Preble fancied he would have done in similar circumstances. "Would to God, that the officers and crew of the *Philadelphia*, had one and all, determined to prefer death to slavery," he wrote to the secretary of the navy. "It is possible that such a determination might have saved them from either." At some level, Porter probably agreed with Preble—as brave a commander as ever wore the uniform.

Bainbridge and Porter hoped they would not have a long time to contemplate their disgrace. Prolonged captivity seemed unlikely. The bashaw would certainly want to ransom them for cash as fast as he could. And President Jefferson would undoubtedly want to end the embarrassment quickly and pay for their release. Of course, reaching an agreement between the two governments might still be difficult. The price the bashaw demanded might be excessive, and Preble might not have enough of a squadron left to force the bashaw's hand. The prisoners would then have to brace themselves for a long confinement. As it turned out, Karamanli insisted on receiving $3 million, a sum that was preposterous, and guaranteed a long incarceration, unless the navy freed them by force.

The Americans now had no idea how long their imprisonment would last, or how Karamanli would treat them. They hoped he would keep them in good health because of their ransom value, but they could not be sure. The Tripolitan secretary of state, Sidi Mohammed D'Ghies, took charge of them. Fortunately, he recognized their worth, and from the beginning, treated them decently. He spoke fluent French, which greatly eased communications. The rest of the Tripolitans followed his example, at least at the start.

Porter, Bainbridge, and the other officers were housed in the comfortable residence of the former American consul. They gave their parole not to attempt an escape, which permitted Karamanli to relax his guard somewhat. They were left pretty much on their own. The moody, depressed Bainbridge occupied a separate room and kept largely to himself, writing letters, and letting Porter and Lieutenant Jacob Jones supervise the other officers. Porter and Jones organized a school for the midshipmen, expanding their knowledge of seamanship, mathematics, navigation, gunnery, and even fleet sailing.

D'Ghies allowed the Danish consul, Nicholas C. Nissen, to attend to the officers' basic needs. An industrious, sensitive man, Nissen improved their lives immeasurably, supplying bedding and food, handling their mail, and bringing them books. Porter spent much of his leisure time studying. He had always been preoccupied with improving his mind. Although not formally educated beyond elementary school, he was already well-read. With books provided by Nissen, Porter now studied history, French, English grammar, and drawing.

As might be expected, the crew received quite different treatment. Kept apart from the officers, hands were locked in a single large, dank cell in the basement of the castle. Later they were moved to a primitive warehouse in a different part of the city, where they had to lie on the damp, cold ground, eat bad bread, and do hard labor. Their drivers constantly beat them. The slightest infraction resulted in being bastinadoed, that is, beaten on the soles of the feet with a hard stick. This brutal treatment resulted in nine deaths. Meanwhile, the *Philadelphia*'s carpenter and other skilled workmen, such as blacksmiths, riggers, and sail makers, were compelled to help restore the frigate. The distress of any individual crewmember could be relieved if he converted to Islam, but in the long months of captivity and suffering, only five did.

Meanwhile, Bainbridge managed to send letters to Preble at Malta explaining what had happened. The bashaw allowed the letters to be transmitted. His agents scrutinized the contents before forwarding them, of course, but Bainbridge fooled the censors by using invisible ink on part of the paper. The alert censors soon found out, but then Bainbridge changed to another type of invisible ink the Tripolitans failed to detect, and his messages got through. He urged Preble to either recapture or destroy the *Philadelphia*.

Preble did not need any prodding; he had been studying the matter since the surrender and had concluded there was no real chance of retrieving the frigate. He settled on a plan to demolish her and chose young Stephen Decatur Jr. to lead the expedition. It was a fitting appointment, for Decatur's father, Revolutionary War hero Stephen Decatur, had been the *Philadelphia*'s first captain, and had superintended her construction.

On February 16, 1804, Decatur and a carefully picked crew of volunteers slipped into Tripoli's harbor in a captured Tripolitan ketch (*Mastico*) that Preble had renamed *Intrepid*. They took the *Philadelphia*'s guards by surprise, and burned the frigate, destroying her beyond repair and escaping amid a shower of gunfire from angry Tripolitans ashore. Despite the fire and the fusillade from dozens of shore batteries, Decatur suffered only one wounded and no deaths.

Porter and the other captive officers saw the flames and were overjoyed, even though they knew the bashaw would retaliate against them. He did, removing them from the comfort of their residence and confining them to a dungeon in the center of the castle, where no air or light could penetrate except through a small iron grate in the ceiling. In addition to foul air and terrible food, they were plagued by noxious reptiles.

The new treatment was so severe that Porter now considered the officers released from their promise not to escape, and they made three attempts, which he led. All were thwarted, however. The bashaw was furious, but the prospect of ransoming them restrained him. So too did the likelihood of ransoming the rest of the crew, although they were treated even more harshly now as well.

Unfortunately for Porter and the other prisoners, the burning of the *Philadelphia* and Preble's subsequent attacks on Tripoli did not secure victory. It was not until June 3, 1805, nineteen long months after the *Philadelphia*'s surrender, that Tobias Lear, an experienced diplomat who had once been George Washington's private secretary, signed a peace treaty and obtained the prisoners' release. Lear was able to reach an agreement with the stubborn bashaw because President Jefferson finally sent a fleet with enough firepower to force Karamanli's hand. The fleet arrived off Tripoli on September 10, 1804, but its commander, Commodore Samuel Barron, who superseded Preble, was ailing and ineffective, so the war dragged on inconclusively. It was not until the spring of 1805 that Commodore John Rodgers finally used American naval superiority off Tripoli to force Karamanli to come to terms. As part of the peace treaty, the bashaw received $60,000 in ransom money for 293 prisoners—a tiny fraction of what he had originally demanded. The hostages, although they had been cruelly treated at times, were in surprisingly good health.

In June 1805, a naval court of inquiry examined all the evidence concerning the *Philadelphia* disaster, including testimony from her officers. It judged Bainbridge's actions reasonable under the circumstances, a verdict that President Jefferson endorsed and the country accepted.

The ordeal had a lasting impact on Bainbridge and Porter. They may have been exonerated, but the cumulative effect of an ignominious defeat and long captivity, made a permanent imprint on their psyches. Bainbridge, given his history, suffered the most. "I have zealously served my country and strenuously endeavored to guard against accidents," he wrote to Preble, "but in spite of every effort misfortune has attended me through my naval life—Guadeloupe and Algiers have witnessed part of them, but Tripoli strikes the death blow to my future prospects." Porter was less open about his feelings, but he was also deeply affected in a way that would influence his decisions, particularly in battle, from then on.

The widespread acclaim heaped on Stephen Decatur Jr. for his daring raid on the *Philadelphia* was also a source of dismay for Porter and Bainbridge. Preble wrote to the secretary of the navy urging that Decatur, for his gallant service, be promoted immediately from lieutenant to captain as an incentive for all naval officers. Needless to say, Preble did not express the same boundless admiration for Bainbridge and Porter.

Bainbridge was particularly apprehensive about Preble's opinion. It had taken some time after the *Philadelphia*'s capture for communication between the two men to be established, and for Bainbridge to know for certain that Preble was receiving his letters. That period of silence had been torture for the captive. When letters finally began arriving from Preble, they had been reassuring. The commodore, not wanting to add to Bainbridge's burdens while he was in captivity, repeatedly gave him expressions of support, but Bainbridge worried that Preble might not mean them.

In fact, Preble had mixed feelings. His first reaction on hearing what had happened was to find fault. He thought that if Bainbridge had fought to the death instead of surrendering, he could have saved the men and the ship. After all, it was floated off the reef less than two days later. But on learning the exact circumstances facing Bainbridge and Porter, Preble relented and understood, to a degree, that they really had no other choice. Preble remained ambivalent, however. He undoubtedly felt that he would have handled the matter better than they did.

Continuing to be concerned about Preble's feelings, Bainbridge stayed in close touch with him, hoping that Preble would not change his mind and openly criticize him. Bainbridge worried—far more than Porter—about the judgment others placed on his conduct. Bainbridge wrote to his wife on November 1, 1803, about, "an apprehension which constantly haunts me, that I may be censured by my countrymen. These impressions, which are seldom absent from my mind, act as a corroding canker at my heart."

Porter was a changed man as well. He spoke less than Bainbridge did about his searing experience. But there is no doubt that surrendering an American frigate to a pirate state, spending nineteen months in captivity, and securing his freedom only by being ransomed, had a profound impact, and he craved an opportunity to redeem himself.

AFTER THE FINAL VICTORY OVER TRIPOLI, PORTER REMAINED IN the Mediterranean for two more years in command of his old ship *Enterprise*. During that time an incident occurred that the Admiralty would remember for years. It happened in the British port of Valetta in Malta, where Porter had the *Enterprise* anchored. A young, undoubtedly drunk, English tar came by in a rowboat shouting obscenities at the *Enterprise*. He was so intemperate that Porter hauled him aboard and gave him twelve lashes before sending him home. Sir Andrew Ball, the governor of Malta, was livid. He ordered Porter to remain in the harbor until the incident was reviewed. Porter ignored him, and despite threats that the *Enterprise* would be fired on if she attempted to leave, Porter sailed her past the formidable array of guns guarding the harbor entrance without incident. The Admiralty was furious that he had been let go. His name would be remembered in the Royal Navy for years. Whitehall had a score to settle.

PRIMED FOR BATTLE

O N APRIL 22, 1806, PORTER WAS PROMOTED TO MASTER Commandant. The following year he finally returned to the United States, arriving in New York in October 1807. He had been away for over six years.

The next few months were a busy time for him. He became fast friends with young Washington Irving, whose literary prowess was just beginning to be recognized in New York with the publication of his satirical magazine *Salmagundi*. Sea officers with extensive combat experience fascinated Irving. His father had once been a petty officer in the Royal Navy. Porter for his part admired Irving's erudition. They became part of a group of accomplished young men who partied together at various New York taverns, and at Crockloft Hall, the New Jersey estate of the fabulously wealthy Gouverneur Kemble.

Porter was also occupied with navy business. He was appointed to sit on no less than four courts-martial, all concerned with the *Chesapeake-Leopard* affair of June 22, 1807. A raw nerve was struck in the American psyche when the 50-gun British warship *Leopard*—caught up in a dispute over impressment—unexpectedly fired three broadsides into the unprepared 36-gun *Chesapeake*, killing three men and wounding fifteen others.

Enormous animosity was aroused in America against Britain and might have precipitated a war if President Jefferson had not moved deftly to defuse the issue.

Commodore James Barron had been in charge of the *Chesapeake* at the time, and he was criticized for the unprepared state of his ship and for how he handled the situation generally. He hoped a court-martial would absolve him of blame. Commodore John Rodgers was president of the court, and after carefully examining the evidence, eleven officers found Barron guilty of failing "on the probability of an engagement, to clear his ship for action." His sentence was a heavy one—suspension from the navy for five years without pay. Porter took an active part in the proceedings, asking more questions than any other officer, pressing Barron hard, and supporting the verdict.

On February 22, 1808, the courts-martial were over, and Porter turned to more pleasant business, traveling to Chester, Pennsylvania, where on March 10 he married seventeen-year-old Evelina Anderson (he was now twenty-eight). Although her family was eventually pleased with the match, at the moment they were uncertain about Porter. They thought Evelina could do much better. Two months earlier, when David went to Chester to ask for Evelina's hand, her brother Thomas had informed him—none too gently—that marriage was out of the question. Whereupon, Porter flew into a rage, shouting, "Sir, you are meddling in a matter that does not concern you. I came here about marrying your sister, I didn't come to marry you, and damn you if you don't leave the room I'll throw you out of the window." Many years later, Porter's son, Admiral David Dixon Porter wrote, "Young Anderson, who had a strong sense of humor, often related this incident to show Captain Porter's rough way of wooing, which was, in fact, his impulsive manner of doing everything."

Porter had already received orders to take command of the New Orleans naval station, and so only a week after the wedding, the young couple embarked on the long trip from Pennsylvania to Louisiana. It was to be their only honeymoon. The newlyweds arrived in New Orleans on June 17, 1808, and were happy that David's father was stationed there. In late 1807, so that he could be near his son, the navy had given the Revolutionary War hero a warrant as a sailing master and assigned him to the New Orleans naval station.

The elder Porter was good friends with a man who would become important to his son. George Farragut, fifty-two, and Porter were serving together in the navy's tiny New Orleans station and soon discovered they had a lot in common. Like Porter, Farragut had fought on the patriot side during the American Revolution, even though he was a native of Spanish Minorca. Farragut had been a privateer, and later became a member of the state navy of South Carolina, where he performed heroically during the battles of Charleston and Savannah. Later, he fought as a guerrilla with Francis Marion. After the Revolution, Farragut and his family settled in Tennessee. They remained there until March 1807, when he was appointed a sailing master in the United States Navy and sent to New Orleans, where his friend William Claiborne was governor of the Province of Louisiana.

But tragedy soon struck the Porters and the Farraguts. On a hot summer's day in 1808, Porter was fishing on Lake Pontchartrain when he collapsed from sunstroke. He would have died right there had Farragut not been fishing nearby. Quickly realizing what had happened, Farragut took Porter to his house, where his wife, Elizabeth, cared for him. Tragically, while she was nursing him, she contracted yellow fever and passed away on the same day that the elder Porter also died—June 22, 1808. Five days earlier, on June 17, Master Commandant David Porter Jr. had arrived to take command of the New Orleans Station. He was devastated by his father's death. To make matters worse, he soon contracted yellow fever himself, only narrowly avoiding the same fate as Elizabeth Farragut.

While recovering from the loss of his father and from the fever, Porter tried to assist George Farragut with the enormous task of caring for his five grief-stricken children. Farragut was a man of great inner strength, and he held together, but the burden of the children was beyond his capacity, and when Porter offered to take two of them and bring them up as his own, George reluctantly agreed. Thus, in February 1809, nine-year-old James Glasgow Farragut and one of his sisters became members of the Porter household.

Young Farragut would during the Civil War become the first admiral in American history and a great hero. But that was much later. At the moment, he had to move into the Porters' house, which he did with great reluctance. In time, he became, in essence, the Porters' son, although he was never actually adopted. From the beginning of their relationship, David Porter treated Farragut as if he was his own child, and in recognition of that unselfish care, James later changed his name to David Glasgow Farragut.

In spite of his relationship with Porter, Farragut remained close to his father. They would spend many days together on Lake Pontchartrain, where young Farragut acquired an extensive knowledge of sailing and a love for life on the water. At the end of Porter's two-year tour in New Orleans, Farragut, in what must have been a heartrending decision for the boy and his father, remained with Porter, traveling with him back to Chester. Farragut's sister, who had also been a member of the Porters' household in New Orleans, stayed behind in the city with Porter's sister, Margaret.

Aside from the personal tragedies, Porter's time in New Orleans was exceptionally stressful. He was tasked with doing the near impossible: enforcing President Jefferson's embargo in an area swarming with smugglers, pirates, and corrupt politicians. And on top of that, he had to deal with General James Wilkinson, the military commander in Louisiana, who was as devious and dishonest an officer to ever wear the uniform.

Luckily, during his stay in Louisiana, Porter met someone whose friendship helped him over the roughest patches. Navy purser Samuel Hambleton became his closest friend and confidant and would later serve as his prize agent.

When Porter's tour was up, he and his family set sail for Green Bank, their great stone mansion on the Delaware River, arriving on August 3, 1810. They must have been overjoyed to see the old house. It would be the first opportunity they had to live in it. It would also be the first time young Farragut was separated from his father.

Being back in Chester in a comfortable mansion did not mean that Porter had lost his zest for action. Far from it. He wasn't home for long before he was writing to the secretary of the navy, Paul Hamilton, requesting promotion to captain and assignment to a frigate. He had to wait for his ship and his promotion, however. It was peacetime, and the navy was not expanding. He would not receive orders to take command of the *Essex* until August 1811, and he was not promoted to captain, a rank commensurate with his new position, until June 1812.

With war looming, Porter suggested to Secretary Hamilton that when fighting broke out, the *Essex* should be sent to the Pacific to harass British whalers and merchantmen. Porter's request was ignored, however. When the War of 1812 actually began, he was ordered to join Commodore John Rodgers's squadron in New York. In pursuance of these orders, Porter brought the *Essex* into the city during the second week of June 1812, but she needed extensive repairs, and Rodgers decided not to wait for her, taking the rest of his squadron to sea on June 21, 1812. Porter was left on his own.

Commodore Rodgers, the navy's senior officer in command, had gathered nearly the entire serviceable American fleet (only five warships) for the first cruise of the war. His flagship was the 44-gun heavy frigate *President*. Commodore Stephen Decatur sailed with him, in command of the 44-gun *United States*. Rodgers's plan was to attack a huge convoy of British merchantmen (over a hundred) traveling from Jamaica to England. He never found the convoy, but he did succeed in drawing the British fleet at Halifax away from the coast of the United States in search of him. (His departure had been no secret.) This allowed 516 American merchant vessels then at sea to return safely to their home ports. They had no idea war had been declared, and would have been easy prey for the British fleet had it been waiting for them off Boston, New York, Philadelphia, and other major ports.

Unhappy to be stuck in port while the war he had been preparing himself for finally had begun, Porter was nearly frantic to get the *Essex* repaired and out to sea. Luckily, Captain Isaac Chauncey, with whom Porter had served in 1803 on the *New York*, was in charge of the New York Navy Yard. He had the *Essex* repaired and ready for action in a remarkable three weeks. Porter put to sea on July 3. As he stood out from Sandy Hook, he could not have been in a better mood. The previous day he had finally received notice of his appointment to captain, and since Commodore Rodgers had already left New York, Porter was on his own. He immediately went on the hunt and found plenty of action. The crew, which he had been training hard since first taking command, performed brilliantly. The greatest prize was, of course, the *Alert*, taken on August 13. But as we have seen, there were other triumphs, too, during this unusually productive cruise. In mid-September, the *Essex* arrived in Chester laden with laurels, her captain and crew filled with great expectations.

When Porter dropped anchor near his home in Chester on September 14, he expected to refurbish, resupply, and put right back to sea. He soon learned that his victory over the *Alert* was the first of the war. That was great news, but the disparity in size between the two combatants made him continue to downplay his success and to crave more than ever a one-on-one battle with a frigate.

On October 6, while supplies were dribbling in, and Porter was hard at work on the *Essex*, he began receiving his orders. Instructions from Bainbridge described Porter's assignment in the commodore's three-ship squadron. The next day, he was given Bainbridge's plan for how they were going to rendezvous. On October 8 a letter from the secretary of the navy confirmed the arrangements. Porter could not help but be pleased that the president had finally settled on a new strategy for the navy, and that the *Essex* would play an important part. He preferred being on his own, of course, not having to share laurels and prize money, but joining Bainbridge was the next best thing.

Porter was also happy that Madison was finally using the navy for commerce raiding, instead of relying exclusively on privateers. Like most naval officers, he had no respect for privateers. "I detest the idea of trusting to our privateers for the destruction of British commerce," he wrote to Samuel Hambleton; "are we to become a nation of buccaneers, a nest of villains, a detestable set of pirates? When a general system of piracy is countenanced by our government, when the whole maritime defense of a nation consists of buccaneers, farewell national honor, farewell national pride! Then we sink to the level of the bashaw of Tripoli, and the emperor of Haiti."

Porter did not anticipate that refurbishing the *Essex* would take very long, if supplies arrived from the Navy Department as quickly as he hoped. The ship needed a new suit of sails, the standing rigging replaced, and the bowsprit taken out and fished. She also needed as many supplies as she could hold, including double clothing for the crew, fresh fruits, vegetables, and lime juice to fight scurvy. Ammunition also had to be replenished and leftover gunpowder examined. It should have taken no more than two or three weeks to accomplish all of this, but since supplies were slow in coming, the work dragged on until the end of October. Part of the reason for the delay was that another warship, the eighteen-gun sloop of war *Wasp*, was being readied for sea in nearby Philadelphia at the same time that the *Essex* was. Her skipper, Jacob Jones, needed supplies as much as Porter did. Years of neglecting the navy were now taking their toll.

Porter feared that if he delayed much longer, a British blockade would trap him in the Delaware. "If we do not get out soon," he wrote to Hambleton, "we shall all be kept in until winter, as the British force has been so much augmented." Porter's recent run-in with the three enemy warships off the tail of Georges Bank had heightened his fears. He was convinced that Britain was making a determined effort to close all the principal American ports. He told the secretary of the navy that, having run into the three-ship squadron, the *Essex* was already "cut off from New York and Rhode Island," which is why he had put into the Delaware River.

He was so worried about being blockaded that even while repairs were still being made on the *Essex*, he sailed her down to the Delaware Capes looking for intelligence about the British fleet. His fears intensified when he spoke a merchantman who told him that an enemy squadron was nearby. Porter feared that if he didn't get to sea right away, he would be stuck in the Delaware for a long time.

His concern was unwarranted, however; he was in no immediate danger. The British had not even begun to mount their blockade of the American coast. After Porter's last cruise, he could have easily put into Boston, New York, or Newport. The enemy ships that the merchantman was warning him about actually constituted nearly the entire usable British fleet at Halifax, and it was searching for the American squadron commanded by Commodore John Rodgers, not patrolling off New York or Narragansett Bay. Britain would not have a blockade in place until the middle of 1813, and even then, it would be far from complete.

Porter blamed Secretary of the Navy Hamilton for the delay in getting supplies to the *Essex*. "The neglect of the Department is unpardonable," he wrote to Hambleton. "There must be a change or we never can expect to do anything except on our own responsibility; there is no energy, nor will there be while a pint of whiskey can be purchased in the District of Columbia—it is shameful."

Secretary Hamilton's drinking problem had been bandied about Washington for years. It was rumored that nothing got done in the Navy Department after lunch, although that was an exaggeration. President Madison was aware of the problem, but even after war had been declared on June 18 Hamilton remained in charge of the department. Keeping Hamilton was a measure of how unimportant the navy was to the president at the time.

Porter's urge to be back at sea in search of glory was demonstrated again when a challenge to a sea duel came on September 18 while he was waiting impatiently for the *Essex* to be ready. The challenge was delivered in an unusual way. The *Democratic Press*, a Philadelphia newspaper, published what was purported to be a letter from Sir James Yeo, captain of the British frigate *Southampton*, stationed in the Bahamas. It read: "Sir James Yeo [presents] his compliments to Captain Porter of the American frigate *Essex*—would be glad to have a *tete a tete* anywhere between the Capes of the Delaware and Havana, where he would be pleased to break his own sword over his damned head and put him down forward in irons."

Yeo, it seemed, wanted to goad Porter, whom the British had a special dislike for, into a one-on-one fight. Porter's handling of a well-publicized row in New York City at the start of the war had aroused the Admiralty's ire. And Whitehall remembered Porter from an old incident at Malta involving the lashing of a drunk and disorderly British tar.

The latest episode involved John Erving, a sail maker's mate aboard the *Essex*. On June 26, eight days after the United States had declared war, Porter called upon the crew of the *Essex* to take the oath of allegiance to the United States, but Erving refused. He protested that he was an Englishman and could not do so. Immediately, one of his shipmates contradicted him, swearing that Erving was an American from Barnstable, Massachusetts. Erving admitted that he had lived in the United States since 1800, but insisted that he was still a British subject, and if he were caught fighting against his country he would be hanged as a traitor. Porter wasn't pleased, but he refused to whip the man and kept his irate crew from beating him. That didn't end the matter, however. When some of the *Essex* men asked the captain's permission to tar and feather Ervin and put him out on the streets of New York with appropriate labels affixed to his body, Porter, in his usually impulsive way, said yes.

The treatment of Erving angered the British consul in New York, and he quickly became involved. He asked the New York police to safeguard Erving, declaring him to be a British subject. The police did intervene, protecting Erving while the consul arranged passage for him to Halifax.

Porter strongly objected to letting Erving go, pointing out that he could be a spy and might report to the enemy all he knew about the American navy. Porter's superiors did not support him, however. Secretary Hamilton found his actions deplorable, and sent him a blistering rebuke, telling him that "mobs should never be suffered to exist on board a man of war." Needless to say, the secretary's scolding did not sit well with Porter, who continued to believe that releasing Erving was a mistake.

The wide publicity afforded this latest controversy added to the rancor the Admiralty felt toward Porter. Their Lordships promised to chastise him at the first opportunity. He was aware of their enmity, and he gloried in it.

Yeo's challenge, thus, came as no surprise. Porter assumed it was genuine and lost no time penning a reply: "Captain Porter of the U.S. frigate *Essex*, presents his complements to Sir James Yeo . . . and accepts with pleasure his polite invitation. If agreeable to Sir James, Captain Porter would prefer meeting near the Delaware, where Captain Porter pledges his honor to Sir James, that no American vessel shall interrupt their tete a tete. The *Essex* may be known by a flag bearing the motto, '*Free trade and sailors' rights,*' and when this is struck to the *Southampton*, Captain Porter will deserve the treatment promised by Sir James."

Porter pleaded with Secretary Hamilton not to prohibit him from accepting Yeo's challenge. When Hamilton made no objection, Porter rushed down to the Delaware Capes during the last week of September and hovered off them briefly before sailing back to Chester. The loud-talking, but cautious Yeo never appeared. He may have had second thoughts about his chances against the *Essex*. The *Southampton* was the oldest frigate in the Royal Navy, having been built in 1757. She carried thirty-two guns, but she would have had a hard time against the American frigate. The *Southampton*'s long guns might have been a factor in her favor. Despite being old, if she were skillfully handled, she might have given the *Essex* a real battle. As it was, for one reason or another, Captain Yeo did not appear.

CHAPTER

5

THE *ESSEX*

PAST AND PRESENT

I N OCTOBER 1812, CAPTAIN DAVID PORTER WAS ANXIOUS TO get to sea, but he had serious reservations about the *Essex*. What he objected to most was her armament. She carried forty 32-pound carronades and six long 12-pounders, a total of forty-six guns. The mix of weaponry was the exact opposite of what he wanted. Carronades were most effective as supplements to a main battery of long guns; they were not intended to be a frigate's primary weapon. As far back as October 12, 1811, Porter had written to Navy Secretary Hamilton complaining that carronades remained "an experiment in modern warfare. . . . I do not conceive it proper to trust the honor of the flag entirely to them." A little over a month later, after he had returned from a short cruise, Porter wrote to Sam Hambleton, "I am much pleased with my ship, and I wish I could say as much for her armament—She is armed with carronades which in my opinion are very inferior to long guns."

Porter remained so disgruntled that he asked Secretary Hamilton on October 14 to give him another ship, preferably the twenty-eight-gun *Adams*, sitting in the Washington Navy Yard. Porter told Hamilton that because of her inadequate armament and "bad sailing" the *Essex* was the "worst frigate in the service." Porter's hyperbole did not move Hamilton. The secretary did not take the complaint about her poor sailing seriously, but faulting her battery of carronades had validity, which Hamilton was aware of. Nonetheless he turned down Porter's request for another ship. The *Adams* was not ready to go, and even if she were, there wasn't enough time to make a switch before Porter had to leave and join Bainbridge.

The carronade was a relatively new weapon. The Carron Iron Company had developed it during the American Revolution in their massive iron works (the largest in the world) on the Carron River near Falkirk, Scotland. Made of cast iron, carronades were short and smoothbore with one-third the weight of a conventional long gun, but with explosive power. They were placed on a sliding rather than a wheeled carriage, and a turn screw achieved their elevation rather than quoins (wooden wedges). The screw was mounted on a lug underneath the barrel. Carronades required a smaller crew to operate, were easier to aim, and fired faster. At short range (less than 500 yards) they could be devastating. The British gave them the name "smasher" because of their ability to create clusters of deadly splinters when employed against an enemy's wooden works, and their ability, at very close range, to drive through the hull of a ship as large as a frigate.

Without a doubt, carronades had real advantages, but at long distances they were ineffective, and this was what bothered Porter. Until the *Essex* got close to an enemy, she was at risk. An alert British commander could cripple her with long guns (the main battery on all British frigates) before she got near enough to employ her carronades. An adverse wind, or anything else (such as enemy fire) that affected her ability to sail, could make the *Essex* a sitting duck. "Was the ship to be disabled in her rigging in the early part of an engagement," Porter complained to Secretary Hamilton "a ship much inferior to her in sailing and in force, armed with long guns, could take a position beyond the reach of our carronades, and cut us to pieces without our being able to do her any injury."

Porter knew that if the *Essex* tangled with an enemy frigate, he would be forced to run in close to her, blast away with his carronades as he went, and hope their devastating firepower would force a surrender. If not, he would have to board and fight it out hand to hand. His only hope would be to overwhelm the enemy with numbers, which is why he had an unusually large crew for the size of his ship—319 officers and men, including thirty-one marines.

The *Essex* had not been designed to carry primarily carronades. At her commissioning in December 1799, her battery was well balanced with twenty-six long twelve-pounders and ten six-pounders, and her crew numbered 260. Her first skipper, thirty-eight-year-old Captain Edward Preble of Portland, Maine, received permission to substitute nine-pounders for the original six, giving her more firepower but added weight. After the change, Preble was well satisfied with her armament. By the time David Porter took command in August 1811, however, that had all changed.

The *Essex*'s vulnerability gnawed at Porter, but he could not convince Hamilton to exchange the carronades for long guns or to give him a different ship. So Porter was forced to work with what he had. He never considered resigning; his sense of duty and desire for fame and prize money were too strong for that.

In spite of his grumbling and penchant for hyperbole, Porter undoubtedly knew at some level that the *Essex*, apart from her carronades, was a fine ship. It was one of the subscription warships built during the Quasi-War, just as the *Philadelphia* had been. In the spring and summer of 1798 President John Adams had persuaded a Federalist-dominated Congress—against the strong opposition of Republican leaders Jefferson, Madison, and Albert Gallatin—to approve a new navy department and a substantial fleet to cope with French aggression on the high seas. In a remarkably short time Adams dramatically expanded the navy that George Washington had started in 1794.

Adams also sought help from private citizens, and they responded. Patriotic fervor and the need to protect merchant vessels from French privateers led wealthy citizens in nine seaports along the Atlantic coast—Newburyport, Salem, Boston, Providence, New York, Philadelphia, Baltimore, Norfolk, and Richmond—to build substantial warships and loan them to the federal government. Adams and the Congress helped the effort by requiring the Treasury to issue interest-bearing stock at six percent to the contributors.

The leading merchants of Essex County, Massachusetts raised half the money for their new frigate. Major contributions came from the fabulously wealthy merchant Elias Hasket Derby and from William (Billy) Gray, Jr., chairman of the Salem Frigate Committee. Each donated $10,000. The overall subscription raised $74,700. The total cost of the *Essex*, including her guns and stores, was $154,687. The government made up the difference.

William Hackett, the well-known naval architect, designed the *Essex*. He also designed and built the *Merrimack*, the first subscription warship, in 1798, on the Merrimack River in nearby Newburyport, Massachusetts. Hackett was famous as the architect of the celebrated Revolutionary War frigate *Alliance*. Built in Salisbury on the Merrimack across from Newburyport, she was generally considered the finest warship in the Continental Navy. The *Alliance* and *Essex* were strikingly similar, although the *Alliance* was a bit larger. Both ships were fast.

Enos Briggs of Salem took charge of building the frigate. He sought help from the citizens of Essex County in the *Salem Gazette:*

> Take Notice! Ye sons of freedom! Step forth and give your assistance in building the frigate to oppose French insolence and piracy! Let every man in possession of a White Oak Tree feel ambitious to be foremost in hurrying down the timber to Salem, . . . where the noble structure is to be fabricated to maintain your rights upon the seas and make the name of America respected among the nations of the world. Your largest and longest trees are wanted, and the arms of them for knees and rising timber. Four trees are wanted for the keel, which altogether will measure 146 feet in length, and hew 16 inches square. Please call on the subscriber, who . . . will pay the ready cash.

The citizens of Essex County responded, cutting the great timbers for the ship's hull in the wood lots of Salem, Danvers, Peabody, Beverly, Marblehead, and other nearby towns. Giant trees, felled by expert hands, dropped onto a cushion of snow, and after trimming, were dragged on sleds by teams of oxen through Salem with townspeople cheering as they lumbered by. Paul Revere contributed copper bolts, spikes, staples, and nails, but he could not supply the rolled copper for her all-important sheathing. That would still have to come from England. Revere did not begin his copper mill at Canton, Massachusetts, until 1800. Revere worked with navy agent Joseph Waters, who was responsible for seeing to it that building supplies and provisions, including shot for the carronades and other armament arrived in a timely fashion.

Work progressed rapidly. The ship's keel was laid in April 1799. The launching took place on September 30, 1799 (Revere attended); and she was ready to put to sea the third week of December. Small as frigates go, she displaced 850 tons, slightly more than half of what the largest American frigates, the 44-gun heavyweights, *Constitution*, *United States*, and *President*, displaced, 1,576 tons. ("Ton" was a crude measure of volume, not weight, derived by multiplying length in feet, times width, times depth of hold, and then dividing by one hundred. It was a rough measure by any standard, varying from shipbuilder to shipbuilder.)

The *Essex* measured 141 feet in overall length, with a 118-foot keel, 37-foot beam, and a depth of hold of 12 feet 3 inches. Between her upper, or spar deck, and the gun deck below was six feet at the waist and six feet three inches under the quarterdeck. The height between the gun deck and lower deck was a cramped space of only five feet nine inches. She was built for speed and carried an impressive array of canvas, but her sailing was compromised later by changes made to her armament.

Captain Preble officially accepted her into the navy on December 17, 1799. In his letter to the Salem Committee he noted that "her hull, masts, spars and rigging [were] complete, and [she was] furnished with one complete suit of sails, two bower cables and anchors, one stream anchor, one kedge anchor, one tow line, four boats and a full set of spare masts and spars, except the lower masts and bowsprit."

The *Essex*'s first mission was a challenging test. Captain Preble received orders to sail from Salem to Newport, Rhode Island. There he was to rendezvous with the 36-gun frigate *Congress*, under Captain James Sever, one of President Washington's original frigate captains, appointed in 1794 when the president began the new Federal Navy. The *Essex* and the *Congress* were to proceed to the Sundra Straits and Batavia in the Dutch East Indies, where French privateers were harassing American merchantmen. After dealing with the French marauders, Sever and Preble were to shepherd home any American ships gathered at Batavia. Sever was senior to Preble and would be squadron commander.

The two frigates would be the first American warships to round the Cape of Good Hope and sail across the Indian Ocean to the East Indies.

They would not be the first American ships, of course. Merchantmen had been making voyages from the United States to the Far East since the 1780s—after the Revolutionary War ended. The first to make the voyage to Canton was the *Empress of China*, owned by Robert Morris of Philadelphia (the great financier of the Revolution) and a group of New York merchants. The *Empress of China* left New York on February 22, 1784. Elias Hasket Derby, who made a fortune as a privateer during the Revolution, was also quick to enter the China trade after the war, sending his ship the *Grand Turk* (a former privateer) to Canton in 1785.

Early in the morning on December 22, 1799, the *Essex* stood out from historic Salem Harbor bound for Newport on the first leg of her long journey. The short trip to Rhode Island would be an excellent test for the new frigate, coming as it did in the dead of winter—a treacherous time to be sailing the North Atlantic, when the seas could be nearly as vicious as any in the world. Despite the season, Preble arrived in Newport without mishap in five days. "The ship proves a good sea boat and sails very fast," he reported to Secretary of the Navy Benjamin Stoddert.

To Joseph Waters, the navy agent in Salem, Preble wrote, "I arrived here [Newport] the 27th, experienced some blustering and much moderate weather on my passage, the wind generally contrary. The *Essex* . . . went eleven miles per hour, with topgallant sail set and within six points of the wind." Looking back years later, Preble remembered the *Essex* as "a prime sailer and the best model of a frigate (of her rate) in the Navy."

On January 6, 1800, the *Essex* and the *Congress* departed Newport, beginning their long journey to the Sundra Straits. A powerful storm with high winds, snow, and hail dogged them the first four days, and the two frigates became separated. Powerful gusts stirred the sea into a frenzy, completely dismasting the *Congress*. She probably would have foundered had not moderating weather suddenly granted her a reprieve. With a prodigious effort from her crew, Sever was able to get up a jury rig. On February 24 the *Congress* limped into Norfolk, Virginia, for repairs. Preble, in the meantime, acting more swiftly and surely than Sever, saved his masts, rode out the storm, and continued on to St. Helena Island and the Cape of Good Hope. The contrast between the two ships and two captains could not have been more pronounced. Sever's lieutenants accused him later of poor seamanship. A court of inquiry cleared him, but his reputation—never high to begin with—was hopelessly compromised, and he was soon forced out of the navy.

On March 11, 1800, a little over two months after leaving Newport, Preble put into Table Bay off Cape Town. On the way he stopped at St. Helena, a rendezvous point that he and Sever had agreed upon in case they were separated. When the *Congress* failed to appear, Preble moved on. The *Essex* got a friendly reception from the British in Cape Town. They had seized it from the Dutch in 1795, after revolutionary France made the Netherlands a vassal state. When Preble arrived, the United States and Britain were both engaged in a war with France, and they cooperated to a limited extent when it suited their purposes. Britain had been fighting revolutionary France since January 1793; the United States had been enmeshed in its undeclared naval war with France since 1798.

When the *Essex* pulled into Cape Town, she was in need of repairs and provisions. Preble had no trouble securing both. The repairs were extensive. Much of the iron work had given way; the fore and main crosstrees were broken due to defective wood; and the main shrouds and all the topmast stays, which were of "infamously bad" quality, according to the captain, had to be replaced.

For two weeks, while work went ahead on the ship, Preble joined in the social whirl that enlivened life on the many (mostly British) ships anchored in the harbor. He kept an eye out for Sever and the *Congress* but decided not to wait if they again failed to appear. When the *Essex* was ready to go, the *Congress* had still not arrived, and Preble left without her, sailing across the Indian Ocean to the Sundra Straits and Batavia, where he executed his mission with the élan for which he became famous.

Although he failed to capture any French privateers (which he dearly wanted to do), he did protect American trade for two months, and then convoyed fourteen merchantmen back to the United States, arriving in New York on November 19, 1800. Unfortunately, Batavia was a disease-ridden hellhole, and Preble may have picked up some ailment there, or he might have just been suffering from a severe case of ulcers. Whatever it was, by the time he reached home, he was in far from vibrant health.

After her return, the *Essex* was refurbished and participated fully in the war against Tripoli. A year after the war was over, she left the Mediterranean and sailed back to the United States, arriving on July 27, 1806.

She was then placed in ordinary at the Washington Navy Yard, where she remained until February 1809. During that time extensive work was accomplished under the expert eye of the famous Naval Constructor Josiah Fox, who thought the *Essex* was a fine ship. He liked to point out that, "The white oak timber and plank with which this ship was built is superior in quality to any white oak I have seen made use of in the Navy. It appears to have been cut from trees, young and thriving." When Fox finished with her, the *Essex* was in excellent shape, although she probably received her carronades during this time. Records verifying exactly what was done were lost when the British sacked the capital on August 24, 1814, and parts of the Washington Navy Yard, including warships, had to be destroyed to prevent them from falling into enemy hands.

David Porter took command of the *Essex* in August 1811, and he requested that John Downes be appointed first lieutenant. Porter's relationship with Downes began in 1802 during the Tripolitan War, when Midshipman Downes served with Porter on the frigate *Congress* and later on the *New York*. Porter was impressed with Downes's leadership qualities and his cool courage under fire. Downes was promoted to lieutenant in March 1807.

In the late fall of 1811, Porter took the *Essex* on a shakedown cruise. On Christmas day he ran into an explosive storm that the ship handled with comparative ease. No matter how well she performed in dirty weather, however, Porter remained unhappy with her armament. And his unhappiness did not abate when the war began. His success in the early weeks of the conflict against the *Alert* and the other vessels he had captured did not change his mind about the *Essex*'s carronades.

FIRST RENDEZVOUS

PORTO PRAIA

T HE TIME FOR CAPTAIN PORTER AND THE *ESSEX* TO DEPART
the Delaware River and join Bainbridge in the *Constitution* and
Lawrence in the *Hornet* finally arrived on October 28, 1812. Evelina
Porter had known for weeks that this moment was coming, and she must
have been dreading it. Saying goodbye to her husband was never easy,
but this time it was particularly difficult. David was about to begin a
voyage of indeterminate length that promised to be more dangerous
than any he had undertaken before. Evelina understood to a degree the
requirements of a navy wife in wartime, but this assignment would demand more of her than any had in the past. She had no idea when he
would return, or, indeed, if he would; whether he would cover himself
with glory or be disgraced. His courage and cunning in battle were legendary; he was a fearsome opponent, but he had outsized ambitions that
could cloud his judgment. She must have worried that his prowess in
combat might be compromised by an obsessive desire for fame. One
thing she knew for certain; he'd pursue his dreams of glory without any
regard for their effect on her.

Evelina was standing on the manicured front lawn of Green Bank, the Porters' imposing, graystone mansion overlooking the mile-wide Delaware River. Baby Elizabeth was in her arms, and son William was at her side, standing next to Captain Porter and Midshipman David Farragut—now eleven years old. Evelina was unaware that she was pregnant with their third child, who would be born on June 8, 1813 and named David Dixon Porter. It was possible, even likely, that Captain Porter would be far away when the baby arrived. "I sail on a long, a very long cruise," he wrote to Hambleton, "it may be many months before you hear of my arrival in the U.S. . . . if you hear of me at all."

Green Bank would be of some comfort to Evelina while she waited for David to return. Situated in the middle of picturesque Chester, the mansion was the finest in town. Four and a half years earlier, Evelina's father, Congressman William Anderson, had given it to the young couple as a wedding present. He probably thought that Evelina would need a comfortable place to raise her children while her husband was away at sea.

The *Essex* was anchored in deep water near shore ready to sail. As slack tide approached, Porter gave Evelina and the children a final kiss. With Farragut at his side, he made his way down the long sloping lawn onto a small dock at the water's edge, where the captain's gig was tied up. As soon as he and Farragut were in the stern sheets, the coxswain shouted, "Shove off. Altogether now, give way." Muscled oarsmen pulled into the river navy fashion, their oars striking the water in near perfect unison. In minutes the gig brushed up against the frigate's massive black side, and a bowman hooked a painter onto the starboard main chains. Porter grabbed the ladder amidships and climbed up the side followed by Farragut.

Bosun's pipes squealed, as the captain in his working uniform passed through the entry port. A side party of marines and ship's boys came smartly to attention. First Lieutenant John Downes rendered a formal salute, which Porter returned, before striding toward the quarterdeck, anxious to be underway. He did not waste time inspecting the ship and the crew; he knew Downes would have them well prepared.

As the tide began to ebb, Porter weighed anchor and stood down the Delaware. They were heading for his rendezvous with Bainbridge and Lawrence, who had departed Boston two days earlier. It appeared that

Porter would have no trouble meeting them. A favorable wind and tide carried the *Essex* swiftly past Wilmington and Newcastle. River traffic was increasing, and on every boat curious eyes were undoubtedly glued to telescopes examining the intriguing frigate.

The river soon widened into Delaware Bay. As the *Essex* sped toward Cape Henlopen and the sea, Porter summoned the pilot, who had guided them down the river and bay, and was about to return to Philadelphia. As soon as the door of the captain's cabin closed, Porter, without explanation, ordered the man to hand over any last-minute letters crew members had entrusted to him. After the surprised pilot produced the letters, Porter dismissed him and then examined each letter carefully, looking for usable intelligence about the *Essex*'s mission, particularly her destination. As it turned out, all the letters were innocuous notes to loved ones, except for one that gave the ship's first place of rendezvous as "the coast of Africa." Porter confiscated that letter and all the others without informing the writers. He would not allow anything to compromise his mission. That these were letters to loved ones from men who might not see them again seemed to matter little to him. His duty, as he saw it, was always paramount. Besides, the crew would never know that he had destroyed the letters.

By nightfall, the *Essex* had moved beyond the Delaware Capes and was plowing into rising swells in the Atlantic. A sizable storm was getting up, intensifying with every turn of the glass. During the night the wind hauled around from north to west, and the weather thickened. Porter had to fight hard to avoid running onto the dangerous shoals at Chincoteague. On the morning of October 29, with the wind increasing to a gale, he put the ship under snug sail, and secured the masts by tightening the rigging, which, being new, had stretched considerably. The heavily laden frigate labored in the swollen seas. Her rolling opened waterways that flooded the berth deck, soaking bedding and stores. Water filled the coalhole, and an additional leak appeared between cut-water and stem. The rest of the *Essex* remained tight, however, and by pumping only a few minutes every two hours, Porter kept the ship reasonably dry.

The storm continued into the next day, and then let up, but the weather remained unsettled for another forty-eight hours. As soon as he could, Porter put the ship back in order, replacing oakum (fibers from old cordage treated with tar) in the waterways, drying clothing, airing out bedding, and salvaging stores. He even found time on October 31 to exercise the men at the guns.

Despite the crew's best efforts, so many provisions were lost that Porter was forced to ration what was left, except for water and rum. He hoped to maintain his supply of water by catching every bit he could in the rain awning. But he was forced to cut the bread allowance in half and reduce other provisions by a third. He never considered returning to port. The *Essex* was still in good shape, despite the hammering she had taken from the storm.

THE CAPE VERDE ISLANDS ARE 3,500 MILES FROM THE DELAWARE Capes. Porter estimated it would take the *Essex* a month to make the voyage to Porto Praia, the capital of the archipelago and the first point of rendezvous with Bainbridge. Of course, Porter hoped that enemy merchantmen or, even better, a warship would delay him. Once the weather eased on November 2, he shaped a course to strike latitude 36° 7' north and longitude 58° 54' west (northeast of the Bermudas), which would take the *Essex* across the track of enemy vessels bound to Europe from the West Indies.

Since Parliament passed the Convoy Act in 1798, all British merchantmen were required to sail together in convoys protected by the Royal Navy. If Porter was lucky enough to run into a convoy, the escorting warships would undoubtedly be too much for the *Essex*, but that would not preclude him from picking off a straggler or two. Because merchantmen sailed at varying speeds, keeping them bunched together was impossible. If a convoy was big enough, a skilled raider like Porter with a fast ship could claim a prize or two with relative ease, despite the presence of bigger escorts.

Lookouts aboard the *Essex* kept a sharp eye out, but they spotted few foreign vessels, and those they saw invariably turned out to be Portuguese. Porter chased every ship that remotely resembled a British man-of-war or merchant vessel, but he was consistently disappointed.

While waiting for his opportunity, Porter honed the crew's fighting skills. He tried to compensate for the shortcomings of the frigate's carronades by obsessively drilling the men in small arms. He was determined to make his hands the most accomplished boarders afloat. The crew had already melded into a successful fighting unit during the first cruise of the war, but the *Essex* men had never faced an enemy frigate. Porter wanted them ready for that supreme test. As the ship plowed toward the Cape Verdes, the drills were incessant. David Farragut wrote that "I have never since been in a ship where the crew of the old *Essex* was represented, but that I found them to be the best swordsmen aboard. They had been so thoroughly trained as boarders that every man was prepared for such an emergency, with his cutlass as sharp as a razor, a dirk made from a file by the ship's armorer, and a pistol."

Despite the hard work (and to some extent because of it), morale was high. The *Essex* men, young and old, hungered for glory and prize money, and they were confident their young skipper would secure them both. He had already shown how adept he was at turning patriotic zeal into gold. The money they had coming from the *Essex*'s first cruise was significant, and money from signing bonuses was still in their pockets. And this was just the beginning; they expected Porter to produce far more on this lengthy voyage. The officers, too, had cash from three months' pay the navy had advanced them, and they were eager for more, as was the captain. "My next cruise I hope will be more profitable," he wrote to Hambleton on October 4, 1812, "if they give me any discretion I shall expect to make my fortune."

On November 23, the *Essex* crossed the Tropic of Cancer at 25° 27' north latitude, and 28° 39' west longitude. To relieve the boredom of the trip, Porter permitted a time-honored ceremony to take place. David Farragut and the other neophytes who had never crossed the line before were initiated at the clown court of King Neptune. On November 23 a lookout at the main masthead cried, "Sail Ho." The officer of the deck shouted back, "Where away?" followed by "What does she look like?"

"A small boat on the lee bow," came the reply.

The officer then hailed the stranger and asked what boat she was. The answer was that she was Neptune's, god of the sea, and he wished permission to come aboard with his train, which was speedily granted.

A bosun's mate and his cronies were waiting in the fore-chains. They sprang over the bow and mounted an unsteady carriage made of boards lashed together. Two chairs were tied together in the center of the awkward conveyance to provide a throne for Neptune and his wife, Amphitrite. Four men drew the carriage while others trailed behind with their shirts off and their bodies painted. Others walked along the side with their trousers cut above the knees and their legs and faces painted. Barbers with razors made of iron hoop accompanied them, along with constables and musicians playing band music. They marched onto the quarterdeck, where Neptune dismounted and asked Captain Porter's permission to shave all aboard who had not crossed the line before—provided the king and his entourage were paid with rum. Permission was granted, and the initiation went on all afternoon.

Popular bosun's mate William Kingsbury played the part of Neptune. Under his bleary-eyed direction, the novices were lathered with tar, crude soap, and other disagreeable ointments, after which, one by one, they were forced to sit on a rough spar spread across a huge tub of water. Fixed in this position, each man was shaved in turn with dull razors made of rough wood. The victim was then plunged into the icy water and cleansed. When he arose, dripping wet, he would participate in tormenting the rest of the uninitiated.

As the ceremony progressed, "Neptune . . . and most of his suite, paid their devotions so frequently to Bacchus," Porter recalled, "that before the christening was half gone through, their godships were unable to stand; the business was therefore entrusted to the subordinate agents, who performed both the shaving and washing with as little regard to tenderness as his majesty would have done. On the whole, however, they got through the business with less disorder and more good humor than I expected; and although some were unmercifully scraped, the only satisfaction sought was that of shaving others in their turn with new invented tortures."

The crossing of the line ceremony was a tradition borrowed, as so many were, from the Royal Navy. Not every British officer approved of the tomfoolery, of course. Some thought it, at best, a waste of time; Captain William Bligh had been one of these. Porter, on the other hand, found it harmless fun.

AS THE *ESSEX* CONTINUED ON TOWARD PORTO PRAIA, PORTER paid special attention to the crew's health. The fighting quality of the frigate depended as much on the men's physical condition as it did on their weapons. The *Essex* could not make an extended voyage or win the battles Porter was so assiduously preparing for if the men were incapacitated by ship-borne diseases like typhus (ship's fever), dysentery, malaria, and especially scurvy. Porter might be impulsive at times, quick to anger, even choleric, but he was also smart, thoughtful, and studious. He had spent a good deal of time studying the conditions that maximize the well-being of ordinary sailors. A happy, healthy crew, in his view, was far more effective in a fight than a disgruntled one. Porter's concern for the welfare of his men came from personal experience and outstanding teachers like his father and Thomas Truxtun.

As part of his health regimen, Porter put the crew on three watches instead of two, which allowed the men to get a good night's sleep. Britain's famed explorer Captain James Cook had done the same thing forty-four years earlier—as had other skippers—with excellent results. Under the commonly used two-watch system seamen never had more than four hours' rest. Since their watches changed every four hours, half the crew was always on duty. Organized in three watches, the men could have eight hours of down time. Porter gave strict orders that they not be disturbed unnecessarily. In severe weather or other emergencies, of course, this regulation had to be dispensed with. On these occasions nobody got any rest. But when conditions permitted, which was much of the time, a three-watch system was used. Porter could do this because his crew was experienced enough to compensate for the smaller number of men on each watch under the three-watch system.

Captain William Bligh, whom Porter had studied, used the three-watch system in the ill-fated HMS *Bounty* for the same reason that his mentor Cook had. Bligh had served as master on Cook's third voyage, and he had seen the good effects of organizing daily life around three watches instead of two. The extreme length of the *Bounty*'s voyage from England to Tahiti meant that her crew would inevitably be subject to the ravages of ship-borne diseases, so if Bligh wanted a crew at all, he had to look after the men's health. "I have ever considered this [three watch system] among seamen as conducive to health," he noted in his log, "and not being jaded by keeping on deck every other four hours, it adds much to their content and cheerfulness."

Bligh's concern for the crew's health was heightened by overcrowding on the tiny *Bounty*. Porter had the same problem. A small warship with an unusually large crew made keeping the men in good physical condition exceptionally difficult. On a long voyage a crowded man-of-war was a naturally unhealthy place. "What can be more dreadful," Porter explained in his journal, "than for 300 men to be confined with their hammocks, being only eighteen inches apart, on the berth deck of a small frigate, a space of 70 feet long, 35 feet wide, and 5 feet high, in a hot climate, where the only aperture by which they can receive air are two hatchways about 6 feet square? The situation must be little superior to the wretches who perished in the black hole of Calcutta."

To protect his men against a naturally unhealthy environment, Porter allowed them to sleep on the gun deck with the ports open. As he wrote in his journal,

The regulation of permitting the crew to sleep on the gun deck with the ports open, where they have free circulation of air contributes not a little . . . to the preservation of their health. Most commanders are opposed to this indulgence, in consequence of their supposing their hammocks in the way of the guns . . . but so far from finding a disadvantage in it, I find a great advantage in always having the men near their quarters, when on the slightest alarm they may be ready for action. . . . It must be understood that none are permitted to sleep on the gun deck, but those who are quartered at the guns there; and they are compelled to sling the hammocks opposite their [own] guns.

The sick were not permitted to remain on the gun deck at night. They stayed below on the berth deck. But Porter required that they be brought up to the gun deck every morning and their hammocks slung in a cool place, where they would not be disturbed by men at work.

He also insisted on the utmost cleanliness for everyone on the ship. Each morning he had the crew mustered at their quarters, where their officers inspected them. He recommended bathing at least once a day. Officers were required to show the men an example by doing it themselves. In addition, Porter fumigated the ship every morning. And he ordered the berth deck kept in a clean and wholesome state, putting Lieutenant

Finch in charge. "Lime [was] provided in tight casks for the purpose of white-washing, and sand for dry-rubbing it," he explained, "and orders given not to wet it if there should be a possibility of avoiding it." He insisted "that no wet clothes or wet provisions should be permitted to remain on the berth deck, or that the crew should be permitted to eat anywhere but the gun deck, except in bad weather." Having established the above and other regulations, he "exhorted the officers to keep [the men] occupied constantly during working hours in some useful employment," Between the hours of four and six in the afternoon, however, they were allowed time for amusement—whenever the duties of the ship permitted, of course.

Porter had good wind sails rigged to provide ventilation below as Cook had done. "As we have but few who sleep on the berth deck," he noted, "we have no foul air generated; and it is found that good wind sails, and a little vinegar evaporated . . . are sufficient to keep the air perfectly sweet."

The greatest menace to the crew remained scurvy. In Porter's view, "Sudden and frequent changes of climate, great exposures to inclement weather, violent fatigues . . . unseemliness, bad provisions and waters" were its principal causes. This, of course, was not true. The real cause remained a mystery until twentieth-century science found that a vitamin C deficiency was the culprit. But Porter knew that the way to prevent scurvy had been known since at least the time of Cook's first voyage, which began in 1768.

Cook's experience in the Royal Navy had made him especially sensitive to the problem. When he first entered the service in June 1755, he was shocked by how badly seamen were treated aboard ships of war in the British navy. Getting men to serve was already difficult, and having to resort to the heinous practice of pressgangs was so common, he assumed that once the men were aboard they would be well treated, but the opposite was the case. Most British captains paid no attention to the men's health. Innocent tars fell sick and died from scurvy and other ship diseases at astonishing rates. Conditions were bad enough that large numbers of men looked for every opportunity to desert.

Even more disheartening to Cook was the discovery that skippers in the Royal Navy considered the scourge of scurvy normal. He observed their shocking indifference on his very first voyage in HMS *Eagle*, a 60-gun warship, on patrol from Lands End in England to Cape Clear in Ireland, under a Captain Hamer. To his astonishment, Cook observed dozens of men suffering from scurvy after having been on board only a few weeks. Conditions became so bad that in a few months Captain Hamer was forced to put into port and send 130 men to hospital. They were the lucky ones; at least they were alive. The man who passed for a surgeon had himself died from scurvy. All of this happened while the *Eagle* was in sight of land nearly every day.

Drawing on all the knowledge then available about ways to prevent scurvy, particularly the work of James Lind, Cook implemented a program during three lengthy voyages that was astonishingly successful. Not one man aboard his ships ever died from scurvy during the many years he was at sea.

There was no excuse for any captain in 1812 having this disease ravage his ship, yet through indifference and sheer stupidity, scurvy remained a threat in both British and American warships. Porter was determined not to let it ruin his cruise. Using what he learned from Cook and other writers, and his own experience, Porter hoped his health regime would protect the *Essex* from the ravages of scurvy and other diseases. He was convinced that with "precautions to procure exercise and cleanliness, with proper ventilations and fumigations, with the best provisions, and the purest water, perfectly free from all bad taste and smell, he would command a young, active, healthy, and contented crew." Of course, diet was supremely important, which is why Porter insisted on having lemon, lime, and oranges aboard, along with the best water he could obtain, fresh vegetables, and fresh food in general, especially fish.

He was particularly enthusiastic about the good effects of lemon juice. During his time in the Mediterranean he discovered that it was as cheap as vinegar and quite effective. He bragged that his "men were never affected by the scurvy" as other crews were. "On long voyages through different climates, where the transitions from hot to cold and from dry to wet are very great and frequent, the ravages of the scurvy are more dreadful," he explained in a letter, "and lemon juice is found to be indispensably necessary as a preventative to that disease; for after long use of salt provisions, fresh provisions and vegetables have not always the desired effect, as they frequently bring on dysenteries more destructive to life than the scurvy, indeed, there have been instances of persons on long voyages who have suffered greatly by scorbutic affections that have abstained entirely from the use of salt provisions."

Porter's concern for the well-being of the crew did not lead to any slackening of discipline. He ran a tight ship, but he was fair, and his men respected him. When the voyage began, he announced a general pardon for all previous offenses, and then threatened that the first man he had to punish would receive three dozen lashes. The threat was real. No one doubted it. The captain's tough measures were accepted because if they were to obtain the riches they all sought, the ship would have to perform to his high standards. As an example, he expected the *Essex* to be cleared for action and the crew at their stations, ready to fight within fifteen minutes of being summoned. Hands consistently fulfilled this demanding requirement, knowing how important it would be when faced with an enemy frigate. Porter was also wise enough not to abuse his power. Although he insisted that all orders be obeyed without hesitation or demur, he expected officers to act with civility toward their subordinates, on the grounds that in no way did courtesy detract from discipline.

Later in life, Porter gave this striking description of the powers of a sea captain:

A man of war is a petty kingdom, and is governed by a petty despot. . . . The little Tyrant, who struts his few fathoms of scoured plank, dare not unbend, lest he should lose that appearance of respect from his inferiors which their fears inspire. He has therefore no society, no smiles, no courtesies for or from anyone. Wrapped up in his notions of his own dignity, and the means of preserving it, he shuts himself up from all around him. He stands alone, without the friendship or sympathy of one on board; a solitary being in the midst of the ocean.

As he was wont to do, Porter exaggerated. Carried to extremes, the kind of self-imposed isolation he described above could be self-defeating, and while he was captain of the *Essex* he did not fall into that trap. He maintained the respect of his men without having to stand so far apart from them that he lost the capacity to lead them effectively into battle.

AT SUNRISE ON NOVEMBER 26, A LOOKOUT SPOTTED THE FIRST Cape Verde Island—St. Nicholas, a dry, uninviting place. Porter saw no vegetables or trees, and began thinking that the provisions he needed would not be forthcoming on any of the archipelago's ten islands. Viewed from the sea, they appeared barren and desolate. Erupting volcanoes in ages past and scorching tropical sun had turned them into sterile places inhospitable to vegetation. The largest and most important was Santiago, where Porto Praia, the capital and first place of rendezvous with Commodore Bainbridge, was located.

Not only did the islands have an inhospitable look, but Porter could not be sure of the reception he would get from the authorities. The Cape Verdes were Portuguese colonies, after all, and Britain was Portugal's closest ally. It was true that since Napoleon had invaded Portugal in November 1807 and the royal family had fled with their court to Brazil, the islands had become a neglected backwater of a declining empire. But they were still Portuguese territory, and even though Portugal was supposedly neutral in the war between Britain and America, officials in the islands might not want to traffic with an American warship. There might also be problems with the Royal Navy. Although Porto Praia was not a place where British men-of-war normally stopped, from time to time they did, and one or two might be there now.

On November 27, the *Essex* approached the island of Santiago. As Porter surveyed the countryside, he was disappointed at what he saw. Arid hillsides, sugarcane fields, and banana plantations dominated the landscape. Villages and flocks of goats dotted the mountainsides, but the soil was so poor that no vegetation, except for a scattering of coconut trees, was visible. He was so disappointed that he contemplated just looking into the harbor at Porto Praia and seeing if Bainbridge and Lawrence were there, but not stopping if they weren't. He could make do with the provisions he had and move on to the next point of rendezvous, the island of Fernando de Noronha.

On the afternoon of the 27th, the *Essex*, flying American colors, sailed quietly into Porto Praia. It was a dilapidated place dependent for its livelihood on provisioning a few merchant ships and on the slave trade. Defenses were a sham. Porter estimated that thirty men could take the place without suffering any injury. The only other vessel he saw was a small Portuguese schooner. Bainbridge and Lawrence obviously weren't there, and since this was the day they were scheduled to leave, Porter assumed they had left, but he had to make certain. He sent Lieutenant Downes ashore to visit the governor and find out if any American warships had visited recently, and if supplies were available, although he had not made up his mind if he would remain to receive them. He had not dropped his anchor yet.

Downes returned shortly with news that the governor was taking an afternoon nap and could not be disturbed. The lieutenant governor could not have been more solicitous, however. He promised whatever salutes and other civilities Porter required, as well as information and supplies. He also invited the captain to meet with the governor. Given this unexpectedly warm reception, Porter decided to stay for a time; his ship and crew were in excellent condition, but the men could use a run ashore, and Fernando de Noronha was 1,400 miles away.

Taking advantage of the governor's hospitality, Porter remained for five days. Every member of the crew had time ashore. No enemy warships appeared to ruin their holiday. The governor was at pains to tell Porter that he had good relations with the American merchantmen who visited for supplies, but that British merchants never put in. A few British men-of-war did stop from time to time and annoyed everyone—particularly the governor. He found their officers insufferably haughty.

Porter was able to obtain most of the food and supplies he needed, although not as much water as he would have liked. The surf was so high the crew had difficulty transporting it to the ship. A variety of exceptionally fine tropical fruits were put on board—lemons, limes, coconuts, and an amazing amount of oranges. Porter found them to be the best tropical fruits he ever tasted. Sheep, pigs, goats, fowls, and very fine turkeys were also available, as well as some poor beef. The island's rum was dreadful, but the crew craved it, and many subterfuges were used to obtain it. The natives hid it in coconuts they were sending aboard, draining out the milk and filling the inside with rum. It was impossible to control the amount coming into the ship. Not that Porter made much of an effort. As long as the drinking stayed within reasonable bounds, he allowed the traffic to continue. He also permitted the crew to bring a variety of live animals aboard, from goats to chickens and monkeys. By the time he was ready to sail, he thought of himself as the skipper of Noah's Ark.

IN THE SOUTH ATLANTIC, DREAMING OF THE PACIFIC

ALTHOUGH BAINBRIDGE HAD NOT VISITED THE CAPE Verdes Islands as planned, David Porter continued on to the next place of rendezvous, hoping the *Constitution* and the *Hornet* would be there. On December 2, 1812, he stood out from Porto Praia, steering southeast toward Africa to conceal his actual destination. As soon as he was out of sight he changed course, turning south southwest, making for the next point of rendezvous, the Portuguese penal colony on the island of Fernando de Noronha, 220 miles off the northeast coast of Brazil.

As the voyage progressed, Porter found that the many animals he had allowed aboard were too much of a burden. They were consuming far more water than he had anticipated, and they were causing prodigious sanitation problems. Reluctantly, he ordered all the pigs and young goats killed. The kids had to go because in sucking their mothers they deprived the crew of goat's milk. The monkeys were allowed to live, however. Their skylarking antics in the rigging and upper yards provided much-needed entertainment. Of course, they also consumed precious water. The men were now reduced to a half gallon a day.

As the *Essex* made her way southwest, she ran beyond the northeast trade winds in a few days and entered the flat water, calms, and erratic storms of the doldrums near the Equator. When she reached four degrees north latitude, slight variations in the winds began, hauling from northeast to east by south. Distant lightning was often seen to the southward. At intervals, heavy rain showers came, but only for a few minutes, making it impossible to catch any water, even though the rain awning was spread. Sometimes the rain was accompanied by a little increase of wind, but more frequently by calms. The temperature of the air remained relatively constant, and clouds continued to block out the sun.

Porter noted that all navigators in crossing between the Cape Verdes and the coast of Brazil had remarked on the irregularities of the currents. He believed that the trade winds were the underlying cause of currents in the North and South Atlantic. The *Essex* picked up the southeasterly trades three degrees north of the Equator, not south of it. And, contrary to expectation, the temperature dropped.

On December 11, the *Essex* crossed the Equator at longitude 30° west. Porter had on board what he considered an accurate chronometer. King Neptune did not make an appearance, all the novices having been initiated earlier. The following afternoon at two o'clock lookouts spotted a sail to windward. She appeared to be a British brig of war, and Porter gave chase. At six o'clock the brig sent up a signal, which Porter responded to. Using intelligence he had taken from the *Alert* months before, he gave what he thought was an appropriate answer, but no reply came. Just before sundown the brig hoisted British colors and after dark began making night signals, whereupon Porter beat to quarters and cleared for action. He kept closing with her, and by nine o'clock he was within musket shot. He hailed her through a speaking trumpet, and not wanting to injure her, he ordered her to lower her topsails, haul up her courses, and heave-to to windward. Instead of obeying, the brig's plucky skipper attempted to run to leeward athwart the *Essex*'s stern with a view to raking her and then scooting off. To prevent this, Porter ordered a volley of musket fire, which quickly brought the brig to.

She turned out to be the packet ship *Nocton* out of Rio de Janeiro bound for Falmouth, England, carrying ten guns and a crew of thirty-one. Before Porter sent over a boarding party he warned everyone not to plunder any prisoners. A thorough search of the brig revealed an unexpected treasure—12,000 pounds sterling in metal coinage, or specie ($55,000), money, which Porter took aboard the *Essex*. It could provide him with a considerable degree of independence. The Royal Navy routinely carried large amounts of specie from South America to England. The burgeoning British merchant fleet in South America acquired huge amounts of gold in trade, and skippers always wanted warships to carry their money home. They had been doing a brisk business in Latin America ever since Napoleon had invaded the Iberian Peninsula in 1807 and 1808, and Portugal and Spain had become reliant on Britain for their lives. In the past, Madrid had been able to keep most of Britain's traders out of Latin America, but no longer; and when British merchants accumulated large quantities of gold, London made sure it reached England. The Ministry considered the flow of gold vital. It was financing the Duke of Wellington's army in Spain. He was wisely paying in specie for the supplies he was constantly requisitioning from the countryside.

The following day, December 12, Porter put Midshipman William B. Finch in command of the *Nocton* with Midshipman Thomas Conover as his second. They had orders to sail the packet back to the United States as a prize. The *Nocton*'s captain, master, and passengers were sent aboard her on parole of honor with instructions that should they meet any vessel bound for England or anywhere else, they were free to transfer to her. Porter allowed seventeen prisoners to remain aboard the *Nocton* and added thirteen of his own men (one an invalid) to aid Finch. The seventeen were the youngest and weakest of the *Nocton*'s crew. Porter kept the strongest, more experienced prisoners on the *Essex*. He expected that this arrangement would help Finch keep control.

Unfortunately, the *Nocton* never made it back to the United States. The frigate HMS *Belvidera* (Captain Richard Byron) captured her on January 5, 1813, in heavy seas northeast of the Bahamas and due west of St. Augustine, Florida, in latitude 31° 30' north and longitude 66° west. After a chase lasting three hours and twenty minutes, the frigate—sailing at an impressive eleven knots—caught the unlucky *Nocton* and took her to Bermuda. Finch and his men were incarcerated for a time, before being exchanged with a number of other prisoners.

On December 14, two days after Porter had captured the *Nocton*, an *Essex* lookout spied the Pyramid (Morro do Pico). It is the highest peak in the strikingly beautiful archipelago of Fernando de Noronha, northeast of Cape St. Roque, the easternmost point on the northeastern coast of Brazil. Remarkably thin, the 1,023-foot-high mountain is the tip of a sub-Atlantic range that rose four thousand feet from the sea bed. Amerigo Vespucci, the Italian explorer and cartographer, temporarily in the service of Manuel I of Portugal, was the first European to describe the island, at the start of the sixteenth century.

Using the mountain as a guide, Porter spent the rest of the day making his way toward the archipelago. During the night he continued to windward under easy sail, and at daylight rounded into a good harbor on the northwest side of the archipelago's capital, disguised as a merchantman displaying British colors. Only seven square miles, the main island, although exceptionally attractive, had been turned by the Portuguese into a depressing prison colony. They allowed no females or boats on it. Women were prohibited in order to render the place of exile more horrible.

Now began a game of false identities and coded messages, played with ingenuity and a keen sense of comedy. Porter ordered a boat lowered, and Lieutenant Downes (in plain clothes) went ashore and met with the governor. Downes told him that the *Essex* was the merchant ship *Fanny* (Captain Johnson) from London, via Newfoundland, bound to Rio de Janeiro for a cargo. Downes told him that they had been out sixty days, were short of water, had several men sick with scurvy, and needed supplies, but they could not anchor, because they had lost all of their anchors but one, and their cables were bad.

In two and a half hours, Downes returned with the news that, according to the governor, two British men-of-war had visited the island the previous week—the 44-gun *Acasta* (Captain Kerr) and the 20-gun *Morgiana*. Kerr left a letter for the captain of HMS *Southampton*, who was, not coincidentally, Porter's old antagonist, Sir James Yeo. It was to be dispatched to England at the first opportunity. The governor also gave Downes some fruit as a present for his captain.

Porter sent Downes back with cheese and porter beer for the governor and a message informing him that a gentleman was aboard who knew Sir James Yeo intimately. This gentleman was on his way to England after a brief stop in Brazil and would take charge of the letter.

At three o'clock that afternoon, Downes returned with the letter. It read:

> My dear Mediterranean friend,
>
> Probably you may stop here; don't attempt to water, it is attended with too much difficulty. I learned before I left England that you were bound to the Brazil coast; if so, perhaps we may meet at St. Salvadore or Rio de Janeiro. I should be happy to meet and converse on our old affairs of captivity; recollect our secret in those times.
>
> Your friend, of H.M.'s ship Acasta,
KERR

The rest of the letter was written in invisible sympathetic ink:

> I am bound off St. Salvadore, thence off Cape Frio, where I intend to cruise until the 1st of January. Go off Cape Frio, to the northward of Rio de Janeiro, and keep a look out for me.
>
> Your Friend

The letter was obviously from Bainbridge; the writing was in his hand. It was also obvious that he had never gone to Porto Praia but had traveled directly from Boston to Fernando de Noronha. Porter immediately hoisted in his boat and stood out from the harbor. The penal colony was so depressing he did not want to tarry a single night, even though he could have obtained wood, water, fruits, vegetables, hogs, and even turtles, albeit with difficulty. He threw on all sail and shaped a course southward for Cape Frio, 1,400 miles away, the next rendezvous point.

On December 20, the *Essex* spoke a Portuguese vessel from St. Salvador. The *Constitution* and the *Hornet* had, indeed, put in there on December 13, as Bainbridge said he would. The Portuguese captain confirmed what Porter had learned from the *Nocton*, that the *Bonne Citoyenne*, a British sloop of war carrying a heavy load of specie to London, had sprung a bad leak, and had run into St. Salvador in distress. She was carrying gold belonging to British merchants trading in Buenos Aries on the Rio de la Plata.

Porter thought of racing to St. Salvador and joining Bainbridge, but decided that he was not needed, and Bainbridge might not remain there for long. So far as the war between America and Britain was concerned, St. Salvador was a neutral Portuguese port, and Bainbridge might not be able to touch the *Bonne Citoyenne*. There was also the danger that the 74-gun British battleship *Montague* would be sailing up from Rio with escorts to rescue the *Bonne Citoyenne* and shepherd her to England. The *Montague* was the flagship of Vice Admiral Manley Dixon, commander of Britain's South American Station at Rio. The *Montague* was the most powerful warship on the South American coast, and Porter did not want to run into her. Given all these factors, he thought it best if he went directly to Cape Frio.

It did not take long to get there. On December 25 the color of the water indicated soundings, and at noon a lookout sighted several islands north of the cape. Around four o'clock the cape itself came into view, seventy-four miles east of Rio. Three hundred and nine years earlier, in 1503, Amerigo Vespucci had been the first European to view the cape. Porter thought the waters surrounding it were as good as any for intercepting British commerce. He hove to just off the cape, positioning himself to catch any vessel traveling to or from Rio.

For two days he patrolled under easy sail without spotting an enemy vessel. He did chase a Portuguese brig-of-war he thought was British, and in doing so, came within fifteen miles of the entrance to Rio. That was too close; enemy warships were sure to be in the harbor. He attempted to beat back to Cape Frio, but fresh winds made that impossible, so he decided to remain where he was and take the risk. Vice Admiral Dixon was in Rio at the time, and he had no idea that Porter and the *Essex* were so close. He did not find out until weeks later.

During the few days that the *Essex* patrolled off Rio, she saw little action at first. But there was great excitement when many dolphins began swimming playfully around the ship. Hands were enchanted. They threw lines out, hauling in scores, and having a feast every day. But everything changed on the morning of December 29, when a lookout at the main masthead spotted a sail to windward. Porter grabbed a glass and rushed to the main-top, where he saw a schooner making for Rio. He immediately gave chase, caught up with her, and after firing several shots, brought her to around nine o'clock that night. She turned out to be the British schooner *Elizabeth*. Porter examined her log book, which her captain had failed to destroy, and then questioned the luckless skipper, who told him that he had been on the way to England before a dangerous leak had forced him to turn back. From the schooner's crew Porter learned that the *Montague* was still in the harbor at Rio with her sails unbent, which might mean that Dixon wasn't preparing to depart anytime soon.

Porter also discovered that the *Elizabeth* was part of a six-vessel convoy being shepherded to England by the three-masted, 8-gun schooner *Juniper*. He learned further that three deeply laden ships were slowing the convoy down, and he went after them. Before departing, he turned over command of the leaky *Elizabeth* to Midshipman William Clarke, and gave him six *Essex* men and three prisoners for a crew. Porter told Clarke to pick some port other than Rio to stop into and fix the leaks, and to then sail to the United States. He gave Clarke discretion to go into Rio if he absolutely had to, but Porter obviously did not want to alert Admiral Dixon to the *Essex*'s presence offshore. If Clarke was forced to go into Rio, however, Porter gave him a letter for the American minister there, Thomas Sumter Jr. Porter then raced east after the *Juniper* and her charges, but contrary winds and damage to the *Essex* slowed him down.

Midshipman Clarke, in the meantime, was having problems. He hadn't been aboard the *Elizabeth* long before her leaks worsened, and he was forced to put into Rio after all. The Portuguese authorities refused him sanctuary, however, and he had to burn the ship. He was now stranded in a neutral port that was under effective British control. Clarke stayed clear of Dixon, never providing him information, but word of the *Elizabeth*'s distress and return to Rio spread, and the admiral now knew there was an American raider operating offshore. It took Clarke and his men a year to get home.

On January 2, 1813, Porter stopped a Portuguese brig-of war and finally received news of Bainbridge and Lawrence. The brig had been at Bahia nine days earlier and had put into the harbor at St. Salvador, where she had seen the *Bonne Citoyenne*. The brig's skipper told Porter that when he sortied from the harbor, he was brought to by a big frigate and a sloop of war flying British colors. Porter assumed they were the *Constitution* and the *Hornet*. He had already learned that only three British men-of-war were in this part of South America—the 74-gun *Montague* in Rio; the 32-gun *Nereus* in the Rio de la Plata estuary off Buenos Aires; and the 20-gun *Bonne Citoyenne* at St. Salvador. The following day, January 3, Porter stopped another Portuguese brig, which had also seen two American warships ten days earlier off Bahia.

Convinced now that Bainbridge and Lawrence would remain in the area of St. Salvador to capture the *Bonne Citoyenne* when she sortied, Porter decided to join them. He had learned from the *Elizabeth*'s crew that Admiral Dixon was expecting reinforcements at Rio, which meant that the *Essex* could not remain where she was for long. Before Porter could move, however, he needed to make essential repairs on the ship before they got completely out of control. The main topmast trestletrees and the mizzen topmast trestletrees had both carried away and had to be replaced before the topmasts and topgallant masts on the main and mizzen masts, with all their rigging, came tumbling down. The temporary replacements were about to give way. Porter already had new trestletrees made up so that the work could be accomplished in one long day.

A shift in the wind forced Porter to delay his plan to sail north and meet Bainbridge and Lawrence. A fresh gale had begun blowing from the north, forcing him to sail east. He kept an eye out for the small convoy he had been chasing before and waited for the wind to change. The *Essex* was in latitude 22° 13' 17" south. For six days, from January 6 to 12, however, the wind did not change; it continued blowing obstinately from the north, forcing Porter to remain on his present course until it shifted. The continuously adverse winds caused him to rethink his plan to travel north. Since his supplies were running low, he decided to stand south instead of north, and make for either St. Sebastian Island or St. Catherine's, depending on the wind. It was a critical decision. If he stood south, he would dramatically lessen his chance to rendezvous with the *Constitution* and the *Hornet*.

PORTER HAD NO WAY OF KNOWING THAT MEETING BAINBRIDGE and Lawrence was already impossible. On December 29, Bainbridge, while cruising off the Bahia coast, had fallen in with the British warship of his dreams. At nine that morning the *Constitution* was sailing along the coast just south of St. Salvador when one of her lookouts spotted two sails well off the weather bow. The *Constitution* was alone. Bainbridge had left Lawrence and the *Hornet* just outside the harbor at St. Salvador to blockade the *Bonne Citoyenne*, which Bainbridge had discovered was carrying 500,000 pounds sterling in specie. Lawrence could not attack her while she was in a neutral port, but he was doing everything he could to entice her out.

An hour later, at ten o'clock, Bainbridge saw the two strangers split up. One steered for St. Salvador, but the other sailed toward the *Constitution*. She was the formidable 38-gun British frigate *Java*, and what ensued that afternoon was one of the greatest naval battles in American history. Bainbridge was up against Henry Lambert, a veteran captain with a ship that was markedly faster than the *Constitution*, which gave her an important edge. Of course, "Old Ironsides" had her strengths as well— a more powerful battery, a skipper with an overwhelming need to win, and the remarkable hands that Isaac Hull had trained. They were far more experienced than Lambert's men, a hundred of who were recently impressed.

The gruesome battle went on all afternoon. It ended at 5:30 with the *Java* a complete wreck, wallowing in the sea with all her masts down, her colors struck. Her gallant first lieutenant, Henry Chads, had the baleful task of surrendering. Henry Lambert was below, mortally wounded. A sharpshooter, standing in one of the *Constitution*'s tops, had put a musket ball in his chest. The rest of the *Java*'s crew had suffered mightily as well. Fifty-seven out of 426 were dead and eighty-three wounded. Losses on the *Constitution* were far less. Nine out of 475 were dead and twenty-six wounded, including Bainbridge. Despite the carnage and his own wounds, however, he was more elated than at any time in his life. He had finally redeemed himself, finally wiped away the stain of the *Philadelphia* and the other disappointments in his career. He could now hold his head up among his peers and countrymen.

Bainbridge dearly wanted to bring the *Java* home in triumph, but that was not to be. She was too far gone and had to be destroyed. After removing her crew and burning her, he returned to St. Salvador and released hundreds of prisoners on parole. He then repaired the *Constitution*, but the damages were so extensive that he could not continue his cruise, meet Porter, and proceed to St. Helena. Getting the wounded ship back to America—preferably to her homeport of Boston—would be difficult enough. She would have to run past whatever blockade the British had in place along the east coast.

Bainbridge also had to think about Lawrence and the *Hornet*. He did not know what had happened to them. He worried that Admiral Dixon and the *Montague* might have captured them. When Bainbridge went back to St. Salvador, he could see that Lawrence wasn't there, and he soon discovered that the *Montague* had made a surprise appearance on December 24. Fortunately, Lawrence, who at the time was still blockading the harbor, spotted the *Montague* in the nick of time and ran into the neutral port for protection. During the night he took Dixon by surprise and ran the *Hornet* to the southward out of the harbor.

Once safely away, Lawrence decided against attempting a rendezvous with Porter or Bainbridge at Cape Frio. Instead, he traveled home, which turned out to be a fortunate choice. On the way he captured the 10-gun British brig *Resolution*, and then defeated and sank the 18-gun British war-brig *Peacock*. Three of Lawrence's men were drowned trying to save the crew of the *Peacock*, and many more were saved only by luck as she went down. A heavy sea was running at the time. The American brig *Hunter* out of Portland Maine had been recently captured by the *Peacock*, and Lawrence recaptured her as well. The *Peacock* was one of the finest vessels of her class in the British navy. Afterward, he sailed home with a huge load of prisoners, and a ship that was badly in need of repairs and dangerously low on provisions. Contributing to his load of prisoners were men from the British merchantman *Ellen*, which he had taken outside St. Salvador before Admiral Dixon and the *Montague* arrived. On the way back to the United States Lawrence managed to avoid the British blockade and put into Homes Hole in Martha's Vineyard on March 19, 1813. He was hailed as a great hero around the country, just as Bainbridge was.

The triumphs of Bainbridge and Lawrence were two in a string of six blue-water victories that the much-abused American navy achieved in the opening eight months of the war. The unexpected triumphs stunned London and invigorated President Madison, whose strategy for winning the war was otherwise in shambles. The invasion of Canada continued to be stymied, and Napoleon Bonaparte, whom the president was counting on so heavily, had been badly defeated in Russia, taking the pressure off London to end the American war quickly.

The *Essex*'s triumph over the *Alert* was the first of these remarkable naval victories. Porter had not heard of the others, of course, except for the *Constitution*'s back in August of 1812. Nor did he know yet that his dream of being free to pursue his own path to glory was now a reality. The victories of Bainbridge and Lawrence, and their return home had liberated him, given him the opportunity he had craved for so long.

At the moment, Porter had no inkling of how his fortunes had changed. More mundane matters occupied his mind. The *Essex* was still patrolling off Rio and badly in need of water, wood, and salt; and her crew needed refreshment. Since the *Essex* men had departed the United States, they had been on two-thirds allowance of salt provisions, half allowance of bread, and a full allowance of rum, which was now running dangerously low.

Rum was a particular problem that was much on Porter's mind. He did not dare prohibit its consumption, but it was running so low that he was forced to reduce the daily allowance, which caused the entire crew to balk. The men wanted their grog now, and if it gave out later, they promised to live without it. They declared that if they did not receive their full allowance, they would not take any at all. Porter had his mind made up, however, and would not give in. He called their bluff by declaring that the grog tub would be overturned fifteen minutes after the crew was called to grog. Fear of losing all their allowance led every man to hasten to the tub at the appointed time and the crisis passed.

BAINBRIDGE HAD LISTED THE ISLANDS OF ST. SEBASTIAN AND St. Catherine's as possible rendezvous points, and Porter felt that he had to make for one of them right away. "With my water and provisions getting short, and feeling apprehensive of the scurvy," he wrote later to Bainbridge, "I determined to put into port, and as I had certain intelligence that the British Admiral [Dixon] had sailed from Rio on the 5th of January in pursuit of us I considered it advisable to go to a place where there would be the least likelihood of his getting intelligence of me in a short time, and therefore proceeded to St. Catherine's."

St. Sebastian Island was only two hundred miles south of Rio (a day's run) while St. Catharine's was five hundred, and for that reason a much safer place to put in. St. Catharine's was one of the more congenial spots along the South American coast, the usual stopping place for American whalers, sealers, and privateers.

On the way to St. Catharine's, Porter distributed a portion of the prize money he had taken from the *Nocton*. He wanted the men to have enough cash to purchase what they needed when they reached the island. He had misread his men, however. Instead of being saved for St. Catharine's, the new money ignited a bout of gambling. He put a quick stop to that by punishing anyone asking for or paying a gambling debt, and by giving monies collected to any informer without revealing his name. The gaming ended.

On January 18, Porter spoke to the captain of a Portuguese vessel recently out of Rio. The movements of the British squadron were uppermost in his mind, and he was told that the *Montague* had sailed on January 6 to search for Bainbridge and Lawrence. Actually, the *Montague* had sailed long before January 6, but Porter had no way of knowing that. He believed that more warships were coming to Dixon from England, and guessed that while the *Montague* might have sailed north to St. Salvador, the admiral could have remained at Rio to await those reinforcements. If so, Porter thought Dixon might send one or two of the recently arrived warships to trap him at St. Catharine's. In fact, two of Dixon's warships, the 24-gun *Cherub* (Thomas Tucker) and the 18-gun *Racoon* (William Black), had left Rio while Dixon was away, and searched to the southward for the *Essex*, but could not find her.

Porter was worried that Dixon might stumble on him. So he decided that, no matter how strong the temptation to stay in such an agreeable place as St. Catherine's, he would not remain there any longer than he had to. On January 19 he made the island, bearing southwest, close to the Brazilian coast. He stood for her, and by eight o'clock that evening he was twelve miles away and laid off for the night. In the morning he ran in with light winds to within two and a half miles of the principal fortification and dropped anchor. As soon as he did, a swarm of bumboats rushed to the ship's side with food for sale in small quantities. Regrettably, the prices were outrageously high. Porter discouraged the officers and men from buying anything, but he did not forbid it.

Lieutenant Downes went ashore to establish relations with the Portuguese authorities, and received a warm welcome. Obtaining water was Porter's first priority. Even though the government cooperated, the weather at St. Catherine's was squally with heavy rains, which complicated all the provisioning. The ship had to be moved in order to reach the best watering place. Once his guide led him to it, however, Porter had the *Essex* supplied with water in two and a half days. He also put on board all the wood he needed, and rum, which he had no problem buying at a decent price. But food was another matter. He continued to have a difficult time with the ubiquitous bumboats. They were always about, selling fowl, yams, hogs, plantains, turkeys, watermelons, and onions at ridiculously inflated prices. Porter got so annoyed watching his crew being cheated that he finally intervened and established strict rules for trading. Unfortunately, he found that obtaining the same quantity or quality of goods on shore was impossible because the bumboat men had a corner on the market.

Even though the weather was poor at the moment, St. Catherine's was otherwise an attractive place, blessed with a temperate climate and ideal conditions for growing food. Ten thousand people lived on the island in comfortable houses and lovely villages. The peasants looked well fed and well clad, and the women were handsome. Don Luis Maurice da Silvia, the Portuguese governor, assigned Sergeant-Major Sabine to attend to Porter's needs, which he did with consummate diplomatic skill. Even so, Porter continued to have trouble obtaining all the provisions he wanted.

While work on resupply went forward, a remarkable visitor appeared from the ocean. Some rotten beef had got on board, and Porter threw it over the side, which drew the attention of an enormous shark. Porter thought it measured twenty-five feet. At one point the fish was thrashing in the water with a quarter of a bullock in its mouth—in the exact place where the previous evening some of the crew and a few officers had been swimming. Porter thought that a man would be only a mouthful for the giant.

The island's principal industry, besides supplying ships sailing to and from the Pacific, was the whale fishery. About 500 whales were taken annually from the bay where the *Essex* was anchored. They came to calve and were defenseless. Their oil was deposited in an immense rock tank and shipped to Portugal.

While the *Essex* was being loaded, Porter spoke to the captain of a small Portuguese trader that had left Rio four days earlier. He was told that the *Montague* had captured a 22-gun American warship, which Porter assumed was the *Hornet*, and that the *Montague* was in pursuit of a large American frigate, which Porter thought had to be the *Constitution*. None of this was true. The Portuguese captain went on to tell Porter that a British frigate and two brigs of war had arrived at Rio and more reinforcements were expected. With them, Admiral Dixon could now make a more determined search for the *Essex*. The captain also told Porter that Buenos Aires, then in a state of starvation, was to be avoided, while Montevideo (the future capital of Uruguay) was closed to the *Essex*. Its government was still in the hands of Spaniards loyal to the deposed King of Spain, Ferdinand VII, who was allied with Great Britain. Porter had no way of knowing if the information was true or not, but he had to assume that Dixon was looking for him, and for that reason Buenos Aires and Montevideo where good places to avoid.

All of the enemy activity along the Brazilian coast made Porter anxious to get back to sea. He feared the British would blockade him, or worse, attack the *Essex* in St. Catharine's supposedly neutral harbor. Thus, in spite of the island's temptations, he remained determined to leave as quickly as possible. On January 25, after spending only five days in what all hands (including the captain) thought was a delightful place, Porter fired signal guns for everyone to repair on board. After waiting what he thought was a sufficient amount of time, he hove up and dropped down below the fort, where he anchored to give the officers time to retrieve their clothes, which were on shore being washed. At eight o'clock that evening, he pulled anchor. By dawn the *Essex* was at sea. Two men were left behind. For one reason or another, when the signal was given, they did not return to the ship. Porter waited for a time, assumed that they preferred to stay, and left.

Once out in the South Atlantic, Porter faced the most important decision of his life—where to go from here? Before leaving St. Catharine's he had given Sergeant-Major Sabine a note for Bainbridge should he appear. There was little likelihood that he would, but on the off-chance that he might, Porter wanted him to receive this letter. It read in part: "Should we not meet by the 1st of April, be assured that by pursuing *my own course*, I shall have been actuated by views to the good of the service, and that there will have been an absolute necessity for my doing so." The letter was dated January 20, 1813.

It is hard to imagine that Porter did not have an overwhelming preference for sailing to the Pacific. He had been advocating doing so for years. The possibility must have been on his mind since he left Chester. Everything he had done since the war began indicated how fixated he was on distinguishing himself in some heroic action, and here was his opportunity; there might never be another. Sailing the first American warship into the eastern Pacific was his path to everlasting fame. He could destroy the British whaling fleet there—a great accomplishment in itself—and also have an excellent chance of engaging in a one-on-one battle with an enemy frigate, which was always his main objective.

As far back as 1809, Porter had written to former president Jefferson proposing a voyage to the Pacific. He had visions of being the Lewis and Clark of the sea, highlighting to America the importance of the vast Pacific. Porter sent a copy of the letter to Charles Goldsborough, chief clerk of the navy, who passed it on to President Madison, but like his predecessor, Madison never replied. Porter wrote again to Madison on October 31, 1810, explaining the importance of the Pacific, but again, he was ignored. Still not deterred, Porter wrote on February 7, 1811, to Secretary of the Navy Hamilton that should war break out he wished to be appointed commander of a squadron whose object would be to sail into the eastern Pacific and attack British whalers and merchantmen. Hamilton liked the idea but never followed up on it.

Porter had also urged his plan on Bainbridge. Before the *Essex* left the Delaware River in October 1812, Bainbridge had solicited Porter's opinion on the best mode of attacking the enemy, and Porter had laid before him his plan of sailing into the Pacific. He received a positive response, but in the end Bainbridge decided that patrolling the waters around St. Helena was a better idea. Nonetheless, Porter was convinced that going to the South Pacific would have Bainbridge's approval.

Before making a final decision, Porter asked purser John R. Shaw for an accounting of the provisions on board. They had not been able to obtain all the supplies they needed at St. Catharine's. They did procure wood and water and some refreshments but found it impossible to obtain any sea stock except rum and a few bags of flour. Shaw reported that only three months worth of bread at half allowance were aboard, and this was indicative of the state of the other provisions. Porter talked himself into the idea that only in the eastern Pacific could he resupply the *Essex*. He insisted that no port on the east coast of South America could fulfill his needs without running the risk of blockade, or capture. He also maintained that returning to the United States was out of the question. The American coast would be swarming with British warships, and returning empty handed was diametrically opposite to his instructions to annoy the enemy. He did not seriously consider sailing to the waters around St. Helena, rejecting the idea on the grounds that the state of his provisions would not allow it.

Porter's imagination soared when he thought of what he could accomplish in the Pacific. Wreaking havoc on Britain's whaling fleet would significantly impact her economy. Whalers were so important that the Royal Navy was forbidden to impress men out of them. The British were not expecting the *Essex* in the Pacific. Porter could surprise their whaling fleet before word of his presence reached Admiral Dixon.

Given all these factors, Porter made the final decision to proceed to the Pacific. He wrote later to Bainbridge explaining his thinking:

> [At St. Catherine's] I obtained intelligence of your action with a British frigate, and of the capture of the *Hornet*, of a considerable augmentation of the British force on the coasts of Brazil, and so no hopes of being able to join you except at the last appointed rendezvous and there my stock of provisions would not admit of my going to cruise . . . , to go elsewhere than to the places appointed would be a departure from your instructions and as it now became necessary for me to act discretionary I determined to proceed to the nearest port that would render my supplies certain and at the same time put it out of the power of the enemy to blockade me and thus be enabled to extend my cruise.

Porter claimed that he had no idea where to find Bainbridge at this point. The only realistic way to extend his cruise, he insisted, was to go into the Pacific. Supplies could be obtained at the Chilean ports of Concepción and Valparaiso, and conceivably from enemy whalers, or from privateers—or even from warships. No other course was open to him, he argued, but doubling the Horn. "There appeared no other choice left for me," he wrote, "except capture, starvation, or blockade."

Porter understood well the disadvantages he was operating under. The possible disasters were innumerable, but instead of deterring him, the challenge only stirred his ambition. He ignored for the moment the *Essex*'s battery of carronades and how inadequate they would be in a fight with a British frigate. He knew the Admiralty would be coming after him, especially if he had any success. He welcomed London's attention, but would the *Essex* be up to the task he was assigning her? The remarkable victories of American warships in the early months of the war had been due in large part to their superior gunnery. Porter would not have that advantage. He could only be successful if he closed with an enemy, blasted away with his carronades, and boarded. To do this he would have to rely on the witless behavior of British captains, something they were not noted for, although, of course, the Royal Navy had its incompetents. Nothing was going to deter Porter, however. He was too close to realizing his dream. So he put aside the risks, thought only of what might be accomplished, and pressed on.

He convinced himself that the *Essex* could reach Concepción in no more than two and a half months. He could buy jerk beef, fish, fowl, and wine there—and probably a lot more. He also thought there was a good chance of obtaining supplies from captured whalers and privateers, which would allow him to avoid Concepción or any other Spanish port and keep his presence in the eastern Pacific a secret for as long as possible.

CHAPTER 8

DOUBLING CAPE HORN

A ND SO THE FATEFUL DECISION TO DOUBLE CAPE HORN
(2,500 miles south of St. Catharine's) and sail into the Pacific was
made. Porter did not reveal his intentions to the crew right away, but
some of the men had been around the Horn before, and when they saw
the ship heading south, they sensed where the captain was going. Word
got around quickly. Dreams of fat prizes and Polynesian women aroused
every imagination.

The rigors of Cape Horn still lay ahead, however. The *Essex* would be
the first American warship to double the Horn. Of course, it was a little
ridiculous bragging about being the first American warship when European—especially Spanish—ships had been plying the Pacific for centuries.
And American whalers and sealers had been in the eastern Pacific for years,
going back to the 1780's. It was an American sealer, the *Topaz* (Captain
Mayhew Folger), for instance, that rediscovered Pitcairn Island in February
1808 and answered the question of what had happened to Fletcher Christian, his mutinous comrades, and HMS *Bounty*.

As the *Essex* plowed south, the temperature dropped steadily. Storms
and generally poor weather plagued the crew. The cold began to be a

problem. Woolen clothing that Porter had thoughtfully brought aboard was now a necessity, and blankets were needed at night.

On January 28, the *Essex* reached latitude 34° 58' 09" south and longitude 51° 11' 37" west. Porter began preparing for the passage around the Horn. He unbent and put below all the light sails (sky-sails, royal studding-sails, and other sails that were fit only for tropical weather). He also ordered the royal-masts and rigging sent down; unreaved all the running rigging that was not absolutely necessary; sent every heavy article out of the tops; and diminished the weight aloft in every way he could. All the shot went below, except for six to each gun on the gun deck, and he removed the guns from the extremities to amidships, set up the main rigging, and bent the storm-stay-sails.

From January 28 to February 2, 1813, the weather was unsettled and wintry, but the crew remained in good spirits. Porter was more than a little pleased with their health. His strict health regimen was working exceptionally well. The ship was now three months into her voyage, and the crew had had but seven days in port, yet no sign of the dreaded scurvy had appeared.

The *Essex* was running fast, at times making nine knots an hour. On February 3, they reached latitude 42°14' 30" south and longitude 59° 9' 51" west. Porter decided it was time to make a formal announcement of where they were going, although everyone aboard had by now probably guessed. Even so, to have the rumor officially confirmed created a stir. The captain's clerk posted this electrifying notice on the bulletin board:

> Sailors and Marines:
>
> A large increase of the enemy forces compels us to abandon a coast that will neither afford us security nor supplies. . . . We will therefore, proceed to annoy them, where we are least expected. What was never performed, we will attempt. The Pacific Ocean affords us many friendly ports. The unprotected British commerce on the coast of Chili, Peru, and Mexico, will give you an abundant supply of wealth; and the girls of the Sandwich Islands, shall reward you for your sufferings during the passage around Cape Horn.

The following day, February 4, the wind hauled around to the south-west during the afternoon, creating a disagreeable cross sea. For the next six days, until February 10, the wind was variable, coming from all points of the compass, but mostly from the southwest. At times it blew so hard that Porter had to reduce the *Essex* to a single storm staysail. Albatrosses and other birds that frequent the high latitudes appeared around this time. The *Essex* men tried various methods of catching them, but none worked.

Porter had to admit that, in spite of his former complaints, he was impressed with how well the *Essex* was performing during the heaviest blows and worst seas. He felt confident now in her capacity to handle the horrendous passage around the Horn. As added precautions, he took the spare spars from the spar deck to the gun deck, and put two long 12-pounders below. With the *Essex* as prepared for rough seas as Porter could make her, she drew closer to the dreaded land at the end of the earth. On February 11, she was at latitude 51° 13' south and longitude 63° 53' west—between Tierra del Fuego, the archipelago at the southern tip of South America, and the Falkland Islands.

Porter kept steering toward the Strait of Le Maire—the eighteen-mile-wide passage between Tierra del Fuego and Staten Land (Isla de los Estados). He feared that the treacherous passage through the infamous Strait of Le Maire would be too dangerous, and decided to avoid it by sailing east of Staten Land, one of the more godforsaken places on the planet. In his opinion, no part of the world was more horrible than Staten Island. He never considered winding his way through the dangerous Strait of Magellan.

There were precedents for choosing Le Maire. In March 1741, Lord George Anson, during his famous voyage, had decided to ignore the Strait of Magellan and sail his six-ship squadron through the Strait of Le Maire, rather than to the east of Staten Island. Porter had studied Anson's historic journey and wished to make the name *Essex* as well known in the Pacific as the *Centurion*, Anson's flagship, was. Porter admired Anson's single-minded determination to capture a Spanish treasure ship and bring it to England, which he eventually did. But Porter thought little of Anson's seamanship. The admiral lost all his ships, except the *Centurion*, and 80 percent of his men. It took him three horrific months just to round Cape Horn. Deaths from scurvy and other diseases were heartrending.

Porter wanted to avoid Anson's mistakes, and he had so far. Much had been learned since Anson's day about how to keep a crew healthy, of course, so it is more than a little odd that Porter continually made reference to Anson's problems in his journal. Porter also mentioned Spanish Admiral José Alfonso Pizarro, who sailed in pursuit of Anson with a small fleet, but was defeated by storms. He never found Anson, and returned to Spain with only one ship. Other than the fact that these two admirals were well known—especially Anson—Porter's references to them, although more than a little strange, were apparently for the purpose of having the reader compare his superior seamanship to theirs, even though their voyages were made decades earlier, when many fewer ships had rounded Cape Horn, and much less was known about navigation and ship-borne illness.

Captain Cook on his first voyage in 1768 had the same decisions to make about how to get safely around Cape Horn. He decided to sail through the Strait of Le Maire, believing it to be a better route than traveling to the east of Staten Island or through the extremely difficult Strait of Magellan. It took Cook three tries before he made it through the Strait on his fourth attempt.

Sailing to the east of Staten Island, although appearing to be a safer route than either Cook or Anson chose, was still fraught with danger. Forty miles long and nine miles wide, the island was seventeen and a half miles off the eastern extremity of Tierra del Fuego, separated from it by the Strait of Le Maire. With forbidding mountainous peaks, some of which rose to 2,600 feet, Staten Island was the tail end of the Andes. The jagged coastline was menacing, containing inhospitable bays and inlets. Numerous small islands and plenty of shoals lay around the coast, creating great hazards for mariners.

As Porter steered to the east of the island, a fine north wind was blowing, and the *Essex* was making seven and nine knots with studding sails set on both sides. On February 13, the wind increased, and the weather became rainy with thick haze. Visibility was soon down to a mile. Porter thought he was about thirty-five miles off Cape St. John, the eastern extremity of Staten Island, but he began to get concerned that he might be closer when the *Essex* encountered a violent ripple that indicated a strong current was running. At the same time he saw an unusual amount of kelp—some of it looking as if it had been drying on the beach for a time—and flocks of birds resembling geese. Lookouts were increased, and Porter prepared to haul his wind.

Suddenly, deadly breakers appeared less than a mile away. The *Essex* was sounding in forty-five fathoms of water, but not for long. Porter reacted fast and hauled on a wind to the eastward. But it was too late. A tremendous sea was running, and the ship was driving forecastle under. There appeared to be no chance of weathering the land, which Porter could see ahead, bearing east by north, running out in small lumps, surrounded by dreadful breakers. If the *Essex* crashed into the rocks, she would be smashed to pieces, and the wind was driving her fast toward them.

In this moment of supreme crisis, Porter moved with desperate speed, managing to set the mainsail and get the ship about. The jib and spanker were then set, but in a few moments the jib was torn to pieces. Nonetheless, Porter had avoided the breakers. But he was far from being in the clear. He felt the currents taking the ship, not to the east, but westward toward the Strait of Le Maire and a deadly lee shore. A gale was blowing, and night was coming on fast. The wind was directly on shore, and a tremendous sea was running. He saw no prospect of keeping off the lee shore except by carrying a heavy press of canvas until the wind changed. The loss of a single spar, or the splitting of a topsail at this critical moment would have doomed the ship.

After standing west northwest for about an hour, the water unexpectedly grew smooth, indicating a sudden change of current, and whales appeared at the side of the ship. Porter thought he was in the Strait of Le Maire. He kept the lead going constantly and found soundings to be regularly forty-five fathoms in a coral bottom. Then, at 7:30, the land was discovered ahead, and on both bows, distant about a mile. They were definitely in the Strait of Le Maire now.

Porter ordered the helm put a-weather and made all sail to the southward. The *Essex* drove through the strait with no difficulty, and by nine o'clock in the morning she was through, to the great relief of all aboard, particularly the captain. They had had a close call. Porter had nothing but praise for the ship. Although she had been at times pitching her forecastle under with a heavy press of sail in a violent sea, she stood the test and brought them through safely.

Staten Island and the Strait of Le Maire were only a prelude, however. Cape Horn and its savage winds and seas lay ahead. But Porter felt prepared. Guns had been put below, spars had been taken from the upper deck, the weight aloft had been reduced, the best sails had been bent, and preventer shrouds were up to secure the masts. As the *Essex* entered the most dreaded passage on earth, Porter felt that she was ready.

Before long, they were there, and as the *Essex* approached the Horn, the sea was unexpectedly smooth with a pleasant breeze blowing from the north. Porter allowed himself thoughts of a speedy passage. Haze partially obscured his view, as he steered southward. On February 14, the horizon was mostly clear and the wind from the west; the sun was out, and except for dark clouds in the north, the weather was pleasant. They were in latitude 55° 58' 47" south, and longitude 67° 16' 18" west.

Cape Horn itself was soon visible, and it did not bear the prospect of the repulsive monster of their nightmares. Its rocky cliffs thrust boldly up from the sea. Their pointed tops, although treeless, were covered with a thin mantle of greenish-brown grass. The land looked strangely benign. The sea, the temperature, and the sky, were the opposite of what they had expected. For a blissful moment they thought the worst was behind them. Their pleasant interlude did not last long, however. The black clouds that were hanging over the Cape suddenly burst upon them with a fury. In a few minutes they were reduced to a reefed foresail, and a close-reefed main topsail, and in a few hours to storm staysails. The full fury of the Horn's violent winds and irregular seas was now upon them, threatening at every roll of the ship to jerk away their masts.

Using the winds coming from the north, Porter steered south to get as much offing as possible, thinking that the terrible weather might be a consequence of local currents producing high winds and irregular seas. He was soon disabused of that idea, however; the farther away from land they got the worse the gale and the sea became. In these latitudes winds whipped around the globe from west to east unimpeded, bringing violent storms of a magnitude and frequency seldom seen in any other part of the world.

For the next four days, from February 14 to 17, the *Essex* sped south. Soon they lost sight of the land. The wind blew hard from the northwest, and with it came heavy, cold rain and a dangerous sea. They were often under a close-reefed main topsail and reefed foresail, and were frequently reduced to storm staysails. By keeping a point free, however, Porter found that the *Essex* made little leeway, and he was able to gain a considerable amount of westing. Since he carried as much sail as he could, the ship was often flooded, as the sea broke over her.

The days were cold, wet, and miserable. Some men were frostbitten; Porter himself suffered from the chill. Hands were constantly at work, making and unmaking sail. Every opportunity to increase speed was grasped, but often moderate weather would be succeeded within minutes by fierce winds and hail, requiring them to shorten sail. The crew had no shoes and their woolen clothing was insufficient. To make matters worse, the rum from St. Catharine's was soon gone.

On February 18, a violent storm struck, greater than anything they had experienced before, threatening the bowsprit and masts. As morning wore on, the storm worsened, forcing Porter back to the main storm staysail and then to bare poles. Despite the furious winds and tremendous head sea, however, he hoped for an opportunity to set enough sail to steer north. The opportunity presented itself briefly around twelve o'clock when the wind hauled around to the southwest. Making doubly sure that the yards were secure, Porter set close-reefed fore and main topsails, and a reefed foresail, with a view to passing the western most point of Tierra del Fuego and sailing into the calmer waters of the Pacific.

For the next few days, he continued to make progress west. On February 21, he estimated that the *Essex* was at latitude 57° 30" south and longitude 77° west. It seemed to him that this was as far west as Cook had traveled on his first voyage before steering northward for the Pacific. Porter was certain they had passed the most difficult tests. He estimated that the *Essex* had gone from the Strait of Le Maire to this point faster than any ship in history, in spite of the westerly gales. He thought that all their sufferings and anxieties would soon be over. Unfortunately, he could not be certain where they were. He had been navigating by dead reckoning. No opportunity of taking lunar observations had presented itself, and his chronometer, because of the cold, was of no use.

Late on February 21, the wind shifted again to the northwest. Porter took advantage of it, racing south and west, making almost two degrees of longitude in twenty-four hours, trying to make certain the ship had achieved as much westing as possible. He figured he was now in longitude 79° 20" west—four degrees west of the western most point of Tierra del Fuego. But he had been cruelly deceived. Just when he decided that now was the time to stand to the north, he was able to make a lunar observation that showed unmistakably that the *Essex* had reached only longitude 75° 20" west—not enough to get around Cape Pilor, the westernmost point of Tierra del Fuego.

Disappointed as he was, Porter pressed on to make more westing, worrying all the time about the crew's spirits. They seemed to be holding up, however. They still had fresh water, but food grew so scarce they were forced to eat their pet parrots and monkeys. They had not been long in these terrible seas, but the crew's desire for fresh food was so strong that a rat was esteemed a delicacy.

Fortunately, the *Essex* continued to perform better than expected. On February 24 Porter, to his immense delight, found that they had reached longitude 80° west, and as the wind shifted to the southwest, he thought their sufferings were now truly over. He began to develop schemes for annoying the enemy, and at the same time, returning home with immense wealth.

For four days, the weather remained benign—sunny skies and a relatively calm sea. The wind continued to blow hard from the southwest, and on the last day of February the *Essex* had reached latitude 50° south.

Their fortunes soon changed, however. During the morning of February 28, the wind increased to such velocity that a full gale was blowing, and by noon Porter reduced the ship to a storm staysail and close-reefed main topsail. The wind blew from the west during the afternoon "and blew with a fury far exceeding anything we had yet experienced," he recorded, "bringing with it such a tremendous sea as to threaten us at every moment with destruction and appalled the stoutest heart on board."

The terrifying gale persisted. "The ship [was making] a great deal of water," he wrote, "and the sea [increasing] to such a height as to threaten to swallow us each instance; the whole ocean was a continuous foam of breakers. The heaviest squall I have ever before experienced, has not equaled in violence the most moderate intervals of this hurricane," he declared.

Birds, kelp, and whales appeared in sufficient quantities to make Porter fearful that they were near the coast of Patagonia. He was forced to keep as heavy a press of sail as he could in order to stay off the rock-encrusted shore, which he felt in his bones was near.

The explosive storm continued through March 1 and 2—horrifying days. The ship's violent jerking caused many to fall and bruise themselves. Porter had three severe falls that hurt him badly. "The oldest seaman in the ship," he recalled, "had never experienced anything equal to the gale."

By March 3, the crew was exhausted. Many were ready to give up and submit to fate. Yet the worst was not over. At three o'clock that morning, with only the watch on deck, an enormous sea broke over the ship, greater than any they had experienced before, deluging her. Huge quantities of water smashed in the gun deck ports, flooding the area where the men were sleeping, washing them out of their hammocks. A boat was driven into the wheel, but did not smash it. Another boat was swept off its davits. Spare spars were washed from the chains and the headrails. The crew was in shock; it seemed certain that the ship would founder. One of the prisoners, the boatswain from the *Nocton*, shouted that the ship was sinking. And it seemed for all the world that it was. David Farragut remembered that "this was the only instance in which I ever saw a real good seaman paralyzed by fear at the dangers of the sea. Several of the sailors were seen on their knees at prayer."

Miraculously, the men at the wheel stood firm, and others held their stations as well. The crew, it seemed, was not ready to give up. "Most were found ready to do their duty," Farragut observed. They were called on deck, and they came promptly, led by William Kingsbury, the boatswain's mate who had earlier played King Neptune. Farragut wrote that he would long remember "the cheering sound of [Kingsbury's] stentorian voice, which resembled the roaring of a lion rather than that of a human being, when he told them: 'Damn [your] eyes, . . . put [your] best foot forward, as there [is a] side of the ship left yet.'"

Porter, though severely bruised, led the fight back. Downes, Kingsbury, and other courageous spirits assisted him, and they managed to get the *Essex* before the wind and save her. As they did, the storm began to weaken, and in the morning Porter was able to set a reefed foresail. He was enormously grateful to the stout-hearted who had done their duty and behaved so bravely in the most extreme circumstances. He rewarded them by advancing each one grade, filling up the vacancies opened by those sent in prizes and the two men who had been left behind at St. Catharine's. At the same time, Porter rebuked others for their timidity.

Porter was more than a little gratified that the *Essex* had held up so well. After three days of incessant pounding and some truly frightening moments—water pouring in and floating nearly everything—she remained sound, and still a potent man-of-war. Even though she had shipped several heavy seas that would have proved destructive to almost any other ship, she was still in working order. And Porter had been able to avoid throwing any big guns overboard, which was the last extremity he would have resorted to.

Repairs went ahead rapidly. There were remarkably few. The *Essex* had gone through all this torment, and she had lost only the spritsail and the bees of the bowsprit. These were fixed quickly, and in a short time the frigate was shipshape and ready to fight again.

The men were another matter. Totally drained, they had reached their limit. Another onslaught would have sent them to Davy Jones. Mercifully, none came. The weather was actually pleasant on March 5—better, in fact, than any they had experienced since passing the Falkland Islands. At meridian the *Essex* was in latitude 39° 20' south. The day was clear, and the men had an excellent view of the spectacular, snow-covered Andes in the distance. Albatrosses were about the ship, and what a wonderful sight they were. As they moved north, parallel to the Chilean coast, squalls and cold rain tormented them from time to time, but for the most part, they experienced temperate weather and fine breezes, allowing the *Essex* to travel at an excellent rate of speed.

Porter was in an exuberant mood, reflecting on what the *Essex* had accomplished— doubling the infamous Horn in record time. Only thirteen days had elapsed since she passed Le Maire Strait on February 13, and reached the Pacific in the latitude of the Strait of Magellan. Perhaps as remarkable as anything else, through all of these trials, the crew's health remained excellent. Scurvy had not made an appearance—not a single case.

CHAPTER 9

NAVIGATING CHILE'S POLITICAL WATERS

A S THE WEATHER GREW MORE BENIGN, THE SHOCKS OF CAPE Horn faded in the minds of the Essex men, and they began looking forward to what lay ahead in the harbor and waterfront haunts of Valparaiso. Porter ran north with the Humbolt current, steering first for Mocha Island, 120 miles south of Concepción and twenty miles off the Chilean coast. The island was famous among Nantucket whalers as the habitat of Mocha Dick, an aggressive white sperm whale of gigantic size— the inspiration for Herman Melville's Moby Dick.

On a clear day, Mocha Island was visible from a great distance, and on March 6 it came into view twenty miles away. A lush, oval-shaped paradise six miles long and three and a half wide, it was a joyous sight after what the *Essex* had been through. A small mountain range covered with a dense virgin rainforest ran from north to south, its highest peak rising to nearly a thousand feet. On the north side hills tapered off gradually to the water's edge, almost touching the dangerous rocks that extended a quarter mile into the sea. On the west side a treacherous reef nine miles long made landing hazardous.

The waters surrounding Mocha teemed with whales, seals, penguins, and aquatic birds. British and American whalers and sealers, as well as privateers and smugglers were naturally attracted to the area. It was not uncommon for a whaler to catch as many as eight sperm whales in these waters, yielding hundreds of barrels of oil.

Mocha was uninhabited, but it had not always been. The Spanish built a settlement here in 1544, but harassed by ferocious indigenous people known as Mapuches, the dons abandoned it. Sir Francis Drake landed in 1578, and the Mapuches attacked him as well, slashing his face, leaving an ugly scar as a permanent reminder of his visit. Since 1673, however, the island had been unoccupied. Threats of a Spanish attack forced the Indians to withdraw.

The Mapuches dominated the huge area of Chile south of the Bío Bío River—the country's second largest. The Bío Bío flowed from the Andes to the Gulf of Arauco near Concepción. The Spanish fought the Mapuches from time to time, but never conquered them. In fact, the fiercely independent Mapuches did not become part of Chile until the 1880s.

Porter thought he could scoop up enough prizes around Mocha to secure the provisions he required, allowing him to steer clear of both Concepción and Valparaiso. Leery of the kind of reception the *Essex* would receive, he hoped to avoid both ports. As far as he knew, Chile was still a Spanish colony, and after Napoleon invaded Spain in the spring of 1808, Britain had become her close ally. The *Essex*'s sudden appearance in either port would alert the British to her presence in the Pacific.

As the *Essex* approached Mocha, an abundance of wild life came into view, but no enemy vessels, which was a great disappointment. The island itself, however, was anything but disappointing. It looked as if it could provide all the water, wood, meat, vegetables, and fruit the *Essex* needed. Magnificent black and white sandy beaches offered suitable landing places. Porter soon found good anchorage on the eastern side, two miles offshore, where the *Essex* had shelter from westerly and southerly winds, but not those coming from the north or the east. Fortunately, the prevailing winds were from the south and west, so he felt comfortable dropping his hook there.

No sooner was the anchor secure than Porter and some of his officers were rowed ashore by a few lucky sailors. The officers had their spyglasses out, and as they surveyed the island and beaches, they were surprised to see wild hogs and horses. Their mouths salivated. Getting ashore proved more troublesome than they anticipated, however. A heavy sea was running, beating hard against the beach and the rocks that skirted the shore, creating a turbulent surf. As they looked for a safe place to land, seals and colorful birds surrounded their boats. After a brief, but intense search, Porter ran up on a pristine sandy beach.

With muskets in hand, the officers and seamen stepped from the boats and set out after the animals. By dusk, they had killed and dragged down to the boats ten hogs and some young pigs, but no horses. They were about to shove off when a splendid drove of wild horses came running along the beach in plain view. Porter quickly changed plans and hid with the men behind the boats, waiting in ambush, weapons ready.

One of their members was missing, however. A seaman named James Spafford had wandered into the woods. No one had noticed; all eyes were on the game rushing by. When the horses were within range, Porter and the others fired. One of the animals fell, wounded, while the others ran off. The seamen rushed to the bleeding animal with clubs and were in the process of killing it when a musket shot rang out, and Spafford, the gunner's mate, who was standing apart from the others at the edge of the woods, fell, blood percolating from his chest. Nearsighted Lieutenant Stephen Decatur McKnight, who was aiming at the fleeing horses, had shot Spafford instead. McKnight was aghast when he heard Spafford cry, "Sir, you have shot me! I am a dying man; please carry me on board, that I may die under my country's flag." McKnight was heartbroken, as were the others. Spafford was one of the most popular and trusted men on the *Essex*. They took him back to the ship, hoping for the best, but when Surgeon Robert Miller examined him, he concluded Spafford had no chance of surviving.

The incident cast a pall over the ship. Although all hands had fresh meat for dinner, it was hard to enjoy while poor Spafford was below fighting for his life. Porter decided not to linger at Mocha. After letting the men have a run on shore, he took in what provisions were easily obtained and prepared to get underway. The island had an abundance of fresh water, wood, and food. The forested hills that ran down to the water's edge made obtaining wood easy, and the picturesque streams that rushed down the west side to the beaches provided sweet water, although at times heavy surf and the dangerous reef made getting casks off tricky. Meat and fruit were easily obtained as well.

Porter was impatient to leave, however, and he cut short operations. Hands were downcast because of Spafford, and since no British vessels were about, and the weather looked as if a gale was getting up, he decided to weigh anchor on the morning of March 7 and move on to nearby Santa Maria Island in Arauco Bay not far from Concepción. British whalers and smugglers were reported to frequent the waters around this island as well.

As Porter steered for Santa Maria, navigating proved difficult. Thick fog often enveloped the ship, and the gale, which was now battering them, made the going slow. He had only a single, largely inaccurate, chart to guide him, along with a few crew members who had been in these waters before. Their memories were vague, however. He hoped to obtain more serviceable charts from his first capture. Until then he'd have to be careful.

At five o'clock that afternoon, during a brief respite from the storm, a lookout caught a glimpse of Santa Maria. Porter judged that they were only ten miles from the island's southwestern extremity, but high winds and haze made running in for an anchorage dangerous. He'd first have to send in a boat, but the violence of the wind made that impossible. Reluctantly, he decided to pass Santa Maria, and with the ship pitching deeply, he stood north. The gale was intensifying when he arrived off Concepción. He felt that he could not bring her to safely, so he ran past the city. By the morning of March 8 the wind had calmed down, but by then the *Essex* was in latitude 35° 40' south—considerably north of Concepción.

Porter was not unhappy with his new location. He assumed that enemy vessels would be plying the waters between Concepción and Valparaiso, and that he could capture at least one, which would allow him to keep the sea for a while and not be forced into Valparaiso for supplies.

The *Essex*'s new position continued to frustrate Porter, however. The weather was abysmal. Thick fog often cut visibility down to a mile or less, requiring him to keep well offshore—too far to have a realistic shot at intercepting coastal traffic. He did see large schools of whales, and he hoped that British hunters would be pursuing them, but he saw none. From March 8 to 11 heavy fog continued to plague the *Essex*, hiding whatever vessels may have been in the area. Porter's irritation mounted. The *Essex* had traveled all this distance, and he had seen no other ships. He would have been happy to find a boat of any kind—a Spaniard, even—that might give him intelligence of British vessels, but none appeared.

The unexpectedly dreary landscape—whenever he got a glimpse of it—also disappointed him. In fact, since they had left Mocha Island, the desolate appearance of the countryside was a surprise. He was anticipating something far better—handsome villages, well-cultivated hills, fertile valleys, but what he saw was quite different and depressing. On March 12 a favorable wind moved the fog to leeward, and they could see the ironbound coast with the majestic, snow-capped Andes in the distance. The grandeur of the lofty peaks did little to cheer Porter, however; he felt nothing but gloomy solitude.

The following afternoon, the *Essex* was twelve miles southwest of Valparaiso, and at 8 P.M. Porter hove to, hoping to intercept a ship bound there. But none appeared, and at daybreak on March 14 he gave up and decided to look into Valparaiso Bay, which was concaved, more of a recess in the coast than an enclosed port. The Point of Angels marked its southwestern extremity. From there it ran eastward for three miles before turning north. Since the prevailing winds blew from the south during the entire year, the bay provided excellent protection for ships, except when the winds came out of the north, as they did from time to time during the winter months (May to October). These could be gale-force, accompanied by heavy seas that rolled in with tremendous power, tearing ships loose from their moorings and driving them onshore. Old, and some not so old, wrecks were strewn on the rocks as stark reminders of what could happen.

Until the *Essex* rounded the Point of Angels, the city and harbor remained hidden, tucked into the southern part of the bay. During the morning of the 14th a stiff breeze was blowing from the southward, allowing the *Essex* to sail around the Point of Angels with ease, and when she did, Porter turned east. Soon, the harbor and city came into view, three miles off the starboard bow. Picturesque hills cut by deep ravines dominated the landscape in back of a long, half-moon shaped white sandy beach. Rising twelve to fifteen hundred feet, the hills were dotted with old, Spanish-styled homes. In front of them, the beautiful old city of Valparaiso stretched along the wide beach.

As Porter glided into the harbor flying British colors (one flag at the gaff and another at the fore), he took note of several large Spanish ships anchored with their sails bent, preparing to leave. Near them, a British whaler was repairing damage she probably had received doubling the Horn. Not far from her was an 18-gun, deeply laden American brig, the privateer *Colt* (Captain Edward Barnewell). She was a reminder that, although the *Essex* was the first ship of the United States Navy to double the Horn, she was by no means the first American vessel, nor, of course, the first ship from Europe. Spain had dominated the eastern Pacific since the sixteenth century. The northern two-thirds of present-day Chile, that is, the land north of the Bío Bío River, had been a Spanish colony since 1541.

The Spanish ships in the harbor concerned Porter. When they sortied, their destination would undoubtedly be Lima, the center of Spanish power in South America for centuries. He did not want them reporting that an American frigate was loose in the eastern Pacific. He began to have second thoughts about dropping anchor. Since the *Essex* was flying British colors, and the Spaniards would not have identified her, he decided to pull out of the harbor and not drop his hook until they left. It also occurred to him that by waiting offshore a few days, he might intercept the British whaler and obtain supplies and intelligence from her.

So instead of setting his anchor, Porter surprised the crew and made all sail. They ran with a strong breeze to the north for four hours, whereupon the wind died. By that time the *Essex* was thirty miles from Valparaiso, and the men were perplexed. Since leaving St. Catherine's, they had been at sea for eight difficult weeks; they desperately needed shore leave. And, of course, the *Essex* needed repairs and replenishment. Porter understood the situation and calmed everyone down by mustering the ship's company and telling them, in his usual animated style, the advantages of waiting a bit before putting into Valparaiso. Young Farragut, who knew how much the lower deck longed for leave, could not believe the response—the men cheered. It was a measure of Porter's charisma.

For some reason, perhaps the obviously deteriorating mental and physical state of the crew, Porter soon changed his mind, and the following day he put back into Valparaiso. Still leery of the reception Spanish authorities were going to give an American warship, he dispatched Lieutenant Downes to confer with the governor of the port and test the waters. Downes was to inform the governor that the *Essex* was an American frigate urgently in need of supplies, because her supply ship had been lost going around the Horn. Porter feared the Chileans would prevent him from obtaining supplies unless he claimed that this was an emergency. And even then, he thought they would be reluctant to sell him water and provisions, unless he softened them with gold from the *Nocton*.

As things turned out, he did not have to worry. Even before he let go his anchor, the governor's barge pulled alongside with Lieutenant Downes, accompanied by the captain of the port and another officer. They were bubbling over with enthusiasm, offering the Americans whatever assistance and accommodations Valparaiso had to offer. Porter was bowled over by the reception. The port captain could not wait to tell him that Chileans were now independent of Spain and that their ports were open to all nations. What's more, he reported, Chileans looked to the United States for inspiration and protection. They needed help, but so did every American vessel in the area. Peruvian warships (sent by the Viceroy of Peru, who was still loyal to Spain) were off shore capturing American vessels bound for Valparaiso. Only a few days before, five American whalers had disappeared close to the port. They were undoubtedly captured, the captain said, and taken to Lima.

Porter was surprised that Chile had a new, pro-American, revolutionary government, and he intended to take full advantage. He had not bothered to inform himself about the breathtaking changes on the Iberian Peninsula during the last five years that had profoundly altered South American politics. In November 1807 Napoleon had invaded Portugal, throwing the Portuguese empire into turmoil. French General Jean-Andoche Junot led an army of 20,000 across Spain (with the permission of the government), crossed the border, and marched on Lisbon against scant resistance. The royal family narrowly escaped, fleeing the capital on November 27, twenty-four hours before the French army arrived. With British warships, under the command of Rear Admiral William Sidney Smith, and the entire Portuguese navy escorting him, the Prince Regent, Joao VI, his nine-year-old son, Pedro de Braganza, and a huge entourage sailed in forty ships for Brazil, where the Portuguese court was reestablished at Rio de Janeiro under British protection. Portugal was Britain's oldest Continental ally, dating back to the Treaty of Methuen in 1703.

In March 1808, Napoleon invaded Spain. Marshall Murat led a French army of 120,000 and occupied Madrid, under the pretext of saving the feuding royal family—King Charles IV, Queen Maria Luisa, and their son, the prospective king Ferdinand VII—from itself. Manuel de Godoy, the queen's lover, had been the de facto ruler of Spain since the middle of the 1790s and advised the frightened royals to flee to South America, as the Portuguese royal family had. They were in the process of leaving—traveling to the port of Cádiz—when hostile crowds at Aranjuez (thirty miles south of Madrid) stopped them and forced them back to the capital. Napoleon was then able to convince Charles, Maria Luisa, Ferdinand, and Godoy—to journey to Bayonne in France to sort things out. Once there, in May 1808, Bonaparte made them all prisoners, holding them in luxurious captivity for several years.

With the royal family captive and a French army in Madrid, the way appeared open for Napoleon to consummate his grand scheme for Spain and her colonies. In June 1808 he installed his brother Joseph on the Spanish throne. In his megalomania, Napoleon assumed the Spanish people, and all the diverse populations of Spain's American empire, would accept this new arrangement. His audacity was mind-boggling. If successful, he would become ruler of, not only the mother country, but her vast domains in America, which included nearly all of South America, almost all of Central America, much of the Caribbean, and important parts of North America, including the present states of Florida, Texas, Arizona, New Mexico, and California.

As part of his grandiose plan, Napoleon had dispatched agents to Spain's American colonies with orders to inspire and frighten them into accepting his brother as king. The agents met with universal resistance, however. Having a French heretic on the Spanish throne infuriated the church, the aristocracy, and just about every other group in Spain and her colonies. Setting aside their endless squabbling, angry Spaniards rose in rebellion. So did all of Latin America. Unfortunately, the opposition was everywhere rallied in the name of the dimwitted reactionary Ferdinand VII.

Napoleon's belief that he could acquire Spain's vast empire on the cheap was a pipedream, given the existence of the British navy. It had been supreme on the oceans since Admiral Horatio Nelson's dramatic victory over the combined Franco-Spanish fleet at Trafalgar in 1805. (At the time, Spain was still allied with France.)

When Chileans received reports of the Napoleonic conquest in 1808, they were slow to react. The ultra-conservative Governor Luis Guzmán died soon after the news arrived, and he was replaced by General Francisco Antonio Carrasco, an elderly monarchist with no political experience and no common sense. He attempted to carry on as if the Bourbons were still in power, forcibly crushing any resistance to Spanish rule. Opposition soon became widespread, however. To many of Chile's elites, unquestioned loyalty to the hapless Bourbons seemed absurd. Their gross incompetence over a twenty-year period prior to Napoleon's invasion had already undermined Spain's authority in Chile, and, indeed, all of Latin America. The ineffectual Charles IV, who had been nominal ruler since 1788, had found himself two decades later in a suicidal struggle for power with his hapless son, the future Ferdinand VII, and Queen Maria Luisa's lover, Godoy. At one point both Charles and his son—oblivious to Napoleon's designs on their country—had mindlessly appealed to the French dictator for help against the other. Opposition to Spanish authority in Chile was difficult to organize, however, since no meetings were allowed in 1808, and there were no newspapers—or even printing presses—in the entire country. The first newspaper in Chile's history, *La aurora de Chile* (*The Dawn of Chile*) did not appear until February 13, 1812.

In the months that followed the cataclysmic events of 1808 in Spain, Chilean political opinion generally divided into two camps—monarchists and republicans. The monarchists were united, and their program had the virtue of simplicity. It called for continued submission to the Bourbons and absolutism. These reactionaries were labeled *peninsulares* because most of them were white Spaniards who had left the mother country to administer her empire, both temporal and spiritual. Their ties to the imprisoned Bourbons, in addition to those of sentiment, were of self-interested officials whose positions and profits depended on continued Spanish rule.

Republicans, on the other hand, were split into violent, irreconcilable, almost feudal factions. While quarreling with each other over who should lead, they advocated independence and a government responsible to the people. Inspired by the revolutions in the United States and France, they supported a complete break with Spain. For the most part, republicans were creoles—well-to-do people of Spanish blood born in America. For decades they had been restive under Bourbon rule. Alexander von Humbolt, the Prussian explorer, geographer, and biological scientist, who knew South America firsthand, wrote that, "since the year 1789, they are frequently heard to declare with pride, 'I am a not a Spaniard, I am an American,' words which reveal the symptoms of a long resentment."

Regrettably, Spain's dependencies had no tradition of self-government. For centuries all Spanish colonies were ruled directly from Madrid. The king appointed a cadre of officials, both secular and ecclesiastical, who ran each colony in minute detail. Every major decision and most minor ones were made in Spain. Without experience in republican government, creoles found working together exceptionally difficult.

Furthermore, neither monarchists nor republicans spoke for the bulk of the population. Spanish America was deeply divided along racial, ethnic, and class lines. No group spoke for the large Indian populations, or for the mestizos (those of mixed Spanish and other racial categories, Indian and/or African), for African slaves, or for other powerless elements in society. The fight over what, if any, regime would replace the Bourbons was strictly among elites.

Chile's struggling republicans were given heart on May 25, 1810. On that day, nationalists deposed the head of the Viceroyalty of the Rio de la Plata in Buenos Aires, the largest Spanish colony in South America, and declared independence. Unrest in Chile grew so strong that General Francisco Carrasco was forced to resign in favor of the equally incompetent eighty-five-year-old General Mateo del Zambrano. It wasn't long before his regime failed as well, and in September 1810, Chilean republicans finally formed a national government of their own. The creoles who orchestrated this change had high hopes for creating a republic similar to the one in the United States. In March 1811 they convened a national congress, but on September 4, 1811, a military junta led by twenty-six-year-old José Miguel Carrera seized power. Proud, impatient, and ambitious, Carrera was from one of the wealthiest and most powerful creole families, but until then, a political unknown. He had fought in Spain against the French and had been imbued with republican ideals, which he sought to install in Chile. But he was in a hurry, and would not wait for his dreams to be realized in a more democratic fashion.

When David Porter steered the *Essex* into Valparaiso Harbor on March 15, 1813, José Miguel Carrera was still in power in the Chilean capital of Santiago, but he was not in full control of the country. Other republican families continued to contest his leadership, and the monarchists, who had a powerful ally in Peru, were still strong. They received encouragement from the Spanish viceroy in Lima, José Fernando de Abascal, a fierce advocate of continued Spanish rule in all of South America. His hand was strengthened by support from Great Britain—Spain's staunch ally.

While these events were transpiring in Chile, the Peninsular War in Spain continued into its fifth bloody year. The Spanish and Portuguese resistance against Bonaparte had naturally looked to Britain for aid, and London had been happy to provide it. In August 1808, the Peninsular War had begun when General Sir Arthur Wellesley (who would become in 1814 the first Duke of Wellington) landed nine thousand men at Mondego Bay, north of Lisbon. The talented Wellesley led the British forces most of the time against a French army that eventually numbered over two hundred and fifty thousand. In spite of this massive force Napoleon's army could not prevail. The Spanish guerrilla resistance, working with the British expeditionary force, continued to frustrate them, and the war dragged on into 1813.

It was not clear what government would eventually come to power in Madrid, if and when Napoleon's army was defeated. But many hoped it would be a constitutional monarchy along British lines, only more democratic. At the beginning of the resistance in 1808, Spanish rebels had formed various regional councils or juntas to provide local leadership. These juntas in turn met in a national council in Seville, which, because of the fighting, moved in January 1810 to the port of Cádiz—a place where British naval power could be used for protection. This national junta, known as the regency council, convened a national congress, or Cortes, in September 1810, and invited representatives of the American colonies to attend. By 1812—with the Peninsula War still raging—the Cortes agreed on a new constitution, which offered partial representation to the Latin American colonies and envisaged a grand empire under a constitutional monarch. The suffrage, theoretically, was broader than anything in Britain, or even in America.

Monarchists in South America wanted no part of this liberal regime, of course. Their power was concentrated in Peru, where the aging Spanish Viceroy Abascal had maintained absolutist control throughout the Peninsular War. Imbued with an uncompromising loyalty to the Bourbons and to Ferdinand VII, Abascal was determined to prevent Spain's South American colonies from becoming independent. He rejected out of hand the reforms of the liberal Spanish resistance in Cádiz.

The monarchists' cause strengthened as Napoleon's power diminished in 1813. The colossal blunder of invading Russia in June 1812 and the stunning defeat of his armies had undermined his capacity. And as his power declined, the prospect of Britain and her reactionary allies putting Ferdinand VII on the Spanish throne markedly increased. By March 1813, when Porter sailed into Valparaiso, the major European powers were mobilizing to prevent Bonaparte from reestablishing his power over Europe, while in Chile, José Miguel Carrera continued to be locked in a struggle against the strengthening monarchists and his republican rivals, among whom was Bernardo O'Higgins.

The immediate threat to Carrera's dictatorship came from Peru and Abascal, who felt a deep obligation to prevent Chile from becoming either independent or liberal. For all of its history Chile had been something of a Peruvian satellite, but, at the same time, Chileans had always maintained a separate identity, and now there was a growing nationalism that made the country's elites think of themselves as ruling an independent nation, distinct from their powerful neighbor and her Spanish master.

When Porter arrived on the scene, things were becoming even more complicated. Abascal was conducting a surprise amphibious invasion of Chile, which, because of the country's primitive communications, the junta in Santiago was completely unaware of. General Antonio Pareja had landed a tiny detachment of royalist troops on the island of Chiloe south of Concepción, planning to move onto the mainland and capture Concepción before attacking Santiago. As Pareja expected, the royalists in the provinces of Chiloé and Valdivia went over to him, swelling his ranks, and Concepción itself soon followed, as did the city of Chillán. By the end of March 1813, Pareja had a force of over five thousand royalists threatening to reestablish Spanish authority over all of Chile north of the Bío Bío River.

Porter had no way of knowing that the Chilean political situation was so fluid, that a clash was about to take place between the Carreras (supported now by their former enemy Bernardo O'Higgins) and Pareja. But even if he had, he had no desire to get mixed up in a complicated colonial war. He simply wanted to replenish the *Essex*, give his men time ashore, and move on.

CHAPTER 10

A PACKED WEEK
AT VALPARAISO

PORTER SET HIS HOOK IN VALPARAISO, ON MARCH 15. BY prearrangement, the *Essex* saluted the town with twenty-one guns, and the town responded in kind. Porter then landed and met American deputy vice-consul Blanco, who rushed news of the *Essex*'s unforeseen arrival to his superior, Joel Poinsett, the consul general in Santiago—seventy-four difficult miles inland. Afterward, Porter made an official call on the governor of Valparaiso, don Francisco Lastra, who gave him a warm reception.

Lastra made a good first impression on Porter. But later, after the American became better acquainted with Chilean politics, he judged Lastra to be an opportunist who supported the Carrera government but would change his allegiance in an instant if it were overthrown. Other government officials Porter met were honest republicans and patriots, he thought, but not Lastra. Neither Lastra nor Porter knew that Peruvian General Pareja had already landed south of Concepción, beginning a counterrevolution that stood a very good chance of restoring monarchist rule to Chile.

Although Porter had arranged with Lastra to resupply the *Essex*, a customs officer made it impossible to actually embark the goods. When word came from Santiago that Porter was to be given everything he wanted, the official, who Porter assumed was a monarchist, backed off. Governor Lastra brought the news to Porter personally, and provisioning went forward expeditiously. The food was exceptionally good and abundant. Apples, pears, peaches, nectarines, melons, onions, potatoes, and vegetables of every description were available. And the prices were much cheaper than at home. Soon, repairs were moving along just as fast. It looked as if the *Essex* would be ready for sea in six days. That would allow Porter to leave—no matter how tempted to stay—in one week. But what a week it was. He packed more into it than any other in his life.

The influential consul general in Santiago, Joel Poinsett, was a big help in making sure that Porter received what he wanted. Poinsett was the senior American official in the southern region of South America. When he received news that an American frigate had arrived in Valparaiso, he was ecstatic. He had heard nothing from his government since the War of 1812 began; in fact, he had heard nothing from Washington for two years. During that time he had reported faithfully to the secretary of state on events and personalities in his area, but had received no dispatches in return.

Occupied with the war against Britain, Washington paid scant attention to South America. President Madison was far more interested in East and West Florida, and to a lesser extent Cuba, Hispaniola, and Texas (all Spanish territory). The president was worried that the British might seize Florida and use it as a base to attack Louisiana and the southeastern part of the United States. To prevent this, and to carry out a long-standing goal of the South, he occupied a portion of West Florida in 1810, and in 1813 he absorbed the rest of the territory, moving troops up to the Perdido River, a narrow, dark stream—almost a creek—fifteen miles west of Pensacola. The Perdido formed the boundary between East and West Florida. Madison did not advance into sparsely populated East Florida, but there was no doubt that his ultimate goal was to annex all of Florida.

The unexpected appearance of the *Essex* raised Poinsett's hopes that Washington was finally looking beyond Florida to his distant part of the world. Madison, of course, had not sent the *Essex*, and his interest in the southern part of South America in 1813 was minimal. That had not always been the case. When he first appointed Poinsett in August of 1810 the president had great sympathy for the South American revolutionaries fighting for their freedom against a reactionary Spanish autocracy. When a revolutionary junta, inspired by America's revolutionary ideas, had been established in Buenos Aires and had taken control of the huge Spanish colony of the Rio de la Plata in May 1810, Madison looked on with satisfaction. He searched for ways to aid all the independence movements in Latin America and dramatically expand American trade in the region.

In 1810, Madison sent Poinsett, for whom he had a high regard, to explore ways to further American interests. Poinsett was a rich, well-educated, gentleman of liberal opinion from Charleston, South Carolina. He had spent years in Europe educating himself, traveling, among other places, to Russia, where he became a favorite of Tsar Alexander, who hoped that Madison would make him the new American ambassador in St. Petersburg. That post went to John Quincy Adams, however. Madison was rewarding him for his vote (as a senator from Massachusetts) in favor of Jefferson's embargo.

Instead of ambassador to Russia, Poinsett was appointed Agent for Seamen and Commerce to the port of Buenos Aires, and also Agent for the Province of Peru and the Province of Chili, positions that did not require Senate approval. Secretary of State Robert Smith emphasized to Poinsett that his primary mission was to promote commercial relations. Knowing that the British were hard at work obtaining privileged trading positions in Portuguese Brazil and everywhere else in Latin America, Madison wanted to compete with them. "With respect to Spanish America generally," he wrote to the American ambassador in London, William Pinkney, "you will find that Great Britain is engaged in the most eager . . . grasp of political influence and commercial [gain, extorting] a preference in trade over all other nations . . . from the temporary fears and the necessities of the Revolutionary Spaniards."

Britain had been trying to increase her influence and trade in Latin America for centuries. The weakness of Portugal and Spain after the Napoleonic invasion offered her the best chance she had ever had. So, in spite of being tied down in Europe fighting France, she stubbornly pursued her old objectives.

Britain's interest in Latin America was so strong that before becoming Spain's staunch ally in 1808, London had debated whether or not to take advantage of Spain's weakness and simply invade her colonies. In 1806 a British force tried to seize Buenos Aires, the capital of the Viceroyalty of the Rio de la Plata. The invaders were resisted and defeated, however. Monarchists fought them, but so, too, did the creoles, who were determined not to trade one imperial master for another. The British tried again the following year with the same result, and finally concluded that their strategy was badly flawed. From then on their goal was to become privileged trading partners, not imperial rulers.

London's task became far easier when Napoleon invaded the Iberian Peninsula in 1807 and 1808. The Portuguese and Spanish monarchs then became totally reliant on Great Britain for survival. London used its influence to dramatically expand its trading privileges in Portuguese Brazil, and then in Spain's Latin American colonies.

While the British continued to fight for the Spanish monarchy, they also maintained friendly relations with the revolutionaries—in case they were successful. Of course, London could not openly support the insurgents, but British agents—often naval officers—quietly kept communications open. The revolutionists, in turn, did everything they could to interest Britain in their favor. They wanted to assure the British that if they dropped their support of the Spanish monarchy, and the revolutions in Latin America succeeded, trade with Britain would continue to flourish.

Madison had a clear idea of British ambitions, and he wanted to thwart them, but his capacity was limited. He supported the insurrectionists to the extent he could, hoping to gain favor with them and not give the British a free hand. Poinsett was expected to inform nationalist leaders that the United States would view their independence movements favorably, but would not ship them arms directly. They could purchase munitions, but they would have to come to the United States to get them.

When Poinsett left for South America on October 15, 1810, he made his way first to Rio de Janeiro, arriving on Christmas day. Another South Carolinian, Thomas Sumter Jr., the American minister plenipotentiary to the Portuguese court, met him. During a lengthy visit, Sumter provided Poinsett with a clear picture of what awaited him in his area of responsibility, and he gave him a letter of introduction to the revolutionary junta now in charge in Buenos Aires. Poinsett arrived there on February 13, 1811, much to the consternation of Viscount Strangford, the head of the British mission in Buenos Aires. Strangford did what he could to thwart Poinsett, but the revolutionary junta was about to declare independence, and they wanted good relations with both America and Britain. They welcomed Poinsett, offering him the same trading privileges granted to the British, much to Strangford's annoyance.

Poinsett remained in Buenos Aires until November 1811, when he left a vice consul in charge and set out for Chile, traveling over the Andes. The government of José Miguel Carrera formally received him on February 24, 1812, and he became deeply involved in supporting Carrera against all his rivals. Even though the political situation in Chile was chaotic, and the regime unstable, Poinsett became a faithful ally of Carrera. He was convinced that Carrera's military dictatorship was only a temporary expedient, that his real goal was establishing a liberal republican regime in Chile. Supporting Carrera against all rivals, however, was contrary to State Department policy. While America was at war with Britain, the United States was officially neutral in disputes between Spain and her colonies.

When the War of 1812 broke out, Madison had changed his South American policy. Defeating Britain became his first priority. When his invasion of Canada in the summer of 1812 failed, and the Napoleonic invasion of Russia later that year failed as well, he was forced to alter his approach to Latin America. His policy now was not to push Spain into becoming an active belligerent alongside Britain, but to remain neutral. To keep Spain at bay, Madison was forced to turn his back on the Latin American revolutionaries. The State Department never kept Poinsett informed of American policy, however, and he threw his wholehearted support behind Carrera.

Without any communication from Washington, Poinsett was left on his own, which allowed the administration to repudiate whatever he did. In spite of the lack of direction, Poinsett carried on as best he could, trying to increase American influence with the few tools he had to work with. And, despite all the difficulties, he made some progress.

The sudden appearance of the *Essex* raised Poinsett's hopes that he could use her to advance Carrera's fortunes. He had visions of using the frigate to check the aggressive Peruvian Viceroy Abascal. "On the arrival [of the *Essex*], I wrote a remonstrance to the viceroy couched in stronger terms, but received no answer," Poinsett wrote to Secretary of State Monroe. Poinsett was unaware that Abascal's invasion of Chile had already begun, and that Monroe would never reply.

Poinsett and Carrera were so enthusiastic about the *Essex*, they got carried away. They assumed, without any evidence, that Madison had sent her to arrange an alliance with the new republic of Chile, and to assist in maintaining its independence from foreign control. Porter encouraged their illusions, even though he had no idea what American policy actually was. He did not disabuse Carrera of the idea that the United States was supporting him, even though Porter's sole object was obtaining provisions.

When news of Porter's arrival reached Santiago on March 15, bells rang in the capital, and illuminations lighted the city throughout the night in celebration. Poinsett arranged an invitation for Porter and his officers to meet Carrera, who called himself the president of the Provisional Republic of Chile. Porter never found time to go to the capital, however. He remained in Valparaiso, busy with the ship and being entertained. He was focusing on repairing and provisioning the *Essex*, in part because during his initial visit with Governor Lastra, he learned that the British battleship HMS *Standard*, a 74-gun behemoth, had stopped at Valparaiso four months earlier. His Majesty's spies would certainly warn the *Standard* of the *Essex*'s presence—if the battleship was still in the eastern Pacific. Her actual whereabouts were unknown, but Porter had to keep her constantly in mind. He was not concerned with the British commander in Rio, Vice Admiral Manley Dixon. It would be some time, he thought, before Dixon could have warships off Chile or Peru.

Actually, the *Standard* had departed the eastern Pacific months before. Admiral Dixon was informed of Porter's appearance in Valparaiso on April 3, 1813—less than three weeks after the *Essex* arrived. But there was nothing Dixon could do about it. He knew that London would be apprehensive about the extensive British whale fishery in the eastern Pacific and would want him to take immediate action against the *Essex*, but his resources were few and his responsibilities many. Perhaps the most important was protecting British trade with Rio and other ports along South America's east coast, seeing to it that homeward-bound convoys reached England, and the specie British merchants had accumulated got to London safely. Destroying the *Essex* would have to wait.

Without Dixon and the *Standard* to worry about at the moment, Porter allowed his men to enjoy Valparaiso for the brief time they were there. He was liberal about shore leave, the only stipulation being that hands had to be back on board when the gun sounded at eight o'clock at night—no exceptions. This rule created no difficulty apart from the carpenter, John S. Waters, who failed to appear at the specified time one evening. Porter dealt with him harshly, not letting him return to the ship at all. According to Porter, he was a worthless fellow anyway, and the ship would not miss him. The gunner, Lawrence Miller, also ran into trouble when he was caught smuggling rum aboard. Since he had broken the rules before, he was confined in irons. While Porter was disciplining the carpenter and the gunner, he was also welcoming aboard, with great satisfaction, three deserters from an English brig lying in port.

Porter was also entertaining Governor Lastra and other notables. During his first audience with the *Essex* commander, the governor, who had himself been a naval officer, expressed an interest in visiting the *Essex*. Porter invited him to come aboard that day. The invitation was accepted, and Lastra arrived with his entourage late in the afternoon—after his siesta. He was given a special tour, and examined every part of the ship with great interest. He appeared to be quite impressed. He had never been on a frigate before, nor had any of his retinue. The visit lasted two hours. Before leaving, the governor invited Porter and his officers to a party the following evening, which Porter eagerly accepted.

The party turned out to be a grand affair. The company and the dinner were fascinating—far more than Porter had imagined they would be. A colorful assemblage of ladies—two hundred of them—were there. At first glance they were enormously attractive, especially to men who had been at sea for so long. On closer examination, however, the women's mouths were oddly repulsive. Porter wondered why. He soon discovered that what hurt their appearance was a slavish devotion to maté, a drink made from an herb sweetened with liberal amounts of sugar that they sucked hot through a silver tube, creating a pleasing sensation, but having a devastating effect on their teeth and making their breath repellent.

Exotic dances followed dinner. Porter and his officers were unfamiliar with them and remained spectators, but they were impressed. The climax startled them, however. Known as the *ballas de tierra*, the dances ended in wild, indelicate, and lascivious motions, until overcome with passion, the participants lost their energy and were forced to sit down. Porter claimed that he did not like the display, although it's hard to imagine that he didn't.

The leading citizens of the town, all of whom were at the governor's ball, invited the Americans to visit their homes, but were reluctantly turned down. Getting the *Essex* ready for departure was consuming nearly all the time Porter and his officers had. Thanks to their unceasing efforts, by noon on March 20 the ship, except for a few articles, was as fully loaded as when she left Delaware Bay. That afternoon, Joel Poinsett, accompanied by one of the president's brothers, don Luis Carrera, and the American consul in Valparaiso, Mr. Heywell, came aboard for dinner.

The following day was Sunday, and Porter decided that after the intense labors of the last few days, the crew needed to relax a bit. He organized an entertainment aboard the *Essex* and invited some of the city's notables. Early in the afternoon he went ashore to escort his guests to the ship, but about three o'clock, when they were assembling on the beach, lookouts spied a frigate in the offing. Porter and his officers immediately turned around and unceremoniously left, jumping into the boats, and racing back to the ship. Poinsett, don Luis Carrera, and several other Americans and Chileans accompanied them to the *Essex*, then returned to shore.

The stranger was a 32-gun frigate, and the *Essex*, under a cloud of canvas, shot after her. The wind soon died, however, and Porter was forced to launch boats and tow the *Essex* out of the harbor, where she regained the wind. In an hour she was alongside the stranger, which turned out to be a Portuguese warship, much to everyone's disappointment, especially the women of Valparaiso, who were looking forward to viewing a great naval battle from the safety of the hillsides. Porter did not get back into port until the morning of the 22nd. When he arrived, an invitation from the governor to attend another grand dinner and ball was waiting. Porter felt he had to accept it.

As anticipated, the ball was lavish. The city's notables and dozens of women turned out in their finest attire. The partying went on until one o'clock, when Porter and his officers returned to the ship, expecting to get underway the following morning. Before they could, however, the governor sent a request that he and some ladies be allowed to come on aboard one last time, and Porter felt he had to accede to the request. The visitors arrived at nine o'clock the next morning and remained until noon.

After they left, Porter prepared to sail, but he was delayed again. An American whale ship, the *George*, had unexpectedly arrived in the harbor. Porter thought her captain might have up-to-date information about Peru and the whaling fleets in the eastern Pacific. He was not disappointed. Captain Benjamin Worth was from Nantucket and had years of whaling experience. He knew as much about the fishing fleets in the eastern Pacific as anyone, and he was anxious to share his information with Porter. Worth told him that word of the American declaration of war had just reached the British whaling ships, all of whom were armed— making some of them powerful small warships. Most, if not all, American whalers had no idea a war was on. They would be easy prey for their British counterparts. Worth wanted Porter to provide protection, and as far as Worth was concerned, the best way to do it was to attack the enemy whalers. Porter agreed. Worth pointed out that the best places to find them were the waters around the Galapagos Islands and off the Peruvian port of Paita.

Porter was more anxious than ever to be underway. Adding to his sense of urgency were the two Spanish ships he had seen when first entering the harbor. They had departed during the week—presumably traveling to Lima—where they would bring news of the *Essex* to the viceroy. Porter wanted to get along to the Peruvian coast and the Galapagos Islands before his enemies had time to react to his presence.

On March 23, just before leaving Valparaiso, Porter wrote to Commodore Bainbridge. He briefly described what had happened to him since leaving the Delaware River on October 26, 1812, and explained what he was doing in Chile. He spoke of the warm reception he had received in Valparaiso.

> I here in six days after my arrival had on board as much provisions wood and water as my ship could conveniently stow, and shall sail on my cruise today—My reception here has been of the most friendly nature, the political state of the country is most favorable to our cause, and every advantage that a port of the United States could afford to us has already

been offered to me by the President & Junto—their cause is liberty and independence, and the arrival of this ship has given them fresh vigor.

Porter sent this report and the few ones that followed via Poinsett, who passed them on to Thomas Sumter Jr., the American minister in Rio. Needless to say, the letters took months to get to their destination.

During this time, Porter's competitive instincts were aroused to a high pitch when he received more accurate reports of the astonishing American naval victories at the start of the war. He yearned to accomplish what his colleagues Bainbridge, Hull, and Decatur had—a great victory over a British frigate. That remained his supreme goal. It was his path to everlasting fame, and a way to blot out forever the stain of the ignominious surrender of the *Philadelphia* long before.

CHAPTER 11

PERU AND THE
ELUSIVE *NIMROD*

WHEN PORTER LEFT VALPARAISO ON MARCH 23, HE SHAPED a course northwest with a flag at the mainmast proclaiming FREE TRADE AND SAILORS RIGHTS. He was making for Peru, hoping to avoid the 74-gun *Standard*, check the viceroy's attacks on American vessels, and do maximum damage to Britain's whaling fleet and privateers. He estimated that there were in excess of twenty enemy whalers in the eastern Pacific, and approximately twenty-three American. The British whalers were entirely at his mercy. The industry's leaders and their political supporters in London had pressed the Admiralty hard to protect the whalers, and their Lordships were keen to do so. But, of course, given the demands placed on the Royal Navy to fight the Napoleonic War, protect a worldwide commerce, and provide other services to a far-flung empire, they could not respond as swiftly or as strongly as they might have liked.

At daylight on March 25, two days out of Valparaiso, a lookout spied a sail to the northeast. Porter gave chase and overtook the stranger, which turned out to be the American whale ship *Charles* out of Nantucket. Her captain, Grafton Gardner, reported that four months earlier a Peruvian privateer had captured him and taken him to Callao (the port city for Lima), where he had only just been released after paying a ransom. Two days before meeting Porter, Captain Gardner had run into more trouble. He was sailing in company with two other American whalers, the *Walker* and the *Barclay*, off the Chilean port of Coquimbo, 280 miles north of Valparaiso. They began to be chased by the *Nimrod*, a British privateer posing as a whaler, and the *Nereyda*, a Peruvian privateer, also disguised as a whaler. The *Walker* and the *Barclay* were captured, but the *Charles* managed to escape. Hoping to surprise the *Nimrod* and the *Nereyda*, Porter crowded on all sail and sped toward Coquimbo.

At eight o'clock that same morning, a lookout spied another sail to the northward, and Porter raced after her with the *Charles* trailing behind. An English jack was flying over the *Charles*'s American flag, indicating that she had been captured by a British ship. By meridian the *Essex* was close enough to see that the stranger was a small warship disguised as a whaler, with whaleboats on her quarters. Seeing British colors displayed on the *Essex*, she raised the Spanish flag and steered toward the frigate. When a mile away, she fired a shot at the oncoming *Essex*, enraging Porter. He almost pumped a broadside into her, but thought better of it when he considered that the *Essex* was flying British colors, and the shot could not have been meant as an insult to the American flag. The stranger mounted fifteen guns and looked like the Peruvian privateer *Nereyda*. She matched the description Captain Gardner had given of the marauder that had chased him and captured the *Walker* and the *Barclay*. Two shots across her bows brought her to.

She was indeed the *Nereyda*, and her second lieutenant soon appeared on the *Essex* with apologies from his captain, who, he claimed, could not present himself because of illness. The nervous lieutenant, assuming the *Essex* was a British frigate, told Porter the *Nereyda* had captured the *Walker* and *Barclay* and was taking them into the port of Coquimbo when the British privateer *Nimrod* suddenly appeared and stole the *Walker* from them, but not the *Barclay*. The *Nereyda* was searching for the *Nimrod* to get the *Walker* back, when she saw the *Essex* and the *Charles*. The lieutenant said that he thought they were the *Nimrod* and the *Walker*. He told Porter that the *Nereyda* had been out of Lima for four months, searching only for American vessels, and that she had on board some of the *Barclay*'s crew, and part of the *Walker*'s, including her captain.

Porter ordered the second lieutenant to return to his ship, and if his captain was too ill, to send over the first lieutenant, along with Captain West of the *Walker* and one of the *Barclay*'s crew members. When West appeared, Porter took him into his cabin and assured him that the *Essex* was an American frigate. West was overjoyed; he could hardly believe his good luck. He told Porter that his ship and the *Barclay* had been loaded with whale oil and were sailing toward Coquimbo to take on supplies before returning to the United States when the *Nereyda* had captured them. They were taken completely by surprise; they had no idea a war was on. The Peruvians were a rough bunch, coming on board and grabbing everything in sight. West told Porter that the *Nereyda*'s captain had sent the *Barclay* off to an unknown port (with her captain, Gideon Randall of New Bedford, Massachusetts, still on board), and that twenty-four American prisoners were on the Peruvian ship. After hearing this, Porter forced the *Nereyda* to strike her colors and took possession of her. Lieutenant Downes went aboard with some men and sent all the Peruvians, including her captain, over to the *Essex*.

Porter now went after the *Nimrod*, which had departed from the *Nereyda* only three days before. Thinking she might be nearby, he stood inshore and looked into Tongue Bay, but she wasn't there. He then looked into Coquimbo, but, again, found nothing. Lieutenant Stephen Decatur McKnight took command of the *Nereyda* that night, with orders to throw her arms, ammunition, and light sails overboard, leaving only her topsails and courses. Porter then sent her Peruvian crew, including her captain, back to their ship and brought her American prisoners over to the *Essex*. When that was done, he sent the *Nereyda* off to Callao with a letter for the viceroy, explaining that Porter had caught the *Nereyda* hunting and plundering American ships, but that he wished "to preserve the good understanding which should ever exist between the government of the United States and the provinces of Spanish America." He was therefore sending the *Nereyda* back to Peru, knowing that his excellency would surely want to punish these criminals. Before the *Nereyda* departed for Callao, Porter removed two whaleboats from her, which she had seized from the American whalers. They would come in handy when he needed to disguise the *Essex* as a whaler. He could also use them in shallow waters.

The *Nereyda* reached Callao with no difficulty, and when Viceroy Abascal read Porter's letter, he was furious. Instead of punishing the *Nereyda*'s skipper, he retaliated by putting sixteen men from the American privateer *Colt*—which the Chilean revolutionary government had purchased and the Peruvians had captured—in irons and sent them to work at hard labor on public projects around Callao.

Porter believed that the capture of the *Nimrod* was of the greatest importance to his mission. She was a serious menace to the American whale fishery. There was no doubt in his mind that London was trying to eliminate American competition in these waters. Porter resolved to thwart them by capturing or destroying all the British armed whalers and privateers he could find, and forcing the rest to stay in port. Captains Gardner and West had already told him there were probably twenty or more enemy whalers along the coasts of Chile, Peru, and the Galapagos Islands, confirming what Captain Benjamin Worth of the *George* had told him earlier in Valparaiso.

If Porter succeeded in driving the British from the eastern Pacific and leaving it open for American vessels, he would be making an enormous contribution to the war effort. Of course, accomplishing this objective would also put money in his pocket—always a high priority for him and his crew. He estimated that the value of a fully loaded British whaler was in the neighborhood of $200,000—a mighty incentive.

Porter advised Captain Gardner to run the *Charles* into Coquimbo and demand the protection of his ship from the government of Chile. He suggested to Captain West that the best course for him was to go with Gardner to Coquimbo and from there travel to Valparaiso and present a claim for damages against the Peruvian government.

After seeing the two captains off, Porter tore after the *Nimrod*, racing northwest for Callao, over 1,500 miles away. He crowded on all sail, planning to capture her and recapture both the *Barclay* and the *Walker*. Located nine miles west of Lima, Callao was the center of Spanish commerce in the eastern Pacific and the most important port along the entire west coast of South America. Porter had to be careful. Callao was well-fortified with batteries, and a flotilla of deadly gunboats that could inflict severe damage in the harbor's calm waters. On the way, Porter altered the appearance of the *Essex* to make her look like a Spanish merchantman. He painted a broad yellow streak around her hull as far as the fore channels, rigged false waist cloths as high as the quarterdeck nettings and painted ports on them, and then he got tarpaulins up and rigged a poop, complete with painted windows. He also painted the quarter galleries different colors.

As the *Essex* sped north, she passed the tropic, and the men saw flying fish for the first time since leaving the coast of Brazil, raising their spirits. On the morning of March 29, a lookout at the main masthead spotted a vessel bound for Callao that looked like an American whaler, possibly the *Barclay*. Porter raced toward the port to cut her off, and as he closed in, he could see that she was indeed the *Barclay*. He wet his light sails in order to hold the wind better and strained forward. The *Barclay* had to pass the island of San Lorenzo in order to get into Callao, and in weathering the point of the island she was becalmed, but the *Essex*—only two and a half miles away now—shot in with the breeze to within one hundred yards of her, lowered boats, boarded, and took possession. Porter then towed her away from the island and out of the harbor in the teeth of contrary winds that had suddenly sprung up.

The *Essex* now inched into Callao. Porter took a good look at the shipping in the harbor, hoping to find the *Nimrod*. But she wasn't there, and, with the wind serving, he departed. Immediately after leaving he turned his attention to the *Barclay*. Her seamen were a sorry lot. Having been seven months at sea without relief, many were sick with scurvy. All of them were anxious to leave their pestilent ship and sign on to the *Essex*, and Porter was willing to have them. He told the *Barclay*'s rough old skipper, Gideon Randall, that he would be permitted to have his men back, but they were too weak to even sail the whaler to Valparaiso. If Randall decided to attempt the voyage anyway he would run the risk of being captured by Peruvian or British raiders. Well aware of the problem, Randall decided to remain in company with the *Essex*. Porter was glad to have him. He could be of considerable value, since he knew the whaling grounds, particularly around the Galapagos, where Porter planned to hunt.

Midshipman John Cowan and eight men were placed on board the *Barclay* to supplement Randall's crew, and both ships steered toward the

Peruvian port of Paita, 625 miles north of Lima. Porter intended to look into Paita for any British vessels before sailing to the Galapagos Islands, where he expected to find a substantial portion of the enemy's whaling fleet. Randall assured Porter, as everyone else had, that the Galapagos were the principal fishing grounds of British whalers.

The following evening, April 4, gunner's mate James Spafford, who had lingered on in great pain since his accidental shooting on the Island of Mocha, died. Before burying him, Porter ordered an inquest to satisfy the crew, and to relieve Lieutenant McKnight. Lieutenants Downes, Wilmer, Wilson, and marine lieutenant John Gamble were appointed to the board of inquest. After considering the matter carefully, they held the grief-stricken McKnight blameless for shooting Spafford, declaring it to have been an accident.

A short time later, a mournful cry, "All hands, bury the dead, ahoy," brought the men to the weather deck. With heads uncovered, they listened in respectful silence as Chaplain David Adams read the traditional service for the burial of the dead. At the conclusion, he pronounced the baleful words, "We therefore commit his body to the deep," and poor Spafford, who had been sewn up in his hammock with two cannonballs attached to his feet, slid down a tipped board placed at the gangway and splashed into the sea.

AFTER QUITTING THE VICINITY OF CALLAO, THE *ESSEX* AND THE *Barclay* stood WNW toward Paita. They kept an eye out for the *Nimrod*, but they never saw her. She seemed to have vanished. On April 6 at three o'clock, a lookout at the mainmast cried out a sail. Porter steered toward the stranger, but soon discovered that the sail was the Rock of Pelado. An hour later a lookout saw another sail and Porter again gave chase. He brought her to at seven o'clock. She was a Spanish brig out of Callao. Believing the *Essex* to be an English frigate, the captain and one of his passengers told Porter that Peru considered Britain an ally and the United States a neutral that could soon become an enemy. It went without saying that Peru considered itself part of Spain. The passenger suggested the Galapagos Islands as the best place to find American and British whalers.

The next morning, April 7, the *Essex* and the *Barclay* continued north toward Paita. In order to search as much of the ocean as possible, they kept apart during the day and could barely see each other's signals. At night they came together. In their journey north they passed near the small islands of Lobos de la Mare and Lobos de la Terre. Fifteen miles apart and well off the coast, they were devoid of vegetation, but the variety and volume of marine and bird life were astounding. Exotic birds covered the barren hills, while seals in great numbers cavorted in the nearby waters. Fish of all kinds were active, pursued by birds, seals, boneters, and porpoises. The same scene was repeated as they entered the Bay of Paita, where the sea boiled with aquatic life. Large fish and seals chasing small fish, were seen with flocks of birds hovering overhead. There may have been whales in the vicinity below the surface, but Porter did not see any.

On April 11, the *Essex* and *Barclay* approached the harbor of Paita with the majestic saddle of Paita mountain in the background. Two crude catamarans approached and their skippers talked with Porter, telling him there were no vessels of interest in the harbor. He took them at their word, turned around, and shaped a course for the Galapagos Islands.

chapter 12

FORTUNE SMILES IN THE GALAPAGOS ISLANDS

T HE GALAPAGOS ISLANDS STRADDLE THE EQUATOR MORE than 500 miles off the Peruvian coast. The south equatorial, or Humbolt, current runs directly to the islands. Sweeping up the west coast of South America from approximately the southern tip of Tierra del Fuego, the famous current curves west at the Equator. In the Age of Sail, together with the prevailing trade winds, the current carried ships comfortably to the archipelago. It was said that it ran more than fifteen miles every twenty-four hours, but Porter suspected the actual rate was much higher, since he frequently met with violent ripples in the sea. The current was darker than the surrounding water, and easily identified. It created a unique climate in the waters around the Galapagos, causing the temperature of the water to rise higher than one might expect and the climate to be milder and drier. Upwelling along the current's route caused the waters around the Galapagos to be remarkably rich in marine life.

Porter used dead reckoning to navigate. The chronometer that had served him so well early in the voyage had been useless since they left St. Catharine's. And he had no good opportunity to correct the dead reckoning by lunar observation since he was traveling in the warmer season (December to May), when rain was frequent—often coming daily—the skies cloudy much of the time, and the water temperature conducive to swimming.

As the *Essex* progressed through the benign sea, Porter prepared the crew and the ship for combat. He put the magazine in good order, and anticipating calms around the islands, he organized seven boats to attack the enemy, assigning ten men to each boat. He assumed that seventy men in seven boats would be more than enough to capture any armed whaler. Lieutenant Downes was in charge of the attack force.

On the morning of April 17, the *Essex* and the *Barclay* arrived off Chatham (San Cristobal) Island, the easternmost of the larger Galapagos. Porter thought it was Hood (Española) Island, but soon discovered that Hood was to the south and steered for it. He was in uncharted waters and had to be careful. Dangerous reefs, irregular, violent currents, as well as heavy swells that could throw a ship on the rocks, were constant hazards. Often the water was so deep near the shore that it was almost impossible to bring a vessel up by her anchors, leaving her at the mercy of a strong current or adverse wind. There were men aboard who had been to the Galapagos before, however, and they helped Porter navigate. He also had British Captain James Colnett's charts (the only ones that existed), although he often found them to be inadequate, and in places dangerously misleading.

Porter undoubtedly exaggerated the inadequacies of Colnett's charts. In fact, Colnett was an accomplished craftsman. From 1772 to 1775 he sailed with Captain Cook on his second voyage of exploration around the world in the *Resolution*. Colnett was a midshipman at the time and could not have had a better tutor than Cook, who was the world's leading cartographer.

Colnett made his charts in 1793, when Prime Minister William Pitt the Younger sent him to explore the eastern Pacific in the merchant ship *Rattler*. Pitt sent him to find harbors where bases could be established to serve the growing fleet of British whalers fishing in what were universally recognized as the richest whaling grounds in the world, containing vast numbers of highly prized sperm whales. Pitt hoped Colnett would find ports that Britain could control, as they did Cape Town and St. Helena. Colnett was well schooled in how to keep a crew healthy on a long voyage, and he knew as much about the eastern Pacific as any officer in the Royal Navy.

During the four years prior to Colnett's voyage, the British developed an intense interest in the whale fishery along the west coast of South America and the Galapagos Islands. The demand for whale oil in Britain, especially sperm oil, was growing so fast in the early 1790s that their whaling fleet had a hard time keeping up.

The pioneering voyage of the British whale ship *Emilia* from 1788 to 1790 had confirmed the rich rewards awaiting those who braved the passage around the Horn to fish in the eastern Pacific. On August 7, 1788, London's largest whaling firm, Enderby & Sons, had sent Captain James Shields in the *Emilia* to ascertain just how plentiful sperm whales were off Chile and Peru. Samuel Enderby was a former American Tory who had fled to London before the Revolutionary War. Captain Shields traveled around Cape Horn, up the western coast of South America, and then to the Galapagos Islands. When he returned to London during the first week of March 1790, he reported that the potential for whaling in the eastern Pacific was vast. His glowing account of large sperm whales abounding in those waters started a rush to the area, led by Enderby, who immediately sent the *Emilia* back, along with the *Atlantic*, *Kitty*, and *Greenwich*. Other London firms sent eight more whalers.

Britain's need for sperm oil was so great that at one time Prime Minister Pitt considered recruiting Nantucket whale men—the finest in the world. He envisioned bringing them to England with their families, establishing them in a port city, requiring them to take an oath of allegiance to the king, and to carry on their vital business from British soil. Pitt talked seriously about the idea with William Rotch, a leading Nantucket whaler, who proposed building a fleet of thirty ships manned by five hundred men. Pitt liked the idea, but English whalers and economic nationalists in Parliament blocked his plans. They were more interested in building a British fleet than handing the business over to Americans. Rotch was not deterred, however. He turned around and set up his colony in Dunkirk under French auspices. Nonetheless, demand for sperm oil remained so high that in

1792 the British permitted a small colony of Nantucket whalers to be established at Milford Haven in Wales. They were required to take an oath of allegiance to the king, but they had no trouble doing it.

Not much time passed after James Shields returned to London in the spring of 1790 before English whalers fishing in the eastern Pacific needed naval bases to protect and service them. As might be expected, Spanish officials were making it difficult, as they always had, to obtain provisions and make repairs in ports along the coast of South America. Spain wanted to keep the aggressive British out of the eastern Pacific. Spanish ports in Chile and Peru were, to all intents and purposes, closed. Bribery allowed some British whalers to use Valparaiso, Calloa, and Paita, but this was an unsatisfactory arrangement from Pitt's point of view, which is why he had dispatched Colnett to find places where Britain could establish her own bases.

American whalers, operating out of ports like New London in Connecticut, Hudson and Sag Harbor in New York, and Nantucket and New Bedford, could have easily supplied Britain's needs. But their oil was kept off the British market by a prohibitively high tariff of 18 pounds 3 shillings per ton on all foreign oil—a duty passed by Parliament in 1783 at the conclusion of the Revolutionary War.

Captain Colnett left England for the eastern Pacific on January 4, 1793, with orders from Pitt to find places where ports could be established for the whaling fleet. Colnett doubled Cape Horn, sailed up the west coast of South America, and continued along the coast of Central America and Mexico to the Gulf of California. He also visited the Galapagos and other islands, but he did not find what Pitt wanted, and he returned empty-handed on November 1, 1794.

Pitt did not give up. Since Parliament would not reduce the tariff on American whale oil, and was determined to rely on the British fleet, he had to devise ways of making whaling voyages more successful without the prospect of having reliable bases from which to obtain succor. In 1795 Pitt tried to deal with the problem by giving shipowners substantial incentives to engage in the whaling business in the Pacific. A bonus was to be awarded to a fleet of whale ships of not less than eight that sailed into the Pacific, stayed between sixteen and twenty-four months, and returned with at least thirty tons of sperm oil and head-matter. The first ship of the eight would receive a bonus of 600 pounds and the other seven 500. Parliament approved the scheme, and it worked well.

In 1811, Parliament extended the rewards for three years to ten additional ships that met the same requirements, then it went even further. Parliament encouraged Americans to move their whaling business to the existing community at Milford in Wales, provided they brought twenty whale ships and their crews, resided in Great Britain for at least three years, and conducted their whaling from there. The owners of these ships were allowed to import whale oil and pay the same duties as if they were British, provided the owner took an oath of allegiance to the king. In addition, the owner would be entitled to any bounties Parliament approved for British subjects.

Considering how important the whaling business was to Britain, the presence of the *Essex* in the eastern Pacific created a great deal of anxiety in London, although the prime minister, Lord Liverpool, would never admit it publicly. But whether he did or did not, the potential of the *Essex* to disrupt Britain's whaling fleet and to simultaneously obtain a distinct advantage for their American competitors was of grave concern. As soon as word of the American intruder reached London in July 1813 (while the *Essex* was in the Galapagos), the Admiralty immediately set out to destroy her, reinforcing Admiral Dixon with eleven additional frigates, including the 38-gun *Targus* (which had specific orders to hunt down the *Essex*) and the 38-gun *Briton*.

Porter for his part was focused on doing maximum damage to the British whalers before any warships could reach him. At the same time, however, he was actively looking to engage an enemy frigate and win a great victory as Hull, Bainbridge, and Decatur had, and by doing so, he was making the Admiralty's task of finding him much easier.

HOOD ISLAND IS THE SOUTHERNMOST OF THE LARGER GALAPAGOS. On April 17 at seven o'clock in the evening Porter found good anchorage (twelve fathoms of water and a clear, white-sandy bottom) and dropped anchor in what is now Gardner Bay on the island's northwest side. Wood was easily obtained there, and he saw large numbers of wondrous land tortoises, ranging in size from three to four hundred pounds. Whalers were accustomed to capturing these creatures by the dozens, often storing up to two hundred aboard their ships. These amazing animals were known to remain alive for as long as a year and a half in a ship's hold without being given water or food, and to be every bit as good to eat as when they were first taken; in fact, aging seemed to improve them.

Porter expected to go into action against enemy whalers the minute he arrived. His men were prepared for battle, in fact, panting for it, thinking of the easy prize money waiting to be had. They did not expect any trouble from whalers, armed or not. The crew's health was exceptionally strong, as it had been since the *Essex* left Delaware Bay. Immediately after setting his hook, Porter dispatched Lieutenant Downes in a whaleboat (purchased from Captain Randall of the *Barclay*) with a dozen well-armed men to scout Gardner Bay. If Downes spotted an enemy whaler, he was to signal, and Porter would unleash his attack boats.

An hour passed in silence, as the *Essex* men waited impatiently for a signal. Then another hour passed, and another. No sign came. Downes eventually returned at ten o'clock empty-handed. The crew was, to say the least, disappointed. Porter had been convinced that at least one, and more likely two, enemy vessels were in Gardner Bay. He returned to Chatham Island and lay to for the rest of the night, utterly frustrated.

The following morning, April 18, Porter weighed anchor and sailed west with an easterly wind for Charles (Floreana) Island. It was famous for its post office—a roughhewn stake driven deep into hard sand with a primitive box nailed to it. A weather-beaten black sign was tacked over the box, on which was painted "Hathaway's Post Office." The box was reputed to be a place where sailors of all nations deposited letters and notices that, they hoped, would eventually be carried home.

Around two in the afternoon, the *Essex* dropped anchor in the harbor at Charles. No other ships were about. Porter sent Downes to the post office, situated near a small beach in the middle of the bay. It rained hard the whole time Downes was pulling for shore. When he finally reached the post office, he found near it articles for distressed seamen—clothes, a tinder box, a barrel of bread, and a cask of water, indicating that little or no water was to be had on the island. The rain simply ran off into the ocean. Downes returned to the *Essex* in three hours with a few papers and some letters confirming that British whalers did indeed frequent these waters.

Porter suspected that finding water would be difficult, if not impossible, on any of the islands, which meant that whalers could not remain for long. He was not expecting to find any humans on Charles or in the entire archipelago. All the islands looked uninhabitable to him. To illustrate just how difficult life was for humans, he recounted a story he had heard of a particular British sailor named Patrick Watkins, an Irishman who deserted his ship and took up residence on Charles. He built a pathetic hut on two acres of ground about a mile from the landing place, where he raised vegetables and exchanged them for rum, or sold them for cash. Watkins's appearance was frightful. He looked like a wild man, and, in fact, he was.

Not long after deserting, Watkins acquired a musket, powder, and ball. Soon after, he captured a few unlucky mariners, whom he used to procure a boat and sail it to Guayaquil in the Viceroyalty of Peru, arriving alone, having killed the others to save the small amount of water aboard. He made his way to Paita, where he hoped to fit in and make a life for himself. Given his appearance, however, the authorities were suspicious the minute they saw him, and the police put him in jail, where he still was when the *Essex* arrived in the Galapagos.

With Watkins's departure, the Galapagos became literally unpopulated. In the succeeding years, that changed. By the time Charles Darwin appeared eighteen years later in HMS *Beagle* to explore the islands, Peruvian merchants had established a tiny, forlorn colony to service whalers.

The difficulty humans found living on the islands gave rise to tales of pirates using them as hideouts and burying treasure. Stories of seamen finding pieces of eight sticking up on sandy beaches were particularly titillating. Captain Colnett contributed to the legend when he wrote in his journal that James Island appeared "to be a favorite place of the buccaneers, as we found not only seats, which had been made by them of earth and stone, but a considerable number of broken jars scattered about, and some entirely whole, in which the Peruvian wine and liquors of that country are preserved. We also found some old daggers, nails, and other implements."

In spite of Colnett's speculations, accounts of buccaneers in the Galapagos were greatly exaggerated. The golden age of piracy occurred during the early years of the eighteenth century, from 1700 to 1726. Action was concentrated in the Caribbean, the Bahamas, and the Spanish Main, not in the eastern Pacific. Doubling Cape Horn was simply too difficult for pirates, compared to the easy pickings available in the West Indies.

AFTER BEING DISAPPOINTED AT CHARLES ISLAND, PORTER SET sail with a fine easterly breeze for Albemarle (Isabela), forty-five miles to the northwest. Eighty miles long, with an irregular shape that resembled a giant seahorse, Albemarle was the largest of the Galapagos. Porter was convinced that Banks Bay off the northwestern part of the island—known as the principal rendezvous of whalers—would yield results. Before noon on April 19, the *Essex* drew within eight miles of the big island, at which point the wind died suddenly, and Porter lowered a boat to explore. As he rowed toward shore, the water was alive with seals, exotic birds, lizards with red heads, odd-looking crabs, and other unusual species.

Two hours after leaving the ship he came across an inviting bay, where he landed and saw an amazing sight—myriads of enormous iguanas of the most hideous appearance imaginable. The grotesque creatures were everywhere, taking up large tracts of ground. In places they completely covered the land. The fearsome beasts kept a close eye on the wary, slow-moving visitors. Porter and his party, their guns and clubs handy, inched toward the animals, but they did not stir. Soon the *Essex* men were among them, but found, to their relief, that their fears were groundless. The ferocious-looking monsters turned out to be the most timid creatures. The *Essex* men clubbed several to death, intending to take them back to the ship, where they might have a feast. When eventually they tasted the meat, it turned out to be delicious. Porter thought it was better than the excellent tortoises.

As they rowed back to the ship, Porter saw innumerable rocks covered with seals, penguins, iguanas, and pelicans, and in the water, hundreds of green turtles. Huge, ferocious sharks were around as well, circling the boat, their black fins sticking ominously above the surface. Sharks were not known to attack boats, but these snapped at the oars, while the men thrust boarding pikes at them. One giant bumped hard against the side of Porter's boat, but then disappeared.

Immediately after reaching the *Essex*, Porter hauled in his anchors and explored the coast of Albemarle a bit more. He then sailed to the much smaller island of Narborough (Fernandina), lying just to the west. The waters between Narborough and Albemarle formed two bays—Banks in the north and Elizabeth in the south. A thirty-five-mile-wide passage connected them. Between March and July these waters attracted huge numbers of whales in search of squid or cuttlefish. Porter was certain he would eventually find whalers here, and he dispatched Downes in a whaleboat to reconnoiter Narborough. As darkness fell, signals flashed continuously from the *Essex* to guide Downes back. He returned at one o'clock in the morning with more depressing news—he had seen nothing.

The *Essex* remained on alert. During the day, seamen and officers manned the yards, searching for prey. Suddenly, on April 23, a cry of "Sail Ho!" electrified everyone. It seemed as if all their hopes were about to be realized. On closer examination, however, the white sails turned out to be objects on shore. The crew became more dejected than ever.

In spite of all the gloom, Porter remained convinced that enemy whalers would soon appear. While waiting, he anchored in Bason cove close to Albermarle in the passage between the two bays, where he found good anchorage and restocked the ship. The men worked hard gathering wood and animals, but they found no water. They did come across an abandoned hut made of stones with no roof. Porter heard later that a marooned English sailor had built the shelter. The poor fellow had been put ashore with nothing but the clothes on his back as punishment for using insulting language to his captain. Being determined and resourceful the sailor built a shelter and survived for a year, eating tortoises and iguanas and other wildlife. He found water dripping down from nearby rocks. When no one came to rescue him, he fashioned a float from seal skins and put out into Banks Bay, hoping a cruising whaler might find him. Sharks circled and bumped against his float, but he kept them off with his paddle. After a harrowing day and night, he happened on an American ship. It was early morning; her crew did not know what to make of the creature that had suddenly appeared alongside. Clothed entirely in seal skin, with a scraggly beard that came down to his chest, an emaciated face, and long, matted hair, the man looked half human and half seal. Fortunately for the marooned sailor, his appearance did not put off the captain, who took him aboard, revived him, and made him a member of his crew.

After restocking the *Essex*, Porter continued exploring the waters around Albemarle. He stopped at one point in an inviting place and set down boats to fish. The men dropped lines, and even without bait, hauled in a large catch. Hooks were no sooner in the water than hundreds of fish came for them. In a short time all their boats were filled with black, red, and yellow grouper, sheepshead, and other varieties they could not identify.

Fishing did not take the crew's mind off British whalers, however. As each barren day passed, morale sank lower. By April 28 patience was running out. The men grew increasingly restless and irritable, thinking they would never find the enemy. Many were convinced that they had been given bad advice. Attitudes changed abruptly, however, when at daybreak on the 29th, the cry of "Sail ho! Sail ho!" rang out from aloft. In a flash all hands were on deck and at their stations. The stranger was a good-sized ship, and Porter sped after her. An hour later he spotted two more vessels in the distance—both large. He was certain they were British whale ships.

With British colors flying, the *Essex* pulled alongside the first vessel at nine in the morning. She was the British whale ship *Montezuma*, under Captain David Baxter, a Nantucket man. Porter invited him on board for a chat in his cabin. Thinking he was on a British frigate, Baxter revealed that the other two ships were armed whalers, the *Georgiana*, carrying six 18-pounders, and the *Policy*, with ten 6-pounders. He also revealed that his ship had 1,400 barrels of sperm oil aboard. The *Montezuma*, which had a British register, belonged to William Rotch's son, Benjamin Rotch, an American from Nantucket, now residing in Milford, England.

While Porter and Baxter talked, Lieutenant Downes moved the *Montezuma*'s men to the *Essex* and replaced them with an American officer and crew. Porter then tore after the other two whale ships, both of which had every sail up, trying to escape. They could not shake the *Essex*, however, and she continued to draw closer. The whalers were given a slight reprieve, when, as often happened in these waters, the wind died. The *Essex* was within eight miles. Porter quickly ordered out the small boats for an attack. Haze was growing thicker, however, and he worried that the enemy might yet slip away.

The attack boats were divided into two divisions with Downes in overall command. He was in the lead boat of the first division with Midshipman Farragut. The three other boats of this division were close behind. Lieutenant McKnight and his men were in the *Essex*'s third cutter; sailing master Cowell and crew were in the jolly boat; and Midshipmen George Isaacs and William Feltus with their men were in the second cutter. Lieutenant Wilmer led the second division in the pinnace. Lieutenant Wilson followed with the first cutter, and marine Lieutenant Gamble managed the captain's gig.

Downes's entire party consisted of fifty men, armed with muskets, pistols, boarding axes, and cutlasses. As the boats rowed, the faster ones slowed their rate of speed in order to keep the group together. At two o'clock in the afternoon they were a mile from the enemy, which hoisted British colors and fired a cannon several times, creating a commotion, but nothing more. Inexperienced gunners were obviously manning the guns. Their shots splashed harmlessly in the water far from their marks

The two *Essex* divisions now came together and rapidly approached the first ship, the larger of the two. Just before boarding, Downes displayed American colors from a pike in the bow and shouted for the whaler to surrender. To his astonishment, he heard cries of "We are all Americans" coming from the ship, and saw her colors being hauled down.

Downes lost no time boarding the whaler and putting an officer and crew aboard. He then raced after the second, smaller ship, which surrendered as easily as the first. The captured vessels turned out to be the former East Indiaman *Georgiana* of 280 tons and the *Policy* of 275 tons. The *Georgiana* had a crew of thirty-five, while the *Policy* had twenty-six men. To Downes's amazement, the greater part of the crews of both ships were pressed Americans, and many of them were eager to sign on to the *Essex*.

Capturing the ships was so easy, despite their armament, that the *Essex* men could scarcely believe their good luck. Porter estimated the three prizes were worth half a million dollars. All doubts the men harbored about achieving their dreams were now forgotten.

The next day, an elated Porter posted the following notice on the bulletin board:

SAILORS AND MARINES,

Fortune has at length smiled upon us, because we deserve her smiles. And for the first time she has enabled us to display FREE TRADE AND SAILOR'S RIGHTS, assisted by your good conduct, she put into our possession near half a million dollars of the enemy's money.

Continue to be zealous, enterprising, and patient, and we will yet render the name of the *Essex*, as terrible to the enemy as that of any other vessel, before we return to the United States. My plans shall be known to you at a suitable period.

D. Porter

The enemy whalers provided an abundance of supplies—cordage, spars, planks, timber, nails, rope, canvas, paints, tar, and every other article necessary for the *Essex*, including food. The whalers had departed England stuffed with three years of provisions, but had not yet consumed half. Their provisions would satisfy the needs of the *Essex* for many months, save for water, which was still lacking.

The United States now had a fleet of four in the Pacific. Porter decided to transform the *Georgiana* into a sixteen-gun warship without altering her appearance as a whaler. She could then be used as both a fighting ship and a decoy. He put Lieutenant Downes in command and gave him a crew of forty-one. Thirty-six came from the *Essex* and five from the captured ships. The large number of seamen from the prizes who had indicated they wanted to join the *Essex* were granted their request. Many were Americans. The few who did not want to join were nonetheless taken aboard the *Essex* as prisoners.

Downes received the *Policy*'s ten guns to add to the *Georgiana*'s six, as well as two swivels, blunderbusses mounted on swivels, and small arms—muskets, pistols, cutlasses, boarding pikes, and tomahawks. Porter put Midshipman William H. Odenheimer in charge of the *Montezuma* and gave Midshipman John S. Cowan command of the *Policy*—two young men who had impressed him with their leadership ability.

Porter spent the next few days repairing the *Essex* and reconnoitering east of Albemarle near James Island. He then decided that separating from Downes would allow them to cover more territory. On May 12 he sent Downes and the *Georgiana* to search for enemy vessels around Albermarle, while he sailed the *Essex* to Hood Island with the other two prizes and the *Barclay*. Downes was to join him there later. After visiting Hood, Porter intended to sail to Tumbes on the Peruvian coast to obtain water. He instructed Downes to join him at Hood, but if he missed him, to proceed to Tumbes and rendezvous there. After Tumbes, Porter planned to beat his way up the Peruvian coast to Lima, and from there travel all the way down to Concepción, before eventually sailing back north to Valparaiso. There he hoped to gain intelligence of British warships hunting him, and, of course, capture whatever enemy whalers, privateers, or merchantmen that came his way.

Downes soon set a course to double the southern point of Albemarle, while Porter steered his little squadron south-southeast for Hood Island. At midday Porter discovered that he was approaching, not Hood, but Charles Island. This finally convinced him that no reliance could be placed on Colnett's chart. He dropped anchor in what he called Essex Bay on the northern coast of Charles, where Hathaway's Post Office was located. He went ashore and discovered unmistakable evidence that other ships had stopped by the post office since his last visit. All the food and water stored there was gone. There was no doubt in his mind that the vessels were English and that their destination was the fishing grounds off Albemarle. Instead of tearing after them, however, he decided to search for water on Charles; his supply was getting dangerously low. He moved to a place on the west side, where he heard water was to be found. It was only six miles from his present location. When he got there he found some water, but it was impure and extremely difficult to get at, so it did not solve his problem.

Three days later, on May 15, Lieutenant Downes and the *Georgiana* unexpectedly appeared. Downes never reached Albemarle. Rapid, confusing currents and general ignorance of the Galapagos stopped him. When he found himself in the vicinity of Charles Island, he decided to look into Essex Bay for enemy vessels, never expecting to find the *Essex* there.

Porter dispatched Downes to go after the whale ships that had left messages at Hathaway's Post Office. He sent Mr. Adams, the chaplain, in two whaleboats to make an accurate survey of a large, unidentified island directly north of Charles. Midshipman Odenheimer went with him, in command of the second boat. Porter told them to return within a week.

While he waited for Adams, Porter continued repairing the *Essex* and adding a huge number of tortoises to her provisions. He also directed that the two prizes be spruced up. He intended to sell them at the first opportunity—probably in Valparaiso. The men, including the prisoners, were given a chance to be on the beach a good deal, and this helped morale. To his great delight Porter discovered what later turned out to be a potent anti-scorbutic on the island—the prickly pear, which grew in abundance and could be easily loaded aboard to help with his constant battle against scurvy.

On the morning of May 20, Adams returned from what he called Porter (Santa Cruz) Island. The following morning at nine o'clock, Porter weighed anchor, planning to pursue a large ship that Adams had narrowly avoided while returning from the island. Adams was certain that she was a well-armed English whaler steering for Albemarle. Porter decided to go after her immediately. Before setting out, he left an uncoded note for Downes, telling him that the *Essex*, after searching for the ship that Adams had seen, was bound for Tumbes. Porter put the note in a bottle and buried it at the foot of Hathaway's Post Office. He then sailed with two prizes and the *Barclay* in pursuit of Adams's ship, sailing all the way to Albemarle, where he dropped anchor and went ashore, climbing a hill to get a panoramic view of the surrounding waters, but no other vessels were visible.

After returning to the *Essex*, he delayed for a time, waiting to see if the ship he was seeking might yet appear. When she didn't, he tacked to the eastward for Hood Island on May 23. The going was tough. He had to fight especially strong currents that nearly drove the *Essex* and her companions aground on Hood. The currents were so contrary they forced him back to Charles Island.

On May 27, Porter left Charles and struggled toward Albemarle. The next day he weathered the island's southern head and soon spotted a sail that looked promising. At the time, the slow-sailing *Montezuma* was in tow, and Porter cast her off while he raced for the stranger. At sunset he could see her plainly from the deck, but he had no hope of catching her before nightfall. She was carrying a full press of canvas, straining to gain distance. The wind continued strong, and Porter kept pressing toward her, hoping to get as close as possible before nightfall. As it fell, he hove to so that his slower companions could catch up, and when they did, he distributed them in a wide area, hoping that one of them would catch a glimpse of the stranger in the morning.

Porter's luck held. At daybreak the *Montezuma* signaled that a ship was to the northward. Porter crowded on sail, but two hours went by before he could see her. He kept after her with the *Montezuma*, but at noon the wind died. Determined that his prey would not escape, Porter lowered three of his fastest boats, filled them with men under the command of Lieutenant Wilmer, and ordered him to sail to the *Montezuma*, which was six miles away, situated between the *Essex* and her prey. When Wilmer reached the *Montezuma*, he was to fill three of her boats with men (giving him a total of six), row to a position astern of the stranger, and keep her in sight.

Wilmer's boats had no sooner left the *Essex* than a breeze sprang up, and Porter resumed the chase. He soon passed his boats and signaled the *Montezuma* to pick them up. As Porter approached the stranger, she hauled close on a wind, and then hove to—exactly what he had hoped she would do. The *Essex* was flying British colors, which deceived the stranger's captain, Obadiah Weir. He was eager for a talk with what he thought was the captain of a British frigate. Weir's vessel was the letter of marque *Atlantic*, a fine fighting ship, the best Porter had seen so far. She carried six 18-pounders and was ostensibly employed in whaling, but her principal business was hunting American competitors.

The *Essex* was soon alongside the *Atlantic*, and when Weir came on board, Porter continued posing as a British captain. His anger mounted when he discovered that Weir was from Nantucket, and he was outraged when Weir told him that the best place to capture American whalers was off Concepción, where he had seen nine of them in a defenseless state. By going there, he told Porter, he could reap rich rewards and destroy the American whale fishery in the eastern Pacific.

Barely able to stifle his anger, Porter asked Weir how he could sail from England under the British flag in an armed ship after hostilities had broken out between the two countries. Weir insisted that he had no difficulty, for although he had been born in Nantucket, he was an Englishman at heart. Porter was disgusted with him, and had great pleasure in introducing him to the unlucky captains of the *Montezuma* and the *Georgiana*, who soon disabused Weir of the notion that he was aboard a British man-of-war.

Weir had been aboard for only a short time when a lookout at the masthead cried another sail. Porter again sprang into action. He signaled the *Montezuma* to come up, took men from her, and put them in the *Atlantic* under Lieutenant McKnight; and then, both the *Atlantic*—reputed to be a fast ship—and the *Essex* sped after the prey. Night came on before they could catch up with her, however, and she disappeared for a time. Luckily, Porter and his lookouts soon found her again with their night glasses (refracting telescopes).

To Porter's surprise, and great pleasure, when night fell, he saw the stranger sailing toward him. Thinking her pursuers could not find her in the dark, she had changed course, coming about, and heading in the opposite direction. Unbeknownst to her captain, she was sailing right into the arms of the *Essex*. As she approached, Porter put a shot across her bows, and she immediately hove to. He ordered her captain to come on board, but he refused until he knew what ship the *Essex* was. Porter responded with a shot between his masts and threatened a broadside. That changed the captain's mind, and he repaired on board. His ship was the excellent letter of marque *Greenwich* of ten guns, employed as an armed whaler. She was the mysterious ship that Mr. Adams had seen. When John Shuttleworth, the *Greenwich*'s skipper, appeared in Porter's cabin, he was obviously drunk. Porter was disgusted with him.

He grew irate when Weir and Shuttleworth failed to conceal their contempt for their captors. Their manners grew worse, even though they were shown to generous quarters. Porter heard so much loud invective against the United States and the captain of the *Essex* that he soon appeared at their door and impressed upon them—face to face—how unpleasant he could make their situation. That got their attention, and they changed their tune, uttering no more ugly epithets.

Lieutenant McKnight took charge of the *Atlantic* with enough men to fight her guns, and since Porter was short of naval officers, he appointed marine Lieutenant Gamble to take charge of the *Greenwich*. This was not only unusual but unique. A marine had never commanded an American warship before. And as it turned out, Gamble was not only the first, but also the last. No marine, before or since, has done so. Porter assigned two experienced seamen to help Gamble run the ship. One of them was a navigator.

Porter now had a fleet of six: *Georgiana, Atlantic, Greenwich, Montezuma, Policy*, and, of course, *Essex*. The potential in prize money was mounting, and so were the spirits of Porter's crew. The last two captures had 800 tortoises crammed into their holds—enough fresh food for the men in all six ships for a month. The captures also had plenty of naval stores—cordage, paint, tar, canvas, and the like. More importantly, the *Atlantic* and the *Greenwich* had in excess of 3,500 gallons of water, which alleviated Porter's immediate need. To be sure, the precious liquid was in the oily casks of whale ships and had an unpleasant smell and taste, but it was usable, and Porter was happy to have it until he found fresher water.

In addition to having adequate supplies Porter also had sufficient men, including prisoners, to man all the ships. He calculated that he had a total of 420, and, miraculously, every one of them was in excellent health, except for the few on the *Atlantic* and the *Greenwich* who exhibited signs of scurvy brought on by indifferent captains. Porter was careful about how hc allocated the prisoners, integrating them into the crews of every ship, and he was pleased with the results. He found them to be as useful as his own men.

Although Porter thought the British tars performed well, he had no use for their captains nor for their uncaring service. The *Atlantic*, he discovered, was the ship that had taken the water and bread placed near Hathaway's Post Office. Captain Weir took them, not because he needed sustenance for his crew, but because he feared men might escape if they knew bread and water were on the island. Britain's tars, it seems, fled from the tyranny aboard their ships whenever and wherever they could, even to uninhabited islands.

On June 6, an awesome sight filled Porter and his crews with wonder. An immense volcano erupted. It was early afternoon when they observed thick, black, cone-shaped smoke rising rapidly from a huge crater on Albemarle Island. The column ascended to a great height before spreading off in grand white curls. The intriguing outburst continued into the evening, illuminating the night sky.

Despite the wondrous sights on these unique islands, by the second week of June Porter had had enough of the Galapagos. He was eager to return to the coast of Peru, fill his water casks, and resume the hunt for whalers along the coasts of Peru and Chile, where he thought the hunting would be as good or better than in the treacherous Galapagos. In addition, and perhaps more importantly, he had no doubt that Admiral Dixon in Rio was aware of the *Essex*'s rampage in the Pacific and would be sending one or more warships to destroy her. Needless to say, Porter was anxious to meet the British hunters.

chapter 13

UNPARALLELED SUCCESS

O N JUNE 8, PORTER PASSED TO THE NORTH OF ABINGDON (Pinta) Island with a fresh breeze. He had all but one of the dull sailing vessels in tow. They were heading for the Peruvian town of Tumbes, close to the Equator in the southern part of the Gulf of Guayaquil, nearly 600 miles north of Lima. Downes and the *Georgiana* were not with him, but Porter left instructions where to find him.

Porter planned to stop at the Island of La Plata on the way to Tumbes. It was seventeen miles off what is now the southern coast of Ecuador, but was then Peru. Legend had it that Captain Francis Drake landed there to bury treasure and divide his plunder. Porter expected to obtain wood and water and leave a message for Downes. The haze was so thick, however, that he did not find the island until the night of June 16.

As the *Essex* approached La Plata the following morning, Porter saw huge schools of sperm and finback whales. He dropped anchor two miles offshore and explored the waters around the island in a whaleboat. It proved a big disappointment. He could not find a comfortable landing place. Before continuing on to the Tumbes River, he left a message for Downes in a bottle and suspended it from the branch of a bush. To make certain Downes did not miss the bottle, Porter painted the letters S.X. on a nearby rock—large enough to draw anyone's attention.

On June 19, the *Essex* ran into the spacious Gulf of Guayaquil and anchored on the south side, a mile off the mouth of the Tumbes River. A considerable sandbar blocked the entrance. As the *Essex* came to anchor, misfortune struck. One of the gunner's crew, John Rodgers, aged thirty-two, one of the best seamen on the ship, was helping to furl the mainsail. Suddenly he lost his balance and plunged headfirst to the deck, smashing his skull. Rodgers's fondness for rum had finally done him in, shocking and saddening the entire ship. Excessive drinking was a problem that never went away for skippers.

Porter now had to turn to the unpleasant business of dealing with the Peruvian authorities. He anticipated that they would be hostile but amenable to bribery. He sent Captain Randall of the *Barclay* upriver to the town of Tumbes to confer with the governor while the *Essex* men got busy bringing wood and water aboard. It was a hazardous business. The waters were loaded with big, hungry sharks and huge alligators; the surf was violent enough to upset rafts. Porter himself shot and killed an enormous, fifteen-foot alligator, placing a musket ball below the joint of the monster's foreleg near the shoulder.

On June 22, Randall returned with the governor and his retinue. The officials, especially the governor, were so wretchedly dressed that it was all Porter could do to stop from laughing. The Peruvians' wardrobe did not hinder negotiations, however. The governor and his men were anxious for money, which Porter supplied, and business went forward with no trouble, as he had anticipated it would. Still, Porter had to be careful; this was not friendly territory. He never went on shore or allowed any of his men to go without being heavily armed and on guard.

The following day, June 23, Porter went into Tumbes, reluctantly returning the governor's visit. The town had about fifty houses or huts and was as wretched as the attire of its officials. Tumbes was built on stilts to protect inhabitants from alligators, but nothing could shield them from swarms of mosquitoes and other insects. Porter spent as little time as possible with the governor and absolutely refused to stay the night.

On returning to the *Essex*, he was confronted with a problem he had long hoped to avoid. Again it had to do with alcohol. The acting second lieutenant, James Wilson, after an abstinence of many months, was drunk again. Everyone liked Wilson, but he had a drinking problem, which Porter had had to deal with more than once. When he was told of Wilson's condition, he went directly to his cabin and advised him that he was under arrest for the remainder of the cruise. Wilson was shaken, reached for a pistol, and attempted to load it. Porter grabbed it from him, but Wilson went for another. Porter was too quick for him, however, and stopped him again. Wilson then told him that he had intended to use the pistol on himself. Porter believed him. He could see the terrible state the poor man was in. It was a sad business; Porter felt sorry for Wilson, and after giving the matter more thought, he decided to give him another chance. Wilson carried on, but he remained terribly unhappy with himself.

On the same day, Porter received a communication from the governor of Tumbes indicating that his superior, the governor of Guayaquil, would not approve of Porter's remaining in the river, and that he should depart as soon as possible. Porter thought this was a demand for more money, a demand he would not meet. But it was also obvious that he was in hostile territory and should leave as soon as he had collected sufficient supplies.

The next day, Lieutenant Downes and the *Georgiana* finally appeared with two prizes and a story to tell. Downes had captured three whalers off James Island in the Galapagos—the 11-gun *Hector* (270 tons), the 8-gun *Rose* (220 tons), and the 8-gun *Catharine* (270 tons). The *Hector* had a crew of twenty-five, the *Rose* twenty-one, and the *Catharine* twenty-nine. Downes had no trouble capturing the *Catharine* and the *Rose*. Their captains had assumed the *Georgiana* was a British ship and drove right up alongside her.

The *Hector* was another matter. She gave Downes plenty of trouble. He had spotted her one afternoon and did not catch up with her until late at night. He ran alongside and shouted for her to strike her colors, but the *Hector*'s skipper cleared for action instead. Downes had only twenty men and boys; the others were on the prizes *Catharine* and *Rose*. Thinking he'd better act fast, Downes fired a shot that smashed into the *Hector*'s stern, and crashed through the interior of the ship, doing considerable damage. He then called for a surrender, but the *Hector* got on more sail and tried to get away, whereupon Downes poured one broadside after another into her, killing two men and wounding six. After receiving five rounds at point-blank range, the *Hector*'s main topmast was down as was most of her standing and running rigging. With his ship a wreck, the *Hector*'s plucky skipper finally struck his colors.

Downes now had seventy-five prisoners—too many to manage safely. He put all of them in the *Rose*—the poorest of the three ships—and sent them on parole to St. Helena Island in the South Atlantic. The British captain pledged that he would take them there and not serve against the United States until regularly exchanged. Downes thought the man would be as good as his word and gave him a passport to St. Helena. Before Downes let the *Rose* go, he transferred her sperm oil to the *Georgiana* and had all her guns thrown overboard.

Before leaving the Gulf of Guayaquil, Porter reorganized his fleet. He converted the *Atlantic*, the best of his captures, into a 20-gun cruiser with Downes in command and christened her *Essex Junior*. Since several more good men from the prizes had volunteered to serve in the American navy, Porter was able to put sixty men aboard her with Midshipman Richard Dashiell as sailing master. The contemporary anti-American British naval historian, William James, claimed that Porter had, with empty promises, enticed His Majesty's innocent seamen out of the prizes to serve on the *Atlantic*. The Admiralty and Parliament thought the same. They would never admit that the principal reason so many of their seamen deserted was the brutal conditions aboard their warships. For a large portion of every British crew, life aboard a man-of-war could be a brutal, dangerous existence. The food was unhealthy and the pay abysmal; threats of cruel, sometimes fatal beatings were routinely used to obtain obedience, and leave was never granted if it was thought the recipient would run away. The torment was unending. Seamen were required to serve for the duration of the war with France, which by 1813 had been going on for twenty years. The problem of desertion in the Royal Navy was endemic. It could never be solved as long as upper-class Britons refused to recognize the tyranny aboard their warships. For ordinary seamen, escape was the only way out, the only way to survive. Thousands ran away, many to the more benign ships of the United States. The Admiralty and its numerous supporters in Parliament refused to admit the obvious.

Those prisoners who did not want to join the American navy had repeatedly asked to be put on shore, and Porter decided that he would be better off without them. He gave them three boats, all of their possessions, and set them free, including the obnoxious captains Weir and Shuttleworth.

Porter next appointed Mr. Adams to be skipper of the *Georgiana* and converted the *Greenwich* into a storeship, putting the extra provisions from all the ships into her, along with twenty guns. He estimated that he had enough supplies for all his ships to last seven months. At the same time he gave command of the prize ship *Montezuma* to Midshipman Feltus, who could not have been happier.

With these matters tended to, Porter, on the morning of June 30, made the signal to his fleet—including the ships in Downes's squadron—to get underway. On July 1, they stood out from the Gulf of Guayaquil, sailing west for the easterly trade winds, which Porter expected to pick up three or four hundred miles offshore. While the fleet sailed west, carpenters and other skilled men worked hard on *Essex Junior*, building up her breastworks and making other alterations to strengthen her as a fighting ship. On July 4, Porter stopped to commemorate Independence Day. *Essex*, *Essex Junior*, and *Georgiana* fired seventeen-gun salutes, and Porter ordered a double ration of grog for all the crews on the nine ships. The rum came from the prizes and was doubly welcome, since the *Essex* men, for some time, had had none at all.

Porter was celebrating more than the national holiday. He was also celebrating the incredible success they had had against the British whale fishery. He was so enthusiastic about their achievements that his horizon broadened, and he changed his mind about remaining on the hunt along the coasts of Peru and Chile. Instead of doing that, he contemplated sailing his whole fleet to Polynesia. His dreams of going there were of long standing. He had mentioned them to the crew before, while they were in the Atlantic standing toward Cape Horn. He had no idea at the time if what he promised would ever come to pass, but now there was every reason to believe that he could finally do what he had been fantasizing about all these years.

To begin with, he decided to divide his fleet and send Downes to Valparaiso while he went back to the Galapagos Islands. He anticipated that Downes would join him there a short time later. More importantly, Porter decided that, after he and Downes met up again, his fleet would travel to the Marquesas Islands, the archipelago in Polynesia. There they would experience the legendary delights offered by the women of these exotic islands.

Porter also thought that, while enjoying the extraordinary female companionship, he could make necessary repairs on the ships, particularly the *Essex*.

Four days later, Downes departed for Valparaiso. The prize ships *Hector*, *Catharine*, *Policy*, and *Montezuma* accompanied him, along with the *Barclay*. Porter instructed Downes to leave the *Barclay* at Valparaiso and sell the other ships, if possible. The *Policy* was loaded with sperm oil. The oil from all the ships had been divided between the *Policy* and the *Georgiana*. Prices for oil at Valparaiso were so low, however, that Porter gave Downes the option of sending *Policy* to the United States, where the oil would bring a much higher price. If she went to America, she was to approach the northern coast in the dead of winter, when severe weather impeded the British blockade.

While Downes was in Valparaiso, Porter expected him to obtain the latest intelligence on any British warships hunting the *Essex*. Porter was certain there would be at least one, and more likely two or more. Porter also gave Downes three letters addressed to Secretary of the Navy Paul Hamilton, dated July 2, 1813. Downes was to give them to Joel Poinsett for transmittal to Washington. Poinsett would undoubtedly do his best to get them there any way he could, by land or sea via Thomas Sumter in Rio, but how long it would take, or even if they would get there at all, was uncertain. Porter had no way of knowing that Hamilton was no longer in charge of the Navy Department. President Madison had finally asked for his resignation in December 1812, replacing him with William Jones of Philadelphia, a respected merchant and banker with a long record of accomplishment.

Porter knew that Washington would be wondering what had happened to him. He had no idea if his brief letter to Bainbridge in March had reached its destination. He also wanted his wife and family to know that he and Farragut were faring well. And he was proud of his accomplishments; he wanted the navy and, he hoped, the whole country to know about them. He told the secretary of the navy,

> Indeed sir, when I compare my present situation with what it was when I doubled Cape Horn I cannot but esteem myself fortunate in an extraordinary degree—then my ship was shattered by tempestuous weather and destitute of everything, my officers and crew half starved, naked and worn

out with fatigue—Now sir, my ship is in prime order abundantly supplied with everything necessary for her. I have a noble ship for a consort of twenty-guns and well-manned, a store ship of twenty guns well supplied with everything we may want, and prizes which would be worth in England two million dollars, and what renders the comparison more pleasing, the enemy has furnished all——.

Porter also wanted the navy to know how well Lieutenant John Downes was performing. In a separate letter to the secretary of the navy, Porter wrote, "If any officer deserves in an extraordinary degree the attention of the department Lt. Downes certainly does."

The letters reached Secretary Jones in December 1813, and they caused a sensation. News about Porter and the *Essex* had been scarce since they left. Reports popped up from time to time, always mixing accurate and inaccurate information, but there had been nothing official. The nation wanted to know what had happened to Porter. Now there was confirmation that he and the *Essex* were not only in the Pacific, as had been suspected, but they were doing brilliantly.

No one was happier with Porter's report than President Madison, who needed cheering up. The war was going poorly for the United States in 1813. The president had renewed his attack on Canada without success, except for the victories of Oliver Hazard Perry on Lake Erie on September 10, 1813, and of William Henry Harrison and Perry at the Battle of the Thames in Lower Canada a short time later. Moreover, Great Britain and her allies had defeated Napoleon decisively at the Battle of Leipzig, throwing him back into France, where his days were numbered. The British would soon be able to turn their whole military might against the United States. From Madison's point of view the future looked bleak. Defeatism was spreading across the country. He was in desperate need of good news—and of heroes. Porter supplied both. The president immediately released Porter's report, and newspapers around the country printed it, boosting morale everywhere.

Secretary Jones lost no time passing the report on to Evelina Porter. She had been writing to him, inquiring about her husband, but he had had nothing to tell her. Now he did. On December 14, 1813, he sent a message to Green Bank:

I have the pleasure to enclose a letter this day received under cover of a very interesting and highly satisfactory dispatch from Captain Porter, dated July 2 last near the Equator on the west coast of South America.

Himself, officers and crew were in [an excellent] degree of health and spirits, abundantly provided with everything necessary for their comfort for eight months in advance, and their success had equaled the most sanguine expectations.

Evelina was filled with joy and relief. He was safe, and more than that, a hero—what he had always strived for. Of course, David wasn't home yet, but, even so, this was wonderful news, considering all the horrible things she feared might have happened to him.

CARRYING PORTER'S LETTERS TO THE NAVY SECRETARY, DOWNES and his fleet set off for Valparaiso on July 8. One of the fleet now had a noteworthy new skipper. In one of his stranger decisions, Porter had given his "de facto son," David Farragut, now age twelve, command of the *Barclay* for her trip to Valparaiso. And to make the assignment even more bizarre, Captain Gideon Randall and his chief mate were left on board to navigate. Porter doesn't mention this unusual arrangement in his journal—as if it were inconsequential. For Farragut, however, it was the major event of his young life. Randall was a fiercely independent old cuss, who wanted his ship back so that he could resume whaling. Instead, he was ordered to navigate the *Barclay* to Valparaiso, and submit to the orders of a twelve-year-old. He was understandably furious, and from the beginning of the voyage he made it plain that he was determined to take back his ship.

As soon as the *Barclay* separated from the *Essex* and stood south with Downes's convoy, Randall made his move. He shouted at Farragut in a voice that was heard throughout the ship, "You'll find yourself off New Zealand in the morning."

At that moment, Farragut recalled,

we were lying still while the other ships were fast disappearing from view; the Commodore going north, and the *Essex Junior*, with her convoy, steering south for Valparaiso. I considered that my day of trial had arrived (for I was a little afraid of the old fellow, as everyone else was). But the time had come for me, at least, to play the man; so I mustered up courage and informed the captain that I desired the main topsail filled away, in order that we might close up with the *Essex Junior*. He replied that he would shoot any man who dared to touch a rope without his orders, he "would go his own course," he shouted, "and had no idea of trusting himself with a damned nutshell," and then he went below for his pistols.

While Randall stomped away, Farragut summoned his "right-hand man of the crew" and explained the situation. He then ordered him in a loud voice to "fill the main topsail."

"Aye, aye, sir!" Farragut's man shouted. The message to the rest of the crew was clear: Farragut was in charge.

"From that moment I became master of the vessel," Farragut wrote, "and immediately gave all necessary orders for making sail."

Farragut warned Randall that if he came on deck with his pistols he would have him thrown overboard. Farragut felt that he "would have had very little trouble in having such an order obeyed." That ended the matter. When Farragut, with Randall in tow, made a report of the incident to Downes, he got firm support. Chastened, Randall pretended that he had not meant what he said. He told Downes that he was only trying to frighten Farragut. Randall and the young skipper then returned to the *Barclay* and "everything went on amicably," Farragut recalled.

While Downes was leading his squadron to Valparaiso, Porter shaped a course back to the Galapagos in search of British whalers. He had been told that three were fishing there and that they were armed and looking for the *Essex*. Porter hoped they were. He did not intend to tarry long in the Galapagos searching for the whalers, however. If he found them right away, fine; but if not, he intended to sail on to the little-frequented Marquesas Islands. The storeship *Greenwich* and the *Georgiana* remained with the *Essex*. When the time was right, Porter intended to send the *Georgiana* to the United States to sell her cargo of sperm oil. He planned to time her departure so that she would have a good chance of arriving along the northeast coast in the dead of winter.

With the prevailing winds and current carrying the *Essex*, Porter easily raised Charles Island on July 12. Recent volcanic eruptions had changed the face of the island, as they had Albemarle and Narborough. The first thing Porter did was send a boat to Hathaway's Post Office, where he found evidence that one British ship, at least, had been there recently. He left a note for Downes and buried it in a bottle at the foot of the post office and then sailed for Albemarle, arriving in Banks Bay at midnight, where he dropped his hook. At daylight he steered to the northward, and at eleven o'clock lookouts caught sight of three large vessels, sailing some distance apart from each other. Porter was ready. He raced after the one in the center, while the others, instead of coming to her aid, fled, or appeared to. That did not surprise him, but he worried that one or both might attempt to take the *Greenwich* and *Georgiana*, who were trailing a considerable distance behind the *Essex*. As he raced toward his prey, one of the strangers did tack to windward of the *Essex* and steer toward the prizes. The *Greenwich* was alert to the danger and hove to, waiting for the *Georgiana* to come up. When the two met, the *Greenwich* took some men from the *Georgiana* and raced after the vessel that was supposedly in pursuit, while the *Georgiana* ran for the *Essex*.

Porter made quick work of the vessel he was chasing—the *Charlton*, a 10-gun English whaler. He then sped after the *Greenwich*, which was now in a gunfight with the ship she had been chasing—the 14-gun *Seringapatam*, a far stronger opponent than the *Charlton*. The *Seringapatam* had a crew of forty and was a fine warship, built for that purpose and converted to a whaler. Her captain had no intention of doing any fishing; he was out to capture American whalers. With the *Essex* gaining ground, the British ship pretended to strike her colors, but then tried to steal away, hoping that darkness would cover her. The *Greenwich* kept after her, however, and with the *Essex* now having come up, the *Seringapatam* was forced to surrender. Immediately, Porter flew after the third vessel and caught her in an hour as darkness was approaching. She turned out to be the *New Zealander* of eight guns.

The *Seringapatam*'s captain, William Stavers, had no papers proving he had a privateer's commission from his government authorizing him to seize enemy vessels. If he could not produce one, he was legally a pirate and could be brought to an admiralty court, convicted, and hung. Porter considered him an outlaw. Unlike his handling of the other enemy skippers, he put Stavers in irons. This did not apply to his crew, however.

They received excellent treatment. In doing so, Porter was returning a favor. He had learned that earlier, when Stavers had captured an American whaler, he had treated her crew well—unlike other British captains. Putting Stavers in irons after he had been so decent to the American whalers might seem like an odd decision, but Porter considered him an able leader, and did not want him leading a prisoner uprising.

The number of prisoners had become a problem. On July 19 Porter dispatched the slow-sailing *Charlton* to Rio under her captain with forty-eight prisoners on parole. The British tars were quick to protest, however; they wanted no part of Rio, where they stood a good chance of being pressed into a man-of-war. Every one of them volunteered for the American service, but Porter, although sympathetic, had enough men, and reluctantly forced them to go.

After they left, he strengthened the *Seringapatam* by putting twenty-two guns on her. He wanted a spare warship in case some dreadful event in these uncharted waters destroyed the *Essex*. If that happened, he could carry on with the *Seringapatam* as his flagship.

When work on the *Seringapatam* was completed, Porter, on July 25, dispatched the heavily laden *Georgiana* to the United States. He wanted to get rid of Captain Stavers, whom he considered a potential threat, and he wanted to allow Lieutenant James Wilson, the officer with the severe drinking problem, a second chance by giving him command of the *Georgiana*. Wilson's seamanship was never in question, and he had performed well in the battle between the *Greenwich* and the *Seringapatam*.

It was a popular decision; Wilson was well liked. The other officers wanted him afforded an opportunity to redeem himself. Porter estimated that it would take five months to reach the northern coast of the United States, which meant that Wilson and the *Georgiana* would be arriving in winter when the British blockade was least effective. Porter estimated her cargo would fetch at least $100,000. He used this occasion to offer some of his men the option of going home. The time of enlistment for many was nearing completion, and he announced that those who qualified could sail back to America with Wilson. None elected to go. Success against the whalers, confidence in Porter, and the prospect of leave on a Polynesian island (which at this point had not been officially announced but was widely anticipated), inspired every man to remain. Needless to say, Porter was gratified.

As the *Georgiana* prepared to depart, the *Essex* gave her a smart salute and three cheers. Everyone hoped that Wilson would have a swift, safe passage. Unfortunately, before he reached the United States, the British frigate HMS *Barrosa* (William H. Shirreff) captured the *Georgiana*, her crew, and all her oil.

At noon on the day that Wilson left, Porter found that his squadron had drifted to the west and was now in longitude 91° 15" west and latitude 1° 8' 25" north. Three days later, at seven o'clock on the morning of July 28, lookouts spotted a strange sail that Porter assumed was a British whaler. He ran up to the main topgallant yard with his glass to get a good look at her and saw that she was close on a wind and had fresh breezes while the *Essex* was practically becalmed with a strong current taking her toward Rodondo Island. Nonetheless, Porter attempted to give chase, but the current nearly ran the *Essex* aground on Rodondo. Only a smart breeze springing up at a critical moment and a quick use of drags saved the ship from crashing into the rocky, perpendicular cliffs on the inaccessible side of the island.

With the *Essex* out of danger, Porter continued the chase, certain she was a British whaler. It was not until 7:30 the following morning, however, that the stranger was seen again from the main masthead. Porter kept after her. In two hours he was only seven miles away, and then, with the mightiest exertion, he approached to within four miles, when his prey lost the wind. It looked as if she was done for. Her captain did not give up, however. He got her boats out, and they towed her. Porter sent two boats after her, the gig and a whaleboat, but cannon shot from the stranger's forecastle kept them at bay.

At four o'clock, both ships were still becalmed. Porter was close enough to see that the stranger had only ten guns and probably a crew of thirty. He did not think there was any possibility that she'd escape. He hoisted out his seven boats, and they went after her. She fired on them ineffectually, while her boats continued towing. *The Essex*'s attack boats kept closing. But just when it appeared that the stranger would be easily overpowered, a breeze sprang up from the east, and she got up every piece of canvas she had and sailed to the northward, while the *Essex* was still becalmed. Porter watched in frustration as his prey moved farther and farther away. By sunset she was hull down, and during the night she completed her escape. Porter thought she was probably either the whale ship *Indispensable* or the whale ship *Comet*. He consoled himself by noting that she was the first enemy who had escaped his clutches. "Such is our nature," he reflected, "that we could not help blaming fortune for thus jilting us, and for this freak of hers forgot for a moment all the favors she had hitherto lavished on us."

On August 4, Porter anchored his ships (now reduced to four: *Essex*, *Greenwich*, *New Zealander*, and *Seringapatam*) in what is now James Bay on James (Santiago) Island. There he spent several days repairing—fixing sails, rigging, and boats, and doing various other jobs that could not be done conveniently at sea. He made a new main topsail for the *Essex*, and wove new cordage from old rope, broke up her hold, cleansed and re-stowed it, and scrapped the ship's bottom, removing a thick accumulation of barnacles and grass. He changed the appearance of the *Essex* as well, and painted the *Seringapatam* to look exactly like her from a distance. And he gave the *Greenwich* the appearance of a sloop of war. He also took all the *Essex*'s gunpowder ashore, sunning and sifting it. He discovered that water had spoiled a third of it by entering the magazine—probably during the passage around Cape Horn or when the rudder coat was damaged off Patagonia. To make up for the loss, he took most of the powder from the *Seringapatam*.

Later, he explored parts of James Island. He noticed for the first time how different the tortoises on this island were compared to those on either Hood or Charles. Charles Darwin would later remark, after it was pointed out to him, that, in fact, tortoises, and many other species of plants and animals, were different on each of the islands, something that would later appear to him to be of great significance as he developed his grand theory of the origin of species.

While the *Essex* was anchored in the bay off James, four of the ship's goats, one male and three females, were allowed to graze on shore. Each day, when the *Essex* men returned to work on the island, they found the goats grazing peacefully, but one day they disappeared, and all efforts to find them failed. Porter assumed they had instinctively searched for the water he believed was in the interior of the island, where the tortoises un-doubtedly found theirs. He speculated what effect this might have on the future and came to the conclusion that the animals would thrive and multiply and offer seamen who landed in the future an excellent resource.

The goats did indeed make a difference on the island, but it was not beneficial. By the year 2000 the descendants of Porter's goats had taken over the island (now known as Santiago). Almost no tortoises were left. The goats had monopolized the water and made it almost impossible for the unique reptiles to survive. In order to save the few tortoises that remained, the government of Ecuador spent huge sums reducing the goat population to zero.

SUDDENLY ONE MORNING IN THE MIDDLE OF AUGUST, PORTER was taken aback by shocking news that gave him incredible pain. His officers reported that twenty-one-year-old Acting Lieutenant John S. Cowan, one of his particular favorites, had been killed in a duel. Porter could not believe it, and he was furious. He could ill afford to lose a good officer, and having it happen in the manner it did was excruciating. Cowan had begun the voyage as a midshipman, and Porter had advanced him because of his leadership abilities. So far as Porter was concerned, dueling was a practice that disgraced human nature.

The duel had taken place on shore at daylight, and Cowan had been killed not on the first round of firing, nor even on the second, but on the third. As angry as Porter was, however, he did nothing to punish the victor; he even attempted to keep his name a secret. But it was generally supposed, although never verified, that marine Lieutenant John Gamble killed Cowan.

Dueling was a tradition in the navy, and setting aside his own strong feelings, Porter felt he had to respect it. A naval officer could not remain in the service for any length of time without participating in a duel. Although Porter had never been a principal himself, he had taken part on more than one occasion as a second. In fact, when Lieutenant Stephen Decatur McKnight's father, Marine Captain James McKnight, had been killed in a duel on October 4, 1802, Porter had been one of his seconds. Navy Lieutenant Richard H. L. Lawson had shot McKnight. Both were serving on the *Constellation*, which was anchored off Leghorn, Italy, with most of the Mediterranean squadron. Porter had been serving aboard the *Chesapeake* at the time.

Porter had had no inkling there was bad blood between Cowan and Gamble. Although living in the closest proximity to both men, he had no suspicion of what was afoot. Because of the psychological distance he felt was necessary to maintain from his officers in the interests of discipline, he lost an able leader who was vital to the success of his difficult mission. The much-esteemed Cowan was buried the same day he was shot, in the spot where he fell near the beach in James Bay. The unnecessary, idiotic manner of his death weighed heavily on the minds of his brother officers and their captain.

CHAPTER 14

THE HUNT FOR THE *ESSEX*

WHILE WAITING FOR DOWNES TO RETURN FROM VALPARAISO, Porter decided to explore more of the islands. Before departing, he left a carefully concealed letter for Downes in a bottle buried at the head of Lieutenant Cowan's grave and a duplicate at the foot of a finger-post that pointed out the grave. Porter left another note in a bottle suspended conspicuously at the finger-post for any British ships that might happen by, giving misleading information. It spoke of how desperate the *Essex*'s condition was. The crew was sick, it said, many had died; the frigate was in terrible condition, and the captured prizes had been either burned or given up to prisoners.

Although Porter was anxious for Downes to return, he did not intend to wait for him indefinitely. He planned to leave for the Marquesas Islands, come what may, no later than October 2. Porter was desperate for intelligence of British movements against him, and he was certain that Downes would provide it, but he thought they could just as well meet up in the Marquesas.

Porter planned to explore the Galapagos unencumbered by the slow-sailing *Greenwich*, *Seringapatam*, and *New Zealand*. He hid them in a small, obscure cove off Narborough Island while he went on a three-week cruise.

He got underway from James Bay on August 20, and by August 22 he had the prizes in place. He put Lieutenant Gamble, commander of the *Greenwich*, in overall charge of the group, with strict orders to keep a sharp eye out for enemy ships from the highest point on the island, and not to attract attention. Fires were prohibited, and guns were to be silent. Porter also ordered Gamble not, under any circumstances, to let the ships fall into British hands. He was to destroy them if he had to and escape to the island in small boats. Of course, this was to be done only if there was no alternative. Porter expected Gamble to fight any attempt to take the ships, and only flee if absolutely necessary.

With all this in place, Porter left his charges on August 24. Fighting sudden shifts of wind and rapid currents, he traveled down the sound between Banks Bay and Elizabeth Bay, then attempted to weather the southern head of Albemarle. But a strong westward current stymied him. He was still there fighting the current on August 29, when finally, the wind shifted to the southward, and he was able to get around and reach Charles Island on August 31, where he dropped anchor.

During the next two weeks, he explored the waters around Charles, Chatham, and Hood islands. On September 14, he was back off the southern tip of Albermarle, where he intended to patrol for a few days. Around midnight, he hove to thirty miles off the island. At daybreak men at the main masthead saw a strange sail to the south. Porter grabbed a telescope and flew up the ratlines to have a look. As he focused, there was no doubt that she was a British whaler engaged in cutting up and processing a whale. She was to windward and drifting toward the *Essex*. Porter let her drift, and as she came toward him he did all he could to give the *Essex* the appearance of a merchantman. He struck down the fore and main royal yards and housed the masts. All the gun ports were shut tight, and he hoisted whalemen's signals that he had obtained from the *New Zealander*. The ruse appeared to be working, until the stranger drew to within four miles and suddenly cut loose her whale carcass, put on sail, and made a desperate attempt to escape. Porter was right after her, and as soon as he was within gunshot range, he blasted away with eight cannon, forcing the whaler to strike her colors. She turned out to be the *Sir Andrew Hammond*, carrying twelve guns, although pierced for twenty. She had a crew of thirty-six, under Captain William Porter, who came aboard the *Essex* and swore that he was certain the *Essex* was a whaler until she was nearly upon him.

The *Sir Andrew Hammond* was loaded with fresh provisions and an abundance of strong Jamaica rum, which Porter distributed liberally to the *Essex*'s crew. The men had not had any since their July 4th celebration. They joyfully swilled all they were allowed. Porter had misjudged how potent the rum was, however, and before long, he had a ship full of drunks. He managed to keep matters under control, however, and passed it all off as harmless, except for one man who got completely out of control— James Rynard, a quartermaster who had been a clever troublemaker for some time.

Porter saw Rynard as a potential leader of a mutiny. When complaints were made, Rynard was habitually in the forefront. The *Essex* was filled with men whose terms of enlistment had expired, or were nearing that point, and Porter had given no evidence that he planned to return to America any time soon. It was conceivable that Rynard might use this to stir up discontent. Porter felt that he needed to make an example of him. To begin with, he confined Rynard in irons and then discharged him, having the purser make out his accounts. He then put him on the *Seringapatam* until they reached a place where he could be put on shore. Treating Rynard in this manner had the virtue of getting rid of a potential mutineer while giving pause to any like-minded hands.

Rynard did not go away so easily, however. He wrote a penitent letter to Porter begging him to overlook his past conduct and asking to be reinstated in the *Essex*. Porter refused, but Lieutenant Downes (after his return from Valparaiso) agreed to accept Rynard in the capacity of a seaman in *Essex Junior*, provided he behaved himself and gave no further cause for complaint. Rynard happily agreed, and the matter was settled.

PORTER EXPECTED DOWNES TO ARRIVE ANY DAY NOW; HE WAS anxious to hear the news he would bring. Lookouts were posted on the high ground north of the port on Narborough. A flagstaff was erected on the hill, and signals were arranged so that *Essex Junior* could see them from either Elizabeth Bay or Banks Bay. As anxious as Porter was to see Downes, however, he was still determined to stand out for the Marquesas no later than October 2.

While Porter waited, he brought the *New Zealander* and *Sir Andrew Hammond* into Port Rendezvous on Albermarle, where he could make repairs and otherwise put the ships in good order. Time passed slowly. Lookouts kept a sharp watch, and then, at noon on September 30 a ship appeared in Elizabeth Bay. A signal shot up to the top of the new flagpole. Porter felt certain that this was *Essex Junior*. His guess was soon confirmed, and by three in the afternoon she was anchored beside the *Essex*. When Downes came aboard with the prize masters and officers who had accompanied him to Valparaiso (including David Farragut), the crew gave a rousing cheer. Needless to say, Porter was overjoyed to see them, and more anxious than anyone to hear the news they brought.

Downes reported that he had sent the *Policy* and her load of sperm oil to the United States because of the low prices in Valparaiso. (Unfortunately, before *Policy* could reach America the British privateer *Loire* captured her.) So far as the *Montezuma*, *Hector*, and *Catharine* were concerned, Downes moored them in Valparaiso, waiting for either a better market or for Porter to decide where to send them. According to Downes, the Chileans had been as friendly and cooperative as they had been before, even though the country was embroiled in a deadly fight with Peru.

The rest of the news from Downes was far more exciting. President Madison had been reelected, and Downes confirmed what Porter had learned earlier, that the American navy, in the first seven months of the war, had indeed won a string of amazing victories (including the *Essex*'s over the *Alert*) in one-on-one battles with the British navy. As encouraging as this news was, Porter was even more interested in the intelligence provided by the American consul at Buenos Aires. The consul informed him that on July 5, 1813, the 36-gun British frigate *Phoebe* (Captain James Hillyar), accompanied by the 24-gun *Cherub* (Captain Thomas Tucker), the 26-gun *Racoon* (Captain William Black), and the 20-gun storeship *Isaac Todd*, had departed Rio de Janeiro with orders, it was rumored, to sail around Cape Horn and into the Pacific. Porter assumed they were coming after him, and nothing could have pleased him more.

In fact, in March 1813, the Admiralty, which had not yet heard of Porter's rampage in the Pacific, had sent Hillyar and the *Phoebe* on a secret mission to what is now Oregon. There they were to capture Astoria, John Jacob Astor's trading post at the mouth of the Columbia River.

Hillyar's orders were "to destroy, and if possible totally annihilate any settlements which the Americans may have formed on the Columbia River or on the neighboring Coasts." The Canadian Northwest Company, operating from their base in Montreal, wanted to eliminate Astor's settlement and set up their own base. The prime minister, Lord Liverpool, had much greater ambitions, however. He was laying the groundwork for a major expansion of British territory in the Pacific Northwest. He wanted to secure Britain's claims to this vast area, claims that were originally established by the exploratory voyages of Cook and Vancouver, and by the remarkable overland explorations of Alexander Mackenzie when he reached the Pacific in 1793, ten years before Lewis and Clark. The large storeship *Isaac Todd*, which belonged to the Northwest Company, accompanied the *Phoebe*. She was to carry on trade with China after Hillyar seized Astor's settlement.

Liverpool had chosen for the mission one of the Royal Navy's premier captains. James Hillyar was an experienced officer with a distinguished fighting record. Born in 1769, he had served in the Royal Navy since the age of ten. He had been on HMS *Chatham* when she captured a French man-of-war off Boston in 1781. In 1783, when he was only fourteen years old, he was promoted to lieutenant. He remained in the navy, serving in various capacities until Britain's wars with France began again in February 1793. He was then stationed in the Mediterranean for a long period, becoming a protégé of Britain's most famous seaman, Admiral Horatio Nelson, who had notably high standards for the officers he favored. Hillyar drew Nelson's attention during the latter's famous defeat of the French fleet in Aboukir Bay near Alexandria in 1798, and on September 3, 1800, when Hillyar led boats from the *Minotaur* and *Niger* in a daring cutting out of two Spanish corvettes in the well-defended harbor of Barcelona. At the time, thirty-one-year old Commander Hillyar was first officer aboard the 32-gun *Niger*. He drew Nelson's attention again in 1803, when he turned down an appointment that would have made him a post captain and guaranteed his future promotion to admiral—if he lived that long. Promotions from post captain to admiral were based strictly on seniority. Hillyar was the sole support of his mother and sisters, and the promotion would have meant an interruption in his pay for an uncertain period of time. After hearing what Hillyar did, Nelson, as a mark of his favor, invited him to dinner, and on January 20, 1804 he wrote to the First Lord of the Admiralty, John Jervis, the 1st Earl of St. Vincent, that "Captain Hillyar is most deserving of all your Lordship can do for him."

Appointed to the *Phoebe* in 1809, Hillyar assisted in the successful British invasion of the Indian Ocean island of Mauritius in December 1810. France had held Mauritius since 1715, calling it Île de France. Success, in fact, had marked Hillyar's entire career. He arrived in Rio on June 10, 1813, much annoyed at the slow sailing of the cumbersome *Isaac Todd*. Admiral Dixon already knew the *Phoebe* was coming. The merchant brig *John* had spoken the *Phoebe* during her passage to Rio and reported to Dixon that she was en route. Dixon welcomed this news since he was about to dispatch one of his scarce warships, the *Cherub*, to guard a convoy of merchantmen sailing to England.

At the last minute, Dixon held the *Cherub* back and waited for the arrival of the *Phoebe*. Embarrassed by Porter's unopposed attacks, Dixon thought he could now send the *Cherub* and the *Racoon* to accompany the *Phoebe* and hunt down the *Essex*. Until this point, he had been utterly frustrated at not being able to go after her—and particularly so since the Admiralty on February 12, 1813, had sent him a message, which he received on April 29, to send at least one warship into the eastern Pacific to protect British commerce, and particularly the whale fishery. At the time, Whitehall did not know about the rampaging *Essex*. Instead the Admiralty was focused on the general collapse of Spanish power in the eastern Pacific and the resultant threat to British ships, as well as the opportunity to expand British interests.

When their Lordships found out about the *Essex*, they did not understand why Dixon had not sent the *Cherub* and *Racoon* after the American frigate long before now. Dixon for his part felt that he did not have enough warships to both go after Porter and continue to protect Britain's burgeoning trade along the east coast of South America.

Needless to say, Dixon was very happy to see Hillyar and the *Phoebe*. He was not privy to Hillyar's secret orders, directing him to seize the American trading post at Astoria. Dixon would have to wait and see what Hillyar's orders were before making a final decision about sending him after the *Essex*. And Hillyar for his part would have to decide whether or not to show his orders to Dixon, since they were so sensitive. At length, he had to disclose them, because stopping the *Essex* had become such a high priority.

Dixon did not know Porter's exact whereabouts. He did know that Porter had been to Valparaiso and had left, and that he had seized at least one Peruvian vessel, but he did not know where Porter had gone after that. He was told that the *Essex* might have headed west with the intent of sailing into the Indian Ocean and joining other American warships like the *Constitution* and the *Hornet*. He was also told that the *Essex* might be sailing back around the Horn, touch at the mouth of the River Plate, and then go home. The Galapagos were also a possibility. Dixon thought it was possible, even likely, that Porter would continue in the eastern Pacific for a time, and be back in Valparaiso sooner or later for supplies and recreation. Neither Dixon nor any of his captains thought the *Essex* would make for the Marquesas Islands.

When Hillyar arrived in Rio on June 10, widespread discontent aboard the *Isaac Todd* was reported to Dixon. Hillyar had had to punish some of her crew during the voyage. Immediately on entering port, two mates had left her and seven seamen deserted, stealing one of her boats and disappearing during a dark night. Dixon found that the ship was badly stowed, had heavy masts and rigging, and far too many guns on her deck. Many crewmembers, including most of her officers, thought the *Isaac Todd* was not safe to sail in, especially around the Horn. None of this fazed Dixon; he got right to work fixing her, and had her repaired and ready to go in short order.

Nearly a month went by, however, before Hillyar and the *Phoebe* departed Rio on July 6, accompanied by the *Cherub*, *Racoon*, and *Isaac Todd*. Although aware of the importance of destroying the *Essex*, Hillyar intended to follow his secret orders and capture Astor's settlement on the Columbia River first. The passage around Cape Horn was predictably difficult. The struggling *Isaac Todd* failed to keep up and got separated from the others. Hillyar thought she had foundered. Nonetheless, after doubling the Horn, he waited a decent amount of time for her, and when she failed to appear, he moved on, setting a course north for the Columbia River. When he was at latitude 4° 33' south and longitude 82° 20' west, he received news from a passing British vessel that the *Essex* had captured the *Isaac Todd*, which, of course, was not true, but he decided at that point to depart from his orders and send the *Racoon* to the Columbia River alone, while he took the *Phoebe* and the *Cherub* and went after the *Essex*. He was supported in this decision by John McDonald, the representative of the Northwest Company on the *Phoebe*. Hillyar did not anticipate that it would take long to find the *Essex*. (The *Isaac Todd* in fact had not foundered, as Hillyar thought, or been captured. It had doubled the Horn and eventually made it all the way to the mouth of the Columbia River, where, after extensive repairs, she began trading Indian furs with China for the Northwest Company.)

Hillyar's expectations about finding the *Essex* quickly turned out to be unfounded. His search for her went on week after anxious week along the coasts of Chile and Peru with no result. Porter had seemingly vanished. Hillyar was frustrated, but no more so than Admiral Dixon and their Lordships at the Admiralty who were hearing alarming reports of all the prizes Porter was taking, and his devastating impact on the British whale fishery. Wherever the *Essex* was, however, Hillyar was confident that she would eventually return to Valparaiso.

Meanwhile, Captain Black sailed the *Racoon* to the Columbia River, arriving on November 30, 1813. There he found, to his great surprise, that the Northwest Company had already taken possession of Astoria, had renamed the fort Fort George, and now flew the British flag over the outpost. No Americans were there. As far as he could tell, their party was completely broken up; they had no settlement on the river or on the coast. He reported that while his provisions lasted, he would endeavor to find what remained of their party and destroy them.

The Pacific Northwest had been of great interest to Britain since the last part of the eighteenth century when Captain Cook had visited there. Spain had a strong interest as well, dating back to the sixteenth century, and so did Russia. The European rivalry nearly resulted in a war between Britain and Spain in 1789 over competing claims to Nootka Island and what became known as Vancouver Island. The United States had a strong interest as well. In May 1792 an American captain, Robert Gray, had been the first outsider to venture into the Columbia River in his ship *Columbia*. At the time, the famous British explorer George Vancouver was in the area, and he and Gray had met and talked about the difficulty of exploring the river. Vancouver decided that it was impossible because of the tricky entrance, but Gray attempted it and succeeded, thus establishing an American claim to the river, the country surrounding it, and, indeed, the entire Northwest. America's interest was heightened significantly after Jefferson sent Lewis and Clark on their famous expedition. Neither the European countries nor the United States thought the Native Americans who abounded in the area would be an obstacle to expansion.

John Jacob Astor, the fur trader, became interested in establishing a trading post at the mouth of the Columbia in 1811–1812. He wanted to trade the bountiful furs of the American Indians in China, and he succeeded in establishing his Pacific Fur Company at the mouth of the river, naming the settlement Astoria. It was this settlement that Captain William Black was sent to destroy. Before he arrived, however, the Pacific Fur Company heard that the British were coming to seize it and decided to sell to the Northwest Company before the Royal Navy arrived and simply took it.

PORTER LEFT THE GALAPAGOS ISLANDS, AS PLANNED, ON October 2, 1813. His performance during the time he was there and that of Lieutenant Downes and the rest of the *Essex* men had been spectacular. Their seamanship had been continuously tested. They had no reliable navigation charts, and the prevalence of fog, strong, tricky currents, and erratic winds made sailing at all times dangerous. That they survived with no major mishaps was a testament to their luck, certainly, but also to their extraordinary courage and skill.

Porter enumerated in his journal all he had accomplished:

> We have completely broken up [the British] whale fishery off the coast of Chile and Peru. . . . we have deprived the enemy of property to the amount of two and a half millions of dollars, and of the services of 360 seamen. . . . We have effectually prevented them from doing any injury to our own whale ships. . . . The expense of employing the frigate *Phoebe*, the sloops of war *Racoon* and *Cherub* [also had to be taken into account].

Porter estimated that the cost of sending three warships after the *Essex* was $250,000. He claimed that by adding the actual captures he made to the value of the American whale ships who were not captured because of his presence, to the cost of sending warships after the *Essex*, less the expenses of the *Essex* for a year ($80,000), his activities cost the British $5,170,000. Whether this fanciful figure bore any relation to reality was of little importance. What mattered was that, without a doubt, Porter had had a significant impact on Britain's whale fishery, as well as on America's. And he did it at a negligible cost to his government.

As much as Porter had accomplished, however, and as fine as his ship and crew had performed, they needed a secure place to refresh. The *Essex*, having been at sea almost continuously for eleven months, required a major overhaul, and her crew, although still in remarkably good health, needed time ashore. The Marquesas Islands were the perfect place for both.

PORTER LEFT THE GALAPAGOS IN THE NICK OF TIME. CAPTAIN Hillyar arrived there three weeks later, on October 23, with the *Phoebe* and the *Cherub*, and stayed for weeks. To begin with, he searched everywhere among the islands for the *Essex*. It took him several weeks, and when he could not find her, he remained for an additional time, hoping she would return. Porter had no intention of going back, however, and Hillyar remained frustrated and anxious. He knew how badly the Admiralty wanted the *Essex* destroyed. When he finally gave up and left the islands, he returned to the South American coast and began again a thorough search there, which consumed even more time. He must have wondered if he would ever find the *Essex*. Porter may have simply gone home, either sailing around Cape Horn or traveling west across the Pacific to the Indian Ocean and around the Cape of Good Hope. It's unlikely that Hillyar ever considered that Porter might be seeking him out as much as he was seeking the *Essex*. The idea would have struck Hillyar as preposterous.

Captain David Porter
(COURTESY OF THE NAVAL
ACADEMY MUSEUM)

The USS *Essex*
(COURTESY OF THE PEABODY ESSEX MUSEUM)

David Glasgow Farragut
at age thirty-eight
(Courtesy of the National
Portrait Gallery)

Lieutenant John Downes
(Courtesy of the Naval
Institute Press)

The burning of
the *Philadelphia*

Commodore William Bainbridge

Evelina Anderson Porter
and her daughter
(COURTESY OF THE NAVAL
INSTITUTE PRESS)

The *Essex* capturing the *Alert*
(COURTESY OF THE NAVAL INSTITUTE PRESS)

Thomas Truxtun
(COURTESY OF THE NAVAL
INSTITUTE PRESS)

Marine Lt. John M. Gamble,
painted later in life when he
was a Lieutenant Colonel
(COURTESY OF THE NAVAL
INSTITUTE PRESS)

Joel R. Poinsett
(COURTESY OF THE NAVAL
ACADEMY MUSEUM)

Commodore
Edward Preble
(COURTESY OF THE
NAVAL INSTITUTE PRESS)

John G. Cowell
(COURTESY OF THE MARBLEHEAD,
MASSACHUSETTS, HISTORICAL SOCIETY)

Captain Porter's drawing of the *Essex* and her prizes
(COURTESY OF THE NAVAL INSTITUTE PRESS)

Captain Porter's drawing
of a woman on Nuku Hiva
(COURTESY OF THE NAVAL
INSTITUTE PRESS)

Captain Porter's drawing
of Mouina, Chief Warrior
of the Taiohae
(COURTESY OF THE NAVAL
INSTITUTE PRESS)

Captain James Hillyar
(COURTESY OF THE NAVAL
INSTITUTE PRESS)

Capture of USS *Essex* by HMS *Phoebe* and HMS *Cherub*
(COURTESY OF THE PEABODY ESSEX MUSEUM)

chapter 15

THE MARQUESAS ISLANDS

"IN VALES OF EDEN"

WHEN PORTER STOOD OUT FROM THE GALAPAGOS WITH A light land breeze on the morning of October 2, he shaped a course due west, hoping to make some new discoveries. Although this route would take him north of the Marquesas, he thought it would add to his luster if he rediscovered some little-frequented islands the Spaniards had visited in the sixteenth century but had ignored (along with the rest of the world) since. Heavy weather, accompanied by a cross sea caused him to revise his plan, however, and he changed course, standing south until he reached latitude 9° south, and then sailed with the prevailing winds west along this parallel, a course that would take him to the Marquesas, 2,500 miles southwest of the Galapagos and 930 miles northeast of Tahiti.

With a powerful enemy squadron now searching for him, Porter's decision to go to the Marquesas made good sense. He knew the British were sure to search the Galapagos, and, of course, Valparaiso and the other Chilean ports. He would have to travel far off the beaten path to find a suitable harbor to fix the *Essex* and give her crew some relaxation. It was extremely unlikely that the British hunters would search for him in the Marquesas.

The list of repairs for the *Essex* was long. Barnacles had to be scraped from the hull; the copper bottom, which in places was coming off, had to be cleaned and repaired. The standing and running rigging needed overhauling, and the ship required a thorough smoking to kill the hundreds of rats that had infested her and had become an intolerable nuisance. The rats were destroying provisions, chewing through water casks, destroying cartridges in the magazine, and eating their way through just about every part of the ship, including clothing, flags, and sails. Smoking the ship was the only way to get rid of them, and it would require removing everything.

The men were as much in need of refreshment as the ship, and the Marquesas, as Porter imagined them, would be an ideal place for accomplishing that as well. Nothing engrossed sailors as much as thoughts of Polynesian women. When, in the late nineteenth century, Robert Louis Stevenson first contemplated making the long journey to the islands, his thoughts were of "undraped womanhood, bedecked with flowers, frisking in vales of Eden." The imaginations of the *Essex*'s crew—and of the captain—were undoubtedly filled with the same vision.

Visiting the Marquesas had its dangers, of course, and Porter was alive to them. The islands were beguiling. Once there, even for a short time, the men might refuse to leave. Mutiny was a real possibility, regardless of the goodwill that currently existed between Porter and his crew. "No part of the world exerts the same attractive power upon the visitor," Stevenson wrote. "The first experience can never be repeated. The first love, the first sunrise, the first South Sea island, are memories apart and touched a virgin sense."

Porter had a high appreciation of the power that Polynesian islands could exert from having studied the uprising aboard HMS *Bounty* in 1789—the Royal Navy's most famous mutiny. After five months on Tahiti, many of the *Bounty*'s tars had become so enamored with Polynesian life that getting them to leave proved impossible, especially when it meant returning to their hard lives in England. The ship's captain, Lieutenant William Bligh, had allowed them unusual liberties, and Tahiti had mesmerized them. Of course, there were other reasons for their reluctance to return home. Sailing under Bligh for months in a tiny ship was unappealing. His faults loomed large in their minds—sudden, unpredictable bursts of temper, flying into a rage over trivial or imagined offenses, and his repeated use of abusive, demeaning language to castigate officers and crew. The men who were the objects of his wrath, particularly officers, found his foul mouth intolerable.

It is likely that Bligh's abrasive, insensitive personality was not, in the end, the main cause of the mutiny, however. It was life on the islands that exerted the most powerful influence. Bligh was convinced that the men's attachment to the women and the easy life on Tahiti were the root causes of his problems. "I can only conjecture," he wrote in his notebook, "that they had ideally assured themselves of a more happy life among the Otaheitans [Tahitians] than they could possibly have in England, which joined to some female connections has most likely been the leading cause of the whole business."

Bligh was undoubtedly right about the source of his woes, but he remained unaware of his own failings. He was so out of touch with, and indeed indifferent to, the feelings of his men that when the *Bounty* left Tahiti on April 5, 1789, he did not have the slightest idea that a mutiny was brewing. He thought the mood aboard ship was buoyant. He fancied that the men were turning their thoughts to home, as he was. When in the early morning of April 28 Fletcher Christian and three others awakened Bligh in his cabin, pressed bayonets to his chest, and warned him not to make a sound, he was taken completely by surprise—utterly flabbergasted. The leaders of the rebellion, like Christian, were men he thought he had favored and promoted and were loyal to him. "I have been run down by my own dogs," he wrote to his beloved wife, Betsy.

The mutineers had firm control of the *Bounty*, and they were determined never to go back to England. Bligh had feared that the unusual length of time the crew spent on Tahiti might undermine discipline, but he could do nothing about it. He had planned a much shorter stay. But because of delays in leaving England, Bligh arrived in Tahiti at the end of October, which meant that his departure would have to be delayed until the eastern monsoon began in May.

Once the *Bounty* left Tahiti, Bligh's insults grated on the disgruntled tars. Twenty-three days after leaving, they could take it no more and seized the *Bounty*, setting Bligh adrift in the middle of the Pacific in a twenty-three-foot launch, crammed with nineteen men and provisions for only five days. At the time of the mutiny, the *Bounty*'s complement was forty-three, and at least twenty-two of them did not support those who seized the ship. But none of them resisted either. Eighteen went meekly into the launch, even though they faced almost certain death. Four others, who made it plain they were with Bligh, were forced to remain on the *Bounty*.

Bligh's chances of survival were practically nil, but incredible luck and seamen's skills of a high order saved him. On August 18, 1789, he reached Coupang (Kupang) on the island of Timor in the Dutch East Indies with all of his men but one, after an amazing forty-one-day voyage of 3,618 miles in an open, overcrowded boat. Eventually, he made his way back to England to tell his improbable tale.

Porter studied Bligh's account carefully, absorbing important lessons that would guide his conduct. To begin with, he was determined not to be taken by surprise, as Bligh had been. He intended to watch for any signs of trouble and planned to react swiftly. He had certain advantages that Bligh did not have. The tiny *Bounty* had no marines on board. She was not on a wartime mission. Bligh's orders had been to gather breadfruit plants and bring them to the Caribbean, where British planters hoped to grow them in abundance and feed them to their slaves. A contingent of marines, acting as the ship's police, might have prevented the mutiny. The *Essex*, on the other hand, had a full complement of marines, and Porter intended to use them.

Porter's plans to avoid a mutiny did not include restricting the men's sexual activity—or his own. He gave the crews wide latitude to satisfy their appetites. He knew this could create problems, but he thought they would be manageable if he did not remain in the Marquesas for too long, as Bligh had on Tahiti. Even so, no matter how long he stayed, mutiny remained a possibility, and Porter intended to be on his guard. Knowing what had happened to Bligh was a constant reminder to stay alert.

Acting in Porter's favor was the crew's knowledge that if they took the *Essex* they would be forfeiting substantial prize money. Even though seamen were notorious for living day to day, thinking only in the present, and not planning ahead, the prospect of losing all that money was sure to give the most disgruntled hands pause.

Another advantage that Porter had that Bligh did not was having observed early in his career how a skillful captain dealt with a mutinous crew.

When he was a midshipman in 1798–99 aboard the *Constellation* during the Quasi-War with France, he saw how Captain Thomas Truxtun reacted to unrest in a crew, and he never forgot it.

Mutiny was in the air in those days. There had been two spectacular mutinies in England during 1797—one at Spithead (the anchorage between Portsmouth and the Isle of Wight), from April 16 to May 15, and the other at the Nore (an important anchorage in the Thames Estuary) from May 12 to June 13.

The mutiny at Spithead involved the entire Channel Fleet, Britain's principal defense force. It was well organized and unusually peaceful. Little blood was shed. The men (actually, two representatives from each ship), in a notably respectful manner, requested an increase in pay (which had not risen since 1652); improved care and compensation for the wounded; better food; an increase in bounties; and the removal of certain unpopular officers. For weeks prior to the mutiny, the leading spokesmen for the tars had made requests for reform to the Admiralty, but they had been ignored. When the men finally took action, they got a response, although the Admiralty was still reluctant to negotiate, even though the requests were obviously reasonable. The situation might easily have gotten out of hand had it not been for Admiral Lord Richard Howe, who intervened at a critical moment, and, in a relatively short time, brought the Admiralty, Parliament, and the mutineers together on reform. The parties were able to reach agreement with minimal bloodshed, although, except for a modest pay increase, little of what was promised actually materialized. With matters apparently settled, the Channel Fleet sailed on May 17, and resumed its blockade off Brest, the major French naval base on the Atlantic. At that point Britain had been at war with France for nearly four and a half years.

Inspired by the apparent success at Spithead, another mutiny occurred on May 12 among warships assembled from various places (not a united fleet like the one at Spithead) at the Nore. The mutineers demanded far more than their more modest brethren at Spithead. The Admiralty, when it considered the additional demands, reacted negatively, and beginning on May 28 took action against the mutineers, starting with cutting off their supplies. Whatever cohesiveness the mutiny had started to crumble. Unlike the protesting tars at Spithead, these mutineers had little public support, and when they felt their cause being undermined, they seriously considered blockading the Thames, or sailing their ships to a neutral, or even a French port. Their talk was so reckless that patriotic seamen soon took over the ships, and the mutiny ended on June 13. Twenty-nine men were hanged, but some of the leaders escaped.

Not long afterward, another sensational mutiny took place in the Caribbean during the night and morning of September 21–22, 1797, aboard the 32-gun British frigate *Hermione*. Its unusual brutality drew the world's attention. There were other mutinies and near mutinies during this time, but this one stood out. The vicious action taken by the crew against a tyrannical skipper remained part of the consciousness of seafarers for years to come, and it directly touched David Porter.

To begin with, the *Hermione* had an infamously cruel captain, Hugh Pigot. His predecessor, Philip Wilkinson, had been just as cruel, if not more so. Thanks to Wilkinson's two-and-a-half-year tyranny, Pigot inherited a sullen crew, which he mindlessly alienated further. The son of an admiral, Pigot had been a privileged character from the start of his career and exhibited no self-control. Unpredictable, a raging sadist, he frequently used strong language—always to demean, never to praise. He was arbitrary in dealing with subordinates, and a heavy flogger in both the *Hermione* and his previous command, the 32-gun frigate *Success*. To make matters worse, he played favorites; certain men escaped his wrath for no apparent reason.

For nine months, Pigot's abusive behavior embittered the already estranged crew, but hands remained obedient until a particularly outrageous incident. At six o'clock on the evening of September 20, 1797, a sudden squall came up, and Pigot ordered the topsails reefed. Topmen were soon at their tasks in difficult conditions, as the masts gyrated in the storm. Pigot observed from below and was unhappy, as he often was, with the men's performance. He screamed at them through a speaking trumpet, and grew enraged. He was especially upset with the ten men working on the mizzen topsail yard. Suddenly, he shouted at them, "I'll flog the last man down," by which he meant that after work on the mizzen topsail was completed, the last man to reach the deck would receive at least twelve strokes from a cat-o'-nine-tails—a common, but brutal, practice that Pigot regularly employed. In their rush to reach the deck, three young, terrified sailors lost their balance and fell fifty feet screaming from the mizzen topsail yard to the deck. Two of them smashed directly into the quarterdeck, nearly at Pigot's feet. The other glanced off Pigot before hitting the hard-as-iron oak planking. Pigot looked at the lifeless, disfigured bodies with disgust and yelled, "Throw the lubbers overboard." The entire ship was shocked. Experienced topmen on the mainmast murmured loud enough for Pigot to hear, and he ordered all of them to be whipped the following day. But that order was never carried out. During the night of September 21, a savage mutiny began, and Pigot, nine officers, and a midshipman were killed and thrown overboard.

The mutineers then sailed the *Hermione* to the Spanish Main, entering the Spanish port of La Guairá just north of Caracas (in present-day Venezuela) and surrendered the frigate to Spain, which, at the time, was Britain's enemy.

The Admiralty went after the mutineers with a vengeance, never closing the books on the case, continuing the search for years. In time, thirty-three of the *Hermione* mutineers were caught and twenty-four hanged after trials. One was exiled to Australia. But over a hundred were never caught, including many of the ringleaders.

It was not clear who planned the mutiny. It appeared to be a spontaneous uprising spurred by recent events like the deaths of the three topmen and Pigot's sacrilegious abuse of their dead bodies. The Admiralty and its numerous supporters in Parliament insisted that Pigot's cruelty was an exception, not the rule, in the Royal Navy. But Pigot's superior, Admiral Hyde Parker, who knew about Pigot's methods, had never reprimanded him for them. Pigot's cruelty was tolerated, if not encouraged, by his superiors' passive acceptance of his methods.

The well-publicized events on the *Hermione* influenced how Captain Thomas Truxtun handled unrest in the 44-gun heavy frigate *Constellation*. Eighteen-year-old Midshipman David Porter watched him and learned an important lesson. The incident began on June 26, 1798, during the *Constellation*'s shakedown cruise. She had a crew of 313, nearly all of whom were inexperienced. Some were already disgruntled at what they thought was Captain Truxtun's excessive discipline.

As the big frigate plowed south along the American coast, Truxtun heard more than the usual grumbling. The complaints were loud enough that he sensed a mutiny might be in the works. Without hesitating, he mustered all hands and read the Articles of War pertaining to mutiny and the severe penalties, including death, that could be awarded to anyone caught trying to foment one. There was no doubt in anyone's mind that Truxtun meant what he said. To emphasize the point, he inflicted a dozen lashes on a marine private for insolence to a superior, including trying to take a pistol from his hands.

A few weeks later, the secretary of the navy informed Truxtun that a letter written by one of his crew to the Speaker of the House of Representatives indicated a spirit of mutiny might exist aboard the *Constellation*. Truxtun acted swiftly again, calling the crew together, and reading off the descriptions of men who had mutinied on the *Hermione*, in case any had gotten aboard his ship. This led to the confession of an able seaman, Hugh Williams, who admitted that he had been one of the mutineers. His admission did not surprise Truxtun, who had thought right along that Williams was a troublemaker. Truxtun got him off the ship quickly, sending him to Norfolk, where he was turned over to the British consul and certain harsh discipline, including possible execution.

Truxtun's fast action impressed Porter. If there was a mutiny being planned on the *Essex*, he was determined to know about it, and deal with it decisively. He intended to remain alert, as Truxtun had, and Bligh had not.

AS LIGHT TRADE WINDS SWEPT THE *ESSEX* WEST TOWARD THE Marquesas, no one but Porter was thinking about mutiny. Fantasies of luxuriating on enchanted Polynesian sands with accommodating women occupied the crew's thoughts. After all, this is what the captain had promised back on February 3, when he announced the ship's destination as the South Pacific. Porter added to the building excitement now by posting a notice on the bulletin board. It read, in part:

> We are bound to the western islands with two objects in view:
>   Firstly, that we may put the ship in a suitable condition to enable us to take advantage of the most favorable season for our return home:
>   Secondly, I am desirous that you should have some relaxation and amusement after being so long at sea, as from your late good conduct you deserve it.

Hands already had a good idea of where they were going, but when the official announcement was made, enthusiasm grew. Porter supposed that for the remainder of the passage, his men could think of nothing but "the beauties of the islands they were about visiting; every one imagined them Venus's and amply indulged themselves in fancied bliss, impatient of our arrival at that Cytherean Paradise where all their wishes were to be gratified." He did not mention his own fantasies, but one can only imagine they were powerful.

Sex was not the only thing on Porter's mind, however. He was alert to the unexpected surprises Captain Cook had encountered during his brief visit to the Marquesas in April 1774. Cook personally led the initial landing party, arriving with outstretched arms seeking friendship. He thought the people were the most beautiful he had ever seen. The men were strikingly handsome, tall, and vigorous, and often covered with elaborate tattoos from head to toe. But what was truly striking was the astonishingly beautiful women he saw. They were as fair as Europeans, and he thought they were without a doubt the best-looking people in the South Seas.

Unfortunately, Cook soon got caught up in a dispute with the natives over trading. Using iron nails as currency, he began trading for food, but some of his midshipmen soon began exchanging more valuable articles with the islanders, who then wanted more than nails. Trading became more difficult, and then impossible after April 8, when some of Cook's men inadvertently shot and killed a thief who had stolen an iron stanchion from the *Resolution*. The dead man's ten-year-old son was in the boat when the incident occurred. Cook tried to make amends, but when he went to the boy's hut the frightened youngster fled. Cook gave up and moved on to the more familiar ground of Tahiti, weighing anchor on April 13, leaving what had become an inhospitable place.

Porter knew the story well, and in the same notice of the *Essex*'s destination, he cautioned the crew:

> We are going among a people much addicted to thieving, treacherous in their proceedings, whose conduct is governed only by fear and reg- ulated by views to their interest. . . . We must treat them with kindness but never trust them. . . . Disputes are most likely to arise from traffic

with them: therefore to prevent these I shall appoint a vessel for the express purpose of trading, and shall select an officer and four men to conduct all exchanges; every other person is positively forbid to traffic with the natives, except through the persons so selected to conduct the trade.

The Marquesans were not used to dealing with strangers like Cook. When he arrived, no other European had visited the islands for two hundred years. The last had been disastrous for the natives. The Spanish explorer Álvaro de Mendaña de Neira had chanced upon the islands on July 21, 1595. He named them Las Islas Marquesas de Mendoza, in honor of the wife of his patron, Don García Hurtado de Mendoza, Marquis de Cañete, the Spanish viceroy of Peru.

The first island in the archipelago that Mendaña saw looked uninhabited. But suddenly, as if from nowhere, outrigger canoes shot out from shore, filled with dozens of people. In fact, the island was densely populated, containing, in all probability, tens of thousands of people. Mendaña was struck by their beauty, as every European and American would be when they first saw them.

Mendaña's chief pilot, Pedro Fernández de Quirós wrote that water, wood, and food were plentiful and the climate pleasant. The houses were made of timber and cane and roofed with leaves. The great canoes were carved from a single tree, and held thirty or forty paddlers. The native men were a bit too dark for his taste, but the women were graceful, light skinned, and strikingly beautiful. Quirós recorded with regret that the Spaniards were quick to use their weapons for real or imagined threats, or just because they could do so with impunity. During the few days Mendaña was on the islands, many natives were killed. Quirós estimated that by the time Mendaña and his men left, on August 5, two hundred natives had been slaughtered.

The Marquesas were spared more European visitors until April 7, 1774. On that day, Cook happened on them while sailing from Easter Island to Tahiti during his second voyage of discovery from 1772 to 1775. After Cook's brief visit, the islands remained isolated until the early 1790s, when explorers, merchants, and whalers put in for refreshment, relaxation, and trade, especially for wood. Outsiders never visited the Marquesas with the frequency they did Tahiti, however, and when Porter considered going there, the islands were still well off the beaten path.

AS THE *ESSEX* DROVE WEST, THE WEATHER AND SEA WERE remarkably pleasant. The air temperature grew hotter, but the heat did not produce squalls, thunder, lightning, or heavy rain, and the current continued to set in a westerly direction, but at a gradually decreasing rate. In spite of the idyllic conditions, Porter was impatient. He could hardly wait to get to the promised land, and to capture a British merchant ship, the *Mary Ann*, which he believed would be waiting there. Downes had seen her in Valparaiso and had heard her captain boasting about stopping in the Marquesas for wood, water, and food, and to refresh his crew before sailing to India. There was no mistaking what "refresh the crew" meant. A British ship sailing from England to India would normally go by way of the Cape of Good Hope, a much shorter route, rather than risk the hazards of Cape Horn. The prospect of Polynesian women evidently had a powerful hold on her captain. Since the *Mary Ann* was actually in Valparaiso and apparently did intend to go to India, Porter thought her captain might be adventurous enough to stop in the Marquesas, although Tahiti seemed a more likely place. In any event, Porter wanted to capture her if he could. The sluggish sailing of the prizes was slowing him down, however, and on October 6 he sent Downes and *Essex Junior* on ahead in case the *Mary Ann* arrived in the islands before the *Essex*.

Uniform good weather continued during the entire passage to Porter's enchanted oasis. On October 23, a lookout at the mainmast shouted, "Land ho! Land ho! Bearing southwest!" The *Essex* was in latitude 9° 6' south and longitude 138° 27' west by his chronometer, which he had begun to use again. Excitement was palpable, every man was full of anticipation, yearning to experience the delights of these magical islands. But what a disappointment this first one was. "A barren lump of rock inaccessible on all sides, destitute of verdure, and about three miles in circuit," was Porter's description.

Disgusted, he moved on, continuing west. The following morning he saw the island of Ua Huka, which, for reasons best known to himself, he called Adams Island. At first he thought it was barren and desolate, like the first one, and he was discouraged, but as the *Essex* drew closer, he saw something breathtaking—fertile valleys, pleasant streams, and clusters of homes, along with natives on verdant hills inviting them to land. Gorgeous trees loaded with luscious fruit were everywhere. Porter felt as if they were about to land in paradise.

Ua Huka was one of five inhabited islands in the Marquesan archipelago. When the *Essex* rounded the southeastern part of the island a canoe appeared suddenly with seven naked, elaborately tattooed men rowing and one sitting in the bow, ornamented with yellow feathers in his hair. They were cautious and would not come alongside until the *Essex* was close to shore. Porter did his best to entice them aboard, but they would not come. He noticed that the foreskin of their penises was drawn tightly back and tied with a strip of bark. It looked unnatural and painful.

Acting as interpreter for Porter was a Tahitian named Tamaha, one of the crew from a captured whaler. Tamaha partially understood the native dialect and was able to communicate somewhat. Porter tried to assure the islanders of his friendly intentions. Remembering that Cook had used iron nails to trade, he lowered pieces of iron, fish hooks, and knives in a bucket attached to a rope to demonstrate his goodwill. Whales' teeth were prized even more, and he offered them as well. In return the natives sent back fish and ornaments, continually using the word *taya*, or friend. They invited the crew to come ashore, where they said the *vahienas*, or women, would welcome them. Nothing could have pleased Porter more. After all, it's what he had come for, dreamed about for months, perhaps years. Now his dream was about to become a reality.

Soon, more canoes filled with men shot out from other coves. They appeared friendly, but would not come near the ship. Porter saw one displaying a white flag, and he reciprocated. At length, when the canoes continued to stay away from the *Essex*, Porter lowered two boats, filled them with armed men, and rowed toward shore. He was in the lead boat. Lieutenant McKnight was in command of the other one. Porter made straight for the beach, while McKnight stood offshore, ready in case of trouble. Heavy surf made the going slow.

As Porter approached the hard-packed sand, large numbers of Marquesans—all adult males, no females or children—crowded the area where he was about to land, observing his boat. War clubs, slings, and spears were in many hands. In a few moments the spears, slings, and clubs were put aside, however, and dozens of natives ran into the water, swimming out to meet Porter's boat before it touched the beach. They had plantains, breadfruit, coconuts, and other produce to exchange for the small iron objects. In spite of this friendly display, Porter sensed that these islanders were leery of visitors. They were also apparently unacquainted with the power of his guns.

He remained in the area for two hours and then rowed to leeward, entering a small cove, where he met fifty males and three young females. They were all naked, but highly ornamented, and the men were elaborately tattooed. Soon their old chief, Othauough, arrived. Porter offered presents, and the Marquesans offered the three women, two of whom looked to be no more than sixteen. Their beauty was dazzling. "The men repeatedly invited us to the shore and pointed to the women and the house near which they were standing," Porter wrote, "accompanying their invitation with gestures which we could not misunderstand; and the girls themselves showed no disinclination to grant every favor we might be disposed to ask."

In spite of the temptation, Porter would not land his boat. Seeing this, Othauough directed the young women to swim out to him, which they were evidently embarrassed to do. Some young men led them to the water, however, and they swam to Porter's boat. When they arrived, Porter took them aboard. He was enchanted by their soft, smooth, surprisingly light skin and their handsome, well-formed bodies. The women made it clear they wanted to go to the frigate, but Porter would not permit it, and when he was finished with them and tried to get them out of the boat one of them cried. Getting them to leave was difficult, but he persisted, and they departed.

This first encounter with what the *Essex* men most wanted from the Marquesans prompted Porter to reflect on the island's young women. They were "willing to gratify every wish," he wrote in his journal:

> Intercourse with strangers is not considered by them criminal, but on the contrary, attaches to them respect and consideration. . . . If there was any crime, the offence was ours, not theirs: they acted in compliance

with the customs of their ancestors; we departed from those principles of virtue and morality, which are so highly esteemed in civilization. . . . Everyone saw an opportunity to indulge himself, which had not for a long time presented itself; and all were determined to take advantage of it, at all hazards, even at the risk of violating every principle of subordination and obedience to orders. The women were inviting in their appearance, and practiced all the bewitching language of the eyes and features, which is so universally understood; and if an allowance can be made for a departure from prudential measures, it is when a handsome and sprightly young girl of sixteen, whose almost every charm exposed to view, invites to follow her. Such was the case with the party with me: they abandoned prudence and followed only the dictates of nature.

Porter anchored off Ua Huka for the night, where five of his prizes joined him, one at a time. Heavy rains and squalls poured down as they dropped their hooks. At daylight Porter was on the move, traveling with the prizes thirty miles west to Nuku Hiva, situated at 9° south latitude and 139° 60' west longitude. At 127 square miles in area, it was the largest and most important of the twelve islands in the archipelago. Porter called it Madison's Island, after his president.

chapter 16

NUKU HIVA

E ARLY IN THE MORNING ON OCTOBER 25, PORTER ENTERED
Taiohae Bay, Nuku Hiva's magnificent harbor in the center of its
picturesque southern coast. He was awestruck by its splendor, as everyone
was when they first saw it. "No description can do justice to its beauty,"
Herman Melville declared. Robert Louis Stevenson was just as enthralled
when he first viewed it. "The land heaved up in peaks and rising vales";
he wrote, "it fell in cliffs and buttresses; its color ran through fifty modu-
lations in a scale of pearl and rose and olive; and it was crowned above by
opalescent clouds. The suffusion of vague hues deceived the eye; the shad-
ows of clouds were confounded with the articulations of the mountains;
and the isle and its unsubstantiated canopy rose and shimmered before us
like a single mass."

Porter renamed Taiohae as Massachusetts Bay. Deep and spacious,
with good landing places, it appeared entirely safe for ships. Pleasant villages were situated near white-sand beaches, the houses interspersed
among coconut trees. The valleys looked highly cultivated and thickly
settled. At either side of the bay's narrow entrance were two rocks that
stuck up high out of the water just off shore, appearing to guard the entrance. Stevenson described them as "the gross statuary of nature." The

natives called them Mataou and Motou-Nui. Porter labeled them East Sentinel and West Sentinel.

After looking into the bay and experiencing winds that at one moment blew fresh and the next vanished, Porter dropped anchor at Taiohae's entrance, until he had a better idea of the bay's characteristics. Later, after he became better acquainted with them, he was completely won over. Despite the baffling winds, he found the bay perfectly suited to his needs, in fact, one of the finest harbors in the world, free from danger, with a depth of water from four to fourteen fathoms and a clear sandy bottom. *Essex Junior* joined him at the entrance to Taiohae later in the day, but she was alone; Downes had been unable to find the British merchantman *Mary Ann*.

Before Downes arrived, Porter had a surprise. The *Essex* was in the process of dropping anchor when a small boat approached with three odd-looking men on board. Porter sensed trouble. He thought they were deserters of one kind or another and up to no good. One of them was naked except for a loincloth and had a heavily tattooed body. He looked as if he had been so long on Nuku Hiva that he had become a native, although he clearly wasn't one. The other two men were deeply tanned, had scraggly hair running down their backs, and long unkempt beards. They attempted to approach and talk, but Porter would not let them near the ship, and they swung back toward the beach. While they did, canoes filled with natives put out from shore and paddled toward the frigate. The three strange men met them, conversed briefly, and then, to the surprise of Porter and his officers who were watching the whole scene with their spyglasses, the canoes turned around and accompanied the three disheveled strangers back to shore.

Porter was apprehensive about what was happening, and his uneasiness grew when he saw more natives gathering on the beach with clubs, slings, and spears. Nonetheless, he was determined to go ashore and establish communications, which he assumed the three unknown men had prejudiced. Prepared for a hostile reception, he ordered four boats lowered with armed sailors and marines, and set off for the beach. As Porter approached land, the natives abandoned the beach, but when his boat ran up on the hard sand, one of the suspect men boldly approached Lieutenant McKnight. When the man got closer, McKnight, to his amazement, recognized him.

The stranger turned out to be a former shipmate, John Minor Maury, from an old Virginia family, and what's more, he was a midshipman in the United States Navy.

Porter was astonished, but more than a little pleased. He was in desperate need of experienced officers, and Maury appeared to be a likely candidate. Porter listened intently as Maury explained how a run of bad luck had left him and his friend John Baker stranded on Nuku Hiva for months. Two years earlier Maury had left the United States on furlough from the navy with Lieutenant William Lewis in the merchant ship *Pennsylvania Packet* bound for Nuku Hiva to obtain a boatload of sandalwood. Lewis intended to trade the lumber in Canton (Guangzhou), China, where a shipload, which could be purchased from the Taiohae for ten whale's teeth, fetched a million dollars.

After several months' work, Lewis sailed to Canton with a full load, leaving Maury and four men to organize another shipload in anticipation of Lewis's return two months later. Unfortunately, the War of 1812 intervened, and British warships blockaded all American vessels trading at Canton. Lewis was trapped, and Maury stranded. He had no way of knowing why Lewis did not return. Only when the *Essex* arrived did he find out what had happened.

During Maury's first months on Nuku Hiva, he and his crew had had a rough time of it. Although the tribe on the beach (the Taiohae) was friendly, the enemies of the Taiohae, attacked from time to time, and three of Maury's men were eventually killed. To protect themselves, Maury and Baker used four coconut trees growing in close proximity to build a tree house, creating secure quarters accessible only by a retractable rope ladder.

When Maury saw the *Essex* sail into the bay, he thought his time of torment was over. Porter's initial rebuff surprised and disheartened him, but he was determined to try again. He and Baker retreated to their tree-house, and kept a sharp eye on the beach, looking for their chance. It came soon after Porter landed, when Maury, to his great relief, recognized McKnight and rushed out to identify himself.

Maury lost no time asking Porter if he could join him, and Porter quickly agreed, provided Lieutenant Lewis did not return before the *Essex* left. Maury was appointed first officer aboard *Essex Junior*, and he proved to be of enormous help, orienting Porter to the very different ways of the islanders, and helping him establish a relationship with Chief Gattanewa, the elder of the Taiohae (or Taeehs, as Porter called them).

The tattooed man who had accompanied Maury earlier turned out to be an Englishman named Wilson. He ingratiated himself with Porter, and since he spoke the language of the Marquesans like a native, Porter used him as an interpreter. Much of Porter's communication with the islanders went through Wilson. Porter thought of him as an inoffensive, honest, good-hearted fellow, well disposed to render every service in his power. Wilson's only failing was a strong attachment to rum.

WHEN PORTER FIRST ARRIVED ON THE BEACH WITH HIS MARINES and armed sailors, the natives had scattered, but they soon returned without their weapons, and he tried to impress on them the power of his arms. He had marines perform a short drill that included firing muskets across the water. The people seemed unafraid, however, apparently unaware of the power of the weapons. Porter also tried to demonstrate his peaceful intentions by distributing iron articles (knives, fish hooks, and the like), which were quickly grasped, but nothing was offered in return.

Afterward, Porter looked up at 2,835-foot-high Mount Muake, which surrounded and dominated the valley. Gathered near the summit were large groups of natives, and he inquired about them. They were Hapa'a, he was told, a neighboring tribe whom the Taiohae had been at war with for several weeks. Porter discovered that the small island was divided into numerous tribes, occupying separate valleys, with no central government. In fact, he had difficulty discerning any political hierarchy or authority anywhere. The valley he now found himself in, Tieuhoy, had six tribes that collectively called themselves Taiohae. Gattanewa was chief of four and had influence over two others, one of which had a chief and the other was a perfect democracy since they had chased away their chief. Their priest became something of a substitute. Porter thought rank in Taiohae society was hereditary, but he did not understand what rank meant to them. It was said that Gattanewa traced his ancestry back fourteen hundred years. He was influential among all the people of the island, and was related to many through intermarriage. Wealth in land, breadfruit, and coconut trees, it seemed, was the primary source of his status, although Porter could not be sure.

The Hapa'a (Happahs, Porter called them) were made up of six tribes. They inhabited a valley in the northwest portion of Massachusetts Bay and maintained complicated relations with the Taiohae that involved conflict at times. Other valleys were heavily populated by a variety of tribes—the Huchaheucha, the Maamatawhoas, and the Attatokahs, as well as the smaller tribes, the Nieekees and Shouemes. On the north side of the island in a long, deep, gorgeous valley called Vieehee were the handsome, well laid-out villages of the fierce, warlike Taipi, whom Melville would later make famous in his novel *Typee*. Porter estimated that together the tribes on the island could produce 19,200 warriors out of a population in excess of 60,000. And this was just on Nuhu Hiva. Taken together, the Marquesas probably had a population of more than 100,000.

WHEN IT CAME TIME TO REASSEMBLE THAT FIRST DAY AND RETURN to the ship, Porter found, not unexpectedly, that all the seamen had disappeared. They were off with women in houses or bushes accomplishing their purposes. The detachment of marines had remained with him, but he could see that this was not going to last long. Women were beckoning them with gestures that were universally understood, and soon the marines threw off all discipline, and gave way to temptation. Porter did not disapprove.

The women beguiled Porter as much as they did his men, and he had no wish to resist his natural tendencies. He was particularly interested in eighteen-year-old Piteenee, granddaughter of Taiohae chief Gattanewa. Porter considered her a great beauty. He alleged that it was his duty to court her. He claimed that his attentions were not reciprocated, however, that she bestowed her affections on other officers—not being content with just one. His story was undoubtedly a way to cover up the fact that she became his live-in girlfriend.

Eventually, Porter gathered his men that day and returned to the *Essex*. When word of the extraordinary entertainment that could be obtained on shore was reported to hands on the ship, they urged the captain to bring the frigate in and anchor it close to the land. He did not resist. The *Essex* was warped up and in a short time secured within half a mile of shore near a white-sand beach at the bottom of the bay. Women stood at the water's edge waving white cloaks enticing the men to come ashore. Soon, boats were sent to bring the women to the ship. In a short time the frigate was filled with females of all ages and descriptions, from sixty years to ten. Some were remarkable for their beauty, but others were not. The ship became a perfect Bedlam, from the time of their arrival until their departure the next morning.

Porter does not mention where David Farragut, who was twelve years old, and the other midshipmen and boys were during the orgy. Farragut reported in his journal that he and the others were sent on board *Essex Junior*, where Parson David Adams was temporarily staying, to keep them "out of the way of temptation as the women were allowed to go on board the *Essex* to the number of four hundred. Ogden, Feltus, and myself continued on board [with] the Parson for three or four days when we returned to the *Essex*."

PORTER WANTED NO PART IN THE POLITICS OR WARS ON NUKU Hiva. What he needed was peace so that he could get on with repairing the *Essex* and enjoying the women. He told the Taiohae (through Wilson) that he had come with the most friendly intentions, and wanted nothing from them but what he paid for. He urged the islanders to look on the Americans as brethren.

It was impossible to communicate this message to the Hapa'a, however. They continued to assume a threatening stance. Porter reluctantly concluded that in order to continue work on the ship (which had already begun) he would have to deal firmly with the Hapa'a. He sent a messenger (one of the Taiohae) to warn the Hapa'a. Despite the war between the two tribes, they communicated regularly. A message could pass without difficulty.

Porter urged the Hapa'a to cease hostilities with the Taiohae while he was on the island. If they did not, he promised to crush them. He added that if they had hogs or fruit to exchange he would welcome trade. He also promised them that as long as they remained peaceful he would protect them from the Taiohae. At the same time, he warned the Taiohae to put aside their weapons, so that he could tell them apart from the Hapa'a. He cautioned them not to appear in his presence with weapons. He pledged that if they followed his dictates, he would defend them against the Hapa'a, or any other tribe.

While the messenger to the Hapa'a was away, Porter looked at possible places to build a defensible encampment so that work on the *Essex* would not be interrupted. He picked a plain in back of the sandy beach where the frigate could be safely anchored in the crystal-clear water nearby. Situated on a prominent hill, the plain was shaded by breadfruit and other trees, and commanded the entire bay. It was also uninhabited. The high ground separated the inhabited parts of the valley from each other. It was something of a no man's land between tribes.

After selecting his strongpoint, Porter unbent the *Essex*'s sails and brought them ashore. He then landed numerous water casts, using them to form an enclosure. When that was completed, he hauled the ship closer to the beach and continued with the repairs. Crews from all the boats were put to work. The men labored hard every day until four in the afternoon. The rest of the day was given over to repose and amusement. One-fourth of the crew was allowed after that hour to go on shore, where they remained until daylight the next morning.

Gattanewa soon paid a visit, coming on board the *Essex* for a chat accompanied by John Maury. The seventy-year-old chief was practically naked, clothed only with a palm leaf about his head and a clout about his loins. He was in a semi-stupor from imbibing too much kava, the island's intoxicating drink made from a root. He impressed on Porter that the two of them were bound together in the most intimate way, that Gattanewa's mother was Porter's mother, and Gattanewa's wife and children were Porter's as well, including conjugal rights. Gattanewa evinced a great interest in whale's teeth, which the Taiohae valued more than any other article.

Gattanewa was more of a patriarch than a chief, an indulgent father among his children. He asked for help against the Hapa'a, but Porter told him that he wanted only peace between the two tribes. He soon changed his mind, however, when the following morning, while his men were hard at work, a large body of Hapa'a descended from the mountain and destroyed two hundred breadfruit trees—the mainstay of the islanders' diet. The Hapa'a then made threatening advances on the camp, moving at one point to within a half mile of the perimeter. Porter ordered everyone back to the *Essex* and fired a few guns that halted the Hapa'a. When Taiohae turned out to oppose them, they retreated.

Porter's messenger to the Hapa'a soon arrived back. He reported that the tribe had ignored his peace overture and threatened an attack in the near future. Porter remained on guard. He ordered that one-fourth of each ship's company be landed each evening with their arms to guard the camp. Despite being on guard duty, he allowed the men, in turns, to stroll about the valley and amuse themselves with the women who had assembled in great numbers outside the enclosure. They went off with any man who gave them a *tie tie*, or present. Porter was astonished to see with what indifference fathers, husbands, and brothers saw their daughters, wives, and sisters fly from one lover to another, as long as they were paid. Porter had a tent erected on shore for himself to better oversee operations and to better enjoy his woman.

While all this activity was going on, the Hapa'a continued to be a threat. Porter became convinced that the only way to have peace with them, and, indeed, with the Taiohae, was to defeat the Hapa'a warriors in battle, and he began to prepare. Additional measures were taken to guard the camp, and enlist the help of the Taiohae. Porter asked Gattanewa, who had been continuously pleading for help against his enemy, to have the tribe bring a cannon to the Taiohae fort on the mountain. It would be quite a task, since the cannon weighed some fifteen hundred pounds. Porter planned to begin his attack on the Hapa'a from there. The old chief was delighted.

On October 28, Gattanewa, accompanied by several warriors, reported to Porter that the six-pounder was in place. Porter was amazed. The terrain looked too difficult to move anything that heavy by hand, but Gattanewa had succeeded rather easily. His men had lifted the cannon up the steep hill slowly on two long poles. When Porter later ascended the mountain himself and saw how treacherous the ground was, he was even more impressed.

With the six-pounder in place, Porter organized a party of forty men and a larger number of Taiohae to climb the mountain, demonstrate his power, and teach the Hapa'a a lesson. Lieutenant Downes was to lead the attack. The Taiohae were to accompany him, carrying, not only their own spears, slings, and arrows, but the weapons of the sailors and marines as well. Downes did not think his men—most of whom were from *Essex Junior*—could climb the mountain with their guns.

Downes was ready to move on October 29, but at the very last minute, there was a hitch. As he was about to march out of the encampment, Gattanewa appeared unexpectedly and told Porter that one of his daughters, who was married to a Hapa'a chief, had come down from the mountain with a peace proposal. Gattanewa urged Porter to take it seriously, but Porter thought some treachery was afoot. He refused to change his mind, and went ahead with the raid, keeping Gattanewa in the compound as a hostage until it was over. The Taiohae were now in possession of valuable weapons that Porter wanted back, and he thought that having their chief in his hands would guarantee that the weapons entrusted to them would not be stolen. Gattanewa was apprehensive about his safety and wanted to know if Porter intended to kill him. Porter assured him that he was safe, but the old man continued to be nervous.

Lieutenant Downes now departed with his men, and began the hard ascent up the mountain. Porter followed his movements with a telescope. As Downes's column crawled slowly forward, the Hapa'a retreated, luring Downes higher and higher. Mouina, the chief warrior of the Taiohae, led the party, but the other Taiohae stayed behind Downes's column.

Mouina was barefoot; his entire body ornately tattooed. Each tribe on the island had their own distinctive tattoos. Acquiring them was extremely painful—begun at age eighteen and continuing until age thirty-five. Women wore tattoos only on their lips, arms, legs, and hands. Lips were done very thinly, and even on the inside to a slight degree. In addition to his striking tattoos, Mouina had the long tail feather of a huge tropic bird attached to the top of his forehead. A large whale's tooth hung from a necklace around his neck and smaller whale's teeth dangled from each ear.

Porter continued to follow Downes's movements as the Hapa'a retreated, taunting the Americans, urging them to follow. By eleven o'clock in the morning, Porter lost sight of the column, and reluctantly put down his glass. While waiting, he received a warning that a large party of Hapa'a was about to attack the camp. Porter had only ten men immediately available to defend it. The alarm sounded; everyone grabbed weapons and took up positions behind the water casks. But nothing happened. Porter sallied forth to examine the territory around the camp but found no Hapa'a warriors. When he returned, he noticed Hapa'a nearby, and used a six-pounder to scatter them.

By four o'clock that afternoon, Downes and all his men were back in camp, dead tired, but victorious. They had ascended the mountain with enormous difficulty. None of them were accustomed to climbing. When they reached the summit they found the retreating Hapa'a assembled in a fortress, ready to make a stand. Downes estimated their number to be three or four thousand. Before he could make a move, a stone suddenly struck him in the belly, knocking him down and halting the whole operation. He recovered quickly, however, and using the cannon that had been so laboriously hauled up the mountain, he blasted open the fort's huge gate. Downes and his men then rushed forward, but a shower of stones and spears rained down on them, slowing their advance. Miraculously, no one was killed, although several were wounded. When they reached the fort, they forced their way in, firing at anyone they met, killing five immediately, whereupon, resistance ceased and a general exodus commenced.

Downes had won an easy victory. The Taiohae collected the five dead bodies and brought them, together with all the booty they could find—drums, mats, calabashes, household utensils, hogs, coconuts, other fruit, and large quantities of a valuable plant they made cloth from—and proceeded back down the mountain to the camp.

When they arrived, Porter released Gattanewa. The old man was now totally convinced of Porter's strength. He was no longer ambivalent about his relations with the Americans. He assumed that the Hapa'a, having been given evidence of Porter's superiority, would establish peaceful relations as well.

Porter was interested in what the Taiohae were going to do with the five bodies they had taken from the fort and carried home. Wilson told him, and this was confirmed by Gattanewa, that sometimes they ate the bodies of their enemies after performing an elaborate ceremony—often days after the warriors were dead and their corpses putrid. Gattanewa said he had never eaten any, nor had anyone in the history of his family. Porter attended the ceremony the Taiohae performed with the bodies, but did not witness any cannibalism.

On November 1, peace talks began. Mowattaeeh, a chief of the Hapa'a and Gattanewa's son-in-law, came to the American camp with other tribe members carrying a white handkerchief, indicating his wish to talk. Porter welcomed them and agreed to peace, provided they would trade hogs and fruit, which he was in constant need of, for iron and other valuables. Gattanewa was pleased with the terms and so were the Hapa'a. Shortly, both tribes brought peace offerings to the encampment in great quantities—hogs, coconuts, bananas, breadfruit, sugarcane, and roots of kava.

Mowattaeeh noticed the tents in the enclosure and remarked how useless they were in keeping rain out. Porter agreed, as did Gattanewa. The Taiohae and the Hapa'a promised to build more suitable houses for the Americans, and a special residence for Opotee (the name they gave Porter). Soon, the other tribes on the island, with the exception of the Taipi and the most distant tribe, the Hatecaahcattwohos in the valley of Hannahow, made peace with the Americans. Porter thought the Taipi decision not to participate was based on confidence in their arms, and the Hatecaahcottwohos in the remoteness of their territory.

Supplies from the natives continued to be brought to the camp in great abundance. In exchange, Porter presented harpoons to the chiefs of each tribe, as well as iron articles for their communities. He was amazed at how harmoniously they divided the iron he gave them. And this was indicative of how they handled all their affairs, as far as he could tell. They appeared to live in the utmost harmony, like affectionate brethren of one family, and the authority of their chiefs appeared to be only that of fathers among children. Porter also noticed that there was no thievery—either inside or outside the encampment—by any of the Taiohae who came in daily contact with Porter's men.

On November 3, an amazing event occurred. Porter had drawn up a plan for housing his men, and was astonished when four thousand natives from different tribes unexpectedly assembled at the camp with building materials. Before night they had built a dwelling house for Porter and another for the officers, a sail loft, a coopers' shop, and a place for the sick, a bake house, a guardhouse, and a shed for the sentinel. The two houses were fifty feet long, connected to each other by a wall twelve feet long and four feet high. The construction was crescent shaped and followed the line laid out by the water casks, which were removed when the sturdy wooden and cane buildings were completed.

Porter was struck by the work ethic he witnessed. "Nothing can exceed the regularity with which these people carried on their work," he wrote in his journal, "without any chief to guide them, without confusion, and without much noise; they performed their labor with expedition and neatness; every man appeared to be master of his business, and every tribe appeared to strive which should complete their house with the most expedition and in the most perfect manner."

As the days went by, Porter and his men came to have a higher and higher regard for the island people. Porter wrote,

> They have been stigmatized by the name savages; it is a term wrongly applied; they rank high in the scale of human beings, whether we consider them morally or physically. We find them brave, generous, honest, and benevolent, acute, ingenious, and intelligent, and their beauty and regular proportions of their bodies, correspond with the perfections of their minds: they are far above the common stature of the human race, seldom less than five feet eleven inches, but most commonly six feet two or three inches, and every way proportioned: their faces are remarkably handsome.

Their sexual behavior was of great interest to Porter. He wrote:

> Go into their houses, you might there see instances of the strongest affection of wives for their husbands and husbands for their wives, parents for their daughters, and daughters for their parents; but at the camp they met as perfect strangers: all our men appeared to have a right to all their women; every woman was left at her own disposal, and everything pertaining to her person was considered as her own exclusive property. Virtue among them, in the light which we view it, was unknown, and they attached no shame to a proceeding which they not only considered as natural, but as an innocent and harmless amusement, by which no one was injured. Many parents considered themselves honored by the preference given to their daughters, and testified their pleasure by large presents of hogs and fruit. . . . With the young and timid virgins, no coercive measures were used by their parents to compel them to make any sacrifices, but endearing and soothing persuasions enforced by rewards, were frequently used to overcome their fears. . . .

The young girls of this island are the wives of all who can purchase their favors, and a handsome daughter is considered by her parents as a blessing which secures to them, for a time, wealth and abundance. After they have advanced in years and have had children, they form more permanent connections, and appear then as firmly attached to their husbands as the women of any other country. . . . But the girls, from twelve to eighteen years of age rove at will . . . unrestrained by shame or fear of consequences.

He convinced himself that venereal disease did not exist in the islands. Actually, venereal disease, brought originally by westerners, was well established in the Polynesian islands. Over thirty percent of the *Bounty*'s crew, for instance, had contracted syphilis and other ailments from their contact with Tahitian women. Nuku Hiva, although it did not have the traffic with westerners that Tahiti did, certainly had venereal infections spread widely among the population.

In spite of enjoying the remarkable sex provided by the islanders and allowing his men the same privilege, Porter, at the same time, regretted that the Marquesans had come in contact with white men at all. Viewing them as people in a state of nature, he was saddened that they could not remain so. And well he might have been, for contact with people like Cook and Porter ultimately brought disaster. In their wake came fatal diseases, heartless exploitation, and heartrending depopulation. In less than fifty years, the remarkable Polynesian society that Porter so admired would be completely gone.

BY THE TIME THE TAIOHAE AND HAPA'A HAD COMPLETED Porter's village, all the provisions, stores, and ammunition had been transferred from the *Essex* to the prizes in preparation for the hardest work on the ship. Killing the rats was the first order of business. Hatches were closed and fires lit in large tubs. Thick smoke soon filled every crevice, choking even the tiniest critter. When the hatches were opened, the crew found over fifteen hundred dead rats, many of them collected around the pots. Hands gathered up the gruesome little bodies and threw them overboard.

After the rats had been removed and the ship cleansed, an oven made of bricks from the prizes was fired up, and it made wholesome baked bread every day for the entire command. Carpenters then set to work caulking seams, while other repairs went ahead expeditiously. Coopers took the best water casks from the prizes and threw out nearly all of the *Essex*'s, which had become rotten. The main topmast was rotted as well, but easily replaced with a spare. The ship's bottom was cleansed of barnacles, grass, and moss. Marquesans helped—diving down and scrapping the bottom with the outer shell of coconuts. The coppering also needed fixing; it was much injured just below the water's surface. The ship was careened slightly so that these repairs could be made. The prizes provided the copper.

The boatswain stripped off all the frigate's rigging so that it could be overhauled and refitted. A rope walk was established at the compound, where a good supply of strong cordage was created from whale line and small pieces of rope. While the work went forward, Porter allowed the men sufficient time for amusement and relaxation, but, curiously, he observed, or thought he observed, that there was less frenzy about the women, who formerly had engrossed the whole free time of the crew. Perhaps he was talking more about himself than the others.

Whatever his feelings about the women, Porter was more than a little pleased with how well his plans were working out. The *Essex* and her prizes would soon be in excellent condition, and he could look forward to a glorious showdown with the British hunters who were still searching for him.

CHAPTER 17

ANNEXATION AND WAR

ITH REPAIRS GOING WELL AND RELATIONS WITH THE tribes friendly, Porter had achieved the great objects for which he had come to the Marquesas. Regrettably, this was not enough for him. He was fixated on crushing the Taipi as well, even though they had left him in peace. The other tribes in their separate valleys had been impressed enough with his strength to be on friendly terms. Only the twelve tribes of the Taipi remained unconquered. Why he felt the need to attack them was not immediately apparent. He claimed that if he did not, relations with the other tribes would be put in jeopardy, although it's hard to see why. Friendly relations with the other tribes were more than sufficient for his stated purposes. If he had come to the island just to repair his ships, enjoy the women, and relax, he would be gone soon. The other tribes would continue to be friendly for another few days. He had no need to crush the Taipi. Nonetheless, plans went ahead to enlist the Taiohae and Hapa'a in a war against the Taipi.

Before proceeding, Porter decided to build a much stronger fort. He first sought the approval of the tribes, and he found them enthusiastic about the idea; it seemed that whatever he proposed they went along with. According to Porter, Gattanewa was so taken with the idea that he asked

if his people could help build the fort, and, of course, his offer was gratefully accepted. Porter used old water casks filled with dirt to form a breast-
work, where he could mount sixteen guns. But not thinking he needed so
much firepower, he mounted only four, which he took from the prizes.
When Porter's strongpoint was completed on November 14, he named
it Fort Madison.

With the fortress finished, Porter's real reason for attacking the Taipi
became clear. He had decided to annex Nuku Hiva to the United States,
and he thought that he needed to subdue the Taipi, as he had the other
tribes, to form the peaceful, united island of his imagination. But he had
no mandate from Washington to conquer Nuku Hiva; it was an outlandish
idea. Nevertheless, he was determined to do it, convinced that it would
add to his luster. The great deeds he had already accomplished fueled his
ambition to rise to even greater heights.

He asked Gattanewa—who could not possibly have understood what
Porter meant—if his people would like to become citizens of the United
States. Gattanewa gave his enthusiastic approval. Porter insisted that Gattanewa and his people wanted to be more than friends and brothers with
him; they wanted to be countrymen. So for Porter, Fort Madison was a
symbol of America's power, tangible evidence that he had taken possession
of the island.

Defeating the Taipi, he believed, would solidify his authority over the
various tribes and make secure the annexation after he left. War plans
went ahead expeditiously. He decided to leave a small contingent of men
to guard Fort Madison, and as soon as the chiefs had their war canoes prepared, he intended to strike the Taipi by land and water.

Before attacking the Taipi, Porter presided over a formal ceremony on
Nuku Hiva that was, to say the least, bizarre, embarrassing, and an outrageous display of arrogance. Porter's critical faculties seemed to have
deserted him as he raised the American flag above Fort Madison on November 19 and formally took possession of Nuku Hiva in the name of the
United States, even though he had no authorization from his government
to do so. Porter claimed that the islanders wholeheartedly approved giving
up their sovereignty, even though they obviously were under the threat of
his guns, and, in any event, had no conception of what he was talking about.

In a staggering display of his ability to hold two opposing beliefs—he formally took possession of the island, firing a seventeen-gun salute, which the shipping in the harbor returned. He then changed the name Nuku Hiva to Madison's Island and read a formal declaration, before signing it.

"Our right to this island," he solemnly declared, is "founded on priority of discovery, conquest, and possession." He claimed that the "natives . . . requested to be admitted into the great American family," which, of course, they had not. He went on to emphasize the importance of constructing a fort capable of mounting sixteen guns, and at the same time formally named his citadel, Fort Madison, and the adjacent harbor, Massachusetts Bay. He claimed to offer the inhabitants "friendly protection."

"The object of this ceremony," he explained, "had been previously and was again explained to the natives. They were all much pleased at being Melleekees, as they called themselves, and wanted to know if their new chief was as great a man as Gattanewa."

Now that the island's inhabitants were subjects of the United States, Porter expected them to be enemies of Great Britain until peace was made between the two countries, even though they had no idea what he meant. He claimed that most of the tribes of the island "have requested to be taken under the protection of our flag, and all have been willing to purchase, on any terms, a friendship which promises to them so many advantages"— excepting, of course, the freedom to pursue their own way of life.

"Influenced by considerations of humanity," he continued, "[this conquest] promises speedy civilization to a race of men who enjoy every mental and bodily endowment which nature can bestow, and which requires only art to perfect, [and] secures to my country a fruitful and populous island, possessing every advantage of security and supplies for vessels, and which, of all others, is the most happily situated, as respects climate and local position."

At the same time that he was taking formal possession of Nuku Hiva, proclaiming the great benefits to the islanders of losing their freedom, Porter wrote in his journal about how devastating contact with Europeans had been to Polynesians. He thought, or rather hoped, that since Nuku Hiva was relatively unspoiled, her people would escape the same fate. How exactly he does not say, and, of course, they did not.

On November 24, Porter made an excursion for a few days to a bay about eight miles from Massachusetts Bay and received a warm welcome from the people, which he took to be their approval of his annexation.

On November 28, Porter set about the final bit of business he thought he had to do before leaving Nuku Hiva for Chile—crushing the Taipi. At three o'clock in the morning he set out in *Essex Junior* to attack, accompanied by five boats filled with armed men, and ten war canoes loaded with warriors. Gattanewa and two other ambassadors were aboard the *Essex Junior* to act as negotiators in the event the Taipi chose to come to terms without a fight. At sunrise Porter was at the Taipi landing place, where ten additional war canoes filled with Hapa'a joined him.

As *Essex Junior* anchored just offshore, large numbers of Taihae and Hapa'a warriors appeared on the mountaintops above the valley of the Taipi with spears, clubs, and slings. Porter thought they numbered in the thousands. His men numbered only thirty-five.

When Porter's force landed on the beach, no Taipi were in sight. They soon made an appearance, however, pelting Porter's party with stones. Porter responded by sending an ambassador with a white flag to offer the Taipi the same terms of submission as those agreed to by the other tribes. The Taipi refused to talk with him or to recognize his white flag. They sent the ambassador back in fear of his life.

Porter now advanced on them with twenty-eight men. He failed to see the Taipi hiding in the bushes ahead. Suddenly, his men heard slings snapping and spears quivering. Miraculously, the shower of missiles that then hit them did not kill anyone. Porter kept advancing, but the Taipi were so carefully hidden he still could not see them. He was now a mile from the water's edge.

The Taiohae and Hapa'a stood by and watched as Porter continued moving forward cautiously. It was abundantly clear that he had not come with enough force and needed to go back and regroup, but he did not want to lose face with the Taiohae and Hapa'a. As if to underscore the danger he was in, a well-aimed stone struck Lieutenant Downes's left leg and cracked it. Porter sent Mr. Shaw, the *Essex*'s purser, with four men to take Downes back to the beach. That left Porter with only twenty-four men. Most, but not all, of his native allies remained spectators. The Taiohae warrior chief Mouina was in front leading, but nearly all the others were either in the rear or watching. Even Mouina was beginning to have doubts about the wisdom of moving forward.

Porter continued to advance, however, and soon came to a river, which he crossed with difficulty, losing all the Taiohae who had stuck with him, except for Mouina and three others. At length, Porter came to a Taipi village, where a seven-foot wall blocked his path. His situation was looking bleaker and bleaker. To make matters worse, he was running out of ammunition. He was forced to send Lieutenant Gamble and four men back to the beach, where they were to take a boat out to *Essex Junior* and obtain more. Porter's party was now reduced to nineteen. While waiting for Gamble to return, Porter carried on a desultory fire at unseen Taipi warriors who were continually throwing stones and spears at him. He was now in danger of losing his entire party and his life, as the Taipi, seeing his hesitation, became bolder. Porter decided he had to get back to the beach, but his retreat could not appear precipitate, otherwise, he feared an attack from the Hapa'a.

When he began to withdraw, the Taipi rushed him, screaming insults, but two of their leaders were instantly shot dead. When others came to drag away the bodies, Porter's men wounded them. This checked them momentarily, allowing Porter to withdraw to the river, with the Taipi following cautiously at a distance. He managed to cross the stream, and to his great relief, the Taipi did not follow, allowing him to get back to the beach with all his men.

Without pausing, he began rowing out to *Essex Junior*, but the Taipi suddenly appeared and attacked the Taiohae who were still on the beach, forcing Porter to reverse course and row back. Fortunately, when the Taipi saw him returning, they ran. He then gathered all his forces and rowed back to Massachusetts Bay. *Essex Junior* followed when the wind served.

Deeply chagrined, Porter believed that his annexation was in jeopardy if he did not return right away with a much larger force and defeat the Taipi. He feared that the whole island would turn against him, including the Taiohae. The skirmish on the beach had provided little intelligence on the real strength of the Taipi. He did not know what was facing him, but he thought that a strike force of two hundred men would be enough to humble them.

He prepared in secret, not wanting help from the natives, since they had proven useless on the last expedition. He originally planned to go back in boats, but decided to travel by land this time, since the boats had been too leaky. He left after dark and reached the summit of the mountain in three hours. He imposed the utmost secrecy, hoping to catch the Taipi by surprise.

By midnight Porter could hear drums beating in the Taipi valley and loud singing. They were celebrating their victory. Since the path ahead was particularly difficult (necessitating a descent down an almost perpendicular cliff) he decided to rest on the mountaintop and wait for daylight. He had just dozed off when rain began to fall heavily. He feared that his muskets and ammunition would get so wet they would be useless. The rain continued coming down in torrents, followed by a cold piercing wind. "Never in the course of my life," he wrote, "did I spend a more anxious or disagreeable night."

At daylight, Porter went about examining the men, their muskets, and the ammunition. He found the guns in remarkably good shape, but half the ammunition was too wet to use. He also spent time looking down the mountainside they would have to travel to reach the Taipi valley. He was astonished at how steep it was and how difficult just descending was going to be. He concluded that it would be foolhardy to try right then and decided to retreat to the Hapa'a valley on the other side of the mountain and wait for better conditions. Before leaving the mountaintop he fired off some guns to demonstrate to the Hapa'a that his force was still potent. "The Hapa'a would not have hesitated in making an attack on us," he wrote.

Porter's party spent the night in the Hapa'a village. People abandoned their houses so that the Americans could have comfortable quarters, but provided no food—no hogs or fruit. In fact, the Hapa'a, who were supposed to be overjoyed at becoming Americans, appeared more and more hostile. Before matters got out of hand, Porter confronted the chiefs, who backed off, and suddenly hogs and fruit appeared in abundance, and everyone, including the women, were friendlier. Nonetheless, Porter remained on guard, posting sentries and having the men sleep with their arms.

The next morning, Porter ascended the mountain again and gazed at the Taipi valley spread out at the bottom of the steep precipice. Nine miles long and three or four wide, surrounded by steep, verdant hills, it looked like a paradise to him. Water cascading from one of the hillsides ran through the valley, forming a delightful stream that flowed to the beach, where Porter had landed a few days before. "Villages were scattered here and there," he recalled, "the breadfruit and coconut trees flourished luxuriantly and in abundance; plantations laid out in good order, enclosed with stone walls, were in a high state of cultivation, and everything bespoke industry, abundance, and happiness—never in my life did I witness such a delightful scene, or experience more repugnancy than I now felt for the necessity which compelled me to punish a happy and heroic people."

The compulsion he felt was peculiar to him, of course. Nothing compelled him to attack these innocent people other than his determination to annex the island. No military purpose was served. Fighting them had nothing whatever to do with refitting and supplying his ships. Slaughtering these people had only one object—his own aggrandizement as the conqueror of Nuku Hiva.

Porter claimed otherwise. He insisted that slaughtering the Taipi was a military necessity because "[we were] a handful of men residing among numerous warlike tribes, liable every moment to be attacked by them and cut off; our only hopes of safety was in convincing them of our great superiority over them, and . . . we must either attack them or be attacked." This was a far cry from his claim that the tribes of Nuku Hiva yearned to become part of America. The Taipi had it in their power to keep him at bay, he insisted; all they had to do was submit. When they refused to give up their liberty, he struck. "The evils they experienced they brought on themselves," he insisted, "and the blood of their relations and friends must be on their own heads."

After briefly resting his party at the summit of the mountain, Porter began threading his way down the tricky mountainside toward the Taipi villages. "Not a whisper was heard from one end of the line to the other," he wrote; "our guides marched in front, and we followed in silence up and down the steep sides of rocks and mountains, through rivulets, thickets, and reed breaks, and by the sides of precipices which sometimes caused us to shutter." Taipi drums were beating and war conchs sounding, as Mouina guided Porter's column toward the Taipi valley. At the bottom of the mountain the Taipi, hidden behind bushes and stone walls, threw stones and then withdrew. None of Porter's men were injured. The column moved on, crossed a river and pushed the Taipi back, killing and wounding a number of warriors.

It was clear that Porter would have to fight every inch of the way through the valley. As he moved slowly forward, the Taipi continued to resist and then draw back. All the while, Porter was consuming ammunition, and he feared running out. With his ammunition gone, the Taipi, with their superiority of numbers, could easily overwhelm him.

As he marched through the valley, Porter set fire to the villages he took and pushed on to the main village, which he thought was splendid. "The beauty and regularity of this place was such, as to strike every spectator with astonishment. . . . their . . . public square was far superior to any other we had met with." Nonetheless, he put it to the torch. The proud Taipi continued to resist to the end; they "fought us to the last," Porter reported with admiration. His force was just too much for them.

Once the work of savaging the Taipi was completed, Porter began the long trek back up the mountain. When he was halfway there, in a spot overlooking the smoking valley, Gattanewa appeared unexpectedly. "The old man's heart was full," Porter reported, "he could not speak, he placed both my hands on his head, rested his forehead on my knees, and after a short pause, raising himself, placed his hands on my breast, exclaimed, Gattanewa!" And then he called Porter Opotee, to remind him that they had exchanged names.

When the column reached the summit of the mountain Porter stopped to survey the damage below. What had been a scene of surpassing beauty and abundance was now misery and desolation. The opposite hills were covered with unhappy fugitives.

Porter moved on to the valley of the Hapa'a, where he spent the night. The next day he returned to the fort on Massachusetts Bay. He had been absent three nights and two days. He sent a message to the Taipi to make peace, which they were now anxious to do. In exchange for peace they agreed to give Porter whatever presents he wanted in hogs and fruit. Eventually four hundred hogs appeared.

With the defeat of the Taipi, Porter believed he had completed his business on Nuku Hiva. He fancied that in seven weeks—even though he could not understand the language of the people or even their customs—

he had completely transformed their ancient society. He believed that he had created a lasting peace among all the tribes, something they had not experienced in their entire history. He pointed out that they could now travel out of their valley to every part of Nuku Hiva in safety. Many old men told him they had never been outside their own valley.

Porter warned them to keep the peace. He promised to leave and return within a year and expected to find the peace he had brought to continue. If not, he assured them his punishment would be swift and severe. "They all gave me the strongest assurances of a disposition to remain on good terms, not only with me and my people, but with one another," he wrote. His capacity for self-delusion was breathtaking.

MUTINY

WHILE PORTER WAS DEALING WITH HIS OTHER PROBLEMS, the possibility of a mutiny was ever present. During the first two weeks of November 1813, a number of British prisoners organized an escape, as it was their duty to do. They planned to seize *Essex Junior* and slip away during the night of November 14, the very day, as it turned out, that Fort Madison was completed. Porter discovered their plan days before, and he was furious. He had been deluding himself that his liberal treatment of the prisoners, especially when compared to Britain's rough handling of American seamen, had brought them over to his side, and they would never attempt an escape. "They had all been permitted to go on shore and on board the different vessels whenever they wished," he wrote bitterly, "on a promise of conducting themselves with propriety, and not absenting themselves so that they could not be found; they were, in fact, admitted on parole, and all restrictions removed."

A seaman named Lawson, formerly a mate on the *Sir Andrew Hammond*, led them. He planned to get the crew of *Essex Junior* drunk on rum mixed with the drug laudanum. Prisoners on the beach were to seize canoes, row out to the ship, board, take her, and put to sea. If complete surprise was achieved, no other ship would be ready to pursue them, and the *Essex*, with no powder aboard, would be helpless to stop them.

The plan was workable, but Porter knew about it almost from the moment it was hatched. Two sentinels, who were guarding the rum, were helping Lawson, and Porter had discovered their activities. Disturbed by what he found, he punished the sentinels severely. He then put the crews and marines on high alert, and warned the marines that if the next neglect of duty merited death, he would not hesitate to shoot the offender. They knew he meant it.

The following evening, Porter discovered just such a neglect and reacted angrily. He was in bed (but not asleep) at the time, and did not hear the marine in the bake house call out "all's well" as he should have. Porter asked why, and the sergeant of the guard, upon investigating, found the marine fast asleep with his musket beside him. Without disturbing the hapless fellow, the sergeant reported back to Porter who grabbed a pistol. With the sergeant and a guard, he strode to the bake house, gripping his weapon. When he arrived, the unfortunate marine was still asleep with the musket by his side. Porter had him seized up and shot him in the fleshy part of the thigh.

Despite the fracas, Lawson still planned to escape on Sunday night, November 14. But as luck would have it, on the afternoon of the previous day, lookouts had seen an unidentified ship at the mouth of the harbor, and Porter sent Lieutenant Downes in *Essex Junior* to see who she was. Before Downes left, Porter took Lawson by surprise, seized him and the other conspirators, put them in chains, and set them to work building a wall around Fort Madison.

On the afternoon of November 15, Downes arrived back and reported that the strange ship was the *Albatross*, an American trader in search of sandalwood for China. She had on board beads and other trinkets to trade with the Marquesans. The *Albatross* proceeded into port, anchored, and then purchased a shipload of the precious wood for practically nothing. When her captain, William Smith, had acquired all his ship could hold, he sold his leftover trinkets at exorbitant prices to Porter's men for cash.

LAWSON AND HIS MATES WERE A SMALL PROBLEM COMPARED TO another, much larger one. The terms of enlistment of many *Essex* men had expired or were about to. Of all the difficulties that Porter faced, this one caused him the most uneasiness. He knew the issue would be raised one way or another, and it had the potential to ruin his mission. He was not taken completely by surprise when trouble arose shortly before the *Albatross* arrived. For example, when the officer of the watch threatened Robert Dunn, a quartermaster, with punishment for neglect of duty, Dunn replied that the time for which he enlisted had expired, and if he was punished he would never do duty in the ship.

Since most of the crew were in similar circumstances, Porter knew he had to deal with Dunn decisively. Immediately after receiving the report on Dunn's insolence, Porter summoned all hands, including Dunn, to the quarterdeck. When all had assembled, Porter ordered Dunn to strip to the waist, and warned him that he would be severely punished, after which Porter promised to banish him from the ship and send him on shore permanently, since he would have his discharge. He then gave an impassioned speech to the crew laying out the evils that would befall everyone if they followed Dunn's example. He acknowledged that many of them were in similar circumstances and could have their discharge on the spot. But if they enlisted again for the cruise, he would give them the usual advance, and on a suitable occasion, three days liberty on shore.

Before Porter could proceed with Dunn's punishment, several officers, petty officers, and seamen intervened. They pleaded that Dunn had been drunk when he made his obnoxious statement and should be pardoned. Dunn swore that he had indeed been drunk and had not meant what he said. He begged to be reenlisted. Porter accepted his excuse and pardoned him. Every man from all the ships then reenlisted, except for one. Porter put him aboard the *New Zealander*, which he intended to send separately to the United States.

Dealing with the problem of expiring enlistments did not remove all the incentives for mutiny, however, particularly as December 13, the date for departure, neared. Porter may have been ready to leave, but many of the men were not. Separating them from what many considered paradise would not be easy. After experiencing the delightful freedom of Nuku Hiva, going back to living in a small space cheek by jowl with as many men as were crowded into the *Essex* was an uninviting prospect. There was such general reluctance to leave that Porter believed it was possible, even likely, that a mutiny would occur. The most dangerous time, he thought, would be just before, or immediately after pulling anchor, and he was on alert, ready to stop any uprising before it got started.

He began preparing the crews for departure by stopping the liberty that hands had been enjoying. They were ordered to remain on board ship and work long hours. The change immediately brought grumbling. The men saw no reason for Porter to push them so hard. And they missed their women. Making matters more difficult, girls lined the beach every day, from morning till night, trying to get the captain to release the men. The young women cried for their lovers, and made every gesture imaginable to entice hands back to shore. While the men watched, their anger grew. They complained of being slaves.

Unable to resist temptation, three lovesick sailors quietly swam to shore one night. Their absence was soon discovered, however, and Porter immediately dispatched marines who caught them on the beach and brought them back. Without hesitating, he put them in irons, and the next morning had them severely whipped at the gangway. He then put them to work in chains with the prisoners. The severity of the punishment caused more murmurings. Porter heard them but felt his decisive action had prevented more serious problems.

He was wrong, however. As December 13 drew closer, discontent grew. Porter realized his error and remained on high alert. On December 9, the crisis he was expecting suddenly erupted. Robert White, a sailor aboard the frigate, was heard to say that the men would refuse to weigh anchor, or if compelled to, would seize the ship within three days. White was a member of the *Essex*'s original crew. Given the level of grumbling on the ship, Porter thought White's threat was not an idle boast, and he reacted quickly, mustering all hands on the larboard side of the upper deck. Shaking with rage, he grabbed a cutlass and placed it ominously on top of the capstan. He then told the assembled crew that everyone's liberty had been revoked, not because they had done anything wrong, but in order to hasten the *Essex*'s departure. This was an obvious lie. Porter had confined the men aboard to prevent happening to the *Essex* what had happened to the *Bounty*. He warned that he would not tolerate anyone going ashore without leave, and should they try to take the ship he would put a match to the magazine, without hesitating, and blow them all to eternity. Knowing Porter, the crew must have taken him seriously. He was determined not to become another Bligh—no matter what.

Porter then declared, "All of you who are in favor of weighing the anchor when I give the order, pass over to the starboard side; you who are of a different determination, stay on the larboard side." Immediately, the entire crew passed over to the starboard side. He then singled out Robert White, who was trembling. Porter's tone was severe as he said to White, "How is this? Did you tell them on board the *Essex Junior* that the crew of this ship would refuse to weigh anchor?"

"No, sir."

"You lie, you scoundrel! Where is the list of the men who visited the *Essex Junior* Sunday?"

Porter made them all step forward and questioned each in turn. "Did you hear of this thing on board of the *Essex Junior*?"

"Yes, sir," replied every man.

Porter then turned to White, "Run you scoundrel for your life."

Terrified, White ran to the starboard gangway and jumped. Farragut, who witnessed the whole dramatic scene, said he thought the captain was mad enough to kill White with his cutlass if he had not jumped.

Luckily for White, a passing canoe picked him up, and he disappeared into the island. Porter let him go. That ended the matter, as far as Porter was concerned, and the men went back to work—"cheerfully," he reported, although that's hard to believe.

PORTER THOUGHT THAT HE HAD TO GUARD AGAINST MORE THAN a mutiny during this time; he thought that he had to secure his new American colony after the *Essex* and *Essex Junior* left. He gave the assignment to Marine Lieutenant John Gamble. Gamble was to remain at Fort Madison with two officers, eighteen enlisted men, and six prisoners to maintain the colony. The two officers were Midshipman William W. Feltus, who had been a member of the *Essex* crew from the start of her voyage, and Acting Midshipman Benjamin Clapp, who had been an officer aboard the *Albatross* and had transferred to the *Essex*. Porter took him on because of his desperate need for officers. Porter left Gamble with three prizes—the

Seringapatam, the *Sir Andrew Hammond*, and the *Greenwich*—and moored them near Fort Madison for safety. He also supplied Gamble provisions for nine months.

Porter instructed Gamble to remain friendly with the natives, and to show them how to produce certain garden vegetables from seeds. Gamble was expected to stay on the island until the *Essex* returned, or until he received further orders, or until five and a half months had elapsed. In the latter case, he was to man and provision two ships, burn the other, and sail to Valparaiso, where he was to sell one of the ships and proceed with all the men, including the prize crews from the different ships then in port, to the United States.

Porter was leaving Gamble the fully provisioned prizes so that the *Essex* and *Essex Junior* would have the option of returning to the island for supplies and repairs after a fight with the British in Valparaiso—the grand one-on-one frigate battle that Porter had made the supreme object of his cruise.

Nothing illustrated how far Porter's hubris had infected his thinking than his orders to Lieutenant Gamble. There was no reason to leave any Americans on Nuku Hiva. The United States had no interest in acquiring the island, but even if she did, the idea that Gamble and a handful of men could secure it against tens of thousands of natives was a cruel delusion.

And there was no reason to establish a base to succor Porter's small squadron after a battle in Valparaiso. Such a battle, after all, was manifestly against the best interests of the tiny American navy, which needed to preserve its warships, not throw them away in useless fighting for the glory of individual captains.

Nonetheless, with no one to respectfully ask Porter to rethink his strategy, he went ahead with his bizarre plans. In preparing for departure, he ordered the remaining 1,950 barrels of sperm oil from the captured ships placed into the *New Zealander*, and he appointed master's mate John J. King commander, directing him to proceed to the United States. This was the third shipload of oil Porter was sending home, giving the crew of the *Essex* further expectations of rich rewards when they finally reached America. John King and the *New Zealander* left Nuku Hiva on December 28, shortly after Porter did. Unfortunately, as she was approaching the coast of the United States, the British frigate HMS *Belvidera* captured her.

chapter 19

SHOWDOWN IN VALPARAISO

THE *ESSEX* AND *ESSEX JUNIOR* WERE STUFFED WITH PROVISIONS when they stood out from Nuku Hiva on December 13, 1813. Aboard were an abundance of wood, water, coconuts, bananas, plantains, and hogs. The ships were bound for Valparaiso and a rendezvous with HMS *Phoebe* and her escorts. Porter insisted that seeking out the British hunters was the best way to fulfill his supreme responsibility to annoy the enemy. Actually, his orders were to engage in commerce-destroying, which implied that he only fight an enemy as powerful as the *Phoebe* if absolutely necessary. Seeking out a British squadron that was bound to be superior was contrary to the policy of the president, not to mention common sense. In fact, the administration was so fed up with captains seeking single-ship combat that Secretary Jones routinely cautioned them not to. He wrote to one of them on December 22, 1813, "The character of the American navy stands upon a basis not to be shaken, and needs no sacrifices by unequal conflict to sustain its reputation. You will therefore avoid all unnecessary contact with the cruisers of the enemy, even with an equal, unless under circumstances that may ensure your triumph, without defeating the main object of your cruise, or jeopardizing the safety of the vessels under your command."

SHORTLY AFTER THEY LEFT NUKU HIVA, AN INCIDENT OCCURRED on the *Essex* that dismayed everyone. A thoughtless boatswain's mate struck Tamaha, the Tahitian who had been such a help to Porter when he first arrived in the Marquesas. The blow came as a complete surprise, injuring Tamaha's pride and heart more than his body. He could not understand why he was beaten; he had done everything in his power to ingratiate himself with the Americans. He felt humiliated and cried at first, but then declared that he would not be struck again.

The ship was twenty miles from Nuku Hiva, and night was approaching. A wind was blowing and the sea was getting up, when, unseen, Tamaha jumped overboard. A seaman heard a splash, but did not report it. Tamaha's absence wasn't noticed until quarters the next morning. Porter hoped that he had taken an oar or something to buoy himself with, but he had no way of knowing if he had, and he feared that he had drowned. Farragut reported many years later that an officer on one of the prizes moored in Taiohae Bay said that Tamaha reached Nuku Hiva in tolerably good health, three days after leaping overboard. Porter did not record how he punished the boatswain's mate, but it's certain that he made the man regret his hasty action.

FOR NINE DAYS AFTER THE *ESSEX* AND *ESSEX JUNIOR* LEFT Nuku Hiva, the winds blew chiefly from north-northeast to northwest. After that, they generally blew from the northwest. Porter sailed east, making nine degrees of longitude the first three days. On December 18, the *Essex* reached longitude 131° west. The rest of the voyage went nearly as well. "Nothing of unusual interest occurred during our passage," David Farragut reported. Porter continually drilled the men in small arms and boarding, something he had done throughout their odyssey. "Every day the crew were exercised at the great guns, small arms, and single stick," Farragut remembered.

As Porter approached the coast of South America, he wrote a letter to Downes, dated January 10, 1814. In it, he revealed why he was hell-bent on going to Valparaiso, and what his strategy would be when they got there. He made it clear that he was determined to engage the British warships that Downes had reported were searching for him—*Phoebe*, *Cherub*, and *Racoon*. Porter did not intend to fight all three at once. If he had the misfortune of falling in with them, he planned "to make my retreat in the best manner I can."

Of course, he was hoping that this did not happen, that he would only have to fight two, or, ideally, one—the big frigate *Phoebe*. "If we fall in with the *Phoebe* and one sloop of war," he advised Downes, "you must endeavor to draw the sloop off in chase of you and get her as far to leeward of the frigate as possible, and as soon as you effect this I shall engage the frigate. "If we meet the *Phoebe* alone and to leeward of us, I shall run along side of her." In this case, Downes was to remain to windward, out of gunshot range and observe. If the *Essex* was getting the better of the engagement, Downes was to do nothing, but if the *Phoebe* was gaining the upper hand, Downes was to intervene and enable the *Essex* to haul off.

If the *Phoebe* was to windward, Porter would attempt to gain the weather gauge (get to windward of her). If he failed, he would try to disable her with his stern guns, so as to obtain an advantage. Otherwise, although he did not say so explicitly, he would do everything possible to avoid giving the *Phoebe* an opportunity to fire on the *Essex* with her long guns, if the *Essex* was unable to respond with her short-range carronades.

In the event they ran across the *Phoebe* and a sloop of war while the *Essex* and *Essex Junior* were to windward, Downes was to "draw the sloop off . . . and leave this *Phoebe* to me," Porter wrote.

"I wish you to avoid an engagement with a sloop if possible," he cautioned Downes, "as your ship is too weak; if, however, you cannot avoid an action endeavor to cut her up so as to prevent her from coming to the assistance of the *Phoebe*.

"I shall in all probability run alongside the *Phoebe* under the Spanish ensign and pendant; should I do so you will show British colors until I hoist the American.

"It will be advisable for you at all times to keep to windward of us," he wrote. This was the ideal position, of course, but it might be impossible to achieve, particularly against seasoned British captains.

Needless to say, instead of planning a grand battle against what would surely be heavy odds, Porter would have been far better off sailing around the Horn with his prizes into the South Atlantic and proceeding home.

If he got into a fight along the way, so much the better. At least he would be following a strategy that had some logic to it.

ON JANUARY 12, A MONTH AFTER LEAVING MASSACHUSETTS BAY, a lookout at the main masthead sighted Mocha Island—normally to windward of Valparaiso. Without stopping, Porter moved slowly north to Santa Maria Island, where he filled his water casks, looked into Concepción, decided not to stop, and proceeded on a leisurely cruise north. On February 3, 1814, he sailed into Valparaiso Bay and anchored off the city.

After exchanging salutes with the battery on old Fort Viejo, he went ashore to pay his respects to the acting governor, Francisco de Formas. The reception was friendly, and the following day, Porter received the governor, his wife, and entourage aboard the *Essex* with a salute. The placid atmosphere of the port belied the fact that since Porter left Valparaiso almost a year earlier, Chile had been in turmoil. Royalists, directed by the viceroy of Peru, had been fighting republicans led by the Carrera brothers, Bernardo O'Higgins, and Juan Mackenna, with neither side being able to win a decisive victory. The American consul general, Joel Poinsett, continued to lend his wholehearted support to José Miguel Carrera, even though it was unclear if the Carreras would survive. The viceroy in Peru had initiated the conflict when he simultaneously invaded Argentina and Chile in 1813, seeking to overthrow their republican governments and returning the countries to Spanish rule. The fighting was intense. By March 1814 the royalists had gained the upper hand. They had captured José Miguel Carrera and his brother Luis, and threatened Santiago.

In this tense atmosphere, Colonel Francisco de la Lastra rose to power. He had been governor of Valparaiso when Porter first arrived in March 1813. A year later, in Santiago (while Porter was again in Valparaiso), he became supreme director of Chile with dictatorial powers. Lastra had been nominally a republican, but, as Porter had sensed the year before, Lastra was ready to align himself with whichever side won. He had no problem pledging allegiance to Ferdinand VII, the Spanish king whom the British were about to restore to his throne. Ferdinand's policy, although unknown in Chile at the time, was to turn back the clock to a time before the American and French Revolutions and make Chile a royalist colony again ruled from Madrid as she had been for centuries.

Communications were so poor in Chile that when Porter arrived in Valparaiso in February, the state of the war between the royalist and republican armies was unknown. No one suspected that in just a few weeks the royalists would gain a significant advantage.

Soon after Porter's arrival in February, he learned of the uncertain political and military situation, which had to be a factor in his thinking, but the British hunters were foremost in his mind. He sent *Essex Junior* to take up a position offshore, where Downes could intercept enemy merchantmen and whalers, while keeping an eye out for hostile warships. Porter was convinced that at least the *Phoebe* and the *Cherub* would appear, and perhaps the *Racoon*. Other warships might be on the way as well. But that might not be the case. He would just have to wait and see. In the meantime, *Essex* and *Essex Junior* were in a high state of readiness.

On February 7, Porter repaid the kindness of the governor and the people of Valparaiso by throwing a party aboard the *Essex*. Lieutenant Downes was invited. He was to anchor the *Essex Junior* in a place that would afford a full view of the sea. As was the normal routine on the *Essex*, one-third of the crew was on shore leave. Dancing continued until midnight, after which Lieutenant Downes returned to his ship and put to sea, taking up his normal station. His crew resumed their regular routine, but there was to be nothing routine about this night. The *Essex*'s crew were in the midst of taking down awnings and flags and generally cleaning up after the party, when *Essex Junior* made a signal—two enemy ships in sight.

George O'Brien, skipper of the English merchantman *Emily*, which was anchored in the harbor, received a signal as well. He leaped into a boat with some men and rowed out to the largest British warship he saw, HMS *Phoebe*, and warned Captain James Hillyar that the *Essex* was in Valparaiso. Hillyar was ecstatic; he had finally found what he had been after all these many months. O'Brien volunteered to help. He had once been a lieutenant in the Royal Navy, but had been broken for misconduct and joined the merchant service. He held no grudges, however, and offered every assistance to Hillyar, even telling him that the entire crew of the *Emily* would volunteer to fight aboard the *Phoebe*.

While O'Brien conferred with Hillyar, a gun sounded on the *Essex* and a signal shot up for all men and boats to return. Within a remarkably short time, every sailor was aboard the *Essex* preparing for battle. Only one appeared drunk.

Porter rowed out to *Essex Junior* to have a look for himself. What he saw—two large British warships, probably a frigate and a sloop of war—was both sobering and exhilarating. He immediately ordered Downes to run the *Essex Junior* into port and take up a position where *Essex Junior* and *Essex* could support each other. When Porter returned to the *Essex* at half past seven in the morning, he found the ship fully prepared for action. At eight o'clock the two British ships entered the harbor, also ready for battle. The larger one, the powerful 36-gun *Phoebe*, kept coming right at the *Essex*, approaching to within a few yards. Her crew was at battle stations.

All was in readiness on the *Essex* as well, the men filled with anticipation. Guns were boused out. Boarders gripped their cutlasses and checked their small arms. Every officer and man had a weapon, standing by for the order to board. The *Phoebe* drew even closer. Just then, the one tipsy youth imagined that he saw a British sailor making faces at him. He shouted that he'd stop the man from making fun of him and went to apply slow-match to his cannon. Before he could, Lieutenant McKnight punched him and sent him sprawling. If the seaman had succeeded in firing, a fierce battle would have ensued, in which Porter and the *Essex* would have had a decided advantage because of the power of their 32-pound carronades, and undoubtedly would have smashed the *Phoebe* into submission.

The British captain was now clearly visible on his quarterdeck in a pea jacket. He was close enough to yell to Porter through a trumpet, "Captain Hillyar's compliments to Captain Porter and hopes all is well."

As men on the *Essex* stood tensely by their weapons, Porter shouted back through his trumpet, "Very well, I thank you, but I hope you will not come too near, for fear some accident might take place which would be disagreeable to you," and with a wave of his trumpet the kedge anchors went up to the yardarms, ready to grapple the enemy.

Playing on the fact that Valparaiso was a neutral harbor, Hillyar had approached the *Essex* close enough to see that she had not been taken by surprise, as he had hoped. She had a full complement of men aboard. George O'Brien's report that a large part of Porter's crew were on shore turned out to be inaccurate, and Hillyar had to quickly adjust his thinking. His gambit had failed. Instead of being unprepared, the *Essex* was ready. Her deadly carronades were close enough to devastate the *Phoebe*. Seeing this, Hillyar suddenly braced back his yards while crying out that if he did fall aboard the *Essex* it would be entirely by accident.

Porter yelled back, "You have no business where you are. If you touch a rope-yarn of this ship, I shall board instantly." At the same time, he signaled Downes on *Essex Junior* to be ready to repel the enemy.

"O, sir," Hillyar shouted to Porter, in a careless and indifferent manner, "I have no intention of getting on board of you."

Hillyar was no stranger to Porter. They had become well acquainted in 1807 when both were serving in the Mediterranean. As Porter recalled, "While [Hillyar's] family resided at Gibraltar, I was in the habit of visiting them frequently, and had spent many happy hours in their company. . . . For Captain Hillyar and his family I entertained the highest respect; and among the American officers generally, no officer of the British navy was so great a favorite as Captain Hillyar."

Nonetheless, Porter was leery of Hillyar's intentions. Hillyar had a well-deserved reputation for ignoring neutrality when it suited his purposes. An experienced commander who had seen plenty of action, Hillyar had demonstrated more than once what few scruples he had when victory demanded that he ignore neutral rights. In 1800, in the port of Barcelona, for instance, he had used a neutral Swedish vessel to sneak boatloads of men into the harbor, past a Spanish battery to attack an unsuspecting enemy in the harbor.

In trying to extricate himself from a potentially disastrous situation, Hillyar luffed up so as to cause the *Phoebe* to take aback, but in so doing, her jib-boom swept across the *Essex*'s forecastle. Porter shouted to all hands to be alert, ready to board if the hulls touched. "At this moment," Porter recalled, "not a gun from the *Phoebe* could be brought to bear on either the *Essex* or *Essex Junior*, while her bow was exposed to the raking fire of the one, and her stern to that of the other. Her consort . . . was too far off to leeward to afford any assistance."

"The *Phoebe* was . . . completely at my mercy," Porter wrote. "I could have destroyed her in fifteen minutes." He wasn't exaggerating; he could have poured two or three raking broadsides into her, tearing her guts out from stem to stern, with no trouble. Powder monkeys held slow matches by the guns. Had Porter given the order, and the *Essex* let go her rounds, her massed boarders could have easily overwhelmed Hillyar.

But the *Phoebe* never touched the *Essex*, and Porter—choosing to observe the rules of neutrality—never fired on him, letting Hillyar off the hook. Oddly, Porter allowed himself to be disarmed by Hillyar's assurances, even though Hillyar's record was well known to Porter. Nonetheless, he allowed the *Phoebe* to extricate herself and move to a less vulnerable position, which Hillyar proceeded to do. He anchored about a half mile astern, beyond the reach of Porter's carronades, but within range of the *Phoebe*'s long 18-pounders.

As soon as the *Phoebe* was in place, Captain Tucker brought the *Cherub* to anchor within pistol shot of the *Essex*. Whereupon, Porter ordered *Essex Junior* to take up a position that placed the *Cherub* between the fire of the two American ships. He wasn't taking any chances.

Porter insisted that respect for Chilean neutrality was his guiding principle. He would never attack Hillyar in the port. If the *Phoebe* had made the first move, he would have been obliged to retaliate, but he would not initiate the action under any circumstances. He liked to point out that since the *Essex* was the inferior ship in point of firepower, his government would not countenance him looking for a fight, but if one came his way, he would eagerly grasp it. Not only would he jump at the opportunity, but the chance of a battle was the reason he had returned to Valparaiso in the first place. He did not need to be there. No military purpose was being served. He was there to have a fight. He might not initiate an engagement, but he would do everything he could to provoke one.

On the following morning, Hillyar noticed that the *Essex* was flying a large banner emblazoned with the words "FREE TRADE AND SAILORS RIGHTS." The message stuck in his craw. He saw it as an "insidious effort to shake the loyalty of thoughtless British seamen." Like most of Britain's upper classes, Hillyar blamed the massive desertions from British warships on American shenanigans, rather than on the tyrannical practices of officers aboard their own men-of-war. With his ire up, Hillyar hoisted an ensign declaring "GOD AND COUNTRY; BRITISH SAILORS BEST RIGHTS; TRAITORS OFFEND BOTH." On seeing this, the *Essex* men swarmed over their rigging and gave a full-throated jeer. Hillyar's crew responded in kind, after which, his little band played "God Save the King." Porter replied with another banner, bearing the motto "GOD, OUR COUNTRY, AND LIBERTY—TYRANTS OFFEND BOTH." This tit-for-tat went on the entire time the two ships were anchored close to each other. The hoisting of rival banners was followed by insults shouted across the water. Songs, and even poetry, were employed to abuse each other, as well as small flags carrying pointed inscriptions.

There was another side to this relationship, however, and it softened the rivalry. On the same day the battle of the banners began, February 9, Captains Hillyar and Tucker paid a visit to Porter at the home of Mr. Blanco, the American deputy vice consul in Valparaiso, where Porter usually stayed while on shore. The meeting went well, and others followed. "A friendly intimacy [was] established," Porter reported, "not only between the commanders . . . but the officers and boats' crews of the respective ships. No one, to have judged from appearances, would have supposed us to have been at war, our conduct toward each other bore so much the appearance of a friendly alliance." During their first meeting, Porter asked Hillyar if he intended to respect the neutrality of the port, and Hillyar replied in convincing fashion, "*You* have paid so much respect to the neutrality of the port, that I feel myself bound in honor to respect it." Porter was satisfied that Hillyar meant what he said.

During their later meetings, Porter made it clear that he wanted a one-on-one duel between the *Essex* and the *Phoebe*, in effect, asking Hillyar to give up his advantages. But Hillyar had no reason to. His responsibility was to remove the *Essex* as a menace to Britain's whalers and commerce. He was a forty-four-year-old veteran who had won enough laurels to feel secure about his reputation. He did not need another victory to prove himself. The Admiralty would judge him on whether or not he got rid of the *Essex*, not on how he did it. His orders from Admiral Dixon required him to destroy a menace to British interests, not to engage in a one-on-one frigate duel. Dixon would not quibble about Hillyar's methods, nor would the Admiralty. But they certainly would if Hillyar relinquished his advantages in order to accommodate Porter. And, of course, if he lost a single-ship duel under these circumstances, he would be subject to severe penalties.

Hillyar could afford to wait. He already had a superior force, and more frigates were on the way. In fact, the Admiralty had already dispatched the powerful 38-gun frigates *Briton* (Sir Thomas Staines) and *Targus* (Captain Philip Pipon) to destroy the *Essex*. To be sure, the *Phoebe* was more powerful on paper than the *Essex* and could take her on with a reasonable chance of success, but naval actions turn on many variables—a lucky shot cracking a vital mast or spar, a cannonball smashing the steering—any number of things could even the odds in the *Essex*'s favor. So Hillyar had every reason to bide his time and blockade *Essex* and *Essex Junior* until he judged he had an overwhelming advantage.

The *Phoebe* and the *Cherub* remained close by *Essex* and *Essex Junior* until their provisioning was complete on February 14. The following day they pulled their hooks, sailed out of the harbor, and began patrolling off Valparaiso Bay, staying to windward, close to the Point of Angels.

Porter for his part continued trying to provoke a single-ship duel. On the afternoon of February 26, when the sea was calm, he towed one of his prizes, the *Hector*, out to sea, hoping the *Phoebe* alone would chase him. Instead, both British ships came after him, standing toward the bay while he was coming out. Not wanting to get far beyond the protection of the neutral harbor, Porter burned the *Hector* and retreated. The British ships continued after him, but he managed to get safely back to his former anchorage.

The following afternoon, February 27, Hillyar tried to turn the tables and lure Porter into uneven combat. He steered the *Phoebe* into the harbor alone—much to Porter's surprise and delight, leaving the *Cherub* to leeward. At five o'clock Hillyar hove to a short distance from the *Essex*, shortened sail, fired a gun to windward, and hoisted a familiar ensign: "GOD AND COUNTRY; BRITISH SAILORS BEST RIGHTS; TRAITORS OFFEND BOTH."

Believing this to be a challenge for the single-ship duel he yearned for, Porter hoisted his own pennant: "GOD, OUR COUNTRY, AND LIBERTY—TYRANTS OFFEND THEM." At the same time he ordered sixty men from *Essex Junior* to join the *Essex* crew, making her numbers 315—more equal to the *Phoebe*'s 320. Porter then fired a gun and got underway, anticipating a deadly fight. In response, the *Phoebe* stood out of the harbor to give the combatants some fighting room—or so Porter thought. He followed, getting closer to her as he went. Suddenly, to Porter's complete surprise, the *Phoebe* bore up before the wind and ran down for her consort.

It was a sensible maneuver, designed to capture the *Essex* at the least possible risk. But Porter was indignant, feeling he had been cheated out of what he most wanted. He fired two guns at the *Phoebe* in a vain effort to bring her to. When that failed, he hauled his wind, and returned to the protection of the port. The *Phoebe*, in company with the *Cherub*, came after him. They entered the harbor, but did not commence an attack. Porter assumed it was because Hillyar respected the neutrality of the port.

Hillyar sent his chivalrous first lieutenant, William Ingram, to the *Essex* under a flag of truce to explain that Captain Hillyar had not issued a challenge. Firing a gun and hoisting a flag, Ingram said, was intended merely as a signal to the *Cherub*. Porter did not believe him. He accused Hillyar of being "cowardly and dishonorable."

During this set-to, the *Phoebe* showed herself once again to be a slow sailor. The *Essex* was obviously the faster ship, and that speed could make a big difference in a one-on-one fight. It could also allow Porter to escape, if it came to that.

Some days later, Porter decided he would make a night attack on the *Phoebe* using the small boats he had employed so successfully in the Galapagos Islands. Given the constant training his men had received in hand-to-hand combat, he was confident they were superior to any British crew, which was probably true. On the night of March 12, all the *Essex*'s boats were filled with armed men, and with muffled oars, they rowed toward the *Phoebe*. Porter was in the lead boat with Farragut. They pulled close enough to hear conversation on the forecastle, which led Porter to believe that Hillyar was waiting for him, whereupon he aborted the mission and rowed back to the harbor.

In fact, Hillyar was unaware of Porter's presence, and the *Essex* men got back to their ship without difficulty. Porter never mentioned the incident in any letter or in his journal. David Farragut gave the details much later. Porter was evidently too embarrassed to mention the non-event. He must have realized later that he had taken Hillyar by surprise after all, and had retreated when he did not have to. Hillyar was informed of what happened sometime later.

On March 14, Porter began a paper war with Hillyar, hoping to prod him into abandoning his caution. He accused Hillyar of trying to encourage men on the *Essex* to desert. Hillyar denied doing so, although, of course, he would welcome any American seaman who left his ship. That Porter thought his transparent gambit would succeed with Hillyar is a tribute to his inflamed imagination.

At length, Porter concluded that Hillyar was never going to fight him one-on-one, and he looked for an opportunity to escape. His sense of urgency increased when word arrived overland from Buenos Aires that the 38-gun *Targus* was on the way, and possibly two other frigates, along with the *Racoon*—back from the Columbia River. In fact, the *Targus* arrived off Valparaiso on April 13.

Porter planned to race out to sea and draw the *Phoebe* and the *Cherub* after him, giving *Essex Junior* a chance to sortie safely out of the harbor. Porter could then rely on his speed to get away. If all went well, he and Downes would rendezvous later. It was a workable plan.

An opportunity arose on March 28. At daylight, winds were light, and Porter had the ship ready for an escape. He had determined from a report by Lieutenant Maury that *Phoebe* and *Cherub*, which were usually stationed to the weather point, or western side of Valparaiso Bay, would be more to leeward, giving Porter an excellent chance to get to windward of them and break free close hauled. Meanwhile *Essex Junior* could slip out to leeward when the two British ships inevitably hauled their wind and chased the *Essex*.

All Porter needed was a stronger breeze, and at noon the wind, which was from the south southwest, freshened before increasing to a strong gale. It blew over the hills and through the ravines in back of the harbor, stirring the bay waters to a frenzy and rocking the shipping. Porter ordered the royals and their masts taken down, and then, at 2:45, the *Essex* suddenly parted her larboard cable, causing her to drag the starboard anchor leeward. Conditions now seemed ideal to go forward with the escape Porter had been planning. He hailed *Essex Junior* to send a boat to take Joel Poinsett, who often was aboard, ashore. Immediately after Poinsett departed, Porter ordered the starboard anchor cable cut, and he was on his way.

At that moment, *Phoebe* and *Cherub* were standing in for the protection of the harbor, providing Porter with an opportunity of getting to windward of them. He took in the topgallant sails, which were set over single-reefed topsails, and stood close hauled for the Point of Angels at the western end of Valparaiso Bay. His chances of breaking free looked excellent. But, as luck would have it, on luffing round the point, a heavy squall suddenly struck the ship. The topsail halyards were let go, but the yards jammed and would not come down. When the ship was nearly gunwale to, the main topmast went by the board, carrying the men on the topgallant yard, Samuel Miller and Thomas Browne (both superb topmen), into the sea, where they drowned.

Porter quickly gave orders to wear ship and clear the wreckage. The mainsail and main topsail were cut from the wreckage to prevent them from acting against the ship as it worked back into the bay. Porter was trying desperately to return the *Essex* to her original anchorage, where she would be safe in neutral territory again. Despite a mighty effort from her crew, however, the disabled ship could not make it back. As an alternative, Porter ran to leeward (east) for about three miles into a small bay called Villa la Mar—about one and a half miles to leeward of the battery on old Fort jel Barron, guarding the east side of Valparaiso Bay. Once there, he let go his anchor in nine and a half fathoms within pistol shot of shore. It was 3:45 P.M. Porter intended to make repairs quickly in what he assumed were neutral waters.

Being in neutral territory did not put a check on Hillyar, however. He was already hot after the *Essex* with the *Cherub* close behind. When he saw Porter drop anchor, he must have been relieved. Hillyar knew he was facing disaster when Porter raced close-hauled for the Point of Angels. The *Phoebe* could never have caught him. Allowing the *Essex* to escape had been Hillyar's worst nightmare. The sudden squall that wrecked Porter's plans saved Hillyar. He did not want to answer to the Admiralty for failing to destroy the *Essex* when she was within his grasp.

Hillyar was saved again when Porter wore ship and ended up anchored on the east side of Valparaiso Bay to make repairs. The *Essex* might have continued eastward into the open sea, where, again, Hillyar might not have caught her, even though she was injured. When Porter dropped his hook, thinking he was safe in neutral territory, Hillyar pounced. Having already had a brush with disaster, he was not going to let this opportunity pass. He now had a chance to engage the *Essex* in an unequal battle with both of his ships. He did not hesitate.

As *Phoebe* and *Cherub* sped toward the *Essex* with motto pennants flying, they made furious preparations for battle. Porter cleared for action as well, but he did not think Hillyar would actually attack him. Nonetheless, he prepared for the worst. He knew that if there was a fight, the *Phoebe*'s long 18-pounders would be critical. The *Cherub* was a different matter. Her principal armament was carronades, just like the *Essex*, which meant that to be effective she had to get close to the *Essex*, where Porter's heavier guns could decimate her. So the *Phoebe*, with her battery of long guns, would carry the brunt of the attack.

Despite the significant advantage he now had, Hillyar remained cautious. He approached deliberately, giving Porter time to run three 12-pounders out of stern ports and rig springs on the *Essex*'s cable, so that she could turn without using her sails. Poinsett, meanwhile, had remained on the scene, and he tried to help. He urged the governor of Valparaiso to use the small battery nearby to defend the neutrality of the port, but he refused. The governor did offer to send an officer to Hillyar and request that he cease firing, should Porter succeed in reaching the common anchorage—an unlikely event, which the governor was well aware of. The political complexion of Chile had changed completely at this point and the authorities were clearly pro-British.

The men from all the ships were ready for a fight. They had been anticipating one for weeks. The ships bristled with hostility. Still, with the decisive battle now at hand, tension gripped every stomach, especially on the *Essex*, where the crew could see the obvious superiority of the enemy. "I well remember the feelings of awe produced in me by the approach of the hostile ships," Farragut recalled. "Even to my young mind it was perceptible in the faces of those around me, as clearly as possible, that our case was hopeless. It was equally apparent that all were ready to die at their guns rather than surrender." In their heart of hearts, however, the brave crew of the *Essex* must have hoped that Hillyar would not violate a neutral port—certainly Captain Porter did.

They hoped in vain. Hillyar was determined to smash the *Essex* right now. As he drew closer, the wind continued southerly but had let up some. He positioned the *Phoebe* under the *Essex*'s stern and the *Cherub* off her starboard bow, commencing a hot fire from both ships at 3:54 P.M. Porter's

12-pounders fired back and were surprisingly effective. A splinter struck Captain Tucker on the *Cherub*, but he kept directing the fight, even though blood was pulsing from his wound. Fire from the *Essex* soon forced Tucker to change positions, but it still looked as if the American frigate stood no chance. During the next half hour, however, Porter's three long 12-pounders, firing out of stern ports, were handled with such skill that both enemy ships were forced to haul off for repairs. In addition to being much cut up in her rigging, and her topsail sheets flying away, the *Phoebe* had lost use of her mainsail, jib, and mainstay.

Hillyar could afford to pause; the *Essex* was trapped—too banged up to attempt an escape—and he needed to change his strategy.

The carnage aboard the *Essex* was indeed dreadful. With only three long guns to oppose two broadsides, Porter had attempted to bring his broadsides to bear with the springs he had hitched to the cables, but they were no sooner hooked up than Hillyar's gunners cut them. Many *Essex* men had been killed in the first minutes of the fight, before her three long twelves in the stern could be brought to bear. Nonetheless, spirits remained high; the men had no quit in them. The ensign flying at the gaff had been shot away, but "FREE TRADE AND SAILORS RIGHTS" continued flying at the foremast. Porter replaced the damaged ensign and put another in the mizzen rigging.

Farragut was stationed beside the captain during this time, along with another midshipman and the sailing master. Two quartermasters attended the wheel. The jobs of those next to Porter were to carry out his every wish amidst the smoke, confusion, and incessant cacophony of an ever-changing battle. "I performed the duties of the captain's aid, quarter gunner, powder boy, and in fact did everything that was required of me," Farragut remembered. He could have added that he was exposed to enemy missiles the entire time, as well as the deadly splinters they unleashed. The first man he saw killed sickened him. "I shall never forget the horrid impression made upon me at the sight of the first man I had ever seen killed. He was a boatswain's mate, and was fearfully mutilated. It staggered and sickened me at first; but they soon began to fall around me so fast that it all appeared like a dream, and produced no effect on my nerves."

When he wasn't employed otherwise, Farragut "assisted in working a gun," often running to bring powder from the boys, and send them back for more "until the Captain wanted me to carry a message; and this continued to employ me during the action."

Hillyar soon returned to the attack, positioning both his ships on *Essex*'s starboard quarter, out of range of her carronades. Porter's deadly stern guns could not be brought to bear either. The punishing blows from *Phoebe* hit the *Essex* hard, while she remained unable to return fire—a sitting duck if ever there was one. Porter was in the exact situation he had most feared, where his short-range carronades could not reach an enemy employing long guns. His only hope was to get a sail up and bear down on the *Phoebe*. But the topsail sheets and halyards had been shot away, as well as the jib and fore topmast staysail halyards. The only ropes not cut were the flying jib halyards. After several frustrating attempts, the crew finally hoisted the flying jib, and Porter quickly cut the cable. With a favorable slant of wind, the *Essex* ran down toward the *Phoebe* with guns blazing, intending to board and fight it out hand to hand. "The firing on both sides was now tremendous"; Porter recalled: "I had let fall my fore topsail and foresail, but the want of tacks and sheets had rendered them almost useless to us— yet we were enabled for a short time to close with the enemy."

The *Cherub* was forced to haul off and continue firing ineffectively from long distance, out of range of *Essex*'s carronades. Hillyar also maneuvered away from the *Essex* as she came toward him. He had no intention of allowing her to crash into his ship and have the American crew swarm aboard. He pulled to a position where his long guns could pummel the *Essex* without fear of being hit in return.

The *Essex* was again helpless. Hillyar's continuous fire smashed many of her guns and created havoc on her decks. The killed and wounded were everywhere. Porter gave up trying to close with Hillyar and decided to run the *Essex* ashore, land the men who were alive, and destroy her. At the moment, the wind was favorable.

As the stricken *Essex* strained toward shore, her decks were strewn with bloody, mangled bodies. She had been on fire several times and was in desperate condition. For a brief moment it looked as if she might make it to the beach. But when she was a hundred feet from it, the wind suddenly, according to Porter's journal, "shifted from the land (as is very common in this port in the latter part of the day)" taking the ship flat aback and paying her head offshore, pointing it directly at the *Phoebe*, where she was "once again exposed to a dreadful raking fire."

At this moment, Lieutenant Downes appeared looking for orders. *Essex Junior*, being too weak to participate, had been spared. Downes was convinced that the *Essex*, in her wretched state, would shortly be taken, and he wanted direction. Porter ordered him back to defend *Essex Junior*, but if that proved impossible, to destroy her if it looked as if she were in danger of being captured. Downes went back, taking with him several of the wounded and leaving three of his healthy men.

All the while, the *Phoebe* kept up a deadly barrage, raking the *Essex*. Porter could not return fire. And the *Cherub*, without having to fear any response from the *Essex*, lobbed in her shots as well. The carnage on the Americans' decks was frightful. Lifeless bodies lay strewn about, their mortal wounds horribly evident—heads cut off, chests shot out, arms sliced in half. Blasphemous oaths from the wounded filled the air, as they writhed in pain from jagged splinters stuck in their bodies every which way, mangled arms, gouged-out eyes, sliced ears. Blood ran everywhere. "The slaughter on board my ship [was] horrible," Porter lamented.

But he was still not ready to give up. He ordered a hawser bent on the sheet anchor, and the anchor cut from the bows to bring her head round. This miraculously succeeded, and the *Essex*'s broadside was brought to bear again. But the hawser soon snapped, and the *Essex* started drifting out of control while the *Phoebe*'s guns kept hammering her.

All the while, fires continued to threaten the *Essex*. Flames were shooting up from the hatchways. Tars rushed up from below, many with their clothes on fire. Their shipmates tore the burning rags off them as best they could. Porter told those having trouble getting their clothes off to jump overboard and douse the flames. On hearing this, many thought the magazine was about to blow up, and they went overboard too. Several of them made it to shore, but others drowned.

Presently, Midshipman Isaacs came up to Porter and reported that quarter-gunner Adam Roach had deserted his post. Porter turned to Farragut and said, "Do your duty." Farragut grabbed a pistol and went searching for the deserter but could not find him. He discovered later that, upon seeing the ship on fire, Roach and six others had taken the only undamaged boat left and rowed to shore. This was not the only time during the battle that Roach appeared to be derelict in his duty. His behavior outraged his comrades. One of them was William Call, whose leg had been hit, and while it hung by the skin with blood spilling from it, he saw Roach on the berth deck, wandering around suspiciously. Furious, Call "dragged his shattered stump all around . . . , pistol in hand, trying to get a shot at him."

Roach's conduct puzzled Farragut. Before the battle, Roach had been a respected man on the ship—the first to grab a cutlass and board an enemy ship. When the *Phoebe* first entered Valparaiso Bay on February 8 and looked as if she might attack the *Essex*, Porter had called for a boarding party, and Farragut saw Roach in the lead "standing in an exposed position on the cathead with sleeves rolled up and cutlass in hand, ready to board, his countenance expressing eagerness for a fight." Farragut concluded that Roach was "brave with a prospect of success, but a coward in adversity." It could have been that Roach and the others were simply avoiding the fires, or they might have objected to Porter's continued resistance in the face of certain defeat, and were unwilling to sacrifice themselves in a mindless slaughter, or, as Farragut suspected, they might have been just plain scared.

The *Essex* had now drifted to a point a half mile from the beach. Most of the men had stuck with Porter, and they continued to fight. But only a hundred remained active. Some of these were wounded and died later. The most pressing problem of the survivors was the fires that threatened to reach the magazine and blow up the ship. There had already been an explosion from gunpowder strewn about below deck. The men turned their attention "wholly to extinguish the flames, and when we had succeeded," Porter wrote, "went again to the guns."

Farragut received orders to bring gun primers up from below. While he was on the wardroom ladder, the captain of the gun directly opposite the hatchway was struck full in the face by an 18-pound shot and fell back directly onto him. They tumbled down the hatchway together. At the bottom Farragut's head struck the hard deck while the other man, who weighed over two hundred pounds, came down on the little midshipman's hips. Had the dead man landed on Farragut's stomach, he would have killed him. "I lay for some moments stunned by the blow, but soon recovered consciousness enough to rush up on deck." When Porter saw him covered with blood, he asked if he were wounded.

"I believe not, sir."

"Then, where are the primers?"

Suddenly realizing that he had completely forgotten why he had gone below, Farragut recovered his wits and went back for the primers. When he returned he saw Porter sprawled out on deck, apparently wounded. He asked if he were injured.

"I believe not, my son, but I felt a blow on the top of my head."

Farragut assumed a cannonball had whizzed by close enough to the captain's head to knock him down and damage his hat, but not his head. Porter got back on his feet right away and resumed command.

Not long afterward, Farragut saw a cannonball coming straight for him while he was standing at the wheel next to Quartermaster Francis Bland. Farragut screamed a warning, but the ball tore off Bland's right leg and Farragut's coattail. Recovering, Farragut dragged Bland below, hoping he could be saved, and then rushed back to the quarterdeck.

The *Essex*'s condition had now deteriorated to the point where the remaining, loyal-to-the-end crewmembers pleaded with Porter to surrender and save the wounded. He responded by going below to check the amount of powder remaining in the magazine, and then sent for the officers of divisions to discuss hauling down the flag. Sadly, only Stephen Decatur McKnight answered the call; the others were either dead or severely wounded. Lieutenant Wilmer was dead, and Acting Lieutenant John G. Cowell was mortally wounded with a leg shot off.

The *Phoebe* and *Cherub*, in the meantime, kept pouring in shot. The stricken *Essex* was still unable to respond. Her cockpit, steerage, wardroom, and berth deck were all packed with wounded. "I saw no hope of saving her," Porter lamented, and, after sending Farragut to make certain the signal book and other important papers had been thrown overboard, he "gave the painful order to strike the colors." It was twenty minutes after six.

In spite of the American flag having come down, *Phoebe* and *Cherub* kept firing. Porter angrily discharged a gun in the opposite direction to indicate surrender, but still the shelling continued. Ten more minutes elapsed before the guns fell silent. Before they did, Farragut, Isaacs, and others worked hard throwing pistols and other small arms overboard to prevent them from falling into enemy hands.

chapter 20

THE BUTCHER'S BILL

PORTER AND FARRAGUT, ALTHOUGH REMAINING EXPOSED
during the entire action, miraculously escaped serious injury. Others
were not so lucky. The butcher's bill aboard the *Essex* was horrific. Of the
255 men at the start of the battle, fifty-eight were killed outright or died
later of their wounds; thirty-nine were seriously injured, another twenty-
seven were slightly hurt; and thirty-one were unaccounted for—a total of
155 either dead, wounded, or missing. Some of the latter drowned while
attempting to swim ashore.

After the surrender, Farragut went below, and he was sickened. The
mangled bodies of his dead shipmates were terrible enough to witness,
but the dying, who were groaning and expiring with the most patriotic
sentiments on their lips, overwhelmed him, and he became faint. He
managed to hold together, however, and as soon as he gathered himself,
he hastened to assist the surgeon, Dr. Richard Hoffman, and his assistant,
Dr. Alexander Montgomery, as well as the chaplain, Mr. Adams, in
staunching and dressing the wounds of his comrades. Among them was
his close friend, Lieutenant John Cowell. "O Davy," Cowell cried, when
he saw Farragut, "I fear it is all up with me." He had lost his leg just
above the knee. Doctor Hoffman told Farragut that Cowell "might have

been saved if he had consented to the amputation of the limb an hour earlier, but when it was proposed to drop another patient and attend to him, he replied, 'No, Doctor, none of that; fair play is a jewel. One man's life is as dear as another's. I would not cheat any poor fellow out of his turn.' Thus died one of the best officers and bravest men among us," Farragut lamented.

The dying men—ordinary jack tars—made an indelible impression on Farragut. He heard them "uttering sentiments with their last breath, worthy of a Washington." All around him, he heard, " 'Don't give up the ship Logan!'—a sobriquet for Porter—'Hurrah for Liberty!' and similar expressions."

Many men bled to death from want of tourniquets. Francis Bland, the old quartermaster whom Farragut had taken below bleeding from an open wound, had succumbed before he could be attended to. When the battle was over, Farragut searched for him to see how he was faring, and was shaken when he saw the lifeless body.

A young Scot named Bissley had a leg shot off close to the groin and applied his handkerchief as a pathetic tourniquet. "I left my own country and adopted the United States to fight for her," he declared. "I hope I have this day proved myself worthy of the country of my adoption. I am no longer of any use to you or to her, so goodbye!" He then leaned on the sill of a port and slid over the side into the water.

A young black slave named Ruff, owned by Lieutenant Wilmer, was so disconcerted by the news that the lieutenant had been shot and tumbled overboard, that Ruff leaped into the sea and drowned.

Porter said of his crew, "More bravery, skill, patriotism, and zeal were never displayed on any occasion."

Captain Hillyar reported only four killed and seven wounded on the *Phoebe*, and one killed and three wounded on the *Cherub*. One of the dead was William Ingram, the *Phoebe*'s gallant first lieutenant, who was struck in the head by a jagged splinter. He was much admired, not only on his own ship, but by the Americans as well, especially young Farragut who was much taken with his demeanor, compassion, and candor. Porter, Farragut, Downes, and all the surviving American officers and crew thought so highly of Ingram they attended his funeral at the governor's castle in Valparaiso.

SOME MONTHS LATER, WHEN PORTER WROTE TO THE SECRETARY of the navy reflecting on the battle and its gruesome toll of American fighters, he had no criticism to offer of his strategy or tactics. "We have been unfortunate, but not disgraced," he wrote. "The defense of the *Essex* has not been less honorable to her officers and crew, than the capture of an equal force; and I now consider my situation less unpleasant than that of Commodore Hillyar, who in violation of every principle of honor and generosity, and regardless of the rights of nations, attacked the *Essex* in her crippled state, within pistol shot of a neutral shore—when for six weeks I had daily offered him fair and honorable combat, on terms greatly to his advantage; the blood of the slain must be upon his head." Porter added bitterly that "I must in justification of myself observe that with our six twelve-pounders only, we fought this action, our carronades being almost useless."

Looking back many years later, Farragut had a different view than Porter's. "In the first place, I consider that our original and greatest mistake was in attempting to regain the anchorage"; he wrote, "as, being greatly superior to the enemy in sailing qualities, I think we should have borne up and run before the wind." Farragut thought that if the *Phoebe* managed to catch the *Essex*, Porter could have taken her by boarding. If Hillyar outmaneuvered the *Essex* and avoided her grasp, the *Essex* could have taken her fire and passed on, replacing her topmast as she went and sailing beyond Hillyar's reach. The slow-sailing *Cherub* would not have entered into the action and would have been left far behind.

Farragut also thought that "when it was apparent to everyone that we had no chance of success under the circumstances, the ship should have been run ashore, throwing her broadside to the beach, to prevent raking, and fought as long as was consistent with humanity, and then set on fire."

Farragut went on to criticize Porter for the way he put on the springs that got shot away. "Having determined on anchoring [instead of running ashore] we should have bent a spring on to the ring of the anchor, instead of to the cable, where it was exposed, and could be shot away as fast as put on."

Farragut did not comment on whether Porter should have been in Valparaiso in the first place, probably because he knew in his heart that being there was a colossal mistake. Porter had no business bringing the *Essex* and *Essex Junior* to any Chilean port. He knew that if he waited long enough, a superior British force was bound to trap him. He was endangering one of America's few frigates and the lives of dozens of good seamen, not for military reasons, but for personal glory. And he never tried to conceal his motives. "I had done all the injury that could be done to the British commerce in the Pacific," he wrote, "and still hoped to signalize my cruise by something more splendid before leaving that sea. I thought it not improbable that Commodore Hillyar . . . would seek me at Valparaiso. . . . I therefore determined to cruise about that place."

AT LENGTH, A BOARDING OFFICER ARRIVED FROM THE *PHOEBE*, an imperious young man, with orders to take possession of the *Essex*. He asked Porter how he would account for the men he had allowed to jump overboard, and in the same breath demanded his sword. "That, sir, is reserved for your master," Porter growled. The officer then escorted Porter to the *Phoebe*, where Hillyar received him with "respect and delicacy," Porter recalled.

Somewhat absentmindedly, Hillyar accepted Porter's sword, only to regret it later and return it. He wrote an apology, saying, "although I omitted, at the moment of presentation, from my mind being much engrossed in attending to professional duties, to offer its restoration, the hand that received will be most gladly extended to put it in possession of him who wore it so honorably in defending his country's cause."

Much controversy arose over Hillyar's conduct of the battle, but David Farragut, reflecting on the matter years later, refused to join in the criticism:

> It has been quite common to blame Captain Hillyar for his conduct in this affair; but, when we come to consider the characteristics of the two commanders, we may be inclined to judge more leniently, although Captain Porter's complaints in the matter will excite no surprise. Porter was about thirty-two years of age at the time, and the "pink of chivalry," of an ardent and impetuous temperament; while Hillyar was a cool and calculating man, about fifty [actually forty-four] years old, and, as

he said to his First Lieutenant, "had gained his reputation by several single-ship combats, and only expected to retain it on the present occasion by an implicit obedience to his orders, viz., to capture the *Essex* with the least possible risk to his vessel and crew."

It was said that William Ingram, the *Phoebe*'s first lieutenant, was critical of Hillyar's tactics before he died. During the fighting Ingram begged Hillyar to relinquish his advantageous position, bear down on the *Essex*, and board her. Ingram maintained that it was deliberate murder to lie off at long range and fire when the *Essex* was obviously unable to respond.

Porter's criticism of Hillyar centered on the attack coming in neutral territory. Theodore Roosevelt, in his study of the naval war of 1812, agreed:

> The conduct of the two English captains in attacking Porter as soon as he was disabled, in neutral waters, while they had been very careful to abstain from breaking the neutrality while he was in good condition, does not look well; at the best it shows that Hillyar had only been withheld hitherto from the attack by timidity, and it looks all the worse when it is remembered that Hillyar owed his ship's previous escape entirely to Porter's forbearance on a former occasion when the British frigate was entirely at his mercy, and that the British captain had afterward expressly said that he would not break the neutrality.

Hillyar, as might be expected, heatedly denied Porter's accusation. He maintained that Porter had already violated the neutrality of the port several times when he "burnt a British ship in the bay [*Hector*]; had come out with his armed boats in the night for the avowed purpose of boarding one of our ships, while his own were enjoying the protection of the neutral flag; and besides these acts had actually fired two shots at the *Phoebe* when much nearer the port than where he was attacked."

If some criticized Hillyar for his conduct before and during the battle, none faulted his treatment of the Americans afterward. It was exemplary—even Porter thought so. "In justice to Commodore Hillyar," he wrote,

"I must observe, that (although I can never be reconciled to the manner of his attack on the *Essex*, or to his conduct before the action,) he has, since our capture, shown the greatest humanity to my wounded, . . . and has endeavored as much as lay in his power, to alleviate the distresses of war, by the most generous and delicate deportment toward myself, my officers, and crew." In keeping with this policy, Hillyar ordered the personal property of the Americans respected. The order was not enforced, however, and much was stolen. The same thing would not have happened to the British, Porter noted, had the battle gone the other way. He liked to point out that this was one of many differences between the two services.

In the immediate aftermath of the battle, Hillyar had the *Essex* and *Essex Junior* taken to the common anchorage in Valparaiso. There he placed Porter and his officers on parole so that they could go ashore unhampered to attend to their dead and wounded. Hillyar had allowed the *Essex*'s wounded to go on shore on parole, with the understanding that the United States would bear all the costs of their hospitalization. The rest of the *Essex* men he placed under guard and confined them to a Spanish merchant ship he had hired for that purpose.

Porter did not expect to receive any comfort from the officials now in charge in Valparaiso, nor did they offer any. Their disinterest was more than made up for by the generosity of Valparaiso's women. The American wounded were housed in a comfortable building that Porter selected for a hospital. Once there, the compassionate women of the city provided for their necessities, and tried their best to alleviate their suffering. The women gave their services voluntarily, expecting no compensation. "Without their aid, I have no doubt, many would have died," Porter wrote. "I shall never forget their gentle humanity."

Farragut volunteered to assist the ship's surgeons in attending the wounded, and his offer was gratefully accepted. "I never earned Uncle Sam's money so faithfully as I did during that hospital service," he recalled.

By April 4, 1814, Hillyar, after discussing the matter with Porter, decided to place the American prisoners on parole and send them home on *Essex Junior*, making her a cartel ship. It was understood that when they arrived in the United States they would be exchanged for an equal number of British prisoners. The *Essex Junior* was to be disarmed, and the United

States was to bear the full expense of the voyage. Hillyar provided Porter with a safe conduct pass, so that British warships blockading the American coast would not detain him.

Porter readily acceded to this generous plan. Not only would it grant his men their freedom, but it would also give them one of their prizes. Any wounded who could not make the trip were to be sent home later by the best conveyance available. Porter suspected that Hillyar wanted to get rid of the prisoners for fear they might cause a problem on the *Phoebe*, which would be carrying a large amount of specie back to England.

Fourteen Americans were not part of this arrangement. Hillyar insisted on detaining Lieutenant Stephen Decatur McKnight, Mr. David Adams, Acting Midshipman James Lyman, and eleven seamen. Hillyar planned to send McKnight and Lyman (not the others) to England so that they could give affidavits in the judicial condemnation (disposition) of the *Essex*. There was little Porter could do but agree. McKnight and the others were put on parole, and forced to wait until May 31, when Hillyar left for Rio in the *Phoebe*, accompanied by the *Essex*. They reached Rio with no difficulty, but McKnight and Lyman then had to wait for a ship to take them to Britain. Adams and the eleven seamen eventually returned on parole to the United States directly from Rio. On August 22, 1814, McKnight and Lyman boarded the *Adonis* (Captain J. M. Molen), a Swedish merchantman bound for Falmouth, England.

Once their business was completed in England, they would be free to return home—still on parole. All was proceeding according to plan, when on October 9, six weeks out from Rio, their journey was unexpectedly interrupted. The *Adonis* was about 300 miles west of the Cape Verde Islands when a lookout spotted a warship that turned out to be the powerful 22-gun American sloop of war *Wasp*, under Master Commandant Johnston Blakeley, one of the navy's outstanding warriors. The *Wasp* stopped the *Adonis* and sent over a boarding party to examine her papers. The sight of their own countrymen coming aboard must have astonished and heartened McKnight and Lyman. They could now avoid going to England altogether.

Blakeley must have been surprised and delighted as well. He never expected to find two colleagues in the middle of the ocean on a Swedish ship. After being away from home since he put out from Portsmouth,

New Hampshire, on May 1, 1814, Blakeley could undoubtedly use the companionship. He allowed Lyman and McKnight to be transferred to the *Wasp*, and all seemed well. Tragically, the *Wasp* was never heard from again. She went down with all hands—lost without a trace—before she reached the United States, after one of the most successful cruises in the history of the navy. In the five months *Wasp* had been at sea, Blakeley had captured seventeen enemy merchantmen and defeated two warships. The reason for his demise has never been uncovered.

The mystery of what happened to McKnight and Lyman was not discovered until six years later. In 1820, McKnight's famous uncle, Stephen Decatur, launched an investigation that caused the *Adonis*'s Captain Molen to come forward with his log. But for Decatur's persistence, nobody would have known that the *Wasp* had taken McKnight and Lyman aboard on October 9.

Now it was time for Porter to take his leave of Hillyar. The American thanked the Briton for his generosity but made it plain that he would never condone the manner in which Hillyar had attacked him. Suddenly, tears welled up in Hillyar's eyes, Porter recalled. "My dear Porter," Hillyar said, "you know not the responsibility that hung over me, with respect to your ship. Perhaps my life depended on my taking her." There was no doubt that the Admiralty had a special interest in ending Porter's career of destruction, and their Lordships could, if Hillyar had been thwarted by some political nicety like the questionable neutrality of Valparaiso, have severely punished him. He was not engaging in idle speculation when he spoke of what hung over him. Besides, he was convinced that Porter had violated Chilean neutrality long before he had.

When *Essex Junior* stood out from Valparaiso on April 27, there were 130 men from the *Essex*'s original complement of 255 aboard. Two of the wounded were left behind, and one of them died, but the other, William Call, miraculously recovered and eventually returned to the United States.

On April 27, the same day that the *Essex Junior* left Valparaiso, the *Essex*, was also ready to sail. In spite of the destructive battle, Hillyar had the *Essex* fully provisioned and ready just thirty days after the fighting. Had Porter known, he would have been amazed. He was too busy tending to his dead and wounded in Valparaiso to keep abreast of what was happening to the *Phoebe* and the *Essex*. As late as July 1814, when he was reporting to Secretary of the Navy Jones, he estimated that "both the *Essex* and the *Phoebe* were in a sinking state [after the battle], and it was with difficulty they could be kept afloat until they anchored in Valparaiso next morning: The battered state of the *Essex* will I believe prevent her ever reaching England."

Hillyar, on the other hand, was always confident that, in spite of her injuries, the *Essex* would make the trip. "Although much injured in her upper works, masts and rigging," he wrote to the Admiralty, "[the *Essex*] is not in such a state as to give the slightest cause of alarm respecting her being able to perform a voyage to Europe with perfect safety."

Hillyar was not exaggerating about the seaworthiness of the *Essex*. She traveled with the *Phoebe* to Rio in late July with no trouble. Admiral Dixon had her carefully examined, and when he was satisfied that she was indeed as sound as Hillyar claimed, he purchased her into the Royal Navy—much to Hillyar's delight. Thomas Sumter Jr., American minister to the Portuguese court in Rio, was deeply saddened by the whole business, but there was nothing he could do except observe.

After organizing a new crew for the *Essex*, Hillyar traveled back to England in the *Phoebe* with his prize and 20,000 pounds in specie, arriving on November 13, 1814, after an uneventful voyage. Since the great war with France was by then over and the war with America was soon terminated as well, the Royal Navy had little use for the *Essex*. Still, she survived until July 6, 1837, as a British warship doing menial tasks, such as holding prisoners, until the Admiralty sold her for scrap—a sad ending for one of the finest warships America produced during the Age of Sail.

SOON AFTER HIS VICTORY OVER PORTER, HILLYAR PLUNGED INTO diplomacy, seeking to restore peaceful relations between Peru and Chile by inducing Chile to become a Spanish colony again. This nearly impossible assignment was one of the reasons London had sent him to Latin America in the first place. Hillyar was supposed to convince Chile's republicans that their interests would be served best by accepting royalists as the legitimate governors in Santiago and ending Chile's fratricidal civil war. His task, which otherwise would have been far beyond his capacity, was made easy by the royalist army, which in March and April of 1814 gained the upper hand. After a year of civil war, both sides were exhausted, but the royalists were for the moment victorious.

Hillyar moved deftly to take advantage of the military situation and the general war-weariness in Chile. He persuaded the viceroy of Peru and the politically malleable Supreme Director of the State of Chile, Don Francisco de la Lastra, to sign the Treaty of Lircay on May 3, 1814, whereby Lastra pledged allegiance to the King of Spain, Ferdinand VII, making Chile a Spanish colony again. Hillyar insisted that he was acting in the interests of the "respected ally of my nation respecting its colonies," and indeed, he was.

Given the new political situation, the American consul general Joel Poinsett was compelled to leave Chile. He asked Hillyar for permission to sail with Porter on *Essex Junior* on April 27, but since Poinsett had been notorious in his support of Carrera, he was persona non grata to the Lastra regime, and Hillyar refused. Poinsett could not get away until the middle of June. He was forced to travel overland to Buenos Aires, and did not reach the United States until July 1815.

The peace that Hillyar arranged between Chile and Peru did not last long. Republicans and royalists were back at each others' throats soon enough. José Miguel Carrera overthrew Supreme Director Lastra, and the civil war resumed. By October 1814, after some intense fighting, the royalists won a decisive victory, restoring Spanish rule once more. The patriots, led by the Carreras and O'Higgins, retreated all the way to Mendoza on the eastern side of the Andes in present-day Argentina, where the governor of the province of Cuyo, José de San Martín, welcomed them.

José Miguel Carrera soon traveled to the United States to seek aid, while O'Higgins and San Martín (the Carreras' rivals) prepared to resume the fight for Chilean independence. The new Spanish viceroy in Santiago, General Mariano Osorio, aided them immeasurably. Following the policy of the restored King of Spain, Osorio instituted a brutally repressive regime that alienated the great majority of Chileans. Taking advantage of Spain's unpopularity, O'Higgins and San Martín in January 1817 led a republican army across the Andes from Mendoza and on February 12 decisively defeated Osorio's royalist force at Chacabuco. General Osorio retreated south, regrouped, and marched on Santiago, but General San Martín met him at the River Maipu near Santiago and totally demolished the royalist army. Half of it was killed and the other half captured, effectively liberating Chile from Spain. A year later, on February 12, 1818, Chilean independence was formally proclaimed.

CHAPTER

21

THE HEROES COME HOME

D AVID FARRAGUT REPORTED THAT THE PASSAGE HOME ON *Essex Junior* was swift and uneventful. "We had, as a general thing, very good weather on our homeward voyage," he remembered, "passing Cape Horn under topgallant studding sails." The weather in early May at these latitudes was still cold, but it did not slow them down. On June 14, 1814, they crossed the Equator. Farragut busied himself tending the wounded. With generally favorable winds, they arrived off New York without incident on July 5—Farragut's thirteenth birthday.

Porter intended to get ashore quickly and request a squadron with orders to rush to the English Channel in hopes of intercepting the *Phoebe* and the *Essex*. A more unrealistic scheme would be hard to imagine. Porter was forced back to reality on July 5 by the 58-gun British razee *Saturn* (Captain James Nash), which brought *Essex Junior* to off Long Island. Porter anticipated that something like this might happen, but he did not expect to be detained for long. He thought that once Nash examined Hillyar's safe-conduct pass, he'd release *Essex Junior*. Nash was the commander of the British blockading squadron off New York, and he treated Porter with the utmost civility at first, furnishing him with newspapers and oranges, which Porter took as a sign that all was well.

Shortly, the *Saturn*'s boarding officer came aboard to examine Hillyar's passport. After a perfunctory review he permitted Porter to proceed. But two hours later, the *Saturn* again brought *Essex Junior* to. A second boarding officer came on board with a party of men and examined Hillyar's safe-conduct pass once more, along with the ship's hold. Porter was bewildered and annoyed. His anger grew when the officer informed him that Hillyar had had no right to issue the passport, and that *Essex Junior* would be detained. Porter immediately objected, telling the officer that this was a gross violation of his contract with Hillyar. He then offered his sword, announcing indignantly that he was no longer bound by the contract made with Hillyar, and would considered himself Captain Nash's prisoner, which meant that he was no longer on parole and would act accordingly. The officer declined to accept the sword and directed that *Essex Junior* spend the night under *Saturn*'s lee.

At seven the next morning, July 6, the *Saturn* and *Essex Junior* were forty miles off Eastern Long Island and about a hundred feet apart with a light wind from the south. Porter was still fuming; he believed that Nash had no intention of liberating *Essex Junior*. Feeling a great sense of urgency, Porter planned an escape. The best time to effect one was immediately after capture. It would be difficult, of course. *Essex Junior* was only a short distance from the *Saturn*, but Porter was determined to risk it.

Before noon, he had a whaleboat lowered, filled it with armed men, and pushed off. Downes was left to accept the consequences, a situation that apparently did not bother Porter. To make matters worse for Downes, before Porter left, he told Downes to inform Captain Nash that British officers were not only personally destitute of honor but had no regard for the honor of each other. After pulling away, Porter kept *Essex Junior* between him and the *Saturn*, hiding the whaleboat.

His departure went unnoticed. He was nearly a mile away before a lookout at the *Saturn*'s main masthead spotted him. Just then, a fresh breeze sprang up, and the *Saturn* crowded on sail, wore ship, and tore after the whaleboat. Before *Saturn* had gotten very far, however, a thick fog miraculously appeared, enveloping Porter's boat, *Essex Junior*, and the *Saturn*. Farragut could hear orders being shouted on the razee, but he could not see her. Porter took immediate advantage, changed course, and made good his escape. As he did, he heard cannon fire from the *Saturn*, but the wild shots never came close to hitting the whaleboat.

Meanwhile, the redoubtable Downes tried to use the commotion over Porter's flight to make an escape of his own. When the providential fog appeared, Downes put on all the sail *Essex Junior* could carry and made for Sandy Hook. Within minutes she was making an impressive nine knots. The fog soon lifted, however, and a lookout on the *Saturn* spotted her to windward. He shouted down to the quarterdeck from a royal masthead. Forgetting about Porter, the *Saturn* fired a gun to leeward and ran after *Essex Junior*. With all the speed Downes was able to achieve, it took the *Saturn* three hours of hard sailing to catch her. Finally, when the *Saturn* pulled to within cannon range, Downes was forced to put his main topsail to the mast and heave to. A boat from the razee was then lowered, and an officer, who had not been on *Essex Junior* before, rowed across to the ship.

He stepped aboard and said sarcastically to Downes, "You drift quite fast. We have been going nine knots for the last three hours, and yet we find you abeam with your main topsail to the mast."

Downes looked at him with a steady eye and said, "Yes."

"And that was Captain Porter who left the ship in a boat, I suppose?"

"It was," said Downes.

"Then by God, you will soon be leaving too, if we don't take your boats from you."

"You had better try that."

"I would, if I had my way."

Downes glared at him. "You impertinent puppy," he said, "if you have any business to do here, do it, but if you dare to insult me again I shall throw you overboard."

Without answering, the young man got into his boat and returned to the *Saturn*. A short time later, another officer, the same one who had first boarded *Essex Junior* the day before, arrived and offered Captain Nash's apologies for the ungentlemanly behavior of the previous officer.

The crew of *Essex Junior* was then mustered, and each man examined in turn to check his name against Hillyar's passport, and for deserters from the Royal Navy. After completing the last interview, the officer turned to one of his own seamen and asked, "Which is the man you spoke of as being an Englishman?"

Suddenly, anxiety gripped every American until the British tar answered boldly, "I never said he was an Englishman."

"But you said you had sailed with him."

"True enough, but it was out of New York."

The officer apologized and returned to the *Saturn*, where Captain Nash countersigned Hillyar's passport. Downes was now free to proceed for Sandy Hook and New York. About sunset, however, he fell in with another British frigate, HMS *Narcissus*, which subjected the entire crew to another examination before countersigning the passport a second time. Downes then continued on. He reached Sandy Hook at 8 P.M.

The night was dark and squally. Downes could not procure a pilot to conduct him into New York, but he proceeded anyway, using a chart for a guide. In the Horseshoe, he hoisted his colors with lanterns and sent a boat on shore with a light. But the light went out and a small battery on shore started firing on *Essex Junior*. It did not stop until the boat returned with another light. In the meantime, not a single shot found its mark.

It was now too late to proceed, and Downes, having convinced the battery that *Essex Junior* was an American ship, furled his sails and anchored for the night. The following morning, July 7, he stood into New York Harbor under full sail with colors flying, only to be fired on by another battery. Its accuracy was no better than the first one, however, and *Essex Junior* sailed on, coming to anchor off New York.

WHILE DOWNES WAS MAKING HIS WAY TO NEW YORK, PORTER was doing the same. But he was delayed. When he set out for Long Island in his whaleboat, he did not know quite where he was. After rowing and sailing sixty long, difficult miles during the night, he finally came within sight of the beach at Babylon early in the morning. The surf was running high, but he managed, with great difficulty, to run the whaleboat up on hard sand. Townspeople assumed he was a British officer, and militiamen quickly assembled. They pointed their muskets at him and took the whole strange boatload prisoner, believing they were British. The militiamen found Porter's story so extraordinary it defied belief. But when he showed his commission, their doubts vanished. They lowered their muskets and gave three cheers. They even saluted their visitors with a one-pound swivel gun. They also gave Porter a large wagon to haul his men to New York.

By four o'clock, Porter was in Brooklyn, where he crossed the East River in the steamboat ferry *Nassau*. When he arrived in Manhattan, Lieutenant Downes was already there. Porter was relieved. He was also exhilarated, as cheering citizens unhitched the horses from the wagon, and with Porter and his men in it, drew it up to City Hall, where a grand celebration commenced. When it was over, Porter was taken to his lodging in Greenwich Street with crowds cheering him along the way. If he had had any remaining doubts about how a defeated captain who had lost his ship and had dozens of men killed and wounded would be received, this reception removed them. The *Boston Gazette* spoke for most of the country when it declared: "The American Navy loses nothing of its justly acquired renown by this loss [of the *Essex*]."

Although Porter and Downes were reunited, they had little time together. Both naturally wanted to get home. When the celebration was over, Porter headed for Chester, and Downes for Canton, Massachusetts. On the way to Chester, Porter stopped in Philadelphia, where he received another rousing welcome. On entering the city the horses were again unhitched from his carriage, and a crowd drew him in triumph to the Mansion House Hotel amidst loud cheering. When he arrived at the hotel, he was carried on shoulders to the reception room, where he received the accolades of the city.

He was still anxious to get home, of course. He remained in Philadelphia only a few hours before moving on to Chester and a reunion with Evelina and his family, which now included a new member, David Dixon Porter, whom Evelina had been pregnant with when David left way back in October 1812.

Porter was overjoyed to see his family, and by the reception he was getting everywhere he went. He later wrote, "On my arrival by land at New York, the reception given me by the inhabitants, as well as those of every other place through which I passed, it becomes me not to record. It is sufficient to say, it has made an impression on my mind, never to be effaced." Adding to his pleasure was the reception he received at the White House. At the end of July, Secretary Jones brought him there for dinner with President Madison, who made it clear that he, like Jones, had a high appreciation of the heroic efforts of Porter and his men—despite their defeat in Valparaiso.

ALTHOUGH PORTER AND HIS CREW WERE ENORMOUSLY GRATEFUL for the applause of their countrymen, they also had an urgent need for money owed them for their service. It had not been forthcoming when they landed in New York, and so they had to borrow to acquire food and lodging. The British had stripped them of everything they had, except for the clothes on their backs. On July 20 six members of the crew wrote respectfully to Porter complaining that "We have now been ten days onshore without one cent in our pockets." He relayed their plea for help to Secretary Jones, who was furious with the Republican politicians in Congress who had voted for the war, but had not properly funded it, leaving the country practically bankrupt. Jones was often without funds for the ordinary expenses of the department such as seamen's wages. On July 25 he provided Porter with $30,000 to pay his crew. Jones also made sure that the navy bought *Essex Junior* for $25,000, which gave the crew and the captain money they badly needed.

GIVEN THE COUNTRY'S WIDESPREAD APPRECIATION OF HIS efforts, Porter was more anxious than ever to have a court of inquiry convened so that he could be officially exonerated for the loss of the *Essex* and so many of her men. On August 11, 1814, Secretary Jones ordered Commodore Stephen Decatur to convene a court of inquiry aboard the frigate *President* in New York harbor. But on August 19 Jones directed Decatur to suspend the court so that Porter and what remained of the *Essex*'s crew could participate in the defense of Baltimore and Washington, where President Madison thought the British would soon attack. They did— Washington on August 24 and Baltimore on September 13.

Porter arrived too late to help with the defense of Washington, but he did participate in a belated attempt to prevent a potent British squadron, under Commodore James Gordon, from sailing back down the Potomac River and joining a much larger fleet, under Vice Admiral Alexander Cochrane, for the attack on Baltimore. Gordon had failed to reach Washington in time to participate in the capture and burning of the capital, but he did sit off Alexandria and force the city, under the threat of destruction, to pay an exorbitant tribute. Gordon then began descending back down the Potomac to join the larger British fleet in Chesapeake Bay. Secretary Jones hoped that Porter, along with Commodores John Rodgers and Oliver Hazard Perry, working separately, could prevent Gordon from getting back to the Chesapeake. If they could, Admiral Cochrane might cancel his planned assault on Baltimore.

Porter and his colleagues made a mighty effort with pitifully inadequate resources, but they could not stop Gordon. They did hold him back long enough, however, to give Baltimore's defenders additional time to prepare. It made a significant difference. The strength of Baltimore's defenses forced Admiral Cochrane's invaders to withdraw after an ineffective bombardment. His humiliating withdrawal, along with the unexpected defeat of British forces at Fort Erie on August 11–12 and at Plattsburgh, New York, on September 11, played an important part in convincing the prime minister, Lord Liverpool, and his cabinet to end the war. Porter and his men, thus, played a not insignificant role in ending the War of 1812 on far better terms than anyone at the time thought possible.

With the war over and Porter an even bigger hero than ever, Decatur's court of inquiry into the loss of the *Essex* appeared pointless and was suspended indefinitely.

chapter 22

LIEUTENANT GAMBLE
AT NUKU HIVA

T EMPORARILY FORGOTTEN AMID THE HORRENDOUS EVENTS
in Valparaiso was twenty-three-year-old Lieutenant John Gamble
and his tiny crew at Nuku Hiva. They had been trying to maintain control of Porter's pathetic caricature of a colony with a wholly inadequate
force. Not surprisingly, the moment the *Essex* and *Essex Junior* departed,
the Taiohae tested Gamble. "The frigate had scarcely got clear of the
Marquesas before we discovered a hostile disposition on the part of the
natives," he reported many months later to Secretary of the Navy Benjamin Crowninshield, who had replaced William Jones.

Porter had assumed that the Taiohae were thoroughly cowed and
would be the least likely tribe to cause trouble. Actually, Gamble had difficulties with them right from the start. A few days after Porter left, the
Taiohae became so insolent that Gamble "found it absolutely necessary,
not only for the security of the ships [*Seringapatam*, *Greenwich*, and *Sir
Andrew Hammond*], and property on shore [Fort Madison], but for our
personal safety, to land my men and regain by force of arms, the many
things they had, in the most daring manner, stolen from the encampment;

and what was of still greater importance, to prevent, if possible, their putting threats into execution, which might have been attended with the most serious consequences on our part from duty requiring my men to be so much separated."

To underscore his determination not to be run over, Gamble captured two chieftains and put them aboard the *Greenwich* until all swine stolen from Fort Madison were returned. His fast action checked the Taiohae for the moment, but a series of subsequent events kept Gamble on edge, prepared for the worst. To begin with, discipline was breaking down among his men, particularly the British prisoners, something that Porter should have foreseen. On January 20 the crew on the *Seringapatam* brought girls on board, which was forbidden. Gamble had issued strict orders not to permit any natives on the ships. He did not want the Taiohae finding out just how undermanned he was. The girls were sent ashore, and the men flogged, but the blatant disregarding of orders was unsettling.

Things were quiet for a time, but on February 28, John Witter, a marine, was found drowned in the surf for no apparent reason. Gamble investigated but failed to discover what had happened. A short time later, on March 6, Isaac Coffin, an escaped British prisoner whom Gamble had recaptured after the *Essex* left, escaped again during the night. Aware that Coffin's companions had freed him, Gamble took eight armed men and searched for him. They found him in a native house, took him back to the ship, and put him in irons. The following morning at ten o'clock, Gamble, with all crew and prisoners assembled, gave Coffin three dozen lashes.

Twelve days later, four men deserted during the night. One was Coffin, who had been set loose from his irons once more. Another was John Robertson, an American prisoner in irons. Two of the four were original members of the *Essex* crew. They took advantage of the darkness, stove in Gamble's blue boat (the fastest pulling boat) in two places, and left the bay in a whaleboat. No one saw them escape except a former prisoner, who had the watch on deck that night and was one of them. The deserters took several muskets, a supply of ammunition, and other articles such as two compasses, clothing, a spyglass, an English ensign, two axes, a grindstone, and a boat sail, all of which would be of considerable use. Gamble had no hope of catching them. "My attempt to pursue them was prevented by their destroying partially the only boat (near the beach) at that time seaworthy," he wrote. The deserters made their way to Santa Christiana (Tahuata) Island, one of the Marquesas, where they hid for months until a British frigate, the *Briton*, picked them up.

By April, Gamble was losing any hope of Porter returning, and on the 12th, he began rigging the *Seringapatam* and *Sir Andrew Hammond* for departure. The remaining men were employed removing everything of service from the *Greenwich* to the *Seringapatam*. While the work went ahead, Gamble sensed that something was wrong, that perhaps a mutiny was brewing, and he ordered the remaining muskets, ammunition, and small arms taken to the *Greenwich*—the ship he was living on.

On May 7, the uprising he had feared broke out on the *Seringapatam*. He happened to be on board at the time, and even though he was on guard, he was surprised when he was violently attacked. An intense struggle ensued. Gamble was beaten to the deck and had his hands and legs tied. He was then thrown below and dragged to the cabin, where he was confined beneath the floor in a space that had no window or light. Midshipman Feltus and Acting Midshipman Clapp were also knocked down and put in the same place with Gamble, where they were tied down and could hardly breath. The entrance to their tiny space was then nailed down and a sentinel placed over it. After complaining loudly about their inhuman confinement, the three were allowed into the cabin. Gamble was forced to sit on a chest under the skylight with two men guarding him.

The fourteen mutineers lost no time spiking the guns on the *Greenwich* and the *Sir Andrew Hammond* and at Fort Madison. Then they removed the arms and ammunition from the *Greenwich* and put them aboard the *Seringapatam*. They also took everything else of use to them from the other ships and put them on the *Seringapatam*. They sent for Robert White, whom Porter had chased from the *Essex* for mutinous conduct, and bending the topsails, got underway at 6 P.M., standing out of the bay with a light wind off the land. Gamble believed that almost none of the mutineers were Americans. He thought that twelve were Englishmen, six of whom had joined the *Essex*'s crew and six who had remained prisoners.

There was also a foreigner, and the American, Robert White, making a total of fourteen. Midshipman Feltus had a different view of who the fourteen were. According to him, six were prisoners, four were former prisoners who had joined the *Essex* crew, and four were Americans. The four Americans were Thomas Belcher, James Bantum, Martin Stanley, and Robert White. Feltus was undoubtedly correct.

When the mutineers were moving slowly out of the bay, an unfortunate accident happened. Lewis Ronsford, a clumsy sentinel who was guarding Gamble, Feltus, Clapp and two other prisoners, mishandled a pistol he was carrying and shot Gamble in the left heel a little below the ankle bone. When the mutineers on the deck above heard the shot, they immediately assumed the worst, grabbed muskets, and pointed them down the skylight. They were about to fire at Gamble and the others, when Ronsford shouted that he had discharged his weapon in error. Somewhat relieved—they did not want to kill their captives—the mutineers backed off. But Gamble was left with a dangerous wound.

By nine o'clock, the *Seringapatam* was safely out of the bay. The night was dark and the wind blowing fresh. The mutineers decided to get rid of Gamble and his companions, Midshipmen Clapp and Feltus, and seamen William Worth, and Richard Sandsbury. They put them in a leaky boat, gave them a keg of gunpowder, and three old muskets, which Gamble had asked for. While the *Seringapatam* disappeared into the night, Gamble and the others rowed for the *Greenwich*, bailing for six long miles, fighting to keep the boat afloat, before finally making it back to the ship, exhausted, but feeling lucky that the mutineers had not killed them and dumped their bodies overboard.

Two days later, Gamble and his remaining men were hard at work making preparations to leave for Valparaiso. They were assisted by George Ross and William Brudenell, Americans who by chance were on Nuku Hiva collecting sandalwood. While Gamble's men were moving supplies from Fort Madison to the *Sir Andrew Hammond*, the Taiohae—urged on by Wilson, the tattooed Englishman with a fondness for rum, whom Porter had trusted and used as an interpreter—attacked them, murdering Midshipman Feltus, John Thomas, Thomas Gibbs, and William Brudenell. Not everyone was killed, however. Peter Caddington, a marine, and

William Worth jumped into the water and started swimming for the ship with the Taiohae after them.

Seeing what was happening, Midshipman Clapp and three others put off in a boat to rescue them, while Gamble fired grape and canister shot at the attackers from the ship. Caddington was badly wounded as he struggled forward, but Clapp managed to pick up both him and Worth and return to the ship safely, with the Taiohae working hard to intercept them. The Taiohae did not stop either. They kept on coming and tried to board the *Greenwich* and *Sir Andrew Hammond*. But Gamble, who was on the *Sir Andrew Hammond*, drove them off with a cannon.

Meanwhile, Wilson and hundreds of Taiohae were overrunning Fort Madison. They tried to get the spikes out of the guns as quickly as possible and turn them on the *Sir Andrew Hammond*, where Gamble and the rest of his men were—with the exception of John Pettinger, a sick man aboard the *Greenwich*.

Gamble—still in excruciating pain—was running low on ammunition. He knew he had to get the *Sir Andrew Hammond* out of the bay before Wilson succeeded in readying the shore battery. Before leaving, Gamble sent a boat to retrieve Pettinger and burn the *Greenwich*. When the boat returned with Pettinger and the *Greenwich* was blazing, Gamble made a run for it. Having already bent the jib and spanker, he cut his anchor (not being able to pull it), and, even though it was a dark night and the only light was coming from the burning *Greenwich*, a providential breeze carried him clear of the bay. Gamble had eight pathetic souls on board—"one cripple confined to bed," he wrote, "one man dangerously wounded, one sick, one convalescent (a feeble old man recovering from the scurvy) and myself, unable to lend any further assistance, the exertions of the day having inflamed my wound so much as to produce a violent fever; leaving Midshipman Clapp and only two men capable of doing duty." To make matters worse, just six cartridges remained.

"In that state," Gamble recorded, "destitute of charts, and of every means of getting to windward, I saw but one alternative; to run the trade winds down, and, if possible, make the Sandwich [Hawaiian] Islands," a perilous journey of two thousand miles. After struggling out of Taiohae Bay, Gamble, who was using a crutch to walk, lost no time getting up topsails. His chances weren't good. But as luck would have it, against horrendous odds, he succeeded, reaching the Sandwich Islands on May 25, after a passage of seventeen incredibly difficult days—"suffering much from fatigue and hardships" the entire way, Gamble remembered.

On May 30, Gamble came to anchor in Waikiki Bay off the island of Oahu. As he had hoped, a few Americans were there, including Captain Nathaniel Winship and some officers from other ships who were anxious to help. "I received every assistance their situations would afford me," he reported.

Hawaiians supplied Gamble with fresh meat, vegetables, and fruit. They expected in return that he would take their chief man and some others with their property to the big island of Hawaii, which was to windward. The weather was too boisterous for the Hawaiians to make the journey in their canoes. Gamble hired nine men to supplement the crew of the *Sir Andrew Hammond* and sailed for Hawaii to meet the king of the islands and request provisions from him, after which Gamble intended to sail to Valparaiso, following Porter's original instructions.

Unfortunately, on the passage to the Big Island, the fates turned against Gamble once more. On June 13, 1814, he ran into a British warship of some size. Incredibly, she turned out to be none other than the 24-gun *Cherub*, fresh from her victory in Valparaiso. After the battle with the *Essex*, Hillyar had ordered the *Cherub*'s Captain Tucker to take on board provisions for five months and race to the Sandwich Islands "to use your utmost endeavor to distress the enemy by capture or destruction of his vessels." Hillyar had gotten word that American merchantmen had congregated there, waiting for the war to end.

In spite of Gamble's protestations, Tucker seized the articles Gamble was transporting for the Hawaiians, including a valuable canoe. The goods were intended as tribute for their king. It was obvious that Tucker's principal object was not capturing American merchantmen but enriching himself in any way he could before returning to Valparaiso and then Rio de Janeiro. After robbing the Hawaiians, Tucker moved on to the island of Kauai, looking for more booty. He was in luck. The American merchant vessel *Charon* was there and was easily captured. Goods from other vessels were deposited on the island as well, which Tucker took, stuffing as much as he could into the *Cherub*.

On July 15, Tucker departed Hawaii and traveled to Tahiti, where he expected to find refreshment of every sort for himself and his crew—but not for their American prisoners. He had little consideration for Gamble, and even less for his men, who were robbed and cruelly handled. "My men were treated in a most shameful manner," Gamble reported.

Tucker departed Tahiti on August 23 with the *Sir Andrew Hammond*, the *Charon*, and the *Cherub* and stood east for a month, dropping anchor in Valparaiso on September 23. An English brig and the *Montezuma*, one of Porter's first prizes, were anchored in the port, along with several Spanish vessels, and to Gamble's surprise and chagrin, the old Spanish flag was flying above the forts. Gamble and Midshipman Clapp were allowed to go ashore, but not the rest of their men. Gamble and Clapp went immediately to the home of the American deputy vice consul, Mr. Blanco, who had been of such service to Porter. To his great surprise, Gamble discovered that as many as twenty (the exact number was uncertain) of the *Essex*'s old crew were still living in difficult conditions in the city. Some of them had even enlisted in the Chilean army. When Porter learned about them much later, he thought they were the men who had jumped overboard or otherwise fled the *Essex* during her monumental battle with the *Phoebe*. He had no sympathy for them. As far as he was concerned, they had brought their problems on themselves by their own misconduct.

On October 18, 1814, the *Cherub* left Valparaiso Bay with her two prizes and the prisoners bound for Rio. Tempestuous rain and hailstorms plagued them as they rounded Cape Horn. They got around, however, arriving in Rio on November 28. Gamble and Midshipman Clapp were allowed to leave the ship, but no other prisoners could. Tucker kept them on board until December 14, when, Gamble recalled, "the prisoners were sent ashore, having received the most rigorous treatment from Captain Tucker during their long confinement in his ship, and the greater part of them, like the natives, left destitute of everything, save the clothes on their backs." Gamble found sixty American prisoners of war in Rio, being kept track of by Thomas Sumter Jr., the American minister. Like all the others, Gamble had only one thought in mind—going home, but Sumter offered little hope of getting them there quickly.

Gamble did not leave Rio until May 15, 1815. Midshipman Clapp and five men accompanied him. Another man had died of smallpox. During the voyage, one of the men died, but the others reached New York on August 27, 1815, after a passage of one hundred days that took them first to France. A few days later, Gamble wrote long letters to Porter and to Secretary of the Navy Crowninshield, explaining what had happened to him and his men after the *Essex* and *Essex Junior* left Nuku Hiva on December 13, 1813.

Porter's guilt at his treatment of Gamble was pronounced. He tried to make up for it by lavishly praising him, but the record of Porter's hubris and bad judgment and their consequences for Gamble and his men could not be erased.

Epilogue

FOUR LIVES AFTER THE WAR

DESPITE DAVID PORTER'S SHORTCOMINGS, WHEN HE RETURNED home from the Pacific, the great majority of his countrymen greeted him as a hero, as did President Madison. The war was going badly for the president in 1814. Defeatism was widespread, and London was reacting to the abdication of Napoleon on April 14, 1814, as though Britain now had the capacity to work her will on the United States in a short time with relatively few resources.

Madison, with good reason, feared a large-scale invasion that would have incalculable consequences. The British were still furious with America for declaring war in June 1812 when they were most vulnerable to Napoleon. In the spring of 1814, after Napoleon had abdicated unconditionally, a vengeful Britain intended to crush the United States and permanently weaken her. Madison vowed to resist the British to the last. Remembering the sacrifices he had observed as a young man being borne during the War of Independence, he was not about to give in. In the darkest moments of the Revolutionary War, Washington had been determined to fight on no matter what. He would never submit. Madison was of that mind now in the darkest hour of the War of 1812. Porter's spirited defense of the *Essex* struck a responsive chord in the president, who was determined never to

263

give in himself. Madison overlooked Porter's failings and concentrated on his brave resistance, declaring in his Message to Congress in 1814, that the loss of the *Essex* was

> hidden in the blaze of heroism with which she was defended. Captain Porter, . . . whose previous career had been distinguished by daring enterprise and by fertility of genius, maintained a sanguinary contest against two ships, one of them superior to his own, . . . until humanity tore down the colors which valor had nailed to the mast. This officer and his comrades have added much to the rising glory of the American flag, and have merited all the effusions of gratitude which their country is ever ready to bestow on the champions of its rights, and of its safety.

It was a handsome tribute. No one could gainsay that those who fought the battle in Valparaiso were heroes; these were men who did their duty in an exemplary manner, and who deserved the plaudits of their country-men. Whether the *Essex* should or should not have been where she was at the time was beside the point. The example of the men who defended her was what stood out. They created a brilliant legacy for those who came after them.

WHILE PRESIDENT MADISON WAS USING THE EXPLOITS OF THE *Essex* men to help rally the country during the difficult summer and fall of 1814, no one imagined that the war would be over by the end of the year. The assumption that the fighting would go on into 1815 and beyond was universal. David Porter, John Downes, David Farragut, and James Hillyar expected to be engaged in the struggle for a long time. At most they anticipated a brief furlough before receiving new orders to go back into battle.

When the peace treaty was signed on December 24, 1814, in Ghent, Belgium, and the war ended abruptly, the four officers were completely surprised. So was the president. He was also extremely grateful. For him, having to carry on the fight when the country desperately wanted peace was an uninviting prospect. In fact, he had been trying hard to end the war since at least February 1813, when it had become clear that his strategy wasn't working. Napoleon had been defeated in Russia, taking the pressure off Britain to negotiate an end to the war with America, and the Canadian invasion that Madison had initiated and persisted in had been repulsed with minimal effort from London.

No matter how much Madison desired peace during 1813 and 1814, however, the British would not oblige him. They were angry that he had declared war in June 1812 when they were most vulnerable to Napoleon. As far as they were concerned, Madison had stabbed them in the back when their very existence was at risk, and they intended to repay him by permanently weakening America. They changed their minds, however, in the fall of 1814. In that season it became obvious, after American victories at Fort Erie, Plattsburgh, and Baltimore, that the United States was too strong to be easily subdued, and that Europe's problems would continue to occupy Britain for years. Given this new reality, the prime minister, Lord Liverpool, his foreign minister, Lord Castlereagh, and their cabinet colleagues moved quickly to end the war. They did not want to be fighting the United States while they were tied down on the European continent.

The peace that Liverpool obtained was widely popular in Britain, where people were dead tired of war. They had been fighting the French since January 1793. Their only respite had been during the period of the Treaty of Amiens, which lasted only fourteen months, from March 1802 until May of the following year.

The United States was as ready to end the fighting as the British, if not more so, and when the peace treaty arrived in Washington in February 1815, it was greeted with universal applause.

Terminating the war did not mean the careers of Porter, Hillyar, Downes, and Farragut, were ending, however. Relatively young when they returned home as heroes, they could look forward to prominent roles in the futures of their navies. As it turned out, though, only three, Downes, Farragut, and Hillyar realized their potential. David Porter never achieved the prominence that everyone expected of him. Following the war, he served for nine years at the highest levels of the navy, and was a respected figure. But then he became embroiled in a controversy that he exacerbated, escalating it unnecessarily into a confrontation with his superiors that led him to resign forever from the navy he loved, and even leave the country more or less permanently.

JOHN DOWNES DID NOT EXPERIENCE THE SAME UNFORTUNATE fate as David Porter. His career was notable for steady advancement and continuing respect from his peers. His remarkable performance in the Pacific did not go unnoticed. Fearless, charismatic, intelligent, steadfast in the performance of his duty, Downes was recognized throughout the rest of his life as one of the navy's preeminent officers. His close friend Isaac Hull described him as "one of our most respectable and amiable commanders." David Porter, to his credit, never lost an opportunity to praise Downes. Although while serving together, Porter never consulted him about strategy, and handed him unusual, often difficult assignments, he constantly sang his praises.

In recognition of Downes's accomplishments, the navy promoted him to master commandant in July 1813, although he did not receive the good news until he returned from the Pacific. The secretary of the navy acknowledged Downes's outstanding abilities again when he awarded him command of the 18-gun brig *Epervier* in 1815. It was a choice assignment. The *Epervier* would be part of a ten-ship squadron, the most powerful yet assembled under the American flag. Commodore Stephen Decatur was leading it to the Mediterranean to quash Algeria, which had been at war with the United States since 1812, trying to take advantage of America's preoccupation with Britain. Decatur also intended to chastise the other three Barbary pirate states—Tripoli, Tunis, and Morocco—at the same time.

Decatur's squadron sailed from New York on May 20, 1815. A month later, on June 17, Downes played an important part in capturing the 46-gun super-frigate *Mashuda*, the most powerful Algerian warship. Two days later, Decatur fell in with the 22-gun Algerian brig *Estido*, which fled into shallow waters. He sent Downes in the *Epervier*, supported by the brig *Spark*, and the schooners *Torch* and *Spitfire* after her. They quickly brought her to. Decatur then moved on with his squadron to Algiers, where he dictated peace. He then turned on the other Barbary states and forced them to agree to peace as well, ushering in a new era in the Mediterranean. Downes provided invaluable help throughout.

Decatur was so impressed with him that he made him skipper of his flag-ship *Guerierre*.

After returning home, Downes was promoted to captain on March 5, 1817 and given command of the frigate *Macedonian*. At the end of the following year he sailed her on an important mission to South America, where he remained until 1821, performing superbly under tough conditions. His job was to protect American shipping along the western coast of South America, particularly the coasts of Chile and Peru, where the fighting between monarchists and patriots was still going on. After Chile had declared independence in 1818, General San Martín used it as a base from which to attack royalist Peru. He was aided by former British captain Thomas Cochrane (the model for Patrick O'Brian's Jack Aubrey).

Both sides were seizing American shipping. Peruvian royalists routinely attacked vessels flying the Stars and Stripes, but so too did Chilean privateers, turned pirates. Downes was ordered to put a stop to the seizures, but maintaining neutral rights among warring countries was not easy. He also had to be careful of Cochrane trying to advance British interests. In these confusing circumstances Downes managed to remain strictly neutral and at the same time save a number of American ships and seamen, acquitting himself exceptionally well.

Not long after returning home, he had to watch helplessly in 1825 as his friend David Porter threw away his career. Downes was appointed to serve on the court-martial that convicted Porter. There was little Downes could do for him, however. The court was stacked with Porter's enemies. Nonetheless, Downes remained close friends with him and continued to loan him money. Porter always lived in high style, far beyond his means. The sums were substantial—$4,500 on one occasion and $1,500 on another.

The next important assignment for Downes was command of the Mediterranean squadron. He sailed for Gibraltar in the USS *Java* in 1828 and remained until 1830. His orders were to protect American commerce. Since the departure of Decatur and Bainbridge in 1815 the United States had kept a force in the Mediterranean to guarantee the peace, beginning a long tradition. America has had a fleet there ever since.

After his stint in the Mediterranean, Downes was soon appointed skipper of the 44-gun, 500-man heavy frigate *Potomac*. On June 27, 1831, he received orders to transport the new American ambassador, Martin Van Buren, to England, after which Downes was to proceed to the Pacific by way of the Cape of Good Hope and assume command "of the naval forces on that station," headquartered in Valparaiso. The sloop of war *Falmouth* and the schooner *Dolphin* were to accompany him.

President Andrew Jackson changed his orders on August 9, 1831, however. He sent Downes directly to Sumatra in the East Indies via the Cape of Good Hope to put a stop to the attacks of Malay pirates on American shipping engaged in the lucrative pepper trade. Jackson and the country had been stirred up by an attack in February 1831 that Malay pirates made on the American merchant ship *Friendship* out of Salem, Massachusetts. The first officer and two seamen were killed while the skipper, Charles Endicott, and the rest of the crew were ashore. Endicott managed to reclaim his ship and sail back to Salem, where community leaders demanded that President Jackson do something.

Responding to these calls and his own outrage, Jackson ordered Downes to proceed directly to Sumatra, and after ascertaining what had happened, obtain "prompt redress" so that "the guilty perpetrators [are] made to feel that the flag of the Union is not to be insulted with impunity."

After a long, but uneventful trip, Downes arrived off the village of Quallah Battoo on February 5, 1832. During the voyage he trained 250 of his men on the *Potomac* as an amphibious force, in case that was necessary, much as Captain Porter had done on the *Essex*. Soon after Downes arrived, he determined that ascertaining exactly what had happened would be impossible, as would negotiating with the obviously hostile rajahs.

He decided instead to attack and bombarded Quallah Battoo. His well-trained landing force of sailors and marines assaulted four forts, capturing them after a two-and-a-half-hour battle in which as many as a hundred or more natives were killed and two Americans. When Downes was through, the rajahs promised never to attack American merchantmen again—a promise that was kept only briefly.

With his mission complete, Downes sailed across the Pacific, stopping among other places at Honolulu before traveling to Valparaiso. There he learned that his attack on Quallah Battoo had created a political brouhaha in Washington. Jackson's political enemies, while not criticizing Downes and his heroic men, faulted the president for initiating a conflict without Congressional approval. Responding to the loud criticism, Navy Secretary Levi Woodbury wrote a private letter to Downes complaining of his aggressive tactics. Downes was surprised. He felt that he had scrupulously adhered to his orders. When he arrived home in May 1834, after circumnavigating the globe, the criticism from Jackson's opponents had subsided, and the president gave the popular commodore his full support.

Downes was gratified, and he soon retired from active sea duty, having spent the greater part of a thirty-four-year career at sea. From 1835 to 1842 and then again, from 1849 to 1852, he served as commandant of the Charlestown Navy Yard in Boston, another choice assignment for someone of his age. In between those commands, he was Boston's port captain. And from 1852 to 1853 he was a lighthouse inspector. Downes died in Charlestown on August 11, 1854, at the age of seventy, still one of the Navy's most respected figures.

DAVID FARRAGUT LOVED THE NAVY EVERY BIT AS MUCH AS John Downes. He remained in the service his entire career. During the years following the War of 1812, his devotion was often tested, but no matter how trying, he persevered. Had it not been for the Civil War, however, Farragut would undoubtedly have ended his career as an obscure captain.

During the Civil War, he became a national hero, but that was a long time after he returned home on parole in *Essex Junior*. After being formally exchanged and released from parole in November 1814, he was assigned to the new 74-gun *Independence*, Commodore William Bainbridge's flagship. In March 1815 Farragut sailed to the Mediterranean with Bainbridge, who was assuming command from Decatur. Much to Bainbridge's chagrin, when he arrived he discovered that Decatur had already subdued the Barbary pirate states. Bainbridge wanted that honor for himself. There was nothing left for him to do, however, and he returned home, leaving part of his squadron in the Mediterranean to maintain a continuing American presence.

The following spring, Midshipman Farragut was assigned to the 74-gun *Washington* for three years (1816–1819). Her skipper, Captain John O. Creighton, made an indelible impression on him. Creighton, it turned out, was a sadistic martinet. Farragut had never seen anything like him in the service, or even thought there could be such a captain in the American navy. It was not uncommon, Farragut reported, for the officer of the deck on the *Washington* to call up the whole watch and give them two or three dozen lashes apiece for the real or imagined fault of one man, or sometimes for a mere accident. At times, for some minor infraction, hands were forced to wait eight or ten hours for their meals. On one occasion, Farragut recalled, the entire crew was kept on deck all night for several nights in succession. Farragut thought Creighton was the worse disciplinarian in the navy and a disgrace to the service. The contrast with Porter and all the other officers Farragut had served under was striking. He vowed never to resort to Creighton's methods, and he never did.

During 1818, while serving in the Mediterranean, Farragut was able to spend nine happy months with Charles Folsom, the American consul in Tunis, where he studied English literature, French, Italian, and some Arabic. He had a gift for languages and later learned Spanish as well. Like David Porter, Farragut believed in constantly improving his mind.

In the fall of 1819, Farragut was appointed acting lieutenant aboard the brig *Shark*, after which he returned home, landing in November 1820. Farragut's career then proceeded slowly. He was promoted to lieutenant in January 1825, but was not made commander until 1841. He did not attain the rank of captain until 1855. He probably would have retired without achieving any fame were it not for the Civil War.

When the war started, Farragut was faced with the most important decision of his life—which side he would fight on. He was a southerner, born in Tennessee, and he had lived in Norfolk, Virginia, most of his adult life, but he was adamantly opposed to secession and said so publicly. During the difficult winter of 1860–1861, he chose nation over state. He never hesitated. On December 20, 1860, when South Carolina seceded from the Union, followed by Florida, Mississippi, Alabama, Georgia, Louisiana, and Texas on February 1, 1861, creating the Confederate States of America, Farragut did not approve. He hoped that Virginia would not follow suit, but when she did on April 17, 1861, he and his family left Norfolk and moved to Hastings-on-Hudson, New York. He traveled the day after the vote to secede.

Not only did he leave the South, but he intended to fight to preserve the Union, and fight he did, becoming one of the greatest heroes in American history. Initially suspect because of his southern birth and longtime residence in Virginia, he did not receive orders until the very end of 1861, when he was given command of the West Gulf Blockading Squadron. Secretary of the Navy Gideon Welles said of Farragut that he had "innate fearless morale courage." Indeed he had.

Farragut's orders directed him to blockade the Gulf Coast from St. Andrews Bay off Panama City to the mouth of the Rio Grande, and to capture New Orleans. President Abraham Lincoln planned to blockade the Confederate States and split them by gaining complete control of the Mississippi River. Seizing New Orleans was essential.

On February 2, 1862, Farragut left Hampton Roads in his flagship, the USS *Hartford*, and sailed south, determined to capture New Orleans as quickly as possible. He knew it would be difficult, but he was confident that he could take it, and he did not wait long. On April 24, 1862, after cutting a chain-and-hulk barrier strung across the Mississippi, he led a flotilla past strongly defended Forts St. Stephen and Jackson—the strong points guarding the southern approaches to the city—through heavy fire, and soon stood off lightly defended New Orleans. A contingent of Farragut's marines, led by Captain Theodorus Bailey, then marched without opposition to the city's custom house and raised the American flag. New Orleans was in Union hands. President Lincoln and the Congress were overjoyed, and to honor Farragut they created for the first time in the nation's history the rank of rear admiral, which they awarded him on July 16, 1862.

Gaining control of the rest of the Mississippi was not as easy. The Confederates put up a desperate fight. Vicksburg and Port Hudson were the keys, and the Union attacked them from the north and the south, by land as well as water. Farragut was in the thick of the fight with David Dixon Porter, David Porter's son, and General Ulysses S. Grant. They finally forced the surrender of Vicksburg on July 4, 1863, and Port Hudson on July 9, cutting the Confederacy in two.

Farragut distinguished himself again in the battle for Mobile Bay in 1864, the last Confederate port remaining open on the Gulf of Mexico.

The bay was stoutly defended. Farragut had a hard time getting in and silencing the three forts defending it, as well as the Confederate ships guarding it, particularly the ironclad *Tennessee*. He persisted, however, as he always did, and won a great victory on August 5, 1864, shutting the port, although the city of Mobile, which was inaccessible to Farragut's ships, remained in Confederate hands until the end of the war.

During the battle for Mobile, Confederate mines (known as torpedoes) were a particular problem, and for a time stymied the Union advance, but Farragut is said to have uttered the famous order, "Damn the torpedoes, full speed ahead," which proved to be a key in moving his fleet forward to victory. Whether he said those exact words, he certainly shouted something similar, and his monumental determination to prevail carried the day. Winning the battle for Mobile Bay was the high point of Farragut's career. It was "one of the hardest victories of my life," he wrote, "and the most desperate battle I ever fought since the days of the old *Essex*." To honor him, Congress created the new rank of vice admiral, and President Lincoln awarded it to him on December 21, 1864.

Farragut's victory at Mobile, coupled with Sherman's in Atlanta, counteracted a wave of defeatism spreading in the North. It contributed to Lincoln's reelection and played an important part in winning the war, all of which made Farragut a greater hero than ever.

He remained in the navy after the war. The new rank of admiral was created for him. He was awarded it on July 25, 1866, and given command of the European Squadron from 1867 to 1868. He died on August 14, 1870, at Portsmouth, New Hampshire.

JAMES HILLYAR'S SUBSEQUENT CAREER WAS ALSO MARKED BY uninterrupted success, although he never achieved the prominence of David Farragut. When he arrived home from South America on November 18, 1814, he was greeted as a hero. His accomplishments in the Pacific were impressive. He had secured British control of the mouth of the Columbia River and furthered Britain's ambition to acquire the entire Oregon Territory, a significant accomplishment in itself. But he accomplished much more. He arranged a peace between Chile and Peru that secured Spanish rule in both countries, albeit temporarily—a seemingly impossible task. And he had captured the *Essex*, restoring the dominance of

Britain's commerce and whaling in the eastern Pacific. The Prince Regent (George III's son who was fulfilling the duties of Monarch for his incapacitated father) and the Admiralty, not to mention Parliament and the public, were loud in their applause.

Although an accomplished fighter, Hillyar was also extraordinarily generous to his opponents. David Porter and his surviving men were able to come home and receive the acclaim of the president and their countrymen only because of the thoughtfulness of Captain Hillyar. After he had performed his grim task of defeating the *Essex*, he did everything he could to ease the burdens of the *Essex* men and their captain. His lack of rancor, his sense that he was performing a distasteful duty for his country and had no personal animosity toward his foe, was symptomatic of the man. He was in every respect a professional.

For his various accomplishments in the Pacific, both diplomatic and military, Hillyar was knighted (Companion of the Bath) in June 1815. In subsequent years, he continued to exhibit the same abilities he had shown against Porter in Valparaiso. In January 1834, he was made Knight Commander of the Bath, and on January 10, 1837, he became a rear admiral. On July 4, 1840, he was awarded the prestigious Knight Grand Cross. His domestic life was as unruffled as his naval career. Two of his sons, Charles and Henry, both became admirals. Hillyar died on July 10, 1843 at the age of seventy-four, still a much respected figure in the Royal Navy.

DAVID PORTER'S CAREER AFTER THE WAR OF 1812 DID NOT FOLLOW the same path of uninterrupted success as those of Downes, Farragut, and Hillyar. And, as one might expect, his problems were largely of his own making. At the conclusion of the war, and for nine years thereafter, the future looked bright for him. His exploits during the war had won him the respect of Washington's political and naval elite. In recognition of his prowess, President Madison appointed him to the Board of Navy Commissioners, a prestigious body of three senior officers that Congress had created early in 1815 to assist the secretary of the navy with the burgeoning work of the department.

The navy's senior captain, John Rodgers, was chairman, and he had recommended Porter. Rodgers had a high regard for him, going back to their days in the *Constellation* under Captain Truxtun during the

Quasi-War with France. Rodgers described Porter as "a man of far more than ordinary talents, indefatigable in whatever he undertakes and added to these, his acquirements, professional as well as more immediately scientific, are respectable." The president and Secretary Crowninshield, both of whom had a high opinion of Porter, readily agreed.

Rogers also recommended Isaac Hull, the navy's most esteemed officer, and he was duly appointed as well. Hull did not remain long as a commissioner, however. In July 1815 he took command of the Charlestown Navy Yard, a position he much preferred, and Stephen Decatur took his place on the Board of Commissioners.

Unlike his friend Hull, Porter considered being appointed one of the three commissioners a signal honor, and he threw himself into the new assignment. There was much to do. The commissioners turned their attention to improving the navy's officers—their regulations, standards, and training, and they worked hard improving ships, guns, and yards, all of which needed attention.

Porter loved being in Washington. He purchased a grand 110-acre estate known as Meridian Hill, where he threw lavish parties, living far beyond his means. Eventually he found himself in financial trouble and had to borrow money. His friend John Downes was an easy and generous target, as was his old friend and prize agent, Sam Hambleton. Friends weren't enough, however, and Porter was forced to return to active sea duty in order to acquire more income.

The navy was happy to accommodate him. The secretary, Smith Thompson, had just the spot. On December 31, 1822 Porter was appointed to succeed James Biddle as commander of the West Indian Squadron. It was a difficult assignment. Pirates and freebooters were running wild in the Caribbean, inflicting heavy losses on American commerce. The great Spanish Empire that had existed in the Americas since the sixteenth century had collapsed, and Spain was left with just a tenuous hold on Cuba and Puerto Rico. She had lost everything else. When Porter took over in 1822, Spain was still at war with her former colonies in the Caribbean, Mexico, Colombia, and Venezuela. She had only a pitifully small force in the area, just one frigate and a few smaller warships. Her former colonies had even less. Privateers did the fighting, but they were indistinguishable from pirates. Corrupt Spanish officials worked with the outlaws, capturing the shipping of every nation.

Porter had been viewing the chaos in the Caribbean for some time and knew how he was going to approach the problem. The first thing he did was assemble a fleet that could actually work against pirates. Biddle had had little success because his ships were too big to run into the shallow inlets, creeks, and rivers where the outlaws hid. Once Porter had his fleet up and running, he made substantial progress, particularly around Cuba and Puerto Rico. He was constantly battling a hostile climate, and the corruption of Spanish officials, but he had important help from the British West Indian Squadron. London wanted to get rid of the pirates as much as Washington did.

Despite the severe handicaps, Porter continued bringing order to the Caribbean until November 14, 1824, when an incident occurred that changed his life. On that fateful day he led 200 men and marched on Foxardo, a town in Puerto Rico. He was on a mission to chastise some corrupt Spanish officials for their rough handling of Lieutenant Charles T. Platt, commander of the *Beagle*, a schooner in Porter's squadron. Platt had visited the town in search of goods stolen from an American firm. He never got the goods, but he did get arrested and thrown in jail for three hours before being released.

Porter thought he had authority to land on Spanish territory in pursuit of thieves in the guise of Spanish functionaries. He threatened to destroy Foxardo if he did not receive an apology, whereupon the corrupt official in charge apologized profusely, made a peace offering of horses, which Porter refused, and the matter appeared settled.

When Porter made his report to the new secretary of the navy, Samuel Southard, he expected to be congratulated. Instead he was relieved of command and ordered to Washington for an investigation. Captain Lewis Warrington, one of the navy's premier fighters, replaced him. Porter was flabbergasted and outraged. Southard was following the lead of John Quincy Adams, who was at the time both secretary of state and president-elect. Adams had reacted angrily when informed of Porter's invasion of Spanish territory, not in hot pursuit of pirates, but to avenge an insult to one of his officers, who was, moreover, it turned out, in civilian clothes at the time. Adams thought that what Porter did was highhanded and could have foreign policy repercussions. What was worse, Porter had in the past repeatedly been disrespectful to Southard. The secretary was happy that Porter was in trouble.

For reasons that are not entirely clear, Adams was overreacting. Although Porter's actions were rash, they did no real harm. Spain was not upset; she ignored the incident. Nothing was heard from Madrid, nor from the governors of Cuba or Puerto Rico. The matter should have been dropped. Focusing on Porter's conduct made it more likely to become a problem in Spanish-American relations than it otherwise was.

After Adams became president in March 1825, he insisted on a court of inquiry and then a court-martial of Porter. But after giving the matter more thought he sought a way out, suggesting to Porter's brother-in-law Joseph Anderson that an apology from Porter could solve the problem. Unfortunately, Porter refused to apologize, and in his usually intemperate manner, carried on a vitriolic attack on the president and the secretary of the navy in public, which made it appear that he was arrogantly undermining the principle of civilian control of the military, which indeed he was. He published letters he had received from the secretary and took the president to task in a venomous pamphlet, *An Exposition of the Facts and Circumstances which Justified the Expedition to Foxardo.*

Adams had no choice, then, but to proceed with the court-martial. Porter was found guilty of disobedience of orders, conduct unbecoming an officer, and insubordinate conduct. Influenced by all that Porter had done for the navy and the country, however, the court gave him the lightest possible sentence—a six-month suspension from the navy with full pay.

Porter was apoplectic over a verdict he considered grossly unfair. He categorically rejected the court's finding, and wrote that he could never again "associate with those who were led by men in power to inflict an unrighteous sentence." Refusing to accept the court's light punishment, Porter, in a highly emotional state, resigned from the navy on July 1, 1826, after twenty-eight years in uniform. It's hard to believe that he really wanted to leave the service he had devoted his life to, and that his father and uncle had served so well, but resign he did, vowing never to return.

Continuing to be highly distraught, he left the country and his family and went to Mexico to become head of their pathetic, practically nonexistent navy. Perhaps he had in mind following the example of British Captain Thomas Cochrane, who found service as head of the Chilean navy after being falsely accused of participating in a swindle and being dismissed from the Royal Navy.

Whatever Porter's thought process, he had some success reforming and expanding the Mexican navy, but he continued to be stymied by an impossible political situation and rampant corruption. He wanted to return to the United States, and when John Quincy Adams lost the presidency to Andrew Jackson in 1828, Porter resigned from the Mexican navy and returned to America. In Washington, he got a friendly reception from President Jackson, who thought the previous administration, particularly Adams, had treated Porter badly.

As sympathetic as Jackson was, however, it took a long time to find a suitable position for Porter. The problem was not the president's but Porter's. He was difficult to please. To begin with, Jackson generously offered to reinstate him in the navy, which would have solved all of Porter's problems, but he rejected the idea out of hand, refusing to serve with those who had condemned him.

Months went by with Porter turning down one offer after another. Then in April 1830 Jackson proposed making him consul general to the Barbary States in Algiers. Porter accepted that position, but before he got there, the French occupied Algeria and incorporated it into France. Porter was out of a job again.

He remained in the Mediterranean for several months with nothing to do until Martin Van Buren, the secretary of state, offered him the post of chargé d'affaires to the Ottoman Empire. Porter immediately accepted. It was now 1831. From then until his death in 1843, he remained in Constantinople, returning to the United States for only a few months during 1838–1839 to urge Van Buren to promote him to minister resident in the Ottoman Empire, which Van Buren did in March 1839. Other than that one short visit home, Porter remained alone in Constantinople. His marriage had been in ruins for some time. The only family members he saw regularly were his sister Mary Brown and her family.

He evidently preferred self-imposed exile. He would have been welcomed back to America at any time and could have performed useful service in the navy. In fact, there had been no good reason for him to leave the navy in the first place. He could have swallowed hard and accepted the light sentence of the court-martial. Indeed, he could have avoided a court-martial altogether had he been more courteous to President Adams. And he certainly could have accepted Jackson's generous offer to reinstate him in the navy. He might have done all those things and remained in the service that was his true home. No one ever questioned his exceptional talents as an officer—courage, daring, a fine mind, and exceptional leadership ability. But it was outsized ambition and excessive pride that stood in the way of the great fame David Porter sought and left him alone in Constantinople with nothing to do but nurse imagined grievances. There he died on March 3, 1843, age sixty-three.

ACKNOWLEDGMENTS

IT IS A GREAT PLEASURE TO THANK ALL THE GENEROUS PEOPLE who have helped me write this book, beginning with my agent, Rob McQuilkin of Lippincott Massie McQuilkin. From start to finish, he offered priceless counsel. No one in the business works harder and with more effect than Rob. My wife, Kay, read the entire manuscript, contributing invaluable ideas. So, too, did Vice Admiral George Emery, U.S. Navy (Retired). He analyzed the entire first draft closely and shared his incomparable knowledge. No one knows more about the naval aspects of the War of 1812.

I was blessed with marvelous editors at Basic Books, beginning with Lara Heimert, the publisher. Her careful reading of the original drafts, invaluable insight on how best to organize the material, and wise criticism, were indispensable. Gifted, sharp-eyed writer and editor Norman MacAfee followed her with advice on every detail of the manuscript, generously sharing his great expertise. Assistant editor Katy O'Donnell provided constant help with good cheer and always good advice. I would also like to thank the manager of editorial production at Basic Books, Michelle Welsh-Horst, who saw the book through the various stages of editorial production.

My nephew, Michael Daughan, who has a special interest in, and wide knowledge of the early navy, read the manuscript and offered his trenchant criticism. I am grateful to him. And also to my daughter Mary Daughan Sheft and her husband, Mark, for their continuous support. My brother William (Jerry) Daughan, who worked for the navy for many years, also provided help, as he always has. Support also came from old friends, David Lafayette, an old navy hand and superb writer; John Couture who served with the 82nd airborne during the Cuban Missile Crisis, and his wife, "Toots"; Howard Ladd, whose knowledge of the South Pacific is extensive, and Nikki Whitney, a writer of uncommon ability.

GLOSSARY

Abaft: to the rear of.
Aft: toward, or in, the stern of a vessel.
Astern: behind a vessel.

Ballast: any heavy substance used to maintain a vessel at its proper draft or trim, or its stability.
Beam: the breadth of a ship at its widest part.
Beam Ends: a ship lying so far over on its side that the ends of her beams are touching the water and she is in danger of capsizing.
Beat to quarters: a marine drummer calling a crew to its battle stations.
Bilge: the lowest point of the hull, usually containing foul water.
Binnacle: box on the quarterdeck near the helm that houses the compass and has drawers where telescopes are kept.
Bomb vessel: a small ketch used to hold mortars for hurling bombs.
Boom: a long spar used to extend the foot or bottom of a specific sail.
Bouse: to pull out.
Bow: the forward part of a ship.
Bow chasers: long guns placed on both sides of the bow to allow firing ahead.
Bower: large anchor placed at the bows of a ship
Bowsprit: a spar extending forward from the bow or stem of a ship to carry sail forward and to support the masts by stays.
Braces: ropes attached to the end of yards that allow them to be turned.
Brig: a two-masted, square-rigged vessel.

Broach to: to veer a ship's stern suddenly to windward so that her broadside is exposed to the wind and sea, putting her in danger of capsizing.

Bulkhead: a partition separating compartments on a vessel.

Cable's length: 600 feet.

Capstan: a vertical, cleated drum used for moving heavy weights powered by capstan bars pushed by hand.

Carronade: form of cannon used to throw heavy shot at close quarters.

Chasers: a chase gun.

Chevaux-de-frise: a piece of timber or an iron barrel traversed with iron-pointed spikes or spears or pointed poles, five or six feet long, hidden under water, and used to defend a passage.

Clew: a lower corner of a square sail or after lower corner of a fore-and-aft sail.

Clew garnets: one of the ropes by which the clews of the courses of a square-rigged ship are hauled up to the lower yards.

Clew line: a rope by which the clew of an upper square sail is hauled up to its yard.

Clew up: to haul a sail by means of the clew garnets, clew lines, etc., up to a yard or mast.

Close-hauled: sails pulled tight to allow a ship to sail close to the wind.

Collier: ship carrying coal.

Con: steer.

***Consolato del mare*:** the right to take enemy goods from neutral ships.

Coppering a warship: sheathing with rolled copper.

Corvette: warship with flush deck, slightly smaller than a frigate.

Courses: the lowest sail on any square-rigged mast.

Cutter: a broad, square-sterned boat for carrying stores and passengers and either rowed or sailed.

Double: To pass or sail round, so as to reverse the direction of motion; as to *double* the Horn.

Fall off: to steer to leeward, or away from the direction of the wind.

Fascines: a long bundle of wooden sticks bound together.

Fire ship: a vessel carrying combustibles sent among enemy ships to set them on fire.

Fleches: a salient outwork of two faces with an open gorge.

Fore-and-aft rig: having, not square sails attached to yards, but sails bent to gaffs or set on the masts or on stays in the midship line of the vessel.

Forecastle: that part of the upper deck of a ship forward of the foremast.
Foremast: the mast closest to the bow.
Forereach: to gain upon.
Frigate: a three-masted, square-rigged warship carrying a full battery of from 20 to 50 guns on the main deck and having a raised quarterdeck and forecastle.

Gaff: the spar upon which the head, or upper edge, of a fore-and-aft sail is extended.
Gallant: third highest sail on a square-rigged ship above the top sail and course.
Grape-shot: small iron balls held together by a canvas bag that act like shotgun pellets.
Gunwale to: tipping until the gunwale, or upper side of a vessel, is level with the water.

Halyards: a rope or tackle for hoisting and lowering sails, yards, flags, etc.
Hawse: the bows of a ship.
Hawser: a large rope for towing, mooring, securing a ship.
Heel: (noun) the lower end of a mast, a boom, the bowsprit, etc.
Heel: (verb) to tilt or incline to one side.

Inshore: near the shore or moving toward it.

Jib boom: a spar that serves as an extension of the bowsprit.
Jibe: to shift a fore-and-aft sail or its boom suddenly and with force from one side of a ship to the other until the sails fill on the opposite side. A maneuver done when a vessel is running with the wind and changes direction.

Kedge anchor: a small iron anchor used to hold a ship fast during changes of tide and to tow a ship forward during a calm by dropping the anchor forward and pulling the ship toward it.
Knot: a unit of speed equivalent to one nautical mile or 6,080.20 feet an hour.

Larboard: the left-hand side of a ship when facing toward the bow. The opposite of starboard. Also called "port."
Lateen sail: a triangular sail, extended by a long yard slung to the mast and usually low.
Lee: the quarter toward which the wind blows.
Lee shore: a shore on the lee side of a vessel, potentially dangerous in a storm.

Letter of marque: a license granted by a government to a private person to fit out an armed vessel to cruise as a privateer.

Lifts: chains or ropes used to hold yards to masts.

Line-of-battle ship: see "sail of the line."

Luff: to turn the head of a vessel toward the wind.

Mainmast: the large center mast of a three-masted ship.

Maintop: the platform above the head of the mainmast in a square-rigged ship.

Main topmast: a mast next above the mainmast.

Merlon: one of the solid intervals between embrasures or openings of a battlement or parapet.

Mizzenmast: the aftermost mast in a two-masted or three-masted ship.

Offing: Position of a ship at a distance from the shore.

Pay her head offshore: to cause a ship to sail to leeward or away from the wind.

Play upon: fire at.

Port: the left-hand side of a ship when facing toward the bow. The opposite of starboard. Also called "larboard."

Pounders: refers to the weight of a cannonball.

Powder monkey: a ship's boy.

Privateer: an armed private vessel operating under the commission of a government.

Prow: the bow of a vessel.

Quarter deck: that part of the upper deck abaft the mainmast reserved for officers.

Ratlines: one of the small traverse ropes attached to the shrouds and forming the steps of a rope ladder.

Razee: a sail of the line that has had one of its decks removed to transform it into a heavy frigate.

Redoubt: small enclosed work of varying size used to fortify hills and passes.

Reef: that part of a sail which is taken in or let out by means of the reef points, in order to regulate the size of a sail.

Reef point: one of the pieces of small rope used in reefing a sail.

Royal: a small sail immediately above the topgallant sail.

Sail of the line: largest of the warships, carrying from 50 to 120 guns, large enough to have a place in the line of battle. Most often a 74-gun ship with three decks. Also called ship of the line.

Scow: a large flat-bottomed boat, having broad, square ends.

Sheet: a rope that regulates the angle at which a sail is set in relation to the wind.

Slow-match: a slow-burning fuse used to ignite the powder charge in a cannon.

Spring on her cable: a line leading from a vessel's quarter to her cable so that by hauling in or slackening it she can be made to lie in any position.

Spring tide: a tide greater than usual, occurring at full moon and new moon.

Starboard: the right-hand side of a ship when facing toward the bow. The opposite or larboard or port.

Starboard tack: the course of a ship when the wind is coming over the starboard side.

Stern: the rear end of a vessel.

Stern Sheets: the space at the stern not occupied by the thwarts of an open boat.

Stream anchor: a small spare anchor.

Strike the colors: surrender.

Studding sail: used in a fair wind to extend the sails on a square-rigged ship.

Swivel: a small gun fixed on a swivel on a stanchion so that it can be rotated. Usually shoots a one-pound ball.

Tack: to change direction by bringing the head of a vessel into the wind and then shifting the sails so that she will come up into the wind and then fall off on the other side until she is sailing at about the same angle to the wind as before but on the opposite tack.

Taffrail: the rail around a ship's stern.

Tender: a vessel employed to attend larger ships, to supply them with provisions etc.

Topgallant: a mast or sail situated above the topmast and below the royal mast.

Topmast: the second mast above the deck.

Topsail: the sail above the course.

Trim: to adjust sails and yards to get the best effect from the wind. Also, to arrange ballast, cargo or passengers so that the ship will sail well.

Veer: to alter the course of ship by turning away from the direction of the wind.

Warp: to move a ship by hauling on a line, or warp.

Wear: to go about or change direction by turning the head of a vessel away from the wind.

Weather gauge: the position of a ship to the windward of another, giving an advantage in maneuvering.

Wherry: a long light rowboat, sharp at both ends.

Windward: the point or side from which the wind blows.

Yard: a long, narrow, cylindrical, tapered, wooden spar that supports and extends a sail.

AUTHOR'S NOTE: The majority of the above definitions are based on *Webster's New International Dictionary of the English Language*, edited by William Neilson, 2nd ed. (Springfield, MA: Merriam, 1938).

NOTES

Prologue

2   *Nothing Porter did had the slightest effect on the* Alert: Captain David Porter to Secretary of the Navy Paul Hamilton, Sept. 3, 1812, in William S. Dudley, ed., *The Naval War of 1812: A Documentary History* (Washington, DC: Naval Historical Center, Department of the Navy, 1985), 1:443–447.

2   *Porter quickly put up the* Essex's *helm:* Porter to Hamilton, Sept. 3, 1812, in Dudley, ed., *Naval War of 1812,* 1:444; William M. James, *The Naval History of Great Britain: During the French Revolutionary and Napoleonic Wars* (Mechanicsburg, PA: Stackpole Books, 2002; first published in 1817), 6:88–89.

3   *The* Alert *turned out to be a former collier:* Porter to Hamilton, Aug. 15, 1812, in Dudley, ed., *Naval War of 1812,* 1:218–19.

3   *Porter sent First Lieutenant John Downes:* Porter to Hamilton, Sept. 3, 1812, in Dudley, ed., *Naval War of 1812,* 1:445–46.

4   *Porter took the* Alert's *officers and the better part:* Porter to Hamilton, Sept. 2, 1812 in Dudley, ed., *Naval War of 1812,* 1:443–47.

6   *standing beside the hammock of Midshipman David Farragut:* Loyall Farragut, *The Life of David Glasgow Farragut* (New York: Appleton, 1879), 16–17.

6   *Porter now turned for home to Chester:* John Hill Martin, *Chester and Its Vicinity* (Philadelphia: William H. Pile & Sons, 1877), 313.

6   *Porter knew before the uprising that having:* Porter to Hamilton, Sept. 5, 1812, in Dudley, ed., *Naval War of 1812*, 1:462–63; Farragut, *Life of David Glasgow Farragut*, 17.

8   *As the* Essex *traveled home, Porter felt:* Porter to Hamilton, Sept. 3, 1812; Porter to Bainbridge, Sept. 8, 1812, in Dudley, ed., *Naval War of 1812*, 1:443–47 and 468–69; Porter to Hambleton, September 7, 1812, in David Dixon Porter, *Memoir of Commodore David Dixon Porter of the United States Navy* (Albany: J. Munsell, 1875), 97.

Chapter One: President Madison's War Plan

9   *David Porter's victory over the* Alert *came as a surprise:* Dudley, ed., *Naval War of 1812*, 1:180–82.

11   *America's second War of Independence:* George C. Daughan, *If By Sea: The Forging of the American Navy from the Revolution to the War of 1812* (New York: Basic Books, 2008), 236.

14   *Rodgers had written on June 3:* Commodore John Rodgers to Secretary Hamilton, June 3, 1812, in Dudley, ed., *Naval War of 1812*, 1:119–22.

15   *Stephen Decatur, the navy's most celebrated captain:* Captain Decatur to Secretary Hamilton, June 8, 1812, in Dudley, ed., *Naval War of 1812*, 1:122–24.

15   *It was a course recommended by his friend William Jones:* Secretary of the Navy to Commodore John Rodgers, Sept. 9, 1812, in Dudley, ed., *Naval War of 1812*, 1:471.

15   *Once Porter reached the Delaware River he was informed*: Bainbridge to Porter, Oct. 13, 1812, in Dudley, ed., *Naval War of 1812*, 1:527–28.

Chapter Two: The Making of a Sea Warrior

18   *mostly in privateers:* David Dixon Porter, *Memoir of Commodore David Porter*, 8.

18   *The elder Porter's sea stories stirred the imagination:* Washington Irving, *Analectic Magazine* (Sept. 5, 1814), 22.

18   *In 1875, he would write of his father:* David Dixon Porter, *Memoir of Commodore David Porter*, 10.

18   *Young Porter began his naval career in 1796: Federal Gazette* (Baltimore), March 1796; David Dixon Porter, *Memoir of Commodore David Porter*, 10–11.

18   *This was young Porter's first encounter with impressment:* David Dixon Porter, *Memoir of Commodore David Porter*, 12–13.

19   *Given his family background and experience:* David Porter, *Constantinople and Its Environs* (New York: Harper & Brothers, 1835), 2:10.

19   *In fact, Porter could not have found a better teacher:* Retired Vice Admiral George Emery, "Thomas Truxtun: First Mentor of the Federal Navy," *Pull Together: Newsletter of the Naval Historical Foundation* (Fall/Winter 2010–2011): 12–14.

19   *Porter did not get along with one particular officer:* David Dixon Porter, *Memoir of Commodore David Porter*, 19–20.

19   *On February 9, 1799, the* Constellation *became embroiled:* Eugene S. Ferguson, *Truxtun of the Constellation: The Life of Commodore Thomas Truxtun, U.S. Navy, 1755–1822* (Annapolis, MD: Naval Institute Press, 1982), 162–67. For a contrary view of what happened to Rodgers and Porter after the battle, see Charles Goldsborough, *The United States Naval Chronicle* (Washington, DC: James Wilson, 1824), 132–33, and David Long, *Nothing Too Daring: A Biography of Commodore David Porter, 1780–1843* (Annapolis, MD: Naval Institute Press, 1970), 9.

20   *As the Quasi-War progressed, Porter continued:* David Dixon Porter, *Memoir of Commodore David Porter*, 29–37; Long, *Nothing Too Daring*, 12–13.

21   *Porter's next ship was the* Constitution: Long, *Nothing Too Daring*, 14.

21   *The Quasi-War with France ended on March 3, 1801:* Ferguson, *Truxtun of the Constellation*, 164–72.

22   *When Sterrett arrived in the Mediterranean with Porter:* Long, *Nothing Too Daring*, 21.

24   *Together with the shallow draught* Vixen: The *Vixen* was designed by Benjamin Hutton and built in Maryland, as the *Enterprise* had been.

24   *Bainbridge and Porter worked well together:* David Dixon Porter, *Memoir of Commodore David Porter*, 56–57.

Chapter Three: Disaster in Tripoli

25   *David Porter was anxious to distinguish himself in Tripoli:* Daughan, *If By Sea*, 353–54.

26   *Soon after, Bainbridge became involved:* David Long, *Ready to Hazard: A Biography of Commodore William Bainbridge, 1774–1833* (Hanover, NH: University Press of New England, 1981), 63.

27   *The* Philadelphia *and the* Vixen *arrived off Tripoli:* Bainbridge to Preble, Oct. 22, 1803, in Dudley W. Knox, ed., *Naval Documents Related to the*

United States Wars with the Barbary Powers (Washington, DC: 1939–1944), 3:159.

27 *"My motives of ordering her off Cape Bon":* Bainbridge to Preble, Nov. 1, 1803, in Knox, ed., *Naval Documents*, 3:171.

27 *"At 9 A.M., about five leagues eastward of Tripoli":* Bainbridge to the Secretary of the Navy, Nov. 1, 1803, in Knox, ed., *Naval Documents*, 3:171–72.

27 *"About 11 o'clock [I] had approached":* Porter testimony during Court of Inquiry on *Philadelphia*, June 29, 1805, in Knox ed., *Naval Documents*, 3:189–94.

28 *They both recognized that the* Philadelphia *was in serious danger:* Bainbridge to Secretary of the Navy Robert Smith, Nov. 1, 1804, in Thomas Harris, *The Life and Services of Commodore William Bainbridge, United States Navy* (Philadelphia, 1837. Reprint, Whitefish, MT: Kessinger, 2007), 80; Bainbridge to Preble, Nov. 1, 1803, in Knox, ed., *Naval Documents*, 3:171.

28 *Reacting quickly, Bainbridge, at Porter's urging:* Bainbridge to Secretary of the Navy, Nov. 1, 1803, in Knox, ed., *Naval Documents*, 3:171–72.

29 *With Porter continuing to advise him:* Porter to Midshipman Henry Wadsorth, 3/5/1804 (while Porter was in prison), in Knox, ed., *Naval Documents*, 3:475–76.

29 *Four hours went by in this desperate struggle:* Porter testimony at the Court of Inquiry, in Knox, ed., *Naval Documents*, 3:190.

29 *Their situation was now desperate:* Porter to Henry Wadsworth, March 5, 1804, in Knox, ed., *Naval Documents*, 3:290; Court Inquiring into the loss of U.S. Frigate *Philadelphia*, in Knox, ed., *Naval Documents*, 3:190–194 and 475–76.

29 *"In such a dilemma, too painful to relate":* Bainbridge to Preble, Nov. 12, 1803, in Knox, ed., *Naval Documents*, 3:174.

29 *"Some fanatics," Bainbridge told Preble:* Ibid.

30 *Before surrendering, Bainbridge ordered all the arms:* Christopher McKee, *Edward Preble: A Naval Biography, 1761–1807* (Annapolis, MD: Naval Institute Press, 1996; first edition, 1972), 180.

30 *Unfortunately, Bainbridge's humiliations were compounded:* William Ray, *Horrors of Slavery, or, American Tars in Tripoli* (Troy, NY: Printed by O. Lyon for the author, 1808), 82; David Long, *Sailor-Diplomat: A Biography of Commodore James Biddle, 1783–1848* (Boston: Northeastern University Press, 1983), 21–22.

30 *Around six P.M., the Tripolitans swarmed:* Bainbridge to Tobias Lear, U.S. Consul General, Algiers, Feb. 8, 1804 (received April 21, 1804), in Knox, ed., *Naval Documents*, 3:177.

30 *To add to Porter's misery and shame:* Bainbridge to Preble, Nov. 6, 1803, in Knox, ed., *Naval Documents*, 3:173; McKee, *Edward Preble*, 180.

31 *"If my professional character be blotched":* William Bainbridge to Susan Bainbridge, Nov. 1, 1803, in Thomas Harris, *The Life and Services of Commodore William Bainbridge, United States Navy* (Philadelphia: Carey Lea & Blanchard, 1837), 91–93.

31 *"Would to God, that the officers and crew":* Preble to the secretary of the navy, Dec. 10, 1803, in Knox, ed., *Naval Documents*, 3:180.

32 *With books provided by Nissen, Porter now studied history, French:* David Dixon Porter, *Memoir of Commodore David Porter*, 63.

32 *As might be expected, the crew received: Journal of Surgeon Jonathan Cowdery, U.S. Navy, from Oct. 31, 1803 to March 1804*, in Knox, ed., *Naval Documents*, 3:529–32.

33 *Meanwhile, Bainbridge managed to send letters:* Long, *Nothing Too Daring*, 26–27; Frederick C. Leiner, *Millions for Defense: The Subscription Warships of 1798* (Annapolis, MD: Naval Institute Press, 2000), 71.

33 *On February 16, 1804, Decatur:* Surgeon John Ridgely to Susan Decatur, Nov. 10, 1826, in Knox, ed., *Naval Documents*, 3:425.

33 *The new treatment was so severe:* Chipp Reid, *Intrepid Sailors: The Legacy of Preble's Boys and the Tripoli Campaign* (Annapolis, MD: Naval Institute Press, 2012), 114–121.

34 *"I have zealously served my country":* Bainbridge to Preble, Nov. 12, 1803, in Knox, ed., *Naval Documents*, 3:174.

35 *Preble wrote to the secretary of the navy:* Edward Preble to Secretary of the Navy Robert Smith, Feb. 1804, in Reid, *Intrepid Sailors*, 106–7.

35 *Bainbridge worried—far more than Porter—about:* Bainbridge to Susan Bainbridge, Nov. 1, 1803, in Knox, ed., *Naval Documents*, 3:178.

35 *After the final victory over Tripoli, Porter remained:* Long, *Nothing Too Daring*, 32–34.

Chapter Four: Primed for Battle

37 *Porter was also occupied with navy business:* Spencer C. Tucker and Frank T. Reuter, *Injured Honor: The Chesapeake-Leopard Affair, June 22, 1807* (Annapolis, MD: Naval Institute Press, 1996), 140–188.

38 *On February 22, 1808, the courts-martial were over:* John Hill Martin, *Chester (and its vicinity) Delaware County, in Pennsylvania . . .* (Philadelphia: William H. Pile and Sons, 1877), 85–87; David Dixon Porter, *Memoir of Commodore David Porter*, 72.

38   *Porter had already received orders to take command:* Long, *Nothing Too Daring*, 37–38.

39   *Young Farragut would during the Civil War:* Charles Lee Lewis, *David Glasgow Farragut: Admiral in the Making* (Annapolis, MD: United States Naval Institute, 1941), 1–21; Alfred Thayer Mahan, *Admiral Farragut* (New York: D. Appleton and Co., 1892), 1–5.

40   *With war looming, Porter suggested:* Long, *Nothing Too Daring*, 58.

41   *Commodore Rodgers, the navy's senior officer:* George C. Daughan, *1812: The Navy's War* (New York: Basic Books, 2011), 82.

41   *Unhappy to be stuck in port while the war:* Ibid., 59–60.

42   *"I detest the idea of trusting to our privateers":* Porter to Hambleton, nd, in David Dixon Porter, *Memoir of Commodore David Porter*, 99.

42   *Her skipper, Jacob Jones, needed supplies:* Jones did not get the *Wasp* to sea until October 13.

43   *Porter feared that if he delayed much longer:* Porter to Hambleton, Oct. 4, 1812, in David Dixon Porter, *Memoir of Commodore David Porter*, 91.

43   *"cut off from New York and Rhode Island":* Porter to Secretary of the Navy Hamilton, Sept. 5, 1812, in Dudley, ed., *Naval War of 1812*, 1:462.

43   *His concern was unwarranted, however:* Porter to Hamilton, Oct. 2, 1812 in Dudley, ed., *Naval War of 1812*, 1:505–6; Porter to Hambleton, Oct. 4, 1812, in David Dixon Porter, *Memoir of Commodore David Porter*, 91; Daughan, *1812*, 53–67.

43   *Porter blamed Secretary of the Navy Hamilton:* Porter to Samuel Hambleton, Oct. 4, 1812, in David Dixon Porter, *Memoir of Commodore David Porter*, 91.

44   *Porter's urge to be back at sea:* Lewis, *David Glasgow Farragut*, 40–41.

44   *The latest episode involved John Erving:* Porter to Hamilton, June 28, 1812; Hamilton to Porter, June 30, 1812, in Dudley, ed., *Naval War of 1812*, 1:171–76.

45   *The wide publicity afforded this latest controversy:* Rear Admiral George Cockburn to Vice Admiral Sir Alexander F.I. Cochrane, July 17, 1814 in Michael Crawford, ed., *The Naval War of 1812: A Documentary History* (Washington, DC: Naval Historical Center, 2002), 3:136–137.

45   *Yeo's challenge, thus, came as no surprise:* John Randolph Spears, *The History of Our Navy from Its Origin to the Present Day, 1775–1897* (New York: Scribner's, 1897), 2:46; Lewis, *David Glasgow Farragut*, 47–48.

45   *Porter pleaded with Secretary Hamilton:* Long, *Nothing Too Daring*, 69–70.

Chapter Five: The *Essex:* Past and Present

47 *In October 1812, Captain David Porter was anxious:* Porter to Hamilton, Oct. 12, 1811, in Long, *Nothing Too Daring*, 60.

47 *"I am much pleased with my ship":* Porter to Hambleton, Nov. 20, 1811, in David Dixon Porter MSS., Library of Congress, vol. 2.

47 *Porter remained so disgruntled:* Porter to Hamilton, Oct. 14, 1812, in Dudley, ed., *Naval War of 1812*, 1:528.

48 *Porter's hyperbole did not move Hamilton:* Porter to Hamilton, Oct. 14, 1812, in Dudley, ed., *Naval War of 1812*, 1:528; Porter to Hamilton, Oct. 12, 1811; Hamilton to Porter, Oct. 31, 1811, in Long, *Nothing Too Daring*, 60–61.

49 *The* Essex *had not been designed to carry primarily carronades:* Knox, ed., *Naval Documents Related to the Quasi-War*, 7:366.

49 *Her first skipper, thirty-eight-year-old Captain Edward Preble:* Captain George Henry Preble, *The First Cruise of the United States Frigate* Essex, *Under the Command of Captain Edward Preble* (Essex Institute Historical Collections), 10:12.

49 *In spite of his grumbling and penchant for hyperbole: Essex Institute Proceedings*, 2:74–78; Philip Chadwick Foster Smith, *The Frigate* Essex *Papers: Building the Salem Frigate, 1798–1799* (Salem, MA: Peabody Museum of Salem, 1974), 19–36.

50 *William Hackett, the well-known naval architect:* Howard I. Chapelle, *The History of American Sailing Ships* (New York: Bonanza Books, 1935), 94.

50 *Enos Briggs of Salem took charge of building the frigate: Salem Gazette*, Nov. 23, 1798; Ralph D. Paine, *The Ships and Sailors of Old Salem* (Chicago: A.C. McClure & Co., 1912), 231–32; Frederick C. Leiner, *Millions for Defense: The Subscription Warships of 1798* (Annapolis, MD: Naval Institute Press, 2000), 163; Philip Chadwick Foster Smith, *The Frigate* Essex *Papers: Building the Salem Frigate, 1798–1799* (Salem, MA: Peabody Essex Museum, 1974).

50 *The citizens of Essex County responded:* Paine, *Ships and Sailors of Old Salem*, 232–33.

50 *Giant trees, felled by expert hands:* Leiner, *Millions for Defense*, 163; Smith, *Frigate Essex Papers*, 94.

50 *Paul Revere contributed copper bolts:* Esther Forbes, *Paul Revere and the World He Lived In* (Boston: Houghton Mifflin, 1942), 378–80.

50 *Revere worked with navy agent Joseph Waters:* Frances Diane Robotti and James Vescovi, *The USS* Essex *and the Birth of the American Navy* (Holbrook, MA: Adams Media Corporation, 1999), 23–43.

51   *Work progressed rapidly:* Bern Anderson, *Surveyor of the Sea: The Life and Voyages of Captain George Vancouver* (Seattle: University of Washington Press, 1960), 241.

51   *The* Essex *measured 141 feet in overall length:* Smith, *Frigate* Essex *Papers*, 290–91.

51   *She was built for speed and carried:* Chapelle, *History of American Sailing Ships*, 94.

51   *Captain Preble officially accepted her:* Quoted in Paine, *Ships and Sailors of Old Salem*, 237.

52   *The first to make the voyage to Canton:* Dorothy Schurman Hawes, *To the Farthest Gulf: The Story of the American China Trade* (Ipswich, MA: Ipswich Press, 1940).

52   *"The ship proves a good sea boat":* Preble to Stoddert, December 29, 1799, in Knox, ed., *Naval Documents Related to the Quasi-War*, 4:578–79.

52   *To Joseph Waters, the navy agent in Salem, Preble wrote:* Preble to Joseph Waters, Dec. 29, 1799, in Knox, ed., *Naval Documents Related to the Quasi-War*, 4:579.

52   *Looking back years later, Preble remembered:* Christopher McKee, *Edward Preble* (Annapolis, MD: Naval Institute Press), 68.

52   *On January 6, 1800, the* Essex *and the* Congress: Christopher McKee, *A Gentlemanly and Honorable Profession: The Creation of the U.S. Naval Officer Corps, 1794–1815* (Annapolis, MD: Naval Institute Press, 1991), 417.

53   *On March 11, 1800, a little over two months:* Robotti and Vescovi, *USS* Essex *and the Birth of the American Navy*, 56; Leiner, *Millions for Defense*, 168.

53   *For two weeks, while work went ahead:* McKee, *Edward Preble*, 71.

53   *After her return, the* Essex *was refurbished:* Robotti and Vescovi, *USS* Essex *and the Birth of the American Navy*, 123.

54   *When Fox finished with her:* Smith, *Frigate* Essex *Papers*, 191–93.

Chapter Six: First Rendezvous: Porto Praia

55   *The time for Captain Porter and the* Essex: Porter to Hambleton, Oct. 4, 1812, in David Dixon Porter MSS., vol. 2, Library of Congress.

56   *"I sail on a long, a very long cruise":* Porter to Hambleton, Oct. 19, 1812, in David Dixon Porter, *Memoir of Commodore David Porter of the United States Navy* (Whitefish, MT: Kessinger Publishing, nd., reprint of 1875 edition published in Albany, NY by J. Munsell), 101.

56   *The* Essex *was anchored in deep water near shore:* Captain David Porter, *Journal of a Cruise* (Annapolis, MD: Naval Institute Press, 1986, reprint

of 1815 edition published by Bradford and Inskeep, Philadelphia), 277.

57   *By nightfall, the* Essex *had moved beyond the Delaware Capes:* Porter, *Journal*, 10.

58   *Porter estimated it would take the* Essex: Ibid., 25.

59   *David Farragut wrote that "I have never since been":* Captain A.T. Mahan, *Admiral Farragut* (New York: D. Appleton and Co., 1892), 30.

59   *"My next cruise I hope will be more profitable":* Porter to Hambleton, in David Dixon Porter MSS, Library of Congress, vol. 2.

59   *On November 23, the* Essex *crossed the Tropic of Cancer: Journal of Midshipman William W. Feltus Kept on Board the US. Frigate Essex,* Pennsylvania Historical Society; Lewis, *David Glasgow Farragut,* 54; Porter, *Journal,* 28.

60   *As the* Essex *continued on toward Porto Praia:* Mahan, *Admiral Farragut,* 17–18.

61   *"I have ever considered this [three watch system] among seamen":* quoted in Caroline Alexander, *The* Bounty: *The True Story of the Mutiny on the* Bounty (New York: Viking, 2003), 83.

62   *"What can be more dreadful," Porter explained:* Porter, *Journal,* 42.

62   *To protect his men against a naturally unhealthy environment:* Ibid. 40–42.

63   *Porter also had good wind sails rigged:* Ibid., 43.

63   *The greatest menace to the crew remained scurvy:* Porter to Dr. Barton, Surgeon of the Frigate *Essex,* Dec. 31, 1811, Newport, in Porter Papers, United States Naval Academy Museum, Annapolis, MD.

63   *Cook's experience in the Royal Navy:* Alan Villiers, *Captain James Cook* (New York: Penguin, 1969), 23.

64   *There was no excuse for any captain in 1812:* Porter, *Journal,* 40.

64   *He was particularly enthusiastic about the good effects:* Porter to Dr. Barton, Dec. 31, 1811, Newport, in Porter Papers.

65   *Later in life, Porter gave this striking description:* Porter, *Constantinople and Its Environs,* 2:10–11.

66   *At sunrise on November 26, a lookout:* Porter, *Journal,* 29–30.

Chapter Seven: In the South Atlantic, Dreaming of the Pacific

69   *David Porter continued on to the next place:* Porter, *Journal,* 43–44.

70   *On December 11, the* Essex *crossed: Journal of Midshipman William W. Feltus,* Dec. 13, 1812.

71   *Unfortunately, the* Nocton *never made it back:* Lieutenant William B. Finch

to Secretary of the Navy Jones, Feb. 13, 1813, in Dudley, ed., *Naval War of 1812*, 2:684–85.

72   *On December 14, two days after Porter:* William Jones to Commodore William Bainbridge, Oct. 11, 1812, in Dudley, ed., *Naval War of 1812*, 1: 512–15.

72   *Now began a game of false identities and coded messages:* Thomas Harris, *The Life and Services of Commodore William Bainbridge, United States Navy* (Philadelphia: Carey, Lea, & Blanchard, 1837), 138–39; William Jones to Commodore William Bainbridge, Oct. 11, 1812, in Dudley, ed., *Naval War of 1812*, 1: 512–15; Porter, *Journal*, 51–54.

73   *On December 20, the* Essex *spoke a Portuguese vessel:* Porter, *Journal*, 56–57.

74   *It did not take long to get there:* Dixon to Croker, March 19, 1813, in Gerald S. Graham and R.A. Humphreys, eds., *The Navy and South America, 1807–1823: Correspondence of the Commanders-in-Chief on the South American Station* (London: Naval Records Society, 1962), 85–86; Porter, *Journal*, 58.

74   *During the few days that the* Essex *patrolled off Rio:* Long, *Nothing Too Daring*, 78; Porter, *Journal*, 59–60; Dudley ed., *The Naval War of 1812*, 2:690.

75   *On January 2, 1813, Porter stopped a Portuguese:* Porter, *Journal*, 60–63.

76   *Porter had no way of knowing that meeting Bainbridge and Lawrence:* Daughan, *1812*, 140–45.

78   *Bainbridge also had to think about Lawrence:* Ibid., 135–49.

79   *At the moment, Porter had no inkling:* Porter, *Journal*, 63–65.

79   *"With my water and provisions getting short":* Porter to Bainbridge, March 23, 1813, in Dudley, ed., *Naval War of 1812*, 2:689.

80   *On the way to St. Catharine's, Porter distributed:* Porter, *Journal*, 65.

80   *On January 18, Porter spoke to:* Ibid., 68–77.

83   *As far back as 1809, Porter had written to former president Jefferson:* Porter to Jefferson, Aug. 17, 1809, in J. Jefferson Looney et al., eds., *The Papers of Thomas Jefferson: Retirement Series* (Princeton: Princeton University Press, 2004), 1:443–49.

83   *Porter sent a copy of the letter to Charles Goldsborough:* Charles Goldsborough to James Madison, Sept. 20, 1809, *Papers of James Madison: Presidential Series*, 1:388; J.C.A. Stagg, *Borderlines in Borderlands: James Madison and the Spanish-American Frontier* (New Haven: Yale University Press, 2009), 185–90.

83   *Still not deterred, Porter wrote on February 7, 1811:* David Porter to Secretary of the Navy, Feb. 7, 1811, USND, vol. I, LRMC (Letters Received

by Secretary of the Navy from Masters Commandant, USND); Long, *Nothing Too Daring*, 58.

83 *Porter had also urged his plan on Bainbridge:* Porter, *Journal*, 72–73.

84 *He wrote later to Bainbridge explaining his thinking:* Porter to Bainbridge, March 23, 1813, in Dudley, ed., *Naval War of 1812*, 2:688–89.

84 *Porter claimed that he had no idea:* Porter, *Journal*, 73–74.

85 *Porter understood well the disadvantages:* Ibid., 74.

Chapter Eight: Doubling Cape Horn

87 *It was an American sealer, the* Topaz: Alexander, *The* Bounty, 346–48.

87 *As the* Essex *plowed south, the temperature dropped steadily:* Porter, *Journal*, 79–81.

88 *The* Essex *was running fast:* Ibid., 82.

89 *The following day, February 4:* Ibid., 89.

90 *Captain Cook on his first voyage in 1768:* Richard Hough, *Captain James Cook: A Biography* (New York: W.W. Norton, 1994), 73.

90 *Sailing to the east of Staten Island:* Porter, *Journal*, 84–86.

92 *Staten Island and the Strait of Le Maire:* Ibid., 90.

92 *Before long, they were there:* Ibid., 91–98.

94 *The terrifying deluge persisted:* Ibid., 98.

95 *Birds, kelp, and whales appeared:* Ibid.

95 *David Farragut remembered that:* Farragut, *Life of David Glasgow Farragut*, 20; Mahan, *Admiral Farragut*, 22.

95 *Miraculously, the men at the wheel stood firm:* Farragut, *Life of David Glasgow Farragut*, 20

95 *Porter, though severely bruised, led the fight back:* Porter, *Journal*, 101–5.

Chapter Nine: Navigating Chile's Political Waters

97 *Porter ran north with the Humbolt current:* Edouard A. Stackpole, *Whales and Destiny: The Rivalry between America, France, and Britain for Control of the Southern Whale Fishery, 1785–1825* (Amherst: University of Massachusetts Press, 1972), 275–76.

98 *Porter thought he could scoop up enough prizes:* Porter, *Journal*, 101–2.

98 *As the* Essex *approached Mocha:* Farragut, *Life of David Glasgow Farragut*, 21; Porter, *Journal*, 108.

99 *The incident cast a pall over the ship:* Farragut, *Life of David Glasgow Farragut*, 21.

100   *As Porter steered for Santa Maria:* Porter, *Journal*, 112.

101   *The unexpectedly dreary landscape:* Ibid., 113–14.

102   *Young Farragut, who knew how much:* Farragut, *Life of David Glasgow Farragut*, 21–22.

102   *For some reason, perhaps the obviously deteriorating:* Porter, *Journal*, 116–17.

103   *Porter was surprised that Chile had a new, pro-American:* John Lynch, *The Spanish American Revolutions, 1808–1826* (New York: W.W. Norton, 1973), 1; Alan Schom, *Napoleon Bonaparte* (New York: Harper, 1997), 453–72.

105   *When Chileans received reports of the Napoleonic conquest in 1808:* Luis Galdames, *A History of Chile*, translated and edited by Isaac Joslin Cox (New York: Russell & Russell, 1964, first published in 1941 by the University of North Carolina Press), 173.

105   *Alexander von Humbolt, the Prussian explorer:* Quoted in Lynch, *Spanish American Revolutions*, 1.

108   *When Porter arrived on the scene:* Galdames, *History of Chile*, 178.

Chapter Ten: A Packed Week at Valparaiso

111   *"With respect to Spanish America generally":* Madison to Ambassador Pinkney, Oct. 30, 1810 in Ralph Ketcham, *James Madison* (Charlottesville: University Press of Virginia, 1990), 502; Secretary of State Robert Smith to Joel Roberts Poinsett, Aug. 24, 1810, in Poinsett Papers, 1785–1851, Historical Society of Pennsylvania, Guide 512, Box 1, 1800–1817.

111   *Britain had been trying to increase her influence:* Charles K. Webster, ed., *Britain and the Independence of Latin America, 1812–1830: Select Documents from the Foreign Office Archives*, two vols. (London: Oxford University Press, 1938), 1:3–12; Robert Harvey, *Liberators: Latin America's Struggle For Independence* (Woodstock, NY: Overlook Press, 2000), 8–13.

112   *While the British continued to fight for the Spanish monarchy:* Poinsett to Secretary of State James Monroe, Sept. 15, 1814, Poinsett Papers, Historical Society of Pennsylvania, HSP Guide 512, Box 1.

112   *When Poinsett left for South America on October 15, 1810:* J. Fred Rippy, *Joel R. Poinsett, Versatile American* (New York: Greenwood, 1968, reprint of 1935 edition by Duke University Press), 36–42; Samuel Flagg Bemis, *The Latin American Policy of the United States* (New York: Harcourt, Brace & World, 1943), 31.

113   *Without any communication from Washington, Poinsett:* Poinsett to Monroe, Sept. 10, 1814, Poinsett Papers, Historical Society of Pennsylvania, Box 1.

114 *Poinsett and Carrera were so enthusiastic about the* Essex: Porter, *Journal*, 120–21.

114 *When news of Porter's arrival reached Santiago:* Ibid., 138.

114 *Actually, the* Standard *had departed:* Captain Peter Heywood to Dixon, April 3, 1813, Dixon to Croker, April 30, 1813, in Gerald S. Graham and R.A. Humphreys, eds., *The Navy and South America, 1807–1823: Correspondence of the Commanders-in-Chief on the South American Station* (London: Navy Records Society, 1962), 86–87.

115 *Without Dixon and the* Standard *to worry about at the moment:* Porter, *Journal*, 127.

115 *Porter was also entertaining Governor Lastra:* Ibid., 121–25.

116 *The following day was Sunday: Journal of Midshipman William W. Feltus*, March 22, 1813.

117 *An American whale ship, the* George: Stackpole, *Whales and Destiny*, 338–39.

117 *On March 23, just before leaving Valparaiso:* Porter to Bainbridge, March 23, 1813, in Dudley, ed., *Naval War of 1812*, 2: 688–89.

Chapter Eleven: Peru and the Elusive *Nimrod*

119 *He estimated that there were in excess:* Porter, *Journal*, 211.

121 *Porter now went after the* Nimrod: *Journal of Midshipman William W. Feltus*, March 25 and 26, 1813; Porter, *Journal*, 131–34.

122 *The* Nereyda *reached Callao:* Samuel B. Johnston, *Three Years in Chile* (Erie, PA: R.I. Curtis, 1816), 122; Dudley, ed., *Naval War of 1812*, 3:740n.

122 *Porter believed that the capture of the* Nimrod: Porter, *Journal*, 135–37.

122 *After seeing the two captains off: Journal of Midshipman William W. Feltus*, March 13, 1813.

123 *As the* Essex *sped north:* Porter to Hamilton, July 2, 1813, in Dudley, ed., *Naval War of 1812*, 2:697–99; Porter, *Journal*, 139.

123 *Porter now inched his way into Callao:* Porter, *Journal*, 143.

124 *After quitting the vicinity of Callao:* Ibid., 145–47.

Chapter Twelve: Fortune Smiles in the Galapagos Islands

127 *Porter used dead reckoning to navigate:* Porter, *Journal*, 149–50.

128 *On the morning of April 17:* Ibid., 162.

128 *Porter undoubtedly exaggerated the inadequacies:* Stackpole, *Whales and Destiny*, 129.

129   *Britain's need for sperm oil was so great:* Eric Jay Dolan, *Leviathan: The History of Whaling in America* (New York: W.W. Norton, 2007), 168.

131   *Considering how important the whaling business:* Kevin D. McCranie, *Utmost Gallantry: The U.S. and Royal Navies in the War of 1812* (Annapolis, MD: Naval Institute Press, 2011), 185.

131   *Hood Island is the southernmost:* Porter, *Journal*, 150, 175–76.

132   *Porter expected to go into action:* Ibid., 152–54.

133   *Porter suspected that finding water:* Ibid., 155–59.

133   *Captain Colnett contributed to the legend:* Captain James Colnett, *A Voyage to the Northwest side of North America: The Journals of James Colnett* (Vancouver, BC: UBC Press, 2004, reprint of 1798 edition).

133   *The golden age of piracy occurred:* The best study of pirates is Colin Woodard, *The Republic of Pirates: Being the True and Surprising Story of the Caribbean Pirates and the Man Who Brought Them Down* (New York: Harcourt, 2007).

134   *After being disappointed at Charles Island: Journal of Midshipman William W. Feltus*, April 24, 1813.

136   *After restocking the* Essex, *Porter:* Porter, *Journal*, 167–70.

136   *Fishing did not take the crew's mind off:* Farragut, *Life of David Glasgow Farragut*, 23; *Journal of Midshipman William W. Feltus*, April 29 and 30, 1813.

137   *Capturing the ships was so easy:* Porter, *Journal*, 180.

138   *Downes received the* Policy's *ten guns:* Ibid., 177–94.

140   *After returning to the* Essex, *he delayed:* Ibid., 200–201.

142   *Weir had been aboard for only a short time:* Ibid., 197–202.

143   *Porter now had a fleet of six:* Ibid., 203–7.

Chapter Thirteen: Unparalleled Success

145   *On June 8, Porter passed to the north of Abingdon:* Porter, *Journal*, 214–21.

146   *On June 22, Randall returned:* Ibid., 223–25.

147   *On the same day, Porter received: Journal of Midshipman William W. Feltus*, June 25, 1813; Porter, *Journal*, 226–28.

148   *Downes now had seventy-five prisoners:* Captain David Porter to Secretary of the Navy Hamilton, July 2, 1813, in Dudley, ed., *Naval War of 1812*, 2:697–99.

148   *Before leaving the Gulf of Guayaquil:* William James, *The Naval History of Great Britain During the French Revolutionary and Napoleonic Wars* (Mechanicsburg, PA: Stackpole Books, 2002, originally published in London by Richard Bentley, 1822–1824), 6:284; Daughan, *1812*, 17–22.

148 *Those prisoners who did not want to join:* Journal of Midshipman William W. Feltus, June 25, 1813; Porter to Hamilton, July 2, 1813, in Dudley, ed., *Naval War of 1812*, 2:697–99.

149 *With these matters tended to:* Porter, *Journal*, 229–30.

150 *Porter also gave Downes three letters addressed to:* Porter to Secretary of the Navy Hamilton, July 2, 1813, in Dudley, ed., *Naval War of 1812*, 2:697–99.

151 *Porter also wanted the navy to know how well:* Ibid., 2:701.

151 *The president immediately released Porter's report:* See, for instance, *Boston Patriot*, Dec. 22, 1813; *Boston Gazette*, Dec. 23, 1813; *National Intelligencer*, Dec. 20, 1813.

151 *Secretary Jones lost no time passing:* Secretary Jones to Evelina Porter, Dec. 14, 1813, David Dixon Porter Mss., Library of Congress, vol. 2.

152 *Carrying Porter's letters to the navy secretary:* Farragut, *Life of David Glasgow Farragut*, 26–27; Lewis, *David Glasgow Farragut*, 77–78.

153 *While Downes was leading his squadron:* Porter, *Journal*, 230–34.

155 *After they left, he strengthened the* Seringapatam: Dudley, ed., *Naval War of 1812*, 2:702.

156 *At noon on the day that Wilson left:* Porter, *Journal*, 237–41.

157 *On August 4, Porter anchored his ships:* Ibid., 243.

157 *Later, he explored parts of James Island:* Ibid., 255.

158 *The goats did indeed make a difference:* Paul D. Stewart, *Galapagos: The Islands That Changed the World* (New Haven: Yale University Press, 2006), 51.

158 *Suddenly one morning in the middle of August:* Long, *Ready to Hazard*, 20.

159 *Porter had no inkling there was bad blood:* Porter, *Journal*, 252–53; Alexander, *The* Bounty, 351.

Chapter Fourteen: The Hunt for the *Essex*

161 *While waiting for Downes to return:* Porter, *Journal*, 255–58.

162 *With all this in place, Porter left:* Ibid., 269–70.

163 *Porter expected Downes to arrive any day now:* Crawford, ed., *Naval War of 1812*, 3:712.

164 *The rest of the news from Downes:* Porter, *Journal*, 271–72.

164 *In fact, in March 1813, the Admiralty:* Admiralty to Hillyar, March 12, 1813, in Dudley, ed., *Naval War of 1812*, 2:710–11.

165 *The Canadian Northwest Company:* Kenneth McNaught, *The Penguin History of Canada* (London: Penguin, 1988), 64–65.

165 *The large storeship* Isaac Todd: Gerald S. Graham and R.A. Humphreys, eds., *The Navy and South America, 1807–1823: Correspondence of the*

Commanders-in-Chief on the South American Station (London: Spottiswoode, Ballantyne and Co., 1962), 93; Kevin D. McCranie, *Utmost Gallantry: The U.S. and Royal Navies at Sea in the War of 1812* (Annapolis,
MD: Naval Institute Press, 2011, 181.

167 *Dixon did not know Porter's exact whereabouts:* Dixon to Croker, June 9,
1813; Dixon to Croker, June 11, 1813; Captain Heywood to Dixon, May
10, 1813; Brown and Watson (British agents) to Captain Heyward, April
8, 1813; in Graham and Humphreys, eds., *The Navy and South America*,
90–92.

167 *When Hillyar arrived in Rio:* Dixon to Croker, June 21, 1813, in Graham
and Humphreys, eds., *The Navy and South America*, 93.

167 *Nearly a month went by, however, before Hillyar:* Report of Captain William
Black of the *Racoon* to Croker, Columbia River, Dec. 13, 1813, in *Oregon
Historical Quarterly*, xvii (1916), 147–48; McCranie, *Utmost Gallantry*,
184.

168 *Hillyar's expectations about the* Essex: Captain William Bowles to Croker,
Sept. 5, 1813; Hillyar to Croker, March 30, 1814, in Graham and
Humphreys, eds., *The Navy and South America*, 141.

168 *Meanwhile, Captain Black sailed the* Racoon: Report of Captain William
Black of the *Racoon* to Croker, Dec. 15, 1813 in Graham and Humphreys,
eds., *The Navy and South America*, 149.

168 *The Pacific Northwest had been of great interest:* Frederick Merk, *The Oregon
Question: Essays in Anglo-American Diplomacy and Politics* (Cambridge,
MA: Harvard University Press, 1967), 1–29.

169 *Porter enumerated in his journal:* Porter, *Journal*, 273–77.

170 *Porter left the Galapagos in the nick of time:* Hillyar to Croker, Jan. 24,
1814, ADM 1/1949/186; McCranie, *Utmost Gallantry*, 184.

Chapter Fifteen: The Marquesas Islands: "In Vales of Eden"

171 *When Porter stood out from the Galapagos:* Porter, *Journal*, 281.

172 *When, in the late nineteenth century, Robert Louis Stevenson:* Robert Louis
Stevenson, *In the South Seas* (London: Penguin, 1998, first published in
1896), ix.

172 *"No part of the world exerts the same attractive power":* Ibid., 5–6.

173 *"I can only conjecture":* Quoted in Anne Salmond, *Bligh: William Bligh in
the South Seas* (Berkeley: University of California Press, 2011), 215–16;
Alexander, *The* Bounty, 357.

173 *Bligh was undoubtedly right:* Quoted in Alexander, *The* Bounty, 155.

173 *The mutineers had firm control:* Ibid., 107.

173 *Once the* Bounty *left Tahiti:* Ibid., 140.

174 *At the time of the mutiny, the* Bounty's: Ibid., 171.

174 *Bligh's chances of survival were practically nil:* Lieutenant William Bligh to the Lords Commissioners of the Admiralty, Aug. 18, 1789, in *William Bligh & Edward Christian: The* Bounty *Mutiny* (New York: Penguin Books, 2001), 72.

174 *Porter studied Bligh's account carefully:* Alexander, *The* Bounty, 77.

175 *Mutiny was in the air in those days:* N.A.M. Rodger, *The Command of the Ocean: A Naval History of Britain, 1649–1815* (New York: W.W. Norton, 2004), 446–47.

175 *Inspired by the apparent success at Spithead:* Ibid., 447–50.

176 *Not long afterward, another sensational mutiny:* John Wetherell, *The Adventures of John Wetherell*, ed. by C.S. Forester (New York: Doubleday, 1953).

176 *For nine months, Pigot's abusive behavior:* The best account of the mutiny is Dudley Pope, *The Black Ship* (New York: Henry Holt, 1963); see also Rodger, *Command of the Ocean*, 452.

178 *As light trade winds swept the* Essex: Porter, *Journal*, 284.

179 *"the beauties of the islands they were about visiting":* Ibid.

179 *Cook personally led the initial landing party:* J.C. Beaglehole, *The Life of Captain Cook* (Palo Alto, CA: Stanford University Press, 1974), 375–79.

179 *But what was truly striking:* Ibid., 275.

179 *Unfortunately, Cook soon got caught up:* James Cook, *The Journals*, Philip Edwards, ed. (New York: Penguin, 2003), 339–44.

179 *Porter knew the story well:* David Dixon Porter, *Memoir of Commodore David Porter*, 168.

180 *The first island in the archipelago that Mendaña:* J.C. Beaglehole, *The Exploration of the Pacific*, 3rd ed. (Palo Alto, CA: Stanford University Press, 1966), 66.

180 *Mendaña's chief pilot:* Ibid., 68.

180 *The Marquesas were spared more European visitors:* Greg Dening, *Island and Beaches: Discourses on a Silent Land: Marquesas 1774–1880* (Chicago: Dorsey Press, 1980).

181 *As the* Essex *drove west:* Porter, *Journal*, 282.

181 *In spite of the idyllic conditions:* Ibid., 286.

181 *Disgusted, he moved on, continuing west:* Ibid., 289–90.

182 *Soon, more canoes filled with men:* Ibid., 290–93.

183 *This first encounter with what the* Essex *men:* Ibid. 293–98.

184 *Porter anchored off Ua Huka for the night: Journal of Midshipman William W. Feltus*, Oct. 25, 1813.

Chapter Sixteen: Nuku Hiva

185 *"No description can do justice to its beauty"*: Herman Melville, *Typee* (New York: Penguin Classics, 1996; originally published 1846), p. 12; Hershel Parker, *Herman Melville, A Biography, Volume I, 1819–1851* (Baltimore: Johns Hopkins University Press, 2005), 211.

185 *Robert Louis Stevenson was just as enthralled:* Robert Louis Stevenson, *In the South Seas* (London: Penguin, 1998, first published in 1896), 6–7.

185 *Porter renamed Taiohae as Massachusetts Bay: Journal of Midshipman William W. Feltus,* Oct. 25, 1813; Porter, *Journal,* 300–301.

186 *After looking into the bay: Journal of Midshipman William W. Feltus,* Oct. 26, 1813; Porter, *Journal,* 443–44.

186 *Before Downes arrived, Porter had a surprise:* Diana Fontaine Maury Corbin, *A Life of Matthew Fontaine Maury, U.S.N. and C.S.N.* (London: Sampson, Low, Marston, Searle, and Rivington, 1888), 11–13.

188 *The tattooed man who had accompanied Maury:* Porter, *Journal,* 303–4.

188 *When Porter first arrived on the beach:* Ibid., 320–24.

189 *When it came time to reassemble:* Ibid., 306.

189 *The women beguiled Porter:* Ibid., 308.

190 *Porter does not mention where David Farragut:* David Farragut, *Some Reminiscences of Early Life,* quoted in Lewis, *David Glasgow Farragut,* 85 and 324; Farragut, *Life of David Glasgow Farragut,* 27.

190 *Porter wanted no part in the politics or wars:* Porter, *Journal,* 305–6.

191 *While the messenger to the Hapa'a was away:* Ibid., 311.

191 *After selecting his strongpoint:* Ibid., 318.

191 *Gattanewa soon paid a visit:* Ibid., 315.

192 *While all this activity was going on:* Ibid., 317–18.

192 *On October 28, Gattanewa:* Ibid., 326.

193 *Lieutenant Downes now departed: Journal of Midshipman William W. Feltus,* Oct. 29, 1813.

193 *Mouina was barefoot:* Porter, *Journal,* 421–22.

193 *Porter continued to follow Downes's movements: Journal of Midshipman William W. Feltus,* Oct. 30, 1813; Porter, *Journal,* 327–28.

194 *When they arrived, Porter released Gattanewa: Journal of Midshipman William W. Feltus,* Oct. 31, 1813.

194 *Porter was interested in what the Taiohae:* Ibid.; Porter, *Journal,* 329–39.

195 *Mowattaeeh noticed the tents:* Porter, *Journal,* 349–51.

195 *On November 3, an amazing event occurred:* Ibid., 357–58.

196 *As the days went by, Porter and his men:* Ibid., 359.

197 *Over thirty percent of the* Bounty's *crew:* Salmond, *Bligh*, 163.

197 *contact with people like Cook:* Glyn Williams, *The Death of Captain Cook: A Hero Made and Unmade* (Cambridge, MA: Harvard University Press, 2008), 2.

197 *By the time the Taiohae and Hapa'a:* Journal of Midshipman William W. Feltus, Nov. 2, 1813.

197 *After the rats had been removed:* Porter, *Journal*, 361.

Chapter Seventeen: Annexation and War

199 *With repairs going well:* Porter, *Journal*, 366–68.

200 *Before attacking the Taipi:* Ibid., 374–78; *Journal of Midshipman William W. Feltus*, Nov. 19, 1813.

201 *At the same time that he was taking:* Porter, *Journal*, 379.

202 *On November 28, Porter set about:* Journal of Midshipman William W. Feltus, Nov. 29, 1813.

203 *Deeply chagrined, Porter believed:* Porter, *Journal*, 393.

204 *At daylight, Porter went about:* Ibid., 395.

204 *Porter's party spent the night:* Ibid., 397.

205 *The compulsion he felt was peculiar to him:* Ibid.

205 *This was a far cry from his claim:* Ibid., 398.

205 *After briefly resting his party at the summit:* Ibid., 392.

205 *Taipi drums were beating:* Ibid., 400–401.

206 *Once the work of savaging the Taipi:* Ibid., 403.

206 *When the column reached the summit:* Journal of Midshipman William W. Feltus, Nov. 29–Dec. 2, 1813.

206 *With the defeat of the Taipi, Porter believed:* Porter, *Journal*, 405.

Chapter Eighteen: Mutiny

209 *While Porter was dealing with his other problems:* Porter, *Journal*, 369.

209 *A seaman named Lawson:* Journal of Midshipman William W. Feltus, Nov. 16, 1813.

210 *On the afternoon of November 15:* Ibid., Nov. 17 and 18, 1813.

210 *Lawson and his mates were a small problem:* Porter, *Journal*, 371–74.

211 *Dealing with the problem of expiring enlistments:* Farragut, *Life of David Glasgow Farragut*, 29–30.

213 *Porter thought that he had to guard:* Porter, *Journal*, 443.

Chapter Nineteen: Showdown in Valparaiso

215 *The* Essex *and* Essex Junior *were stuffed:* Porter, *Journal*, 281.

215 *Actually, his orders were to engage:* Secretary of the Navy Jones to Master Commandant John O. Creighton, Dec. 22, 1813, in Dudley, ed., *Naval War of 1812*, 2:296–97.

216 *Shortly after they left Nuku Hiva:* Farragut, *Life of David Glasgow Farragut*, 30–33.

216 *For nine days after the* Essex *and* Essex Junior *left:* Ibid., 31; Porter, *Journal*, 438 and 446.

216 *As Porter approached the coast of South America:* Porter to Downes, Jan. 10, 1814, Porter Papers, Naval Academy Museum.

218 *On January 12, a month after leaving:* Porter, *Journal*, 446.

218 *After exchanging salutes with the battery on old Fort Viejo:* Luis Galdames, *A History of Chile*, trans. Isaac Joslin Cox (New York: Russell & Russell, 1964), 177–80.

219 *Soon after Porter's arrival in February:* Porter to Secretary of the Navy Jones, July 13, 1814, in Michael J. Crawford, ed., *The Naval War of 1812: A Documentary History* (Washington, DC: Naval Historical Center, 2002), 3:715–16.

220 *All was in readiness on the* Essex *as well:* Farragut, *Life of David Glasgow Farragut*, 33.

220 *Playing on the fact that Valparaiso:* Ibid., 33–34.

221 *"O, sir," Hillyar shouted to Porter:* Porter, *Journal*, 474–75.

221 *Nonetheless, Porter was leery:* Mahan, *Admiral Farragut*, 32–33.

221 *In trying to extricate himself:* Porter, *Journal*, 475.

222 *But the* Phoebe *never touched the* Essex: Farragut, *Life of David Glasgow Farragut*, 33–34.

222 *As soon as the* Phoebe *was in place:* Porter, *Journal*, 475–76.

222 *Porter insisted that respect for Chilean neutrality:* Ibid., 476–77.

223 *During their later meetings, Porter made it clear:* Dixon to Croker, June 21, 1813, in Graham and Humphreys, eds., *The Navy and South America*, 93–95.

224 *Hillyar could afford to wait:* Hillyar to Croker, Feb. 28, 1814, in ibid., 133–34.

224 *Porter for his part continued trying:* Statement of Master Commandant John Downes, *Niles Weekly Register*, Aug. 20, 1814; Porter, *Journal*, 484–89.

225 *During this set-to, the* Phoebe *showed:* Farragut, *Life of David Glasgow Farragut*, 34; Captain James Hillyar to First Secretary of the Admiralty John W. Croker, June 26, 1814 in Crawford, ed., *Naval War of 1812*, 3:719–20.

226 *On March 14, Porter began a paper war:* Porter, *Journal*, 253–54.

226 *An opportunity arose on March 28:* J. Fred Rippy, *Joel R. Poinsett, Versatile American* (Durham, NC: Duke University Press, 1935), 54.

226 *At that moment,* Phoebe *and* Cherub: A piece of the Log Book of U.S. Frigate *Essex*, printed in the *New York Evening Post*, July 8, 1814 in Crawford, ed., *Naval War of 1812*, 3:725–26; David G. Farragut, "Some Reminiscences of Early Life," in Crawford, ed., *Naval War of 1812*, 3:748–59.

227 *Being in neutral territory did not put a check:* Alfred Thayer Mahan, *Sea Power in Its Relationship to the War of 1812* (Boston: Little Brown, 1905), 2:248.

228 *Despite the significant advantage he now had:* Rippy, *Joel R. Poinsett*, 54; Porter, *Journal*, 462.

228 *The men from all the ships were ready for a fight:* Farragut, *Life of David Glasgow Farragut*, 35.

228 *They hoped in vain:* Hillyar to Croker, March 30, 1814, in Graham and Humphreys, eds., *The Navy and South America*, 140.

229 *Farragut was stationed beside the captain:* Farragut, *Life of David Glasgow Farragut*, 40.

230 *When he wasn't employed otherwise, Farragut:* Ibid., 41.

230 *Hillyar soon returned to the attack:* Porter, *Journal*, 455.

230 *The* Cherub *was forced to haul off:* Ibid., 455–56.

231 *At this moment, Lieutenant Downes appeared:* Ibid., 456.

231 *All the while, fires continued to threaten:* Farragut, *Life of David Glasgow Farragut*, 45.

232 *Roach's conduct puzzled Farragut:* Ibid.

232 *The* Essex *had now drifted to a point:* Porter, *Journal*, 457.

232 *Farragut received orders to bring gun primers:* Farragut, *Life of David Glasgow Farragut*, 41.

233 *Not long afterward, Farragut saw:* Ibid., 43.

233 *The* Essex's *condition had now deteriorated:* Porter, *Journal*, 457–58.

233 *In spite of the American flag having come down:* Farragut, *Life of David Glasgow Farragut*, 41.

Chapter Twenty: The Butcher's Bill

235 *Porter and Farragut, although remaining exposed:* Farragut, *Life of David Glasgow Farragut*, 42.

236 *The dying men—ordinary jack tars:* Ibid.

236 *A young Scot named Bissley:* Ibid., 42–43.

236 *Porter said of his crew:* Porter, *Journal*, 458.

236 *Captain Hillyar reported only four killed:* Farragut, *Life of David Glasgow Farragut*, 39–40.

237 *Some months later, when Porter wrote:* Porter to Jones, July 3, 1814, in Crawford, ed., *Naval War of 1812*, 3:730–39; Porter, *Journal*, 459–60.

237 *Looking back many years later, Farragut:* Farragut, *Life of David Glasgow Farragut*, 38.

238 *"I had done all the injury that could be done":* Porter, *Journal*, 452.

238 *At length, a boarding officer arrived:* Farragut, *Life of David Glasgow Farragut*, 41–42.

238 *Somewhat absent-mindedly, Hillyar accepted:* Hillyar to Porter, April 4, 1814, in Porter, *Journal*, 463.

238 *Much controversy arose over Hillyar's conduct:* Farragut, *Life of David Glasgow Farragut*, 39.

239 *It was said that William Ingram:* Ibid.

239 *Theodore Roosevelt, in his study:* Theodore Roosevelt, *The Naval War of 1812* (New York by Putnam, 1882; New York: Random House, 1999), 167.

239 *Hillyar, as might be expected, heatedly denied:* Captain James Hillyar to First Secretary of the Admiralty John W. Croker, June 26, 1814, in Crawford, ed., *Naval War of 1812*, 3:719–20.

239 *"In justice to Commodore Hillyar":* Porter, *Journal*, 461.

240 *Porter did not expect to receive any comfort:* Ibid., 490.

240 *Farragut volunteered to assist:* Farragut, *Life of David Glasgow Farragut*, 44.

240 *By April 4, 1814, Hillyar:* Hillyar to Porter, April 4, 1814; Porter to Hillyar, April 5, 1814, in Porter, *Journal*, 466–67.

241 *Porter suspected that Hillyar:* Ibid., 491.

241 *Once their business was completed in England:* Stephen W.H. Duffy, *Captain Blakeley and the Wasp: The Cruise of 1814* (Annapolis, MD: Naval Institute Press, 2001), 265–73.

242 *Now it was time for Porter to take his leave of Hillyar:* Porter, *Journal*, 491.

242 *When* Essex Junior *stood out from Valparaiso:* One of the 130 was John Maury. He eventually went back to the United States after the Battle of Valparaiso and was assigned to Commodore Macdonough on Lake Champlain, but he arrived just after his historic fight. Frances Leigh Williams, *Matthew Fontaine Maury, Scientist of the Sea* (New Brunswick, NJ: Rutgers University Press, 1963), 22–25.

242 *Two of the wounded were left behind:* Farragut, *Life of David Glasgow Farragut*, 45.

243 *As late as July 1814, when he was reporting to Secretary of the Navy Jones:*

Captain David Porter to Secretary of the Navy Jones, July 3, 1814, in Crawford, ed., *Naval War of 1812*, 3:730–39.

243 *Hillyar, on the other hand, was always confident:* Log Book of HM Frigate *Phoebe*, April 27, 1814, in Crawford, ed., *Naval Documents*, 3:745; Hillyar to Croker, March 30, 1814, in Graham and Humphreys, eds., *The Navy and South America*, 142.

243 *Hillyar was not exaggerating:* Hillyar to Croker, May 11, 1814, in Graham and Humphreys, eds., *The Navy and South America*, 145.

243 *Since the great war with France:* Robotti and Vescovi, *USS* Essex *and the Birth of the American Navy*, 255–58.

243 *Soon after his victory over Porter, Hillyar:* Hillyar to Don Francisco de la Lastra, Supreme Governor and Director of the State of Chile, April 21, 1814, in Graham and Humphreys, eds., *The Navy and South America*, 143–44; Galdames, *History of Chile*, 181–82.

244 *Given the new political situation, the American consul general:* Long, *Nothing Too Daring*, 163.

244 *The peace that Hillyar arranged:* Galdames, *A History of Chile*, 186–200. O'Higgins had been badly wounded at Chacabuco but recovered.

Chapter Twenty-One: The Heroes Come Home

247 *David Farragut reported that the passage home:* Farragut, *Life of David Glasgow Farragut*, 45.

247 *The weather in early May at these latitudes:* David G. Farragut, "Some Reminiscences of Early Life," in Crawford, ed., *Naval War of 1812*, 3:757; *Boston Gazette*, July 14, 1814; Porter, *Journal*, 490–92.

249 *Meanwhile, the redoubtable Downes:* Farragut, "Some Reminiscences of Early Life," in Crawford, ed., *Naval War of 1812*, 3:757–58.

250 *The night was dark and squally:* Farragut, *Life of David Glasgow Farragut*, 46–48.

251 *The* Boston Gazette *spoke for most of the country:* *Boston Gazette*, July 11, 1814.

251 *Although Porter and Downes were reunited:* *Boston Gazette*, July 25, 1814.

251 *He later wrote, "On my arrival":* Porter wrote this in the second edition of his *Journal*. It is found on p. 493 of the Naval Institute Press edition.

252 *Although Porter and his crew were enormously grateful:* Members of *Essex*'s Crew to Captain David Porter, July 20, 1814, in Crawford, ed., *Naval War of 1812*, 3:369–70.

252 *Given the country's widespread appreciation of his efforts:* See Daughan, *1812*, 353–59, 413–17.

Chapter Twenty-Two: Lieutenant Gamble at Nuku Hiva

255 *"The frigate had scarcely got clear of the Marquesas":* Gamble to Crowninshield, Aug. 28, 1814, in Crawford, ed., *Naval War of 1812*, 3:774.

255 *Porter had assumed that the Taiohae:* Gamble to Porter, Aug. 30, 1815, in Abel Bowen, *The Naval Monument, Containing Official and Other Accounts of All the Battles Fought Between the Navies of the United States and Great Britain During the Late War; and an Account of the War with Algiers* (Boston: Cummings and Hilliard, 1816), 12.

256 *To underscore his determination:* Ibid.

257 *"My attempt to pursue them":* Ibid.

257 *The deserters made their way to Santa Christiana:* Gamble to Crowninshield, Aug. 28, 1815, in Crawford, ed., *Naval War of 1812*, 3:776.

258 *Midshipman Feltus had a different view: Journal of Midshipman William W. Feltus,* May 7, 1814.

258 *When the mutineers were moving slowly out of the bay:* Porter, *Journal* (1822 ed.), 519.

258 *Two days later, Gamble and his remaining men:* Gamble to Crowninshield, Aug. 28, 1815, in Crawford, ed., *Naval War of 1812*, 3:777.

259 *To make matters worse, just six cartridges remained:* Gamble to Porter, in Bowen, *Naval Monument*, 128; Gamble to Crowninshield, Aug. 28, 1815, in Crawford, ed., *Naval War of 1812*, 3:777.

259 *"In that state," Gamble recorded:* Gamble to Crowninshield, Aug. 28, 1814, in Crawford, ed., *Naval War of 1812*, 3:778.

259 *After struggling out of Taiohae Bay:* Gamble to Porter, in Bowen, *Naval Monument*, 128.

260 *On May 30, Gamble came to anchor:* Gamble to Crowninshield, Aug. 28, 1814, in Crawford, ed., *Naval War of 1812*, 3:778.

260 *Hawaiians supplied Gamble with fresh meat:* The mutineers in the *Seringapatam*, in the meantime, succeeded in reaching Australia.

260 *Unfortunately, on the passage to the Big Island:* Hillyar to Tucker, Aug. 14, 1814, in *The Navy and South America, 1807–1823*, 147.

260 *In spite of Gamble's protestations:* Gamble to Porter, in Bowen, *Naval Monument*, 128.

261 *Tucker departed Tahiti on August 2:* Porter, *Journal*, 539–40.

261 *On October 18, 1814, the* Cherub *left:* Gamble to Crowninshield, Aug. 28, 1815, in Crawford, ed., *Naval War of 1812*, 3:778.

Epilogue: Four Lives After the War

264 *Madison overlooked Porter's failings:* James D. Richardson, *A Compilation of the Messages and Papers of the Presidents, 1789–1897*, 10 vols. (Washington, DC: Published by Authority of Congress, 1900), 1:549.

266 *His close friend Isaac Hull described him:* Linda Maloney, *Captain from Connecticut: The Life and Naval Times of Isaac Hull* (Boston: Northeastern University Press, 1986), 288.

266 *David Porter, to his credit:* Daughan, *1812*, 405–11.

268 *"the guilty perpetrators [are] made to feel":* Quoted in Jeremiah N. Reynolds, *Voyage of the United States Frigate* Potomac (New York: Harper & Brothers, 1835), 528.

268 *After a long, but uneventful trip, Downes:* David F. Long, *Gold Braid and Foreign Relations* (Annapolis, MD: Naval Institute Press, 1988), 78–80 and 253–56.

269 *David Farragut loved the navy every bit:* Farragut, *Life of David Glasgow Farragut*, 52–53.

271 *Secretary of the Navy Gideon Welles said of Farragut:* Gideon Welles, *The Diary of Gideon Welles*, vol. I (Boston: Houghton Mifflin, 1911), 230.

272 *"one of the hardest victories of my life":* quoted in Mahan, *Farragut*, 288.

272 *James Hillyar's subsequent career:* William R. O'Byrne, *Naval Biographical Dictionary* (London: J. Murray, 1849), 345–46; J.K. Laughton, "James Hillyar," in *Oxford Dictionary of National Biography*, H.G.C. Matthew and Brian Harrison, eds. (London: Oxford, 2004), 239–40; Piers Mackesy, *The War in the Mediterranean, 1803–1810* (New York: Longmans, Green, 1957), 215–17.

274 *"a man of far more than ordinary talents, indefatigable":* Peabody Museum, BWC Papers: Rodgers to Crowninshield, Feb. 11 and 13, 1815, quoted in Maloney, *Captain from Connecticut*, 264.

276 *"associate with those who were led by men in power to inflict an unrighteous sentence":* Quoted in Long, *Nothing Too Daring*, 249.

SELECT BIBLIOGRAPHY

Primary Sources

Biddle, Charles. *Autobiography.* Reprint, Whitefish, MT: Kessinger, 2006.

Bligh, William. *A Narrative of the Mutiny on Board His Majesty's Ship* Bounty. London: George Nicol, 1790.

―――and Edward Christian. *The* Bounty *Mutiny*. New York: Penguin Books, 2001.

Bowen, Abel. *The Naval Monument, Containing Official and Other Accounts of All the Battles Fought Between the Navies of the United States and Great Britain During the Late War; and an Account of the War with Algiers*. Boston: Cummings and Hilliard, 1816.

Brannan, John, ed. *Official Letters of the Military and Naval Officers of the United States During the War with Great Britain in the Years 1812, 13, 14, 15 With Some Additional Letters and Documents Elucidating the History of That Period*. Reprint. Whitefish, MT: Kessinger, 2008, originally published 1823.

Brooks, George S., ed. *James Durand: An Able Seaman of 1812*. New Haven: Yale University Press, 1926.

Colnett, Captain James. *A Voyage to the Northwest Side of North America: The Journals of James Colnett, 1786–89*. Reprint. Vancouver, BC: University of British Columbia Press, 2004.

―――. *The Journal of Captain James Colnett Aboard the* Argonaut *from April 26, 1789 to Nov. 3, 1791*. Judge Frederick W. Howay, ed. New York: Greenwood Press, 1968; original printed in 1798.

_____. *Voyages of the* Columbia *to the Northwest Coast.* Boston: Massachusetts Historical Society, 1941.

_____. *A Voyage to the South Atlantic and Round Cape Horn to the Pacific Ocean in the Ship* Rattler. London: W. Bennett, 1798.

Cook, James. *The Journals.* Philip Edwards, ed. New York: Penguin, 2003.

Cowdery, Dr. Jonathan. *American Captives in Tripoli.* Boston: Belcher and Armstrong, 1806.

Fleurieu, Charles Pierre Claret. *A Voyage Round the World.* London: Longman, 1801.

Forester, C.S., ed. *The Adventures of John Wetherell.* New York: Doubleday, 1953.

Foster, Sir Augustus John. *Jeffersonian America: Notes on the United States of America Collected in the Years 1805–6–7 and 11–12.* Richard Beale Davis, ed. San Marino, CA: Huntington Library, 1954.

Graham, Gerald S. and R.A. Humphreys, eds. *The Navy and South America, 1807–1823: Correspondence of the Commanders-in-Chief on the South American Station.* London: Spottiswoode, Ballantyne and Co. LTD, 1962.

Hussey, John A., ed. *The Voyage of the* Racoon: *A "Secret" Journal of a Visit to Oregon, California, and Hawaii, 1813–1814.* San Francisco: Book Club of California, 1958.

Knox, Dudley W., ed. *Naval Documents Related to the Quasi-War Between the United States and France,* 7 vols. Washington, DC: US Government Printing Office, 1935–39.

_____. *Naval Documents Related to the United States Wars with the Barbary Powers,* Vol. III. Washington, DC: US Government Printing Office, 1941.

Manning, William R., ed. *Diplomatic Correspondence of the United States Concerning the Independence of the Latin-American Nations.* New York: Oxford University Press, 1925.

Markham, Sir Clements R., ed. *The Voyages of Pedro Fernandez de Quiros 1595–1606.* 2 vols. London: Hakluyt Society, 1904.

Morris, Commodore Charles. *The Autobiography of Commodore Charles Morris.* Reprint. Annapolis, MD: Naval Institute Press, 2002.

Porter, David. *Journal of a Cruise Made to the Pacific Ocean …* Philadelphia: Bradford & Inskeep, 1815.

_____. *Journal of a Cruise Made to the Pacific Ocean …* New York: Wiley & Halsted, 1822.

_____. *Journal of a Cruise.* Reprint. Annapolis, MD: *Naval Institute Press,* 1986.

_____. *A Voyage in the South Seas in the Years 1812, 1813, 1814 …* London. Sir R. Phillips, 1823.

_____. *An Exposition of the Facts and Circumstances Which Justify the Expedition to Foxardo* … Washington, DC: Davis & Force, 1825.

_____. *Minutes of Proceedings of Courts of Inquiry and Court Martial in Relation to Captain David Porter*. Washington, DC: Davis and Force, 1825.

_____. *Constantinople and Its Environs*. 2 vols. New York: Harper & Brothers, 1835.

Robarts, Edward. *The Marquesan Journal of Edward Robarts, 1797–1824*. Greg Dening, ed. Canberra: Australian National University Press, 1974.

Rotch, William. *Memorandum Written by William Rotch in the Eightieth Year of His Age*. Boston: Houghton Mifflin, 1916.

Smith, Philip Chadwick Foster. *The Frigate* Essex *Papers: Building the Salem Frigate, 1798–1799*. Salem, MA: Peabody Museum, 1974.

Stewart, Charles S. *A Visit to the South Seas in the US Ship* Vincennes *During the Years 1829 and 1830 with Scenes in Brazil, Peru, Manilla, the Cape of Good Hope, and St. Helena*. 2 vols. New York: John P. Haven, 1831.

Vancouver, George. *A Voyage of Discovery to the North Pacific Ocean and Round the World, 1791–1795*. W. Kaye Lamb, ed. 4 vols. London: Hakluyt Society, 1984.

Wallace, William Stewart, ed. *Documents Relating to the Northwest Company*. Toronto: Champlain Society, 1934.

Webster, C. K. *Britain and the Independence of Latin America, 1812–1830, Selected Documents from the Foreign Office Archives*. Oxford: Oxford University Press, 1944.

Welles, Gideon. *Diary of Gideon Welles, Secretary of the Navy Under Lincoln and Johnson* … 3 vols. Boston: Houghton Mifflin, 1911.

Newspapers

Aurora
Boston Gazette
Boston Patriot
Columbian Centinel
Independent Chronicle
National Intelligencer
New England Palladium
New Orleans La Gazette
Newburyport Herald
Newport Mercury
Niles Weekly Register
Providence Gazette
Salem Gazette

Secondary Sources

Adams, Henry. *History of the United States of American During the Administrations of James Madison.* New York: Literary Classics of the United States, 1986.

Allison, Robert J. *The Crescent Obscured: The United States and the Muslim World, 1776–1815.* London: University of Chicago Press, 1995.

Anderson, Bern. *Surveyor of the Sea: The Life and Voyages of Captain George Vancouver.* Seattle: University of Washington Press, 1960.

Anna, Timothy E. *The Fall of the Royal Government of Peru.* Lincoln: University of Nebraska Press, 1979.

_____. *Spain and the Loss of America.* Lincoln: University of Nebraska Press, 1983.

Anthony, Irvin, ed. *The Saga of the Bounty.* New York: Dell, 1961.

Ashmead, Henry Graham. *History of Delaware County.* Philadelphia: L.H. Everts, 1884.

Barnes, James. *David G. Farragut.* London: Keegan Paul, Trench, Tubner & Co., 1899.

_____. *Naval Actions of the War of 1812.* New York: Harper & Brothers, 1896.

Bauer, K. Jack. *Ships of the Navy, 1775–1969*, vol. 1. Troy, NY: Rensselaer Polytechnic Institute, 1969.

Beaglehole, J.C. *The Exploration of the Pacific.* Palo Alto: Stanford University Press, 1966.

_____. *The Life of Captain James Cook.* Stanford: Stanford University Press, 1974.

Bemis, Samuel Flagg. *The Latin American Policy of the United States.* New York: Harcourt, Brace & World, 1943.

Benton, Thomas Hart. *Thirty Years View.* New York: Appleton, 1854.

Berube, Claude, and John Rodgaard. *A Call to the Sea: Captain Charles Stewart of the USS Constitution.* Dulles, VA: Potomac Books, 2005.

Billias, George A. *Elbridge Gerry: Founding Father and Republican Statesman.* New York: McGraw Hill, 1976.

Billingsley, Edward B. *In Defense of Neutral Rights: The United States Navy and the Wars of Independence in Chile and Peru.* Chapel Hill: University of North Carolina Press, 1967.

Brackenridge, Henry M. *History of the Late War, between the United States and Great Britain. Containing a Minute Account of the Various Military and Naval Operations*, 4th rev. ed. Baltimore: Cushing and Jewett, 1818.

Bradford, James C., ed. *Command Under Sail: Makers of the American Naval Tradition 1775–1850.* Annapolis, MD: Naval Institute Press, 1991.

Brant, Irving. *James Madison, The President, 1809–1812*. New York: Bobbs-Merrill, 1950.

———. *James Madison, Commander in Chief, 1812–1836*. New York: Bobbs-Merrill, 1961.

Bridges, Lucas. *Uttermost Part of the Earth*. New York: Dutton, 1950.

Brown, John Howard. *American Naval Heroes*. Boston: Brown and Company, 1899.

Brown, Stephen. *Scurvy: How a Surgeon, a Mariner, and a Gentleman Solved the Greatest Medical Mystery of the Age of Sail*. New York: St. Martin's Griffin, 2005.

Bullard, John M. *The Rotches*. New Bedford, MA: Cabinet Press, 1947.

Busch, Briton Cooper. *Whaling Will Never Do for Me: The American Whaleman in the Nineteenth Century*. Lexington: University of Kentucky Press, 1994.

Carpenter, Kenneth J. *The History of Scurvy and Vitamin C*. Cambridge: Cambridge University Press, 1986.

Carroll, Sean B. *Remarkable Creatures: Epic Adventures in the Search for the Origin of Species*. New York: Houghton Mifflin Harcourt, 2009.

Clauder, Anna C. *American Commerce As Affected by the Wars of the French Revolution and Napoleon*. New York: Augustus M. Kelley, 1972, originally published, 1932.

Chapelle, Howard I. *The History of American Sailing Ships*. New York: Bonanza Books, 1935.

Clayton, Lawrence A. *Peru and the United States: The Condor and the Eagle*. Athens: University of Georgia Press, 1999.

Clowes, William L. *The Royal Navy: A History*, 7 vols. London, 1901.

Collier, Simon. *Ideas and Politics of Chilean Independence, 1808–1833*. London: Cambridge University Press, 1967.

Cooper, James Fenimore. *Lives of Distinguished Naval Officers*, 2 vols. Philadelphia: Carey and Hart, 1846.

Darwin, Charles. *The Voyage of the* Beagle. New York: P. F. Collier & Son, 1909.

Dening, Greg. *Islands and Beaches: Discourses on a Silent Land: Marquesas 1774–1880*. Chicago: Dorsey Press, 1980.

Dolan, Eric Jay. *Leviathan: The History of Whaling in America*. New York: W.W. Norton, 2007.

Donovan, Frank Robert. *The Odyssey of the* Essex. New York: David McKay, 1969.

Druett, Joan. *Rough Medicine: Surgeons at Sea in the Age of Sail*. New York: Routledge, 2001.

Duffy, Stephen W.H. *Captain Blakeley and the* Wasp: *The Cruise of 1814*. Annapolis, MD: Naval Institute Press, 2001.

Dye, Ira. *The Fatal Cruise of the* Argus: *Two Captains in the War of 1812*. Annapolis, MD: Naval Institute Press, 1994.

Eckert, Edward K. *The Navy Department in the War of 1812.* Gainesville: University of Florida Press, 1973.

Evans, Amos A. *Journal Kept Aboard the Frigate* Constitution *1812.* reprint. Concord, MA: Bankers Lithograph, Co., 1967.

Evans, Henry. C. Jr. *Chile and Its Relations with the United States.* Durham, NC: Duke University Press, 1927.

Farragut, Loyall. *The Life of David Glasgow Farragut.* New York: Appleton, 1879.

Fleurieu, Charles, P.C. *A Voyage Round the World Performed During the Years 1790, 1791, and 1792 by Etienne Marchand,* 2 vols. Amsterdam and New York: Nico Israel and DaCapo, 1969.

Forester, C.S. *The Age of Fighting Sail.* New York: Doubleday, 1956.

Furnas, J.C. *The Anatomy of Paradise: Hawaii and the Islands of the South Seas.* New York: William Sloane Associates. 1948.

Galdames, Luis. *A History of Chile.* Translated and edited by Isaac Joslin Cox. Chapel Hill: University of North Carolina Press, 1941.

Gilje, Paul A. *Liberty on the Waterfront: American Maritime Culture in the Age of Revolution.* Philadelphia: University of Pennsylvania Press, 2004.

Gill, Conrad. *The Naval Mutinies of 1797.* Manchester, England: University Press, 1913.

Gruppe, Henry E. *The Frigates.* Alexandria, VA: Time-Life Books, 1979.

Hall, Christopher D. *British Strategy in the Napoleonic Wars, 1803–15.* Manchester, England: Manchester University Press, 1992.

Harris, Thomas. *The Life and Services of Commodore William Bainbridge, United States Navy.* Philadelphia: Carey Lea and Blanchard, 1837.

Heawood, Edward. *A History of Geographical Discovery in the Seventeenth and Eighteenth Centuries.* Cambridge: Cambridge University Press, 1912.

Hill, Lawrence F. *Diplomatic Relations Between the United States and Brazil.* Durham, NC: Duke University Press, 1932.

_____. *Brazil.* Berkeley: University of California Press, 1947.

Huntoon, Daniel T. V. *History of the Town of Canton, Norfolk County, Massachusetts.* Cambridge, MA: John Wilson and Son, 1893.

Inderwick, James. *Cruise of the US Brig* Argus *in 1813.* Reprint. New York: New York Public Library, 1917.

Jackson, Gordon. *The British Whaling Trade.* London: Adam and Charles Black, 1978.

James, William. *A Full and Correct Account of the Chief Naval Occurrences of the Late War Between Great Britain and the United States of America.* London: T. Egerton, 1817.

_____. *The Naval History of Great Britain,* 6 vols. London: Richard Bentley, 1837.

Johnson, Robert E. *Thence Round Cape Horn: The Story of the United States Naval Forces on Pacific Station, 1818–1923.* Annapolis, MD: Naval Institute, 1963.

Johnston, Samuel B. *Three Years in Chile.* Erie, PA: R.I. Curtis, 1816.

Keegan, John. *The Price of Admiralty: The Evolution of Naval Warfare.* New York: Viking, 1989.

Langley, Harold D. *Social Reform in the United States Navy, 1798–1862.* Chicago: University of Chicago Press, 1967.

Lefebvre, Georges. *Napoleon: From Tilsit to Waterloo.* Translated by J.E. Anderson. New York: Columbia University Press, 1969. Originally published, 1936.

Leiner, Frederick C. *Millions for Defense: The Subscription Warships of 1798.* Annapolis, MD: Naval Institute Press, 2000.

Lewis, Charles Lee. *David Glasgow Farragut: Admiral in the Making.* Annapolis, MD: United States Naval Institute, 1941.

Lewis, James. *The American Union and the Problem of Neighborhood: The United States and the Collapse of the Spanish Empire, 1783–1829.* Chapel Hill: University of North Carolina Press, 1998.

Lloyd, C. and J.L.S. Coulter. *Medicine and the Navy, 1714–1815*, vol. III. Edinburgh: E. & S. Livingstone, 1961.

Long, David F. *Nothing Too Daring: A Biography of Commodore David Porter, 1780–1843.* Annapolis, MD: Naval Institute Press, 1970.

———. *Ready to Hazard: A Biography of Commodore William Bainbridge, 1774–1833.* Hanover, NH: University Press of New England, 1981.

———. *Sailor-Diplomat: A Biography of Commodore James Biddle, 1783 1848.* Boston: Northeastern University Press, 1983.

Lovett, Gabriel H. *Napoleon and the Birth of Modern Spain.* New York: New York University Press, 1965.

McClellan, Edwin North. *History of the United States Marine Corps*, vol. I. Washington, DC: US Marine Corps, 1932.

McCranie, Kevin D. *Utmost Gallantry: The U.S. and Royal Navies in the War of 1812.* Annapolis, MD: Naval Institute Press, 2011.

McKee, Christopher. *Edward Preble: A Naval Biography, 1761–1807.* Annapolis, MD: Naval Institute Press, 1996. First published in 1972.

———. *A Gentlemanly and Honorable Profession: The Creation of the U.S. Naval Officer Corps, 1794–1815.* Annapolis, MD: Naval Institute Press, 1991.

Macy, Obed. *The History of Nantucket*, 1835; reprint, Clifton, NJ: Augustus M. Kelley. 1972.

Mahan, Alfred Thayer. *Admiral Farragut.* New York: D. Appleton and Company, 1892.

———. *Sea Power in Its Relations to the War of 1812*, 2 vols. Boston: Little Brown, 1905.

Martin, John Hill. *Chester (and Its Vicinity) Delaware County, in Pennsylvania*. Philadelphia: William H. Piles & Sons, 1877.

Merk, Frederick. *The Oregon Question: Essays in Anglo-American Diplomacy and Politics*. Cambridge: Harvard University Press, 1967.

Ormsby, Margaret A. *British Columbia: A History*. Toronto: Macmillans in Canada, 1958.

Paine, Ralph D. *The Ships and Sailors of Old Salem*. Chicago: A.C. McClure & Co., 1912.

Parker, Hershell. *Herman Melville: A Biography*. Baltimore: Johns Hopkins University Press, 2006.

Parsons, Usher. *Sailor's Physician*, 2nd ed. Providence: Field, 1824.

_____. *Physician for Ships*, 4th ed. Boston: Damrell and Moore, 1851.

Parton, Dorothy M. *The Diplomatic Career of Joel Roberts Poinsett*. Washington, DC: Catholic University of America, 1934.

Paullin, Charles O. *Commodore John Rodgers: A Biography*. Cleveland: Arthur H. Clark, 1910.

Philips, James Duncan. *Salem in the Eighteenth Century*. Salem, MA: Essex Institute, 1969.

Pope, Dudley. *The Black Ship*. New York: Henry Holt, 1963.

Porter, Admiral David Dixon. *Memoir of Commodore David Porter*. Albany: J. Munsell, 1875.

Pratt, Fletcher. *Preble's Boys: Commodore Preble and the Birth of American Sea Power*. New York: Sloane, 1950.

Preble, George H. "The First Cruise of the United States Frigate *Essex*," *Essex Institute Historical Collections*, 10, part 2. Salem, MA: Essex Institute Press, 1869.

Ray, William. *Horrors of Slavery, or, American Tars in Tripoli*. Troy, NY: printed for the author by Oliver Lyon, 1808.

Reid, Chipp. *Intrepid Sailors*. Annapolis, MD: Naval Institute Press, 2012.

Riesenberg, Felix. *Cape Horn*. London: Readers Union, 1950.

Rippy, J. Fred. *Joel R. Poinsett, Versatile American*. Durham, NC: Duke University Press, 1935.

_____. *Rivalry of the United States and Great Britain over Latin America*. Baltimore: Johns Hopkins Press, 1929.

Robotti, Frances Diane and James Vescovi. *The USS* Essex *and the Birth of the American Navy*. Holbrook, MA: Adams Media Corporation, 1999.

Rodger, N.A.M. *The Wooden World: An Anatomy of the Georgian Navy*. New York: W.W. Norton, 1986.

_____. *The Command of the Ocean: A Naval History of Britain, 1649–1815*. New York: W.W. Norton, 2004.

Ronda, James P. *Astoria and Empire*. Lincoln: University of Nebraska Press, 1990.

Roosevelt, Theodore. *The Naval War of 1812*. New York: Modern Library, 1999.

Sachs, Aaron. *The Humboldt Current: Nineteenth-Century Exploration and the Roots of American Environmentalism*. New York: Viking, 2006.

Salmond, Anne. *Bligh: William Bligh in the South Seas*. Berkeley: University of California Press, 2011.

Schneller, Robert John. *Farragut: America's First Admiral*. Washington, DC: Brassey's, 2002.

Sobel, Dava. *Longitude*. New York: Walker & Co., 1975.

Spears, John Randolph. *David G. Farragut*. Philadelphia: G.W. Jacobs, 1905.

_____. *The History of Our Navy from Its Origins to the Present Day, 1775–1898*, 5 vols. New York: Scribner's, 1897–1899.

Stackpole, Edouard A. *Whales and Destiny: The Rivalry Between America, France, and Britain for Control of the Southern Whale Fishery, 1785–1825*. Amherst: University of Massachusetts Press, 1972.

_____. *The Sea Hunters: The Great Age of Whaling*. New York: Lippincott, 1953.

Stagg, J.C.A. *Borderlines in Borderlands: James Madison and the Spanish-American Frontier, 1776–1821*. New Haven: Yale University Press, 2009.

Starbuck, Alexander. *History of the American Whale Fishery: From Its Earliest Inception to the Year 1876*. Washington, DC: Government Printing Office, 1876.

Stewart, Paul D. *Galapagos: The Islands That Changed the World*. New Haven: Yale, 2008.

Suthren, Victor. *The Sea Has No End: The Life of Louis-Antoine de Bougainville*. Toronto: Dundurn Group, 2004.

Symonds, Craig L. *Lincoln and His Admirals*. New York: Oxford University Press, 2008.

Tagart, Edward. *A Memoir of Peter Heywood*. London: E. Wilson, 1832.

Takakjian, Portia. *The Frigate* Essex. Annapolis, MD: Naval Institute Press, 2005.

Terra, Helmut de. *Humboldt: The Life and Times of Alexander von Humbolt, 1769–1859*. New York: Knopf, 1955.

Tucker, Glenn. *Dawn Like Thunder: The Barbary Wars and the Birth of the United States Navy*. Indianapolis: Bobbs-Merrill, 1963.

Turnbull, Archibald Douglas. *Commodore David Porter, 1780–1843*. New York: Century Company, 1929.

Valle, James E. *Rocks and Shoals: Order and Discipline in the Old Navy, 1800–1861*. Annapolis, MD: Naval Institute Press, 1980.

Villiers, Alan. *Captain James Cook*. New York: Penguin, 1969.

Whipple, A.B.C. *Yankee Whalers in the South Seas*. New York: Doubleday, 1954.

Williams, Frances L. *Matthew Fontaine Maury: Scientist of the Sea*. New Brunswick, NJ: Rutgers University Press, 1963.

Williams, Glyn C. *The Prize of All the Oceans: The Dramatic True Story of Commodore Anson's Voyage Round the World and How He Seized the Spanish Treasure Galleon*. New York: Viking, 1999.

_____. *The Death of Captain Cook: A Hero Made and Unmade*. Cambridge, MA: Harvard University Press, 2008.

Williams, J.E.D. *From Sails to Satellites: The Origin and Development of Navigational Science*. Oxford: Oxford University Press, 1992.

Withey, Lynne. *The Voyages of Discovery: Captain Cook and British Exploration of the Pacific*. Berkeley: University of California Press, 1989.

Woodard, Colin. *The Republic of Pirates: Being the True Story of the Caribbean Pirates and the Man Who Brought Them Down*. New York: Harcourt, 2007.

Periodicals

Bassett, Charles C. "The Career of the Frigate *Essex*." *Essex Institute Historical Collections* 87 (1951).

Callahan, James M. "American Relations in the Pacific and the Far East, 1784–1900." *Johns Hopkins University Studies in Historical and Political Science* 19 (1901).

Galpin, W. F. "The American Grain Trade to the Spanish Peninsula, 1810–1814." *American Historical Review* XXVIII (1922).

Griffin, Charles C. "Privateering from Baltimore During the Spanish American Wars of Independence." *Maryland Historical Magazine* 35 (1940).

Hunt, Livingston. "The Suppressed Mutiny on the *Essex*." *United States Naval Institute Proceedings* 59 (1933).

Irving, Washington. *Analectic Magazine*. 5 (September 1814).

Merk, Frederick. "The Genesis of the Oregon Question." *Mississippi Valley Historical Review* XXXVI (1949–50).

Merrill, Captain A.S. "First Contacts—The Glorious Cruise of the Frigate *Essex*." *United States Naval Proceedings* (Feb. 1940).

Paullin, Charles O. "Father of Admiral Farragut." *Louisiana Historical Quarterly* (January 1930).

Preble, George, Henry. "The First Cruise of the U.S. Frigate *Essex*." *Essex Institute Historical Collections* 10 (1870).

Quarterly Review 13 (1815).

Stille, C.J. "The Life and Services of Joel R. Poinsett." *Pennsylvania Magazine of History and Biography* 12 (1888).

INDEX

323